THE BEST BUSINESS WRITING 2013

Columbia Journalism Review Books

COLUMBIA JOURNALISM REVIEW BOOKS

Series Editors: Victor Navasky, Evan Cornog, Mike Hoyt, and the editors of the *Columbia Journalism Review*

For more than fifty years, the *Columbia Journalism Review* has been the gold standard for media criticism, holding the profession to the highest standards and exploring where journalism is headed, for good and for ill.

Columbia Journalism Review Books expands upon this mission, seeking to publish titles that allow for greater depth in exploring key issues confronting journalism, both past and present, and pointing to new ways of thinking about the field's impact and potential.

Drawing on the expertise of the editorial staff at the *Columbia Journalism Review* as well as the Columbia Journalism School, the series of books will seek out innovative voices as well as reclaim important works, traditions, and standards. In doing this, the series will also incorporate new ways of publishing made available by the Web and e-books.

Second Read: Writers Look Back at Classic Works of Reportage, edited by James Marcus and the Staff of the *Columbia Journalism Review*

The Story So Far: What We Know About the Business of Digital Journalism, Bill Grueskin, Ava Seave, and Lucas Graves

The Best Business Writing 2012, edited by Dean Starkman, Martha M. Hamilton, Ryan Chittum, and Felix Salmon

The Art of Making Magazines: On Being an Editor and Other Views from the Industry, edited by Victor S. Navasky and Evan Cornog

THE BEST BUSINESS WRITING 2013

Edited by

Dean Starkman,

Martha M. Hamilton,

Ryan Chittum, and

Felix Salmon

Columbia University Press New York

Columbia University Press
Publishers Since 1893
New York Chichester, West Sussex
cup.columbia.edu

Library of Congress Cataloging-in-Publication Data

The best business writing 2013 / edited by Dean Starkman, Martha M. Hamilton, Ryan Chittum, and Felix Salmon.
pages cm.—(Columbia Journalism Review books)
ISBN 978-0-231-16075-9 (pbk.: alk. paper)—ISBN 978-0-231-53517-5 (e-book)
1. Business. 2. Businesspeople. 3. Business enterprises—Corrupt practices. I. Starkman, Dean.

HF1008.B48 2013
330.9'0512—dc23

2012047913

Columbia University Press books are printed on permanent and durable acid-free paper.
This book is printed on paper with recycled content.
Printed in the United States of America

p 10 9 8 7 6 5 4 3 2 1

Contents

Part II. Bad Medicine

Part III. Big Business

Part IV. Bad Business

Part V. Media and Marketing

Part VII. Adventures in Finance

Introduction
Dean Starkman

Compiling the Best Business Writing series each year reliably brings the pleasures of the eclectic and unexpected. But it also can deliver deeper insights into troubling undercurrents in American business life.

Editors get lucky that way sometimes. The great American editor Samuel S. McClure had one of the great "who knew?" moments a century ago while putting to bed the January 1903 issue of his eponymous magazine. Until then, *McClure's* had been an eclectic general-interest magazine, publishing fiction by the likes of Mark Twain and Arthur Conan Doyle and historical narratives about Lincoln, Napoleon, and other figures. This time, reading over the issue, McClure noticed his (soon-to-be-famous) staff had delivered three monumental articles, all on a common theme: the lawlessness and corruption permeating bedrock American institutions. Lincoln Steffens had exposed mob-style rule of Minneapolis's political machine (as he would for St. Louis, Pittsburgh, Chicago, and other American cities); Ida Tarbell had documented the underhanded methods John D. Rockefeller had used to build the Standard Oil monopoly; and Ray Stannard Baker told a chilling tale of union-sponsored thuggery. "We did not plan it so," McClure said in a last-minute editorial.

With that single issue, a new form of American journalism—known as muckraking—was born.

We had a mini-*McClure's* moment when reading over candidates for *The Best Business Writing 2013.* First, we saw Thomas Catan, Devlin Barrett, and Timothy W. Martin's story in the *Wall Street Journal* about a drug epidemic killing more than 15,000 American's yearly. Coke? Heroin? Actually, it was prescription painkillers known as opioids, which are deadlier than *all* illegal drugs combined. At the center of the problem are pain doctors and pharmacies, including name brands such as CVS and Walgreens. Both doctors and pharmacies, we learn, are incentivized to write and fill prescriptions without asking many questions.

Then we came across Peter Whoriskey's story in the *Washington Post* about anti-anemia drugs made by pharmaceutical companies Amgen and Johnson & Johnson. Both companies had lobbied fiercely for the drugs' approval, created incentives for doctors to prescribe ever-larger doses, ignored studies that cast doubt on the drugs' benefits, and understated their risks. Whoriskey details the consequences.

The topper? Mina Kime's chillingly detailed expose of Synthes, a maker of a bone cement that regulators explicitly warned was *not* to be used on the human spine. Yet that's exactly the use the company promoted. The practice was so profitable that Synthes was able to sell itself to Johnson & Johnson for $20 billion before the horrifying consequences for patients became clear.

We highlighted the troubling practices in the nation's medical/pharmaceuticals complex in part 2, titled "Bad Medicine," an important centerpiece for this year's collection. As McClure said, we did not plan it so, but some of the best business journalism we saw was flashing clear signs that Big Medicine may be ignoring the injunction to, first, do no harm.

Readers of the Best Business Writing series, now in its second year, are getting used to such moments. These "BBW" books have themselves quickly become important works of curation: They offer a sort of snapshot of both the state of writing and reporting on business and of the state of business itself. We can offer the opinion that the former is in better shape than the latter.

But the world of American business is an infinitely rich and varied subject, and demonstrating that has become one of the chief virtues of the BBW series. This year's edition is filled with stories of ingenious innovation, entrepreneurial derring-do, wondrous technical achievement, and just plain oddness. One of my favorites is Drake Bennett's behind-the-scenes account of the merger of the airline behemoths United and Continental, a corporate version of elephants dancing. Initial predictions were that the combination couldn't possibly work, but Bennett demonstrates that it did and shows the staggering number of details—from integrating the two NASA-like flight-tracking systems to deciding which coffee to brew and how—that the airline's managers had to navigate to pull it off. The vast majority of reporting on mergers ends when a deal is announced. But that's where Bennett starts, and readers are amply rewarded.

In the category of Catty Reads of the Year, turn to Jessica Pressler's brave foray into the dispute between two warring Manhattan fashion houses, C Wonder and Tory Burch. The first is owned by *Christopher* Burch, ex-husband of Tory, who accuses him of ripping off her ideas. This fashion war of words brought out the long fingernails: "It's a rip-off, Tory knows it, and everyone knows it," Pressler quotes "someone we will refer to as a Friend of Tory," who adds: "The interior is blatantly plagiarized. Then there's the snap bracelets. The wallets. The buttons . . ."

Oy, the buttons! A close competitor among fun reads comes via Ken Bensinger, who stumbled upon one on those marketing ideas that probably seemed like a good idea at the time but morphed into a financial nightmare. This one involves airlines that, decades ago, sold unlimited air travel to customers willing to fork over $350,000 or so, allowing them and a partner to come and go whenever and wherever they pleased. One racked up *30 million* miles. Another created a mini-airline, ferrying passengers to and fro for cash.

Beyond wry features, it was an exceptional year for exposés of abuses of power and lawlessness. (Whether a good year for investigative reporting means business journalism was especially good or business behavior was especially bad is a question for philosophers.) And any list of top probes must start with David Barstow's powerful and devastating *New York Times* investigation of bribery at Wal-Mart de Mexico and cover-ups at the corporate headquarters in Bentonville, Arkansas, that lead straight to the executive suite. Rarely has a reporter gotten so far inside a system of corruption or assembled evidence as voluminous and compelling as Barstow does here. At the heart the story are fifteen hours of interviews with Sergio Cicero Zapata, who recounted how he personally helped organize payoffs and bribery to advance Wal-Mart's real-estate ambitions. This 10,000-word piece will go down as one of the classics of the investigative genre.

But, like I said, this was an exceptional year. A Reuters team of Brian Grow, Joshua Schneyer, and Janet Roberts uncorked a series of stunners on Chesapeake Energy and its CEO, Aubrey McClendon, the riverboat gambler behind the recent rise of natural gas in the United States. It was hard to choose among the stories, but we settled on an installment that exposes Chesapeake's plotting to collude with its top rival to drive down prices for drilling rights in Michigan. Among the documents, which an antitrust official calls a "smoking H-bomb," is one showing McClendon offering to "smoke a peace pipe" to keep prices down and divvying up counties to avoid a bidding war. Rarely do readers get to benefit from evidence, won with great effort and against fierce corporate resistance, so definitive and so damning.

And before we leave the investigative space, I need to mention the agenda-setting *New York Times* story on Foxconn, the enormous Chinese supplier of iPads, iPhones, and other Apple products. Using old-fashioned shoe-leather reporting, the newspaper documents labor-rights abuses, long hours, and harsh working conditions that led to suicides and unrest. The story peels away the brand's glossy image to reveal the often brutal reality of the manufacturing behind it. It led to sweeping reforms at both Foxconn and Apple.

Every year, it seems, one op-ed seems to resonate in the public mind far and above the others. Last year, Warren Buffett altered the public conversation about taxes simply by wondering aloud why his rates were lower than his secretary's. No one seemed to have a good answer. This year, a formerly unknown equity-derivative banker for Goldman Sachs named Greg Smith struck a nerve when he described in a few words why he was leaving his job. Its culture, he said, had finally become too "toxic and destructive" to bear. The pushback from Goldman and its usual amen corner in the business press was furious, but Smith's *cri de coeur* weathered it and stands as an important indictment of financial-industry culture. He touched a nerve by speaking to the public's commonsense understanding—hard-won after the financial crisis—that lax regulation and perverse incentives had led to institutionalized corruption on Wall Street, even at its most prestigious firm. That's why the piece went viral. That's why it's in this volume.

We've included other outstanding examples of lucid commentary and analysis on the economy, high finance, and technology. If you're wondering what "the Whale" was, and why it was such a debacle for JPMorgan Chase, Matt Levine will walk you through it like no one else has done. And Evgeny Morozov, master of the highbrow takedown, flays and fricassees the vacuousness that often passes as wisdom promulgated under the TED brand. Try to read it without laughing out loud.

In a classic work of media scholarship of the seventies, *Deciding What's News*, Herbert S. Gans identified and analyzed what might be described as mainstream journalism's fatal flaw: its tendency to fix its gaze on elites and their activities and to ignore everyone else. He called this "top-down" reporting and showed how it had become journalism's default mode. Journalism done right, we firmly believe, means hearing from *everybody*, which is what we liked about Jeff Tietz's piece in *Rolling Stone* on the precariousness of a middle-class lifestyle, one of the best stories on unemployment that you will ever read. Ditto for Paul Kiel's foreclosure story for ProPublica. And do *not* miss Mac McClelland's first-person account for *Mother Jones* of what it's really like to work in a digital retailer's "fulfillment center," better known as a warehouse.

But, this year, nothing quite had the power of the pieces that were written by nonjournalists: letters about banks and bankers written by everyday people caught up in the debt trap and collected in *The Trouble Is the Banks: Letters to Wall Street*. We picked five; we could have chosen many more. If you read only one, I recommend Deena DeNaro's "Please Don't Harass My Father Any Further."

We hope you enjoy *The Best Business Writing 2013*, the second of what we hope is a long-running series.

Acknowledgments

The editors would like to thank *CJR*'s agent, the indispensible Deirdre Mullane, who came up with the idea of a Best Business Writing series then tirelessly shepherded the process of obtaining rights to all the works, no small job. We also, of course, thank our contributors, who did the real work and did it brilliantly. And we gratefully acknowledge the support of Nicholas Lemann, dean of the Columbia Journalism School; Victor Navasky, chairman of the *Columbia Journalism Review*; Peter Osnos, the magazine's vice chairman; its board, Stephen Adler, Neil Barsky (chairman), Nathan S. Collier, Wade Greene, Joan Konner, Kenneth Lerer, Steve Lipin, Michael Oreskes, Randall Rothenberg, Emily Bell, Sheila Coronel, Howard W. French, and Michael Schudson; and major funders: the Maria Moors Cabot Fund, the Commonwealth Fund, the Harnisch Foundation, Kingsford Capital Management, Peter Lowy, Gary Lutin, the MacArthur Foundation, the Martin & Brown Foundation, Omidyar Network, Open Society Foundations, James Ottaway Jr., the Saul and Janice Poliak Center for the Study of First Amendment Issues, Rockefeller Family & Associates, M&T Weiner Foundation, the Schumann Foundation, and Ted Weschler.

Dean Starkman would like to thank Stanley and Regina Starkman and Alex and Julian. Ryan Chittum thanks Anna, Clara, and Nina.

THE BEST BUSINESS WRITING 2013

Part I

On the Ground

Rolling Stone

This portrait of the new homeless in Santa Barbara vividly captures the devastation wreaked on the American middle class in the Great Recession. Taking us inside the subculture of a local program that provides safe parking spaces for people living out of their cars, Jeff Tietz shows how sudden poverty is often hidden in plain sight. With deep reporting on the mundane but poignant details of his subjects' everyday life now and before it all fell apart, Tietz invests his readers in the people he profiles and shows just how tenuous is the grip so many have on the middle class.

Jeff Tietz

1. The Sharp, Sudden Decline of America's Middle Class

Every night around nine, Janis Adkins falls asleep in the back of her Toyota Sienna van in a church parking lot at the edge of Santa Barbara, California. On the van's roof is a black Yakima SpaceBooster, full of previous-life belongings like a snorkel and fins and camping gear. Adkins, who is fifty-six years old, parks the van at the lot's remotest corner, aligning its side with a row of dense, shading avocado trees. The trees provide privacy, but they are also useful because she can pick their fallen fruit, and she doesn't always have enough to eat. Despite a continuous, two-year job search, she remains without dependable work. She says she doesn't need to eat much—if she gets a decent hot meal in the morning, she can get by for the rest of the day on a piece of fruit or bulk-purchased almonds—but food stamps supply only a fraction of her nutritional needs, so foraging opportunities are welcome.

Prior to the Great Recession, Adkins owned and ran a successful plant nursery in Moab, Utah. At its peak, it was grossing $300,000 a year. She had never before been unemployed—she'd worked for forty years, through three major recessions. During her first year of unemployment, in 2010, she wrote three or four cover letters a day, five days a week. Now, to keep her mind occupied when she's not looking for work or doing odd jobs, she volunteers at an animal shelter called the Santa Barbara Wildlife

Care Network. ("I always ask for the most physically hard jobs just to get out my frustration," she says.) She has permission to pick fruit directly from the branches of the shelter's orange and avocado trees. Another benefit is that when she scrambles eggs to hand-feed wounded seabirds, she can surreptitiously make a dish for herself.

By the time Adkins goes to bed—early, because she has to get up soon after sunrise, before parishioners or church employees arrive—the four other people who overnight in the lot have usually settled in: a single mother who lives in a van with her two teenage children and keeps assiduously to herself, and a wrathful, mentally unstable woman in an old Mercedes sedan whom Adkins avoids. By mutual unspoken agreement, the three women park in the same spots every night, keeping a minimum distance from each other. When you live in your car in a parking lot, you value any reliable area of enclosing stillness. "You get very territorial," Adkins says.

Each evening, 150 people in 113 vehicles spend the night in 23 parking lots in Santa Barbara. The lots are part of Safe Parking, a program that offers overnight permits to people living in their vehicles. The nonprofit that runs the program, New Beginnings Counseling Center, requires participants to have a valid driver's license and current registration and insurance. The number of vehicles per lot ranges from one to fifteen, and lot hours are generally from seven p.m. to seven a.m. Fraternization among those who sleep in the lots is implicitly discouraged—the fainter the program's presence, the less likely it will provoke complaints from neighboring homes and churches and businesses.

The Safe Parking program is not the product of a benevolent government. Santa Barbara's mild climate and sheltered beachfront have long attracted the homeless, and the city has sometimes responded with punitive measures. (An appeals court compared one city ordinance forbidding overnight RV parking to anti-Okie laws in the 1930s.) To aid Santa Barbara's large homeless population, local activists launched the Safe Parking program in 2003. But since the Great Recession began, the number of lots and participants in the program has doubled. By 2009, formerly middle-class people like Janis Adkins had begun turning up—teachers and computer repairmen and yoga instructors seeking refuge in the city's parking lots. Safe-parking programs in other cities have experienced a similar influx of middle-class exiles, and their numbers are not expected to decrease anytime soon. It can take years for unemployed workers from the middle class to burn through their resources—savings, credit, salable belongings, home equity, loans from family and friends. Some 5.4 million Americans have been without work for at least six months, and an estimated 750,000 of them are completely broke or heading inexorably toward destitution. In California, where unemployment remains at 11 percent, middle-class refugees like Janis Adkins are only the earliest arrivals. "She's the tip of the iceberg," says Nancy Kapp, the coordinator of the Safe Parking program. "There are many people out there who haven't hit bottom yet, but they're on their way—they're on their way."

Kapp, who was herself homeless for a time many years ago, is blunt, indefatigable, raptly empathetic. She works out of a minuscule office in the Salvation Army building in downtown Santa Barbara. On the wall is a map encompassing the program's parking lots—a vivid graphic of the fall of the middle class. Kapp expects more disoriented, newly impoverished families to request spots in the Safe Parking program this year, and next year, and the year after that.

"When you come to me, you've hit rock bottom," Kapp says. "You've already done everything you possibly could to avoid being homeless. You maybe have a teeny bit of savings left. People are crying, they're saying, 'I've never experienced this before. I've never been homeless.' They don't want to mix with homeless people. They're like, 'I'm not going over to those people'—sometimes they call them 'those people.' So now they're lost, they're humiliated, they're rejected, they're scared, and they're very ashamed. I'm worried about the psychological damage it does when you have a place and then, all of a sudden, you're in your car. You have to be depressed just from the fall itself, from losing everything and not understanding how it could happen."

• • •

One evening last spring, I visit Janis Adkins in her parking lot at the Goleta Community Covenant Church. When I turn into the driveway, the sun has fallen to the horizon. The other residents haven't arrived yet, and Adkins' van, at the far corner of the lot, seems almost metaphysically solitary, drawn to the parcel of greenery at the asphalt's edge.

Because the night is chilly and the van shell seems to draw the cold inward, Adkins has already tucked herself in, reclining against pillows and a rolled sleeping bag at the back corner of the van, beneath blankets and layers of piled-up fleece clothing. For privacy, Adkins has put silver sunshades in the front windshield; a row of clean shirts and blouses suspended on hangers obscures the lot-facing side window. By the light of a little LED bulb in a camping headlamp, she is reading a novel called *The Invisible Ones*, whose main characters are gypsies.

Adkins has tousled blond-gray hair and the kind of deep, unaffected tan that comes from working outdoors. She grew up in a middle-class family in Santa Barbara but eventually took off to become a river guide in Utah. Adkins engages you frankly, her manner almost practiced in its evenness: few gesticulations, steady intonation. Across the ceiling of the van she has affixed a silken red-and-gold banner that spells out a Buddhist chant of compassion. She practices yoga and meditation and believes in the Buddhist concept of equanimity; she takes comfort in the parable of the Zen ox herder, who tries and fails, day after day, to break a raging ox. When a friend calls to ask how she's doing, she often says, "Still riding the ox."

But the rigors of homelessness—the sudden loss of the signifiers of her selfhood—regularly breach the protection of detachment; the trick for her is regaining it quickly. "When negative thoughts come, it's important to be able to say, 'It's just a thought,'" she tells me. "'Just let it go.' When I get really down, I try to look at a worse-case scenario, like the pictures of the Haiti earthquake. I go, 'What could I do to help?' Things like that drive me forward." She also reminds herself to be grateful: to Starbucks for free cups of hot water, to the YMCA for her discounted membership, to the Safe Parking program. Gratitude snuffs out self-pity.

Before the financial crash decimated the value of her home and her customer base, Adkins had been contemplating selling her nursery, High Desert Gardens, and going to work for a humanitarian or environmental organization. But the suddenness and violence of the recession took her by surprise. The nursery specialized in drought-tolerant plants and offered more than one hundred species of trees. Over the years, she had developed a deep base of horticultural knowledge, and people came from long distances to seek her advice. Business was good enough that she could leave her employees in charge of the nursery and travel for a month or so every summer to escape the harsh Moab heat.

Within two years of the crash, sales had dropped by 50 percent and the value of her land had fallen by more than that. Four banks refused to help her refinance. "Everyone was talking about bailouts," she recalls. "I said, 'I'm not asking for a bailout, I'm asking you to work with me.' They look at you, no expression on their faces, saying, 'There's nothing we can do.'" She had to shut the nursery down and sell everything she could to avoid foreclosure: "I was practically giving stuff away just to try to make some money. Started selling everything that wasn't permanent.

I was going to sell the doors, the windows, the gates if I could, but they told me I couldn't." She decided not to file for bankruptcy: It would have cost her thousands of dollars and require her to give up her van, which she was determined to keep. When she had nothing left to sell to make her mortgage payments, she was forced to put her home on the market, clearing only $4,000 on the sale.

"I was spinning out of control," she says. "I was starting to lose my wits. It's very surreal being at a level of depression where it's easier to think about suicide and dying than it is to bend over and pick something up you're stepping over. It was getting bad enough that my friends started looking at me, going, 'You better get out of here.' The only functional thing I could figure out was to just go. I thought I would go travel and figure out what I wanted to do next. So some friends packed up my house and we converted my van so I could have as much stuff in there as possible, and I just left."

However long it takes to lose everything, to get to the point where you're driving away from your repossessed home, the final unraveling seems eye-blink fast, because there is no way to imagine it. Even if you've been unemployed for a year and are months-delinquent on your mortgage, you still won't have a mental category for your own homelessness; it's impossible to project yourself into the scenario. The reality, when it occurs and endures, seems to have sprung from nowhere.

Without reflection, Adkins drove to a wildlife refuge she knew about in Arizona. She thought perhaps she could get a volunteer job there, something to keep her busy, but she soon realized that the plan would leave her with no way to make ends meet. "I went to a place by this lake and I just stayed there for ten days and cried and slept. I was so bad." Eventually she headed to Santa Barbara. She hoped that old connections might help her find work, but it wasn't long before she began running out of money.

Sitting in her van, we chat a bit about High Desert Gardens and the gypsy book and her volunteer work at the wildlife shelter. Eventually I ask how she gets by. She says that a cousin in town gives her food and cash when she can, and a woman at the church arranges informal gardening work for her. Various people she knows give her their recycling so she can redeem the cans and bottles, and she borrows money from friends and acquaintances, like the manager of the wildlife shelter. Having maxed out her borrowing capacity, though, she is increasingly unable to pay what she owes to places like the YMCA, where she goes to shower. She wouldn't be adverse to dumpsterdiving—"I hear there's good food"—but she's not strong enough to climb the sides.

"I actually tried panhandling a couple months ago," she says. "I was so broke. I had, like, a dollar. And I didn't know what else to do, so I went to the library and Googled 'effective panhandling.'"

"Really?" I ask.

"I wouldn't make that up," she says, laughing. "There were a lot of different strategies. One site said do not dress up, dress down. Look sad. Don't be negative in your signs. Say thank you constantly. Be humble for real, don't be phony-humble."

Adkins couldn't bring herself to look dirty. Then she remembered that after the stock market imploded, guys in business suits had walked through New York's financial district wearing sandwich boards with their résumés on them. "People read them because it's so ridiculous, it's effective," she says. So she picked a strategic thoroughfare in Santa Barbara, dressed for a job interview, and spent her last money making copies of her résumé, laminating one so that drivers could handle it without getting it dirty. She found a four-foot-tall piece of cardboard at a grocery store and wrote on it:

> I'D RATHER BE WORKING
> HIRE ME IF YOU HAVE A JOB

Then she stood alongside the road and held up the sign. The day was so windy it was hard to hold on to. "I was like, 'Please hire me,' and everybody's flying by, trying to ignore you, but this one guy drives up, looks at my résumé, looks at me and goes, 'Very effective. I'll take one of those.' I said, 'Thank you, I really appreciate that,' but I never heard from him. And then a homeless guy came up to me and goes, 'Wow. That ain't gonna work.' I didn't want to talk to him about it. I just wanted to stick my sign out there—I didn't have any more cardboard. And about halfway into it, I just started crying and I couldn't stop. I was so embarrassed. It was incredibly humiliating. You know how a lot of women hold their hand over their mouth when they cry? I started doing that, and that's when I raked in the money. I was sort of scared because there were so many cars that I was boxed in, and I was holding this gigantic sign and I was saying, 'I'd rather work, I'd rather you take my résumé, please help,' and I'm crying and the dollars just started coming out of the windows." But finally she cried herself out, and people stopped giving. She made twelve dollars in three hours, all of it drawn by tears.

"And then I went out the next day and didn't get squat," she says. "I was trying to figure out, 'Should I start crying on purpose?' But how do you cry on purpose?"

• • •

Curtis and Concita Cates spent the better part of a year sleeping in their Nissan Titan pickup with their thirteen-year-old son, Canaan, in the parking lot of the Santa Barbara Community Church. The pickup was one of five authorized vehicles in the lot, which is three miles east of the church where Adkins parks. To the north rise the low peaks flanking San Marcos Pass, and an overflow lot across the street offers a view of the outspread city and the ocean beyond it. The Cateses had met Nancy Kapp by chance at the Salvation Army, where they'd gone in search of food. She'd given them a white permit for the front window of their pickup. When they arrived at the church, they found a Safe Parking porta-potty at the corner of the lot.

The Cateses ended up in the Safe Parking program after losing their jobs almost simultaneously. Curtis installed and repaired fire sprinklers in Phoenix; Concita worked as a pharmacy technician. Their combined income averaged $60,000 a year. Before the Great Recession, they had never been jobless. They lost their home after exhausting their available cash and the money in Curtis' medical savings account. Their oldest child was in college, and they were able to send their next oldest to live with his aunt. With Canaan, they drove to California to stay with relatives. When they arrived, however, they found that another family, also recently homeless, had already moved in. There were now eleven people, all but one of them unemployed, sharing a single small house.

"A bunch of us slept all piled up in a room," Curtis recalls.

"Everyone had their own sleeping habits," Concita says.

"And in the kitchen, you're trying to figure out, 'OK, this is my food. Do I share it?'" Curtis says. "It gets down to little things like that. You would buy milk and have it there for the kids and someone else would take it. It got to the point where people would take our cooler and hide it in their room and save it for their own people."

The situation became unbearable, and the Cateses left without knowing exactly where they were going. "We had some friends, and we'd park in their driveways," Concita says. "Or the side of the road by their house, in case we had to go to the bathroom."

When I visit Concita and Curtis, they have just moved into an apartment subsidized by a federal program known as Section 8. The unit is in a stucco apartment building about a block from Highway 101 and the Union Pacific line that parallels it, on a street marked by modest dilapidation: a listing wooden fence broken by tree roots, a few anarchic yards, a beat-up Chevy Aveo mirroring a beat-up Dodge Stratus. The apartment is clean and relatively spacious but still mostly empty.

Curtis, thickset and goateed, welcomes me at the door dressed in jean shorts and a yellow Arizona State T-shirt. Concita, small and soft-voiced, wears a pink sweatshirt and white sneakers. The living room walls are bare, save for an oversize decorative clock, but it is the one room in the apartment close to being furnished: two couches, two easy chairs, a shaded table lamp on a stand, a coffee table. As I look around, Curtis and Concita tell me where everything came from, seeming a little surprised by how good they've become at acquiring things without money.

"That couch, someone was throwing out," Curtis says, pointing at the one opposite me. "A lady Nancy knows gave us these two chairs and this light."

"We found that little stand over there—someone was throwing it out," Concita says. "And I found that mirror in the dumpster—I was like, 'I'll take that.' "

Curtis points sequentially at items: "Got that from the trash, that from the trash. The TV was given to us by that lady Nancy knew." The TV has a large screen, but its anachronistic bulk is almost jarring. In their place in Phoenix, they'd had a fifty-inch LG flatscreen and a Blu-ray player.

When they first arrived in Santa Barbara, both Curtis and Concita were receiving unemployment benefits, but that was the only income they had, and it didn't cover expenses. They had three mouths to feed and no kitchen to cook in; gasoline was more than four dollars a gallon; they had to make a truck payment; they had cell-phone and auto-insurance bills; they had to do laundry. When they went to apply for social services, they learned that their unemployment benefits made them ineligible for additional aid. Curtis, who had worked construction jobs most of his life, started to haunt building sites. Once in a while he would find a few days' work. "But there's the rock and the hard spot," he says. "If you take the job, you lose your unemployment. You have to reapply, and the money doesn't equal the lost benefits." He was better off collecting cans.

Nancy Kapp describes the moment when formerly middle-class people like the Cateses are forced to turn to social-welfare systems as "the beginning of the demise. These systems don't just fail people—they degrade and humiliate people. They're not solutions. They're Band-Aids on wounds that are pusing and bleeding out."

Government-aid agencies and private charities demand that applicants show a bundle of identifying documents: Social Security card, birth certificate, driver's license. Many people don't have all of the required documents; homeless people often have none. The Cateses were lucky—Concita has a good organizational mind and quickly put together a packet of the necessary documents. But at the aid agencies where they applied, they saw many people—poor, hungry, sick—denied basic services for lack of paperwork.

The next thing welfare applicants must do is disclose every possession and conceivable source of income they have. "I can't tell you how many people come to my office and say, 'I couldn't get food stamps because my car is worth too much,'" Kapp tells me. "OK, you have a car. But you've lost everything—your house, your job, your pride—and all you have left is that car and all of your belongings in it. And they say, 'You still have too much. Lose it all.' You have to have nothing, when you already have nothing."

Janis Adkins hadn't been back in Santa Barbara long before she needed to apply for government assistance. She had never asked for aid before. At the California Department of Social Services, she filled out the form for emergency food stamps.

"I didn't wear my best clothes, but I wore a light blouse and jeans, and I guess I was just a little too dressed up," she recalls. "Because the woman just looked at me and said, 'Are you in a crisis? Your application says you're in a crisis.' I said, 'I'm living in a van and I don't have a job. I have a little bit of money, but it's going to go fast.' The woman said, 'You have 500 dollars. You're not in a crisis if you have 500 dollars.' She said anything more than 50 dollars was too much."

If Adkins had filled her tank with gas, done her laundry, eaten a meal, and paid her car insurance and phone bills, it would have used up half of everything she had. But emergency food stamps, she was told, are not for imminent emergencies; they're for emergencies already in progress. You can't get them if you can make it through the next week—you have to be down to the last few meals you can afford.

"The money's for my phone, it's for gas, it's for my bills," Adkins said.

"Why are you in a crisis," the woman asked, "when you have a phone bill?"

"I need the phone so I can get a job. You can't look for a job without a phone."

"Why do you have bills?" the woman asked. "I thought you didn't have a place to live."

"I live in my van," Adkins said. "I have insurance."

"You have a 2007 van," the woman said. "I think you need to sell that."

"Please, I need a break," Adkins said. "I need some help. I need to take a shower."

"Why didn't you have a shower?"

"I live in a van."

The woman told Adkins to come back when she really needed help.

"I was going into shock," Adkins recalls. "I'm crying and I'm shaking my head: 'No, no. I need to talk to somebody else.' They told me no." By then Adkins was screaming and begging. "I'm surprised they didn't call the cops," she tells me.

When welfare applicants finally prove that they exist and show their material worth to be nothing, they usually receive far less than they need to live on. That's what happened to Curtis and Concita Cates. The maximum amount of aid that a single adult is eligible for in Santa Barbara, they learned, is $291 per month—$200 in food stamps, $91 in cash assistance. The waiting time for Section 8 housing, if you have priority status, is six months to a year. If you belong to the vast majority who don't have priority status—if you're not elderly, disabled, or a veteran with dependents—the wait is between four and eight years.

Most of the social-service systems in the United States function not to help people like Curtis and Concita Cates get back to where they were, to a point of productive stability, but simply to keep them from starving—or, more often, to merely reduce the chances that they will starve. Millions of middle-class Americans are now receiving unemployment benefits, and many find themselves compelled by the meagerness of the assistance to shun opportunity and forgo productivity in favor of a ceaseless focus on daily survival. The system's incoherence and contempt for its dependents fluoresce brilliantly in the wake of a historic event like the Great Recession. When floodwaters cover our homes, we expect that FEMA workers with emergency checks and blankets will find us. There is no moral or substantive difference between a hundred-year flood and the near-destruction of the global financial system by speculators immune from consequence. But if you and your spouse both lose your jobs and assets because of an unprecedented economic cataclysm having nothing to do with you, you quickly discover that your society expects you and your children to live malnourished on the streets indefinitely. That kind of truth, says Nancy Kapp, "really screws with people's heads."

• • •

When Curtis and Concita were living in the parking lot of the Santa Barbara Community Church with Canaan, they used constant forward motion to evade despair. "I just wanted to wake up every morning, see the sunrise and be like, 'Let's go!'" Curtis says. Getting on the road was normalizing: using the truck as it was intended to be used, entering into conventional routines. The family would shower at a friend's or relative's house before dropping Canaan off at school. In the afternoons, he had sports, followed by activities at the Boys & Girls Club. "Spend as much time as you can in school and playing sports," his parents urged. "Wear yourself out."

"My son's a good pretender," Curtis says. "He has a knack for finding used clothes at stores and putting things together. All the kids at school thought he had money because he always dressed nice. He never had any gadgets or anything, but he always tried to make himself presentable."

"But there would be times he would ask for stuff," Concita is moved to say. "And I'm like, 'Do you even realize that we're homeless and living in a car? You want me to go buy you new shoes and clothes?'"

While Canaan was in school, Curtis and Concita would head to the local Employment Development Office to search for jobs online. They applied so diligently that they had to wait for new openings to pop up on job sites. The process was dismally impersonal, and their homelessness cast a pall over the search. Many employers demanded a permanent address—"that was the number-one thing we needed," Curtis says. In job interviews, they tried to hide the fact they were homeless, which often proved impossible. The interviewers assumed—Curtis and Concita could read it on their faces—that there were other causes of their homelessness: mental-health issues, drug addiction, a criminal past.

"You're trying to tell somebody, 'Listen, I'm just the person I was,'" Curtis says. "'I was working, things didn't end up the way they should have, and now I'm homeless. I'm not a dirtbag, I'm not a drug user.' But a lot of times people look at you and give you that vibe." Clothes could also be a problem. Once, sitting in an interview in a dress shirt and dollar tie he'd picked out at a thrift store, Curtis realized he'd forgotten to take the tag off the back of the shirt.

They learned where the free food was. One charity had a weekly farmer's market, so they would line up for fresh produce. For hot meals, which become tremendously valuable when you're on the street, they'd go to a charity called Casa Esperanza. I ask whether they generally had enough to eat.

"Not really," Concita says. "I'm glad my kid did, because he gets free lunches at school, free breakfast. But you don't have anywhere to warm up your food. You buy crackers. Dinner, we improvised and did what we could. A lot of the charity places, it's the same stuff over and over. 'Here's some dry beans and dry rice.' We didn't have anywhere to cook it. Or you would get the same bread; you have the same meal every night, in different forms. For plates and silverware, we'd just use the packaging, or sometimes I'd get it from McDonald's or Taco Bell."

The truck payment—$424 a month—was always a problem. "Without it, we don't have shelter, we don't have transportation, we don't have a way of getting to job interviews," Curtis says. When they got their unemployment benefits, much of the money went straight to the truck payment. "My thinking was, as long as I'm throwing them money every freaking week, maybe it'll keep the repo guy off of us," he says. "And we dodged that, too—we didn't let anyone know where we were at."

Curtis asked people if they needed their houses cleaned or lawns mowed. He offered the services of his pickup. He learned to collect cans and bottles and redeem them at recycling centers. One sunny Monday, he was in a park picking cans out of recycling bins. He looked around and noticed several other homeless men doing the same thing. "Yeah, I'm homeless," he thought.

When the family got back to the church parking lot in the evenings, they didn't want to talk to anybody. "I just wanted to pull up, drop the seats, go to sleep," Curtis says. There was an electrical outlet outside the church, and they had a DVD player and an extension cord, so they could watch movies. They didn't need curtains because "all the breathing steams up the windows." The truck had an extended cab; Curtis and Concita reclined in the front seats and gave the backseat to Canaan: They wanted to make sure he slept well.

It was odd to be confined in such a small space. "Sometimes it was a little too intimate," Curtis says. There were times when Concita wanted to give up. "I'm going to take my son and go back home to my brothers and sisters, and you stay here," she'd tell Curtis. They'd fight, but Curtis would say that they needed to stay together, and ultimately Concita would agree. "I always wanted to be with my family," she says.

The worst moments came when they felt immobilized, indefinitely tethered to the lot. "That's when you really feel like you're going crazy," he says. "You feel the pressure of everything: 'I'm not doing anything. I'm not being productive. I'm not making anything happen.' So any friends we had anywhere, we'd offer to cook and clean for them if we could crash that night. This is how it went every night: 'Let me call so-and-so.' 'Hey, can we crash at your pad?' "

Sometimes, through odd jobs and recycling, they saved enough for a night at a Motel 6.

"That was an 'ahhh' moment," Curtis recalls.

"Just to take a shower and lay in a bed," adds Concita. "But then you have to carry all your personal stuff."

"You have to bring all your clothes and everything you have with you," Curtis says. "You carry your life with you."

"Every day I'd pack everything up, make sure everything's secure and then go off and do everything again," Concita says.

"We were battling depression," Curtis says.

"I was," Concita says. "I'd cry all the time for stupid little things. At the time, it probably wasn't stupid, but I can't think about it—I'm going to cry now." She pauses but doesn't cry.

"It takes a lot of your pride," Curtis says. "It's humiliating to be begging for help. I can see how someone can get discouraged and give up, because I felt that way at times, and I'm a motivated person. I have goals in life. I can honestly see how someone that has maybe other issues could just say: 'I don't even want to deal with this.'"

Things have eased up a bit since their Section 8 apartment came through. Curtis is still collecting unemployment, but Concita found a part-time job at a grocery store. I ask whether they celebrated when they spent their first night in the new apartment. They look at each other. "I think we just collapsed," Curtis says.

"We put air in the mattress and just slept," Concita says. It was a queen-size mattress, and they all slept on it together.

"And for the first two or three weeks, we all still slept in the living room as a family," Curtis says. "No one wanted to go in their rooms. We were so used to being stuck together that we all stayed together. After a while, we started venturing off."

"My son, every now and then, he'll say, 'Mom, can you lay down with me?'" Concita says. "And I'll go in his room until he falls asleep."

For the first month after getting the place, she says, "I didn't want to go anywhere. I didn't want to talk to anybody. I just wanted to be in this house."

"She wouldn't leave," Curtis says.

I am reminded of something Nancy Kapp told me. "Homelessness gets in your bloodstream," she said, "and it stays there forever."

• • •

"Self-possession of mind, bro—that's the only way I got through being homeless," the ex-soldier tells me. We're sitting in his brand-new Section 8 apartment, which resembles the Cateses' in its interior spareness and stucco insubstantiality. Until recently, Sean Kennan—he doesn't want his real name used—spent seven months sleeping in a 1971 Winnebago in the parking lot of the First Presbyterian Church. He had his four-year-old son and five-year-old daughter with him. (Out of respect, Kennan tells me, he doesn't want to discuss the children's mother.) He has agreed to show me the short-radius circle in which poverty had confined him while he and his kids were living in the Winnebago. He's wearing a camo field hat and black army fatigues.

"I put this outfit on for you," he says, "because this was how I rolled when I was in the RV. Combat uniform, black boots. Serious. The seriousness of it. I had three sets of these. I looked at it like I was on duty. I was on duty for my kids."

Kennan is thirty-four and quite short, with a long biker beard, a silver fleck of a nose stud and, almost always, a Wildhorse cigarette in one hand. Edgy energy keeps him in motion; he describes himself as "a very overanalytical individual."

Desperate to get his kids out of a homeless shelter after he lost his job in San Francisco, Kennan heard about the Safe Parking program from a friend. He saved his cash assistance for two and a half months and used the $700 to buy the RV then waited two weeks until the rest of his welfare money came in to get it registered. "I basically plunged all the funds I had into the vehicle and then coped with just food stamps," he says. He and the kids named the RV Big Bertha. The First Presbyterian lot, which sits on a hillside in central Santa Barbara, has five spots in the Safe Parking program. Kennan received a spot at the edge of the lot. "When I rolled in that first night, I was so freaked out—never been to this town, don't know anybody," he says. "On the street, you run into crazy people everywhere. But there were two cop cars in the parking lot—it's a central location, and they were just sitting there waiting for calls. I was superstoked. You got your Safe Parking sticker on your windshield so they never bother you. It was comforting—very, very comforting."

After high school, Kennan knocked around the country for a while and then went to work for a relative in Florida as a vintage-boat restorer. September 11 inspired him to enlist in the army. He'd completed basic training and part of jump school when his back gave out, and he received a discharge. After moving to San Francisco with his kids, he struck up a child-care arrangement with a friend and got a job in the packaging department at the U.S. Mint. It was a good job, but the Treasury Department was cutting back in the wake of the economic collapse, and Kennan couldn't get enough hours to get by. Around the same time, his child-care arrangement fell apart, making it difficult to look for work, let alone hold down a full-time job.

The RV now sits on the street, in front of his new apartment. We stop to look at it on the way out. Kennan has pulled off its roof and walls and begun reframing it. He wants to both work and to care for his kids, he says, and the only way to do that is to have his own business. He'd like to get back to the kind of vintage-boat restoration he did in Florida.

"In essence, what you see out here has a lot of meanings," he says. "Because it's one, a prototype, and two, a backup plan." When the RV is fully rehabbed, he says, it will serve as a mobile advertisement for his restoration business. "There's a lot of people around here who have the money for toys," he says. The backup plan involves the fortification of the RV, survivalist style: waterproofing, solar panels, all-climate functionality. The Winnebago had been in rough shape when he lived in it with his kids, and Kennan had vowed that they would never again have to rely on such dicey shelter.

"Big Bertha has a lot of meaning to my family," he says. "She took care of us, now we're taking care of her."

I ask Kennan if he'll drive my car so I can take notes. As we pull away from the apartment, he says, "Man, I haven't driven a car in so long. This is weird, this is really weird. Just being in a car, period. So low. You're so low." We take Highway 101 northwest, beginning a tour of the world he and the kids inhabited after leaving the homeless shelter and striking out in Big Bertha. "The shelter was almost like those reality-TV shows where you get dropped into a situation," he tells me. "I'd never been on welfare before. I had no clue. I'd just heard people talk about it. What do you do? Die, kill yourself, or turn to drugs—and I do none of that. I got food stamps and cash aid for the kids. I got an old bike with a kid cart so I could get from point A to point B, because I had no transportation. I had a little cover for the cart in case it was raining."

We get off the highway and head down a commercial through street called De la Vina. Once he got the RV, he discovered that the roof leaked, so he bought a tarp and bungee cords to cover the holes. He ripped out the foul carpet ("It was so nasty, bro. It freaked me out to where I thought my kids were going to get sick"), and he strapped the bike and the kid cart to the roof.

"But now, what are you gonna do to shower your children?" he asks. "The very first thing was, 'How do I shower my kids?' " The weather was too cold for a camping shower. When he signed up for the Safe Parking program, Nancy Kapp told him about discounted memberships at the YMCA, and he began showering his kids there.

From De la Vina, we turn in to a strip mall. Kennan pulls into one of the spots where he used to park the RV after he finished shopping at Ralphs Grocery, a nearby supermarket. He often cooked something for the kids here, which sometimes drew complaints from the owners of a Chinese restaurant and a pizza place in the mall.

Getting out of the car, we take a short walk to Mission Creek, which runs under De la Vina and connects the strip mall to Oak Park, where Kennan and the kids would spend the better part of their days after leaving the First Presbyterian lot each morning at dawn. The creek runs clean, between stands of old oaks, with no trash in the bed—a hallmark of Santa Barbara. One of their favorite activities was to walk from Oak Park up the streambed on the way to Ralphs.

"We called it our Journey," Kennan says. "I'd say, 'Hey, who wants to get fruit? Who wants to get vegetables?' We'd go all the way down the creek to Ralphs to get food. The kids loved it." Along the way, they'd carefully clear clumps of sticks and leaves lodged between rocks in the creek bed. Kennan told the kids they needed to do this so "the water could flow properly." This became a serious undertaking, and the regularity of the Journey steadied their lives.

Returning to the car, we drive down to Oak Park. At its edge, a road winds through a little wood; we turn onto it and find the parking spot they occupied most mornings, deep in oak shade and just above Mission Creek. Being here leaves Kennan thoughtful; as if to preclude sentiment, he abruptly pulls out, and we drive along the length of the park: a broad, oak-canopied lawn along the creek, a spacious playground, a wading pool for kids, bathrooms. Kennan points to a public tap near the stream.

"This park has everything, bro, everything you could want," he says with the tenderness, almost wonderment, that people in the Safe Parking program express when talking about any public amenity that affords comfort: clean water, electrical outlets, showers, a safe green space, a good playground.

From Oak Park we turn right onto a road leading back to Highway 101, Kennan excruciatingly conscious of the road's steep grade. He'd run out of gas a few times trying to make it up the hill—the RV's gas gauge was broken—and had to carefully roll downhill to get as close to the nearest gas station as he could. "The major issue was always gas," he says. "The RV was really guzzling gas bad—to the point of over 300 dollars a month just for the small circle we would do around here." The First Presbyterian lot was partway up a steep hill, and every night, the ascent burned a ton of gas: "It sucked, bro." Big Bertha was also bedeviled by electrical issues. O'Reilly Auto Parts offered free battery charging, and Kennan took them up on it every week. "They got kinda tired of it," he says.

We get off the 101, and after a few turns pull into the YMCA parking lot. Kennan used to park at the very edge of the lot, to minimize conspicuousness. The Y is a big, modern, glassy facility, built around a courtyard. With the familiar note of thankful wonder, Kennan says, "They got so much cool stuff in there, bro. So much cool stuff."

We head toward the parking lot at First Presbyterian. The basic routine was to leave the church lot at seven a.m. for Oak Park, where they would play and hike until about three p.m. Then they'd drive to the Y for more activities and a shower. Then errands—battery charging, welfare paperwork, grocery shopping—and finally back to the church lot.

The First Presbyterian Church, ensconced in a neighborhood of mountain views and landscaped mission-style homes, is a large, red-roofed, cream-sided building with stained-glass insets. The smooth parking lot forms a hilltop plateau dotted by a few islands of fit palms; past it, the hill descends to a little valley of tile roofs and treetops. We park in Kennan's former spot, at the back of the lot, and get out. The land falls away just past a chain-link fence. A few weathered blue plastic chairs stand next to a Safe Parking porta-potty.

"We used to sit in those chairs at night and look at the stars," Kennan says. They could hear owls hooting after dark, visible sometimes as shadowy forms in the moonlight. The lot was mostly empty, and Kennan kept to himself. "My kids are my best friends and they consume all my time," he says. "When I parked, that was it. The blinds were drawn, the sun goes down. 'Love you, kids, time to go to sleep.' Seven, seven-thirty, they were out. I would relax for a few minutes, play card games or something on my cell phone, and then I would go down too." Each day had been filled with peril.

"It was a complete disconnection from everything that people are technically connected to," Kennan says. "Under the circumstances that you're in, if you don't have the mind frame to understand that every day is beautiful, you can become bogged down and break. It was six and a half months before I really hit my breaking point." He had applied for Section 8 housing, but nothing had come through. "I was very close to going back to the shelter if the RV broke down," he says. "It was just a baby step up."

He'd already headed for the desert, in search of a cheap trailer park, when he decided to call one last time about the Section 8 housing. "Your name is still on the list, sir," he was told, "but there's nothing available." Later that day, though, he got a call—an apartment had unexpectedly come open. "I almost started to cry, I'll be honest with you," he says.

At first, when the family moved into the apartment, they almost never left. "We hibernated for about a month," Kennan says. "We'd go to the grocery store, but that was about it. We'd watch movies constantly. We just hung out, ate a lot of fruits and vegetables. I'd make a big salad, and everybody got a fork, and we'd just hang out and watch movies and eat. We got over it eventually."

Kennan lights a cigarette and tells me an elaborate story he'd made up for his kids while they were in the homeless shelter. The lights there didn't go out until nine p.m., and the kids were in the upper bunk, so they couldn't fall asleep before then. He'd climb up and tell them stories until the lights were turned off. Soon it was just variations on one story, about a guy named Hippie Bob, who lived on a beach in Hawaii and made bonfires and rode sharks. When the kids asked what the shark's name was, "Jabber Jaws" popped into Kennan's head. Hippie Bob would ride out to a buoy on Jabber Jaws, put on his scuba gear, which was stored there, and Jabber Jaws would take him down to the land of the Snorks, who gave Hippie Bob all the gold they'd amassed from sunken pirate ships. Hippie Bob didn't need the gold, but they insisted he take it, so whenever he visited the Snorks, he brought them beautiful rocks and minerals. Before long, Kennan and his kids made up a theme song to go with the story: "Come along with the Snorks! / So happy to be when we're under the sea . . ." Now, whenever Kennan begins to talk about Hippie Bob, his kids immediately go silent.

• • •

One chilly, rainy morning, I meet Janis Adkins shortly after she's woken up outside the Santa Barbara Community Church—the church to which Curtis and Concita Cates had been assigned. Adkins had parked in the overflow lot on the sly, as she sometimes does, to enjoy the view of the mountains. Wearing a purple shawl and blue Patagonia fleece vest over a fleece shirt, she was beginning to straighten the back of the van. It had been so cold she'd had to sleep in her clothes, and I express surprise that they are unwrinkled. She laughs. "Fleece doesn't wrinkle," she says. It was a valuable trait.

She suggests that I sit in the driver's seat while she finishes getting ready. "What's a common denominator for all of us is we can't use the passenger seat, because it's so full of stuff," she says. I climb in. A shoulder bag holding her résumés is slung over the headrest. Scattered across the front seats: a CVS "Interdental Brush and Toothpick," a bottle of Wellness Formula, a bottle of Wellness Herbal Resistance Liquid, a bright-orange plastic box with a snap lid that reads "Homeopathic Emergency Kit Remedy List," and a nylon pouch full of more supplements and remedies.

She nods at all the homeopathic stuff. "It's hell getting sick in a car," she explains. "So I have an arsenal of things to keep me healthy." The homeopathic emergency kit had been sent by a friend, whom Adkins calls whenever she feels like she's coming down with something.

She begins to brush her teeth, excusing herself a few times to go spit at the edge of the lot. When I ask about water, she says, "Because I was a river guide, you really get used to brushing your teeth without water—you have enough saliva in your mouth."

The weather clears momentarily, and a half-rainbow appears over the hills. I ask if she uses a camp stove. "No," she says. "I'm very afraid of fire—paranoid of fire. I'm scared to use it in the van. And outside—there's no table for it." Because she doesn't cook, she relies almost exclusively on three places for a full, hot afternoon meal: Panda Express, In-N-Out Burger, and Taco Bell. They're the only sufficiently cheap places, and to save gas, she goes to whichever is closest.

"I had a cooler, but I needed block ice, and there's only two places to get it," she says. "Cube ice is more expensive and doesn't last long. Block ice lasts two or three times longer, but the gas to drive to get it is expensive. It's all a balancing act. Everything is done on faith and trust—and that's not a religious thing. You know that you're a heartbeat away from the bush. I have to be able to say to myself, 'OK, you're on "E," you have five dollars in food stamps, and you have a dollar. You're OK.' I have to trust that if I lose fifty pounds I'll still be OK. Something happened to me when I was a little kid and I started saying, 'I'll be OK, I'll be OK.' And I've said it ever since. It's constant in my head."

I get out of the driver's seat and climb into the back. Adkins gets behind the wheel and we head south, to Whole Foods, which has a breakfast bar that can be exploited. "Having a hot meal early is essential when it's this cold," she says. On the way, a sudden anxiety seizes her. "If we see a cop, you lie down," she says sharply—the only time I would hear this tone in her voice. Tickets for seat-belt violations in California start at $142—the equivalent of about twenty-eight meals.

"Shit, I might have to stop and get some gas," she says. "The cheapest gas I can find is down the road. I try not to drive anywhere past this area if I don't have to. Yesterday I had to go downtown, and it took a *lot* of gas."

We pull into a gas station. At the moment, regular gasoline is $4.35 a gallon. Adkins gets out her wallet and looks at the few bills in it and then looks at a minicalendar on the center console. She has $23. "Ten dollars in the tank, and ten dollars for me for cash," she says. I stand with her while she pumps. "I'm getting a whopping 2.29 gallons. That's supposed to get me forty miles. That should last me until Tuesday." She grins. "I live near where I park."

As we turn into the Whole Foods lot, she says, "In my mind right now, I know I'm going to use the bathroom to wash myself, wash my face. And I park far away from the store because I hate having people look in my car. I don't think anyone's going to steal anything in the Whole Foods lot, but . . . it's embarrassing. I'd rather people not know."

We walk into the illuminated, multihued splendor of Whole Foods, briskly passing everything that stands between us and the breakfast bar. Adkins looks a little more careworn than the other customers, but in her sheepskin boots and Patagonia fleece, she doesn't look out of the ordinary. She could be the successful nursery owner she once was, stopping for a healthy breakfast on her way to work.

"It's all by weight, so you get the lightest thing," Adkins says. "Stuff without water. They have this really nice burrito that's really light. I get bacon, and it's less than $4." For her that's not cheap, but it's workable; she can go without another full meal the rest of the day if necessary.

At the register, Adkins pays with a fistful of coins. The cashier patiently counts pennies, nickels, dimes, and quarters. Adkins asks for a cup of hot water. We stop at the condiments stand, where she gets utensils and puts honey in the water in advance of the tea bag she has in the van.

As we climb in, I realize the van smells faintly of slept-on sheets. Adkins is a clean person—she showers and does laundry regularly—but vehicle dwellers live in spaces too small to easily dissipate quotidian odors.

Driving back up to the church lot would burn gas unnecessarily, but the view there is restorative. "Keeping my spirits up is important," she says, almost to herself. "And I can also finish the chores in my car, like packing up the trash, without being looked at."

The lot is empty when we arrive. "Do you want a sea view or a mountain view?" Adkins asks. I choose the mountain view because of the rare snow. She drops a bag of Yogi Vanilla Spice tea into her cup of hot water and eats her breakfast quietly, using the plastic fork she'd picked up at Whole Foods.

As she finishes up, she tells me she'd recently applied for a sales position at REI and had been turned down. She'd gotten to the second round, a group interview, and had gone in thinking it would be ridiculous if she didn't get the job, given her qualifications. "But I was cocky in the group interview," she says. "I should have left my ego outside. Ego is good for getting some things done, but not when it leads to arrogance. And I was probably more nervous than I realized." It must be psychically wrenching, I think, to be at once so impeccably qualified and so helplessly destitute. In any event, more than 200 people had applied for the position.

She pauses, then says, "It's weird. When people find out I'm homeless, it changes how they feel about me. I get declined for jobs. As soon as they learn I live in a van, I'm a thief."

Responding to a job listing online, she had spoken with a woman who wanted to exchange pet care for rent on a trailer she owned. But during the interview, the woman asked where she lived, and Adkins could only evade the question for so long.

"What?" the woman responded. "How old are you? And you have no money?" Adkins tried to caution her against judging homeless people, but she knows that as soon as she has to make that kind of appeal, she's already lost.

Another time, she got an interview for a job as a dog walker. The potential employer was a young woman in her twenties, and Adkins thought she'd be open-minded, so she didn't hide her situation. The woman's face changed instantly. Adkins looked at her and took hold of her hand and gave it a squeeze. "It doesn't change who I am," she told the woman. "I'm still the same person. I'm honest, I've always worked hard and I'll work hard for you." But the woman had already withdrawn, and the next day she reposted the ad.

Curtis Cates, looking back on the time he spent living in his pickup, recognized the impossibility of convincing people that he was still "just the person I was." Sean Kennan recognized that the demands of homelessness create a "complete disconnection" between those living on the streets and the rest of society. Janis Adkins, unable for the moment to see a way out of her homelessness, doesn't have the benefit of hindsight. She would rather not give up on the possibility of being treated normally. "I try to not have the van factor into anything I do," she says. "It's where I live—it's just smaller."

• • •

The Great Recession cost 8 million Americans their jobs. Three years after the economy technically entered recovery, there are positions available for fewer than one out of every three job seekers. In this labor market, formerly middle-class workers like Curtis and Concita Cates and Janis Adkins and Sean Kennan cannot reliably secure even entry-level full-time work, and many will never again find jobs as lucrative and stable as those they lost. Long-term unemployment tarnishes résumés and erodes basic skills, making it harder for workers to regain high-paying jobs, and the average length of unemployment is currently at a sixty-year high. Many formerly middle-class people will never be middle-class again. Self-identities derived from five or ten or forty years of middle-class options and expectations will capsize.

I last see Janis Adkins in the off-leash area of Tucker's Grove Park, near the lot where she parks her van. She takes her dog, Jojo, here several times a week. Jojo is a shaggy, shambolic border collie, sixteen years old and blind and deaf and nearly toothless. Life in the van recently became too hard for him, and a woman Adkins met at the Wildlife Care Network found someone willing to take him in.

The day is mild, and Adkins is wearing the sandals that she's worn almost exclusively in nice weather for two years. We sit on a bench as Jojo snuffles around gimpily. The off-leash area, an ample lawn perforated by gopher holes, forms part of a meadow that ends in green hillsides, with low mountaintops behind—surplus gorgeousness typical of Santa Barbara.

When she returned to the city, Adkins tells me, she went to a plant nursery where she'd worked as a teenager and asked her old boss if he needed help. He said he was letting people go, not hiring them, but she'd gone back three more times; the last time, a few weeks earlier, he'd said, "You still haven't found a job? Come on," and gave her two eight-hour shifts a week at ten dollars an hour. Later, she'd added two more shifts, but the day before, her manager had warned her that unless business picked up, he would have to let her go.

"I wonder whether that was just an out, in case they want to fire me," Adkins says. She pauses. "I've lost a ton of confidence in the last year and a half," she concedes. "It just takes a wedge out of you."

The staff at the plant nursery treat her like an entry-level salesperson. Not so long ago, they might have been her employees. "You learn to let go of the concept of identity, of what 'I' means," she says. "That's a concept people really have trouble with. But it's been important for me. I've let go of my ego—or I'm trying to let go: I could be the dishwasher, I could be the janitor. I'm trying to re-form, trying to allow the job to become me. And I keep referring back to the fact that a lot of people would not allow it. They would hold on to their identity—hard."

Adkins has just gotten her first paycheck from the nursery, but expenses and debts have evaporated it right away. She went to the YMCA to take care of her outstanding balance of eighty dollars, but she could only afford to pay it down by twenty dollars. The young woman behind the desk balked, indignant. Not long afterward, the manager of the Y called her to talk about the balance. He appreciated her payment, he told Adkins. "Why don't we just make it a clean slate?" he proposed.

Adkins stops talking. I look over at her. She has her head in her hands; her shoulders are shaking. Finally, she looks up and wipes her eyes.

"I don't know what happened there," she says. "I think what got me was the recognition that I'm trying. He saw I was trying. He saw I was a responsible person." She pauses. "Because," she says, her voice breaking, "I always have been."

ProPublica

At the heart of the great financial crisis is the mortgage crisis, and at the heart of the mortgage crisis is the subprime crisis. At the heart of the subprime disaster are millions of individual tragedies and an enigma: How did all those mortgages get made? Thanks to government inquiries and civil settlements, we know structural changes in the mortgage industry led to systemic lawlessness and fraud. Still, the best overview of the mortgage tragedy in all its human complexity might be Paul Kiel's story about Sheila Ramos, a fifty-eight-year-old grandmother with custody of three children who used mortgage proceeds to pay bills and start a lawn business until medical problems sent the family into a tailspin. The key to her undoing, however, was a fraudulent mortgage. As Kiel writes: "Ramos's story is remarkable not because it's unique but because it isn't."

Paul Kiel

2. The Great American Foreclosure Story

The Struggle for Justice and a Place to Call Home

Sheila Ramos' grandsons, ten and thirteen, started crying. They wanted to know where the house was. There wasn't one. There was only a tent.

They had flown from Florida, after Ramos had fallen hopelessly behind on the mortgage for her three-bedroom home, to this family-owned patch of rural land on Hawaii's Big Island. There, on a July night in 2009, they pitched a tent and, with no electricity, started a new life.

If Ramos were in her twenties, living off the land might be a marvelous adventure. Hawaii is beautiful, and the weather is mild. In the nearly three years since she moved here, her family has built a semipermanent tent encampment, and they now have electricity. But it's not how this fifty-eight-year-old grandmother, who has custody of her three grandchildren, imagined spending her retirement after working for more than thirty years—nine running her own businesses. She regularly scours the local dump and recycling center for items she can salvage.

The story of how she ended up in a tent is the story of how America ended up in a foreclosure crisis that has not ended, that still drags down the economy and threatens to force millions of families from their homes. Already, banks have foreclosed on more than 4 million homes since the crisis began in 2007. With almost 6 million loans still in danger of foreclosure, 2012 could very well be the worst year yet. Ramos's story is remarkable not because it's unique but because it isn't.

Her story doesn't fit any of the conventional narratives. Ramos is not a helpless victim. She made mistakes. But she didn't take out her mortgages to splurge on luxuries or build a new wing for her house. She took out her first mortgage to live the free-market dream of starting her own business. She took out later mortgages to cope with injuries sustained in a car accident.

Every step of the way, from her first subprime loan to foreclosure, her downfall was abetted by a mortgage industry so profit-driven and disconnected from homeowners that the common interests once linking lender and borrower have been severed. The lending arms of the nation's largest financial institutions helped plunge the country into crisis through their abuses and blunders, and they responded to that crisis with still more abuses and blunders—this time in how they handled people facing foreclosure. For subprime borrowers like Ramos, it has been as hard to work their way out of trouble as it was easy for them to get the loans that started their downfall. The millions of prime borrowers who thought they were doing everything right, only to be caught in a historic wave of unemployment, have been forced to endure a similar gantlet of delays, errors, and traps.

The industry developed tactics of dubious legality—not just robo-signing, which most Americans have heard of by now, but an array of business practices, some dating to the 1990s, that were designed to skirt the law and fatten profits. The federal and state governments largely tolerated these practices until they pushed Ramos into a tent and all of us into the Great Recession.

Even then, the federal government, facing an electorate bitterly divided over how and even whether to help "irresponsible" homeowners, responded in ways that proved ineffective. To be sure, the government's efforts were unprecedented, as Obama administration officials have repeatedly insisted. But those efforts were also halfhearted. Only recently, after the banks admitted to widespread law breaking, did the government launch a response that might prove commensurate with the calamity.

This grandmother's story—outrageous and complex—is our story, the American foreclosure story.

Living the American Dream

Born Sheila Ferguson, Ramos was one of seven children. The family lived in the small town of Haiku on the island of Maui, where her father did maintenance work at state parks. At seventeen, she married a man she'd met in high school, dropped out of school, and had two sons but divorced when she was just nineteen. She kept his surname, Ramos, but wanted a new life. Maui suddenly seemed small and confining, and she wanted "to get off the rock," as she puts it. So she took her two sons, aged two and three, and left for Alaska.

She lived in Anchorage for three decades, building a life with her current partner, David Backus. After getting her GED and an associate's degree in cosmetology, she worked in various salons for several years, doing women's hair and giving facials. From there, she jumped to selling cosmetics in department stores, eventually working her way up to a managerial post at J.C. Penney—a role she loved. "I was a typical corporate diva," she says, always impeccably made up and dressed.

As the years rolled on—she worked at the company for nearly a decade—she gradually became disenchanted. When her brother died at fifty-one, she decided "life was too short" to remain in a job she no longer enjoyed.

What came next was another reinvention. Her partner, Backus, was an electrician with a side business building large concrete vaults that house electrical equipment. Ramos began dabbling with the concrete, mixing and pouring it to make stepping stones for her garden, then planters for small trees. Soon she'd taken charge of the business and landed a contract to supply an Anchorage electric company with the utility vaults. Working in a small warehouse behind the Anchorage house she shared with Backus, she managed two employees as they mixed gravel, cement and water, poured the mixture into 1.5-ton forms, and moved them to a truck to be delivered.

Ramos laughs when she recalls the amazement of friends and family at how she'd exchanged business suits and high heels for old sweatpants and rubber boots. "It broke my heart to give up those suits," she says, but jokes that she'd just traded slinging one type of mud for another.

She gained custody of her three young grandchildren after one of her sons and his wife were imprisoned on drug-related charges. Around the same time, her father had begun suffering from Alzheimer's, so her parents moved in. A friend, Elaine Shearer, remembers seeing Ramos working with concrete behind the house with a baby carrier on her back. Occasionally, when Ramos had to deliver her product at night, the children would join her, sleeping in car seats. Still, the job allowed her to set her own hours and stay close to home.

In 2004, her business took a major hit when another company underbid her and won the contract that had been her principal source of income for six years. Soon after, she packed up and decamped to Florida with her three grandchildren and her eighty-three-year-old, recently widowed mother, ready for warmer weather and another reinvention. Backus remained behind but planned to rejoin the family once he retired.

On the Gulf Coast, about two hours north of Tampa, lies the community of Pine Ridge with well-kept, ranch-style homes, equestrian riding trails, a golf course, tennis courts, and a community center. For less than $300,000, Ramos bought a two-year-old house with 2,600 square feet and a swimming pool out back. Compared to Anchorage, it was paradise.

Using the proceeds from the sale of her parents' Hawaiian home, she was able to buy the house free and clear. No mortgage, no debt.

She wanted the freedom she had enjoyed working for herself. So, in the fall of 2004, she took out a mortgage on her new house for $90,000 and used the money to buy a local lawn-care business. First by herself and then working with one of her sons, she'd mow lawns, cut hedges, and blow debris.

"I love to mow," she says. The business grew to about forty customers, she recalls. "We were doing good."

"A Little Bit More to Catch Up"

In June 2005, Ramos was driving a few miles from the house with her mother and all three grandchildren. A car pulled out from a side road and crossed her lane. Traveling at forty to forty-five miles per hour, Ramos couldn't stop in time, and her minivan plowed into the other car. Ramos suffered a broken arm and injuries to her knee and hip. Her mother and granddaughter, then ten, injured their backs. Her car, little more than a year old, was wrecked. The police report puts the blame on the other driver, a woman who was nineteen years old at the time and visiting from New Jersey.

In a single moment, Ramos had lost her car and ability to work. Customers dropped off one by one. Soon, the mortgage payment of $790 per month that had seemed well within her means became a burden. She began running up debt on her credit cards. About six months after the crash, she remembers, she fell behind by one mortgage payment.

Collection agencies began to hound Ramos. When Shearer visited her friend, "I would hear the calls coming in. It gets to a person after a while. I did see Sheila being worn down." The women had been friends for two decades, but "this was the first time where I heard her calling me and crying and saying, 'Elaine, I don't know where to go, I don't know what to do.'"

It was around the holidays, Ramos recalls, when a postcard came from Equity Trust Mortgage, proclaiming her eligible for another mortgage. She threw out that postcard, but the company ran classified ads at the time under the headline "REFINANCE NOW, LOW RATES" and promising, "Aggressive Programs: Fast Approvals, Fast Closings. Programs from good to poor credit. Non-income OK, limited credit OK. We can tailor a program for you. Call 24 hrs."

Ramos remembers thinking, "Maybe I'll just get a little bit more to catch up." She landed a $140,000 mortgage and paid off the $90,000 one she had used to launch her business.

Before moving to Florida, she'd never taken out a mortgage, she says, and was inclined to trust the mortgage broker, Stan Petersen, who ran Equity Trust Mortgage. He assured her it was OK, she recalls, and she didn't pay much attention to the details when she signed the paperwork.

After the old loan and numerous fees were paid off, the new loan brought her enough to buy a car and pay off her other debt but little else, she says. Then there was the monthly payment: it started at $1,150, more than the one on her last mortgage, which she hadn't been able to pay. She swore off credit cards. Still, she says, the new mortgage left her "just surviving."

It was a subprime loan, so the worst was yet to come. After two years, the initial fixed interest rate of 9.25 percent would switch to an adjustable rate. It could never dip below the initial rate but might rise as high as 14.25 percent. If Ramos attempted to escape the loan by refinancing or selling the house before the rate hike, she'd be liable for a penalty of about $5,000.

Around this time, one of her sons wanted to live on his own. So, five months after getting her new mortgage, Ramos took out another $28,000 loan against her home to purchase a trailer for him. It didn't add to her expenses because her son made the monthly payments.

But Ramos was doing what so many Americans did at that time: using her home as an ATM as the frenzied buying of the bubble years raised the value of nearly every house in the country. From 2004 through 2006, American homeowners extracted nearly $1.5 trillion out of their homes, providing a huge boost to the economy. While a lot of that money went to general consumer spending, particularly home improvements, the largest amount went to pay off other debt. Ramos was typical in using the money from her various mortgages to keep her head above water. Many also used the funds, as she'd done, to start a business.

At this time, she, her mother, and her granddaughter were still being treated for their injuries. She'd hired a lawyer to pursue a settlement with the other driver's insurance company, but that was dragging on. After working for more than thirty years, she was convinced it would be just a little bit longer before she was healthy and back at her business. Instead, she began falling behind on her payments again.

To stay afloat, Ramos borrowed from friends and relatives, which weighed on her, her friend Shearer says. "She was never one to owe anybody anything before."

Ramos would get occasional calls from Petersen, her mortgage broker. "He was like my best friend," she recalls. "He'd say, 'Hi, Sheila, how are you doing?' " He knew about the car accident and that she was struggling, she says. But when she asked whether she should just put her house up for sale, she recalls, he said there was no need because she could get yet another loan, one that would allow her to pay off her current ones plus give her some money to make the first payments on the new loan. That would tide her over until she got the accident settlement and could work again. "We'll send an appraiser out, and we'll get you this loan," she remembers Petersen saying. "You've got plenty of equity, don't worry."

Less than a year after her first big refinance, her second major loan was much larger: $262,000. Her home, however, had been appraised at $403,000, which, if true, meant that it was gaining about $40,000 in value every year. Seen that way, the loan seemed almost conservative.

As with all her other dealings with Petersen, she recalls, he himself did not appear; instead, a woman came in the evening with a stack of papers. Ramos remembers that the woman was running late and hurriedly prompted Ramos to initial or sign her way through. The whole whirlwind ceremony at her kitchen table, she says, took about fifteen minutes.

The new loan was also an adjustable rate mortgage, and her initial monthly payment was about $2,200 per month, nearly triple that of her first mortgage.

To make those payments, she recalls, Petersen had told her she could use the proceeds from the refinance. After paying off her two previous mortgages, the penalties for paying them off early, and various loan fees, she would receive $65,000 in cash.

As Christmas approached, the money had yet to arrive. On December 19, Ramos overdrew her checking account twice when she made two debit-card purchases—for $9.09 and $7.50—at a Winn-Dixie supermarket. The two overdraft fees came to $66. The next day, a $37.50 check and a $35.66 charge at Kmart cost her $66 more in overdraft fees. A day later, a $9.95 purchase brought another $33 overdraft fee.

But that day—December 22—the $65,000 finally landed in her checking account, and it was a new day.

She repaid friends and relatives from whom she'd borrowed thousands. Her bank records show she caught up on her taxes, her cable, Internet, and utility bills. She got her car fixed. She bought Christmas presents. She took her grandchildren to a resort near Disney World "to give them a treat because they'd been so stressed," she recalls.

Within two months, about $30,000 was gone. Looking back today, she can't remember where it all went: "It seems like a dream."

The Wall Street Mortgage Machine

Ramos signed the papers for her $262,000 mortgage in December 2006. She didn't know it, but she was riding the last wave of the subprime boom.

Arranged by her local broker, Petersen, the loan was made by a nationwide subprime lender called Mortgage Lenders Network USA. Months earlier, the company, then the nation's fifteenth-largest subprime lender, had broken ground on a $100 million, 300,000-square-foot headquarters building in Connecticut. But less than two weeks after issuing Ramos's loan, the company stopped funding new ones. It soon furloughed employees. By February 2007, it had declared bankruptcy.

Before it collapsed, Mortgage Lenders Network sold Ramos's loan to Wall Street. The buyer was Merrill Lynch, which bundled it with 6,282 other mortgages totaling $1.4 billion and packaged them into a security, the "Merrill Lynch Mortgage Investors Trust, 2007-MLN1." Investors were invited to buy different classes of the security, arranged from least to most risk. Most of the mortgage loans, like Ramos's, had been made to borrowers with poor credit histories. Nevertheless, the credit-rating agencies Moody's and Standard & Poor's gave AAA ratings to the security's safest classes, meaning they were supposedly investments of the "highest quality, with minimal credit risk."

The 326-page offering document does include warnings. On page 17 it says, "In recent months, delinquencies and losses with respect to residential mortgage loans generally have increased and may continue to increase, particularly in the subprime sector." What's more, most of the loans, like Ramos's, had adjustable rates that might jump after two years, which could lead to more defaults and foreclosures. Also, a decline in housing prices could make it impossible for borrowers to sell their homes or refinance, trapping them in foreclosure. And most of the loans went to people with poor credit.

It goes on. Many subprime lenders like Mortgage Lenders Network were struggling or failing because their loans were performing so poorly. They were also being accused of fraud, the document says, though it just notes the general trend and doesn't say that Mortgage Lenders Network faced that charge.

Despite those caveats, the document asserted that the loans in the pool had been made according to reliable underwriting guidelines, meaning the borrowers' history, assets, and income had been carefully reviewed by Mortgage Lenders Network. "The consumer's ability to pay is of primary importance when evaluating applications," it said. Still, Merrill Lynch could not "provide any assurance that MLN had followed the stated guidelines with respect to the origination of any of the Mortgage Loans."

The security found buyers, including the government-backed mortgage behemoths Fannie Mae and Freddie Mac. In a federal lawsuit filed in September 2011 against Merrill Lynch, the federal agency overseeing Fannie and Freddie claimed the companies were swindled when they purchased the pool that included Ramos's loan (and eighty-seven other securities sold from 2005 to 2007). Merrill has denied wrongdoing.

As in dozens of other cases filed in recent years by investors in subprime securities—often pension funds that were looking for safe, AAA-rated investments—the suit argues that the mortgages were worse than the offering documents represented them to be, leading to large losses.

According to the complaint, the appraisers, working with lenders and brokers, inflated the value of homes. In the case of Ramos's pool, the suit claims that more than a quarter of the loans exceeded the value of the homes, while the offering had said that none did. The offering also misrepresented the number of properties that were actually investments, not primary residences, the suit says. Those are seen as riskier loans because the borrower is likelier to abandon the property.

Then there's the issue of how much money the borrowers were making. While subprime loans were by definition given to people with poor credit histories, those borrowers were supposed to have sufficient income to make their payments. But, the suit charges, many didn't. Lenders and brokers often failed to verify the borrower's income or just made it up.

Sheila Ramos's loan was arranged by Petersen, her broker. Mortgage brokers were the ground troops for the subprime boom. More than 200,000 people began work as mortgage brokers during the boom, according to the Financial Crisis Inquiry Commission's report. Not only did they steer a borrower to a certain lender, they typically prepared the paperwork for the loan. They often purported to be acting in the best interests of the borrower, but they had a financial incentive to steer their customers to more expensive loans. Their compensation was often tied to the interest rate; the higher the interest rate, the more they were paid.

And they had no long-term stake in the loan: "For brokers, compensation generally came as up-front fees," states the FCIC report. "So the loan's performance mattered little."

Fraud was widespread in the industry.

Petersen's company had a big payday for originating Ramos's loan, according to the loan documents. From Ramos, the company received $8,200 in fees just for setting up the loan. But Petersen also got $5,238 from Mortgage Lenders Network for originating a high-interest-rate loan. The company collected a total of $13,438.

Petersen's haul was big even for the boom years. Back then, brokers commonly earned about $10,000 for subprime loans the size of Ramos's, says Fred Arnold, a director of the National

Association of Mortgage Professionals. Rules enacted since the housing crash—particularly by the Federal Reserve—have since restricted how brokers are paid.

Ramos says she clearly explained her situation to Petersen: that she wasn't working because of her injuries and that her family was making do with her mother's Social Security payments and what little other income they could muster. Petersen had the opportunity to verify her meager earnings. The mortgage file, reviewed by *ProPublica*, includes an authorization form allowing Petersen to examine Ramos's bank statements and tax returns.

Fifteen months later, when she was facing foreclosure, Ramos began to investigate the facts of her loan. She requested her loan documentation from Petersen's office, which provided it. She says she was shocked to find that her loan application listed her income as $6,500 per month.

The application, reviewed by *ProPublica*, includes other inaccuracies. It lists her as actively self-employed, but her business had fallen apart by that point. It also states that she was not currently delinquent on any mortgage even though Petersen's company, according to the loan file, had reviewed documentation showing that she was.

She called Petersen, she says, and asked why he'd falsified her income. She recalls his answer: "'Well, you got your loan, didn't you?'"

It was "extraordinarily common" for homeowners who took out mortgages during the boom to be later surprised by what their mortgage brokers had put on their loan applications, says Robert Bridges, a former mortgage loan auditor. His job was to check mortgage files and call homeowners who'd fallen behind on their mortgages to see whether there were any misrepresentations on the loan application. Over the past several years, he's investigated thousands of cases on behalf of mortgage insurance companies that wanted to make sure they didn't pay out on any improperly issued loans. Often, Bridges says, he'd tell a homeowner how much income the loan application said they were making. "They'd go, 'What? Where'd you get that number? If I made that much money, I wouldn't be in this situation.'"

After Ramos found that her income had been misstated, she complained to everyone she could think of. She sent letters and e-mails to the FBI, the Florida governor's office, and the state's Office of Financial Regulation. "My stated income was falsified and none of the information I gave him was confirmed," said her 2008 letter to the FBI Mortgage Fraud Division. Then, echoing what Bridges said he had heard from so many homeowners, Ramos wrote: "He stated my income at 6,500 per month. If I had this I would not need a loan."

Reached on his cell phone, Petersen declined to comment, saying only that "the company's closed." He has not been charged with a crime.

Neither Mortgage Lenders Network nor any of its executives have been charged with a crime, either. But in an unusual court filing, federal prosecutors have confirmed the company's practices are under investigation. In early 2011, the trustee overseeing the liquidation of the company proposed, as a cost-saving measure, destroying a warehouse full of mortgage files. The Justice Department objected, arguing that the files shouldn't be destroyed until investigators had had a chance to thoroughly review them. The company's "loans are the subject of many ongoing investigations," said the submission to the bankruptcy court. Representatives for the defunct company declined to comment.

The mortgages bundled into "Merrill Lynch Mortgage Investors Trust, 2007-MLN1" have not fared well. As of October 2011, about 40 percent of them had been foreclosed on, as shown in the chart, taken from investor reports. Another 21 percent of the borrowers are behind on their payments and facing foreclosure. Moody's and S&P now rate the safest classes of the security—once judged as having "minimal" risk—as having "very high" risk. It's a junk bond.

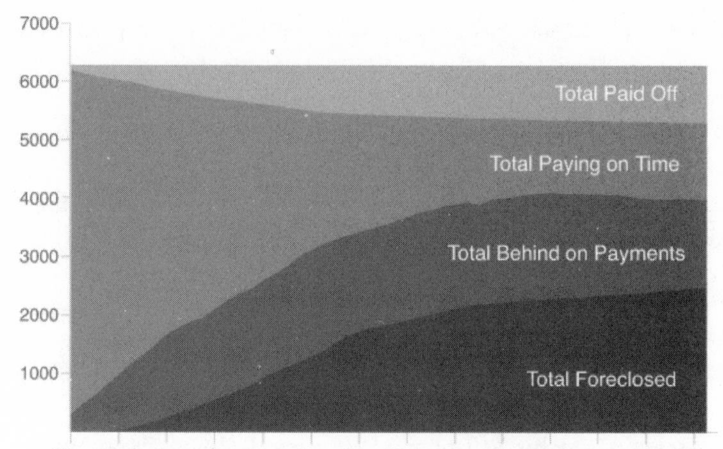

How Homeowners Are Faring in the Security That Includes Ramos's Mortgage
Sources: Deutsche Bank trust reports, ProPublica analysis.

Similar securities have also fared poorly. Among the eighty-eight Merrill Lynch securities targeted by the Fannie Mae and Freddie Mac lawsuit, all have high rates of foreclosure and delinquency. When the suit was filed last fall, on average, a little more than half of the homeowners had either already lost their homes to foreclosure or were in danger of doing so.

The collapse of hundreds of securities like these precipitated the 2008 financial crisis and plunged America into the Great Recession.

The Mortgage-Servicing Industry

One day in the mail, Ramos received a notice that she had missed a mortgage payment. The notice came from a company she'd never heard of, Wilshire Credit Corp. "I was confused," she says, because she'd sent her payments to her lender, Mortgage Lenders Network. Why was this other company, Wilshire, suddenly asking her for payments?

In a bygone era, the bank that made the loan held onto it and collected the payments. In today's system, that's rare. Instead, the job of actually dealing with homeowners and collecting loan payments falls to mortgage servicers.

Serving homeowners is decidedly not the mortgage-servicing industry's focus. Servicers rarely have a stake in the loan itself. They are middlemen, collecting payments from homeowners, keeping a small cut and passing the bulk to investors. They make money keeping costs low. Hiring employees to speak to borrowers about avoiding foreclosure, for example, increases costs and diminishes profits. So, in general, servicers make money by providing as little service to homeowners as possible.

During the housing boom, the industry underwent a dramatic consolidation. In 2004, the ten largest servicers handled about a quarter of the country's mortgages. By late 2008, the five largest handled about 60 percent. It was a high-volume, low-cost business that boiled down to processing payments. Interaction with the customer was minimal and, when it did occur, involved call-center employees who often made as little as ten dollars per hour.

That model hummed as long as relatively few people fell behind on their mortgages. With the housing crash and ensuing recession, everything changed. Delinquent homeowners stopped sending their monthly checks, so instead of processing payments that had come in like clockwork, servicers suddenly had to shoulder the much more expensive tasks of making collection calls, considering the homeowner for some sort of modification or payment plan, and seeking foreclosure if the homeowner fell far enough behind.

Servicers were unprepared. Their employees lacked sufficient training, and there were too few of them. They lacked proper equipment and relied on outdated computer systems. And there was little financial incentive to spend time working with customers. Handling a delinquent loan costs the servicer more than ten times as much as a loan on which the borrower is making the monthly payments, according to an estimate by federal regulators.

Just as Ramos didn't know that Merrill Lynch had bought her loan and then sold it to investors, she also didn't know that Merrill Lynch had selected its own subsidiary, Wilshire, to collect her payments. A small servicer based in Beaverton, Ore., with about 800 employees at the time, Wilshire specialized in handling subprime loans.

In the offering documents for the security that included Ramos's mortgage, Merrill Lynch assured investors that homeowners would be in good hands. Wilshire had ample experience with borrowers who were "experiencing financial difficulties." Their employees were hands-on, prepared for "substantial personal interaction with the obligors to encourage them to make their payments timely, to work with them on missed payments, and to structure individual solutions for delinquent obligors."

Typical for mortgage servicers, those phone calls would come from the company's collections department. At the same time, homeowners would hear via letters and phone calls from Wilshire's "loss mitigation" team, which was charged with deciding whether to foreclose or pursue a "viable workout opportunity." The offering documents give little detail on how foreclosure might be avoided. However, the company said it would be quick in deciding to foreclose if necessary.

Ramos, of course, had taken out the loan *because* she was "experiencing financial difficulties." The loan had bought her time, but how much? She was still injured and unemployed, leaving next to no income for the household, which was now saddled with a $2,200 monthly mortgage payment. Her checking account went one way: down, month after month. By the middle of

2007, little more than half a year after the $65,000 had landed in her checking account, the money was gone.

Nevertheless, she had hope. She'd taken in an elderly family friend with Parkinson's disease to take care of alongside her mother, and his Social Security payments provided a little additional income. One of her brothers had also moved in after discovering he had leukemia. He agreed to help with the payments while he underwent treatment. She started housecleaning because, even with her weak left arm, she could do that work: she and her teenage granddaughter labored together for the few clients she was able to find. Altogether, she figured, it might be enough to make the mortgage and get by. Her lawyers also had finally launched a suit over the car accident, and she was hopeful they'd win some extra damages beyond paying for her treatments.

But she was continually falling behind and catching up, a pattern that began even before the loan funds had run out. She says she often thought she'd made a timely payment only to find that Wilshire considered it overdue. Late charges and other fees made her climb steeper. The company's employees often called and pressed her to make her payments, but she says no one could clearly explain the reason for certain charges or what she needed to do to catch up.

Ramos had entered the maddening, Kafkaesque maze of dealing with servicers. Her complaints echo those of consumer advocates and tens of thousands of borrowers who say servicers routinely lost documents, didn't answer questions, kept homeowners on endless hold, or transferred them to people who knew nothing about their situations. Indeed, servicer errors have often made bad situations worse, sometimes even pushing borrowers into foreclosure. The accounting problems have been exposed in bankruptcy proceedings, which can force servicers to disclose exactly how they handled loans. Bankruptcy judges, who sometimes get so angry they scold servicers from the bench, have penalized companies for improperly processing payments, attempting to collect money they're not owed, and charging unwarranted fees.

"Everyone gave me the runaround," Ramos recalls. When she tried to get answers, she often found herself being transferred to this or that person, only to end up leaving a voice-mail message for someone she knew wouldn't call her back.

"You just don't understand how hard she worked at this," says Shearer, her friend, who recalls watching Ramos spend hours on the phone. "Nobody knew anything, and they'd pass you from one person to the next. It just seemed like she never could get the horse by the tail."

After nearly a full year of falling behind and catching up, Ramos tried to make a payment in March 2008, but Wilshire refused it. At the time, she was less than a month behind, according to payment records kept for investors in the security. But Ramos remembers being told that she was too far behind on her payments to make any more and that she should expect to hear from another Wilshire employee about what would happen next. Ramos had reached the brink of foreclosure. She reached out for help from housing-counseling nonprofits. "My loan company will not work with me Please Please help me save our home," she wrote to one.

A Win-Win

Ramos was part of a growing wave of defaults. Housing prices had been tumbling for more than a year after peaking in 2006, meaning that many delinquent borrowers could no longer sell their homes to get out from under their debt because their homes were now worth less than they owed. For a subprime servicer like Wilshire, the downturn meant that nearly half of the subprime loans it handled were delinquent.

That was a problem for lenders, for the Wall Street banks that had bought such loans, for the investors who'd purchased securities Wall Street concocted out of these loans, and, of course, for borrowers who were losing their homes, their savings, and their creditworthiness. For policy makers, the solution was clear: Get struggling homeowners into affordable loan modifications.

To be sure, modifying a loan by reducing the interest rate, for instance, would mean a loss—or lower profit—for the investor. But if foreclosure was likely to result in even higher losses, then a modification was preferable. Given plummeting home values, a modification would often save the investor money. It seemed like the ultimate win-win.

The earliest governmental program had a modest aim: to make sure the servicer merely considered a modification before pursuing foreclosure. In October 2007, President George W. Bush's administration launched the Hope Now Alliance to provide a forum for servicers and housing counselors to communicate.

"The first step to avoid a foreclosure was for the servicer and borrower to talk to one another," wrote former Treasury official Phillip Swagel in a 2009 narrative of the financial crisis, "but this was not happening in a surprisingly high proportion of instances—some estimates were that half of foreclosures started without contact between borrower and lender or servicer."

So, at the administration's prompting, servicers backed the launch of a hotline (888-995-HOPE) that homeowners could call to speak with a housing counselor, and the companies agreed to send notices to delinquent borrowers about it. President Bush himself recorded a public service announcement encouraging homeowners to call.

But even if a homeowner contacted a counselor and qualified for a modification, there was no requirement that the servicer offer one. In fact, there were no requirements at all for servicers. The alliance was administered by the Financial Services Roundtable, a powerful banking-industry trade group, and headquartered in its offices.

Loan modifications were indeed a win-win for everyone—except the servicers. And it was the servicers who were the deciders. They determined whether homeowners like Ramos got loan modifications.

Servicers earn their main revenue through a small fee for handling each loan, usually between .25 and .5 percent of the principal each year, depending on the type. (Riskier loans like Ramos's netted more.) But servicers have another big income stream: penalty fees and foreclosure-related charges.

Ramos's case shows how lucrative such fees could be. If Ramos had made all of her payments on time, Wilshire would have received only about $1,300 (.5 percent of her outstanding principal) in the first year of handling her loan. But if Ramos was more than ten days late with a payment, it generated a late charge of 10 percent of the overdue payment—in her case, about $220. That amount would then be due on top of what she owed.

Experts say these terms were especially punitive even for subprime loans, which typically gave borrowers more time and penalized them less for being late. While Ramos no longer has records showing how much she paid in late fees, an August 2008 breakdown by Wilshire of unpaid charges on her account shows outstanding late fees of $770 and a returned-check charge of $50—an extra $820 on top of its base of $1,300.

If Ramos or other troubled homeowners could somehow scrape together the money to pay such fees, great. But the true genius of the business model is that it didn't matter whether borrowers could pay the fees. If a homeowner went bust and the house was sold through foreclosure, no problem. The securitization contracts ensured the servicer was first in line to collect.

It was a virtually fail-safe income stream. In 2008, Ocwen, a subprime servicer similar to Wilshire, received about 19 percent of its mortgage-servicing income from such fees. In fact, some servicing executives assured analysts that mounting delinquencies would actually help their companies.

David Sambol, chief operating officer for Countrywide, then the country's largest subprime lender and servicer, pitched this idea to stock analysts during a fall 2007 earnings call. His company, he claimed, would benefit from "greater fee income from items like late charges" and the company's "counter-cyclical diversification strategy" of running businesses involved in foreclosing on homes, such as property-inspection services. As more and more homeowners ran into trouble and then foreclosure, the servicer could count on more short-term income, not less.

In 2010, the Federal Trade Commission sued Countrywide, accusing it of a widespread scheme to profit from delinquencies and foreclosures by hitting homeowners with bogus or marked-up charges. Countrywide settled the suit without admitting any wrongdoing. It agreed to stop overcharging borrowers and pay $108 million to consumers who'd been affected.

Compared to Countrywide, Wilshire was tiny and hasn't been charged with wrongdoing. But the larger economics were the same: If Ramos kept paying, Wilshire made money. If she lost her home, Wilshire made money.

The one option that didn't make financial sense for servicers was spending money on staff and equipment to make sure that homeowners like Ramos were adequately reviewed for modifications. Trained employees would have to spend valuable time analyzing the borrower's situation and, in effect, re-underwrite the loan. Worrying too much about unnecessary foreclosures would cut into servicers' profits. Servicers also worried that investors might object to cutting homeowners' payments and sue to recoup any supposed losses. No forum for servicers and borrowers to "talk to one another" was going to change the fundamentals of the servicing industry: Collect payments or foreclose.

In the rare event that a homeowner did receive a modification, it didn't typically lower the homeowner's payments, according to a 2008 report by federal banking regulators. About a third of the modifications granted in 2008 actually made the payments go up, because all the servicer had done was lump the arrears and fees into the principal and then amortized the new, higher balance over the life of the loan. About a quarter of the time, the payments stayed the same, and only about 42 percent of the time did they actually go down. As a result, most modifications merely delayed foreclosure. By the end of 2009, according to regulators, more than two-thirds of the homeowners who'd received modifications in 2008 had fallen behind again.

In 2008, Merrill Lynch, Wilshire's corporate parent, reacted to the downturn not by expanding but by freezing hiring at Wilshire. No new staff was added, and departing employees were replaced by temp workers, many of whom had scant experience in the mortgage industry. For Merrill, the logic was clear: The bubble had popped; investors were no longer willing to buy packages of subprime loans, so there would be few if any new loans for Wilshire to handle. So what if most of the old loans would now require far more time and effort? Wilshire would just have to make do with the staff it had.

"Dear Valued Customer"

It was through the HOPE Now hotline that Ramos found a housing counselor with Consumer Credit Counseling Service, a large Atlanta-based nonprofit that has since changed its name to CredAbility. She went through all her income and expense information, and the resulting worksheet, prepared by the counselor, shows Ramos with monthly income of $4,700, which was enough to cover her regular monthly mortgage payments (not including fees) as well as her living expenses with about $300 left over.

The counselor told her she was a good candidate for a mortgage modification, meaning that it would not only help Ramos but be in the best financial interest of the investors. Here was a case of that win-win. With home prices plummeting, kicking Ramos out of her home meant a certain loss for investors. Even a generous modification would likely cost them less. All that was required was for the servicer to put its own interests—maximizing fees and minimizing costs—to the side.

Studies have shown that homeowners working with counselors have fared better than those working on their own (a low bar to clear), but counselors have often complained that they spent a lot of their time just trying to get homeowners' applications acknowledged and reviewed. Delays and lost documents have been the rule.

So it went with Ramos and her counselor: Their major hurdles were logistical—getting someone, anyone from Wilshire on the phone and getting that person to acknowledge receipt of documents that they had sent to the company. Ramos' counselor sent the same documents several times, Ramos remembers. Even though Wilshire was a member of the HOPE Now Alliance, Ramos remembers a Wilshire employee telling her that there was no need to go through a counselor: She could simply contact the company directly—which, of course, she'd had no luck doing.

Ramos knew she couldn't rely on Wilshire for help. In the months that passed while she waited for an answer to her application for a modification, she looked for other options. She listed the home for sale with the help of a friend who offered to waive her commission if it sold, but there were no takers. She began searching for a homeless shelter in the area that could take all seven people in the house if they were suddenly evicted but found that no shelter could.

She got help from neighbors. One day, during one of her many conversations with Wilshire employees, she recalls that an employee told her the company might allow her to resume making payments if she made a lump-sum payment of around $5,000. She told one neighbor, Dave Shea, about the offer, and Shea decided to make the rounds in the neighborhood asking for donations.

"I knocked on a lot of doors," Shea said. "I know a lot of folks."

He told them their neighbor was facing foreclosure and needed help getting caught up. One by one, they handed over $50, $100, sometimes several hundred dollars. It wasn't a hard sell, he says. "These people are just willing to help."

Eventually, he delivered about $5,000 to Ramos. Elated, she went with her brother to his credit union to deposit the money and convert it into a cashier's check, she recalls. Wilshire, as do many servicers with delinquent homeowners, required payment with guaranteed funds. They mailed it off, hopeful they'd finally stopped the snowballing growth of her debt, she says. But where those funds went—whether they were deposited and not applied to her mortgage or simply lost—she still doesn't know. How servicers handle payments is often a mystery to homeowners, who often complain that they're lost or misapplied.

On July 12, 2008, Ramos got her first clear response to her efforts to catch up: a summons. "A lawsuit has been filed against you," it said. Wilshire had decided to foreclose.

Ramos's chances for a modification at Wilshire, it turns out, were dismal. In 2009, as part of a report on Wilshire's servicing performance, the credit-rating agency Fitch analyzed how people in Ramos's situation—subprime borrowers who were delinquent in early 2008—had fared. A year later, only about 12 percent had either caught up on their payments or managed to pay off their loans (mostly through selling or refinancing). The rest—fully 88 percent—had already lost their homes, were in the foreclosure pipeline, or were still behind and likely destined for foreclosure.

Bank of America spokesman Rick Simon, speaking for Wilshire because the bank later acquired the company, says the servicer had reviewed Ramos numerous times for some sort of foreclosure alternative. Back in February or March 2008, there had been "a discussion of setting up a formal six-month payment plan," he says, but Ramos hadn't agreed. Ramos has no memory of such a conversation.

The payment plan was Wilshire's preferred solution to delinquency in 2008, according to a Moody's report, and a favorite industry tool: The servicer simply tacked missed payments and fees onto regular payments. The result, of course, was even higher payments for the struggling borrower.

Three months later, in June, Simon says, Wilshire declined Ramos's application for a modification. The company then reviewed her for another payment plan but rejected that, too. Simon declined to provide the reasons for the denials or evidence that Ramos had been notified. Ramos, for her part, doesn't remember ever hearing about any of this before she was sued.

Instead, almost a week *after* Wilshire launched a foreclosure suit, it sent her a letter, which read in full:

> Dear Valued Customer:
>
> In connection with the above referenced loan, Wilshire Credit Corporation ("Wilshire") has reviewed your request for a MODIFICATION. Please be advised that after careful consideration, Wilshire has declined to approve your request.
>
> If you have any questions, please contact us at our toll-free number above.
>
> Sincerely,
> Loan Workout

The Bailout

It was in 2008 that the full force of the foreclosure crisis hit. Housing prices went into free fall—by year's end, Tampa home prices had tumbled about a third from their peak. Foreclosures skyrocketed, rising about 80 percent from 2007. In September, the investment bank Lehman Brothers went bankrupt, and the beating heart of the financial system seized up.

"I felt that this is something like I've never seen before, and the American public and Congress don't fully understand the gravity" of the crisis, legendary investor Warren Buffett recalled in a 2009 interview with the *Wall Street Journal*. "I thought, we are really looking into the abyss."

Though the crisis had spread far beyond real estate, mortgages like Ramos's—bundled, sold, bundled again, insured, and insured against—were the absolute epicenter. Banks and insurance companies carried billions of dollars of mortgage-related assets on their balance sheets, and those assets were plunging in value by the day. Yet HOPE Now, with its goal of encouraging homeowners and servicers merely to communicate, was still the government's chief effort to stem the damage.

For reformers, the near collapse of the financial system and the ascension of an energetic new president whose party controlled both houses of Congress provided an opportunity to act boldly. Until that point, the idea of using taxpayer dollars to stem foreclosures—supported by some Democrats and economists in the Bush administration's Treasury Department—had been a political nonstarter because of the perception that it would reward irresponsible behavior. But in October, Congress passed legislation creating the $700 billion Troubled Asset Relief Program, more commonly known as TARP or simply "the bailout."

The TARP plan, formulated by Bush's Treasury Department, was for the government to buy up the "troubled assets," mainly those securities backed by mortgages that were defaulting in droves. Democrats agreed but pushed for a clause that would mandate the government to modify the loans contained in the assets it purchased. With the government as the dominant owner of the assets, the thinking went, it would be in a position to dictate how they were handled. After the bill passed, the stage seemed set for the government to rescue not only the country's largest financial institutions but also millions of homeowners.

Less than a month after the bill passed, Treasury Secretary Hank Paulson changed course. Buying up the assets would be too complicated and take too long, he decided. The financial system needed quicker intervention. So, the Treasury Department invested directly in the banks. Along with the billions being loaned daily by the Federal Reserve, the move stopped the economy's free fall. But it did nothing to address foreclosures.

Obama's Options

In the wake of that decision, two broad alternatives emerged.

Federal Deposit Insurance Corp. chairman Sheila Bair, appointed by Bush, had been agitating since at least 2007 for modifications. Now, she proposed a system of incentives to make affordable modifications more attractive to servicers and investors. Using a $24 billion pool of TARP funds, the FDIC would pay servicers $1,000 for each modification. That money would help offset the costs of evaluating the borrower and compensate the servicer for forsaking the quick returns from foreclosure. The FDIC would also provide insurance on any modified loans by sharing the loss if the homeowner defaulted again and ended up in foreclosure. For investors, Bair thought, modifying loans through the program would be a no-brainer, and they would lean hard on servicers to push them through. Many Democrats supported the idea.

If the FDIC plan was about dangling carrots, the other option was all stick. Called "cramdown," it relied on bankruptcy courts to force a modification on investors and servicers.

Current law allowed judges to slash credit-card and other kinds of debt (even mortgages on second homes), but the debtor's primary mortgage on a principal residence was off limits. That's why Ramos hadn't declared bankruptcy. She didn't have much debt outside of her mortgage, so at most, declaring bankruptcy might have slightly delayed her foreclosure.

But if the law were changed, then bankruptcy might have made sense for Ramos. A bankruptcy judge would have assessed her financial situation and the true market value of her home. If the judge found Ramos had enough income to keep the home, then he could cram down her debt by reducing the interest rate, the principal, or both.

In fact, the carrot of incentives and the stick of forced modifications probably worked best together: The threat of a bankruptcy judge stepping in would provoke servicers to modify loans. "That was always the thought, that judicial modifications would make voluntary modifications work," says North Carolina representative Brad Miller, one of several Democrats who were pushing cramdown legislation.

Republicans and the banks vehemently opposed cramdown. "It undermines the foundation of the capitalist economy," says Swagel, the former Bush Treasury official. "What separates us from [Russian leader Vladimir] Putin is not retroactively changing contracts."

Banks, of course, didn't want a third party slashing their loans and potentially costing them billions in lost interest and write-downs. "Every now and again an issue comes along that we believe would so fundamentally undermine the nature of the financial system that we have to take major efforts to oppose, and this is one of them," Floyd Stoner, the head lobbyist for the American Bankers Association, told an industry magazine.

Democrats tried and failed to include cramdown in the TARP legislation, in part because then-presidential-candidate Barack Obama, who was leading in the polls and was consulted by congressional leaders, thought something so controversial might "cloud this thing with partisan politics," as he put it, and imperil the bill's passage.

But cramdown's backers remained optimistic. After all, Obama had campaigned on it and, shortly after rejecting the idea of including it in the TARP, had called it "the right thing to do, to change our bankruptcy laws so that people have a better chance of staying in their homes." He promised Democrats he'd "push hard to get cramdown into the law," Miller recalls.

Cramdown would change the law, requiring an act of Congress. But Sheila Bair's incentives could be enacted unilaterally by the executive branch.

Less than a month into his presidency, Obama announced his new plan. "In the end, all of us are paying a price for this home-mortgage crisis," he told a cheering crowd in Mesa, Ariz. "And all of us will pay an even steeper price if we allow this crisis to continue to deepen—a crisis which is unraveling homeownership, the middle class, and the American dream itself. But if we act boldly and swiftly to arrest this downward spiral, then every American will benefit." The program, he promised, would "enable as many as 3 to 4 million homeowners to modify the terms of their mortgages."

Even as he spoke, Treasury Department officials were still scrambling to work out the details—rules and calculations that would bear enormous consequences for millions of homeowners like Ramos and for the American economy. "We didn't have much on paper at that time," Laurie Maggiano, policy director for the new program, would later say.

In the end, the Home Affordable Modification Program, or HAMP, plucked a few ideas from Bair's carrot approach; for example, servicers would receive $1,000 immediately upon granting a modification to erase their incentive to foreclose and compensate them for evaluating homeowners' ability to afford the modified loan. That incentive was not based on hard evidence. "It was just a guess that $1,000 might be enough," says Karen Dynan, a former senior economist at the Federal Reserve.

But the administration's final plan lacked an incentive Bair considered crucial: having the government bear half the loss of any modification that failed. The administration balked. To have taxpayers eat the losses caused by deadbeat borrowers was seen as political dynamite. A Gallup poll taken in the fall of 2008, for example, had found that 79 percent of Americans cited "people taking on too much debt" as the main cause of the financial crisis. ("Banks making risky loans" was second, at 72 percent.) Instead, Treasury designed the system to pay investors for modifications, but only in increments and only if the borrower continued to make payments. The program only "paid for success," the administration boasted. On average, investors could hope to reap about $15,000 in subsidies over five years.

Bair saw another flaw she considered fatal. "In addition to the lack of economic incentives," she later explained, "the operational complexity was mind-boggling. The big servicers do not pay or train their staff as well as they should. The turnover is very high. That's the reality. You really have to make it simple for the program to be operationally effective."

In her view, the carrot needed to be juicy, sweet, and easy to get—because there were no penalties. Servicers didn't have to participate at all; if they volunteered for the program, they signed a contract with the Treasury Department agreeing to follow the rules in return for the incentives.

In the view of many on the left, the program put the government in a weak, almost supine position. But that was still too much for some on the right, who attacked the plan as a bailout for "losers."

The day after Obama announced the creation of HAMP to that cheering crowd in Arizona, CNBC commentator Rick Santelli excoriated the program in a rant that is widely credited as sparking the Tea Party movement, which jolted American politics to the right. "How many of you people want to pay for your neighbor's mortgage that has an extra bathroom and can't pay their bills?" Santelli thundered. Do Americans, he asked, "really want to subsidize the losers' mortgages"?

Cramdown's proponents saw HAMP as merely a first step. Publicly, the administration still supported cramdown, but its supporters saw worrying signs. The White House "kept punting" when Democrats pushed for cramdown to be attached to larger pieces of legislation such as the stimulus bill, says former representative Jim Marshall, a moderate Democrat from Georgia and cramdown backer. In private meetings, Treasury staffers began conversations with congressional aides by saying the administration supported cramdown and would then "follow up with a whole bunch of reasons" why it wasn't a good idea, says an aide to a senior Democratic senator.

The administration feared the consequences for the nation's biggest banks, which had been rescued just months earlier. If too many consumers were lured into bankruptcy, they wouldn't have only their mortgages reduced. They might very well have other debts slashed, such as home-equity loans and credit-card debt. The cumulative effect could devastate the banks, plunging the nation back into a financial crisis.

Cramdown's Democratic supporters needed the president's vigorous support because the measure faced powerful opponents: not just the too-big-to-fail banks but small banks and credit unions. "The community banks went bonkers on this issue," says former senator Chris Dodd (D-Conn.), then head of the Senate banking committee. Democratic leaders offered to exempt smaller banks from the legislation but couldn't reach a deal. After narrowly passing the Democrat-controlled House, cramdown was defeated in the Senate when twelve Democrats joined Republicans to vote against it.

Some, like Rep. Barney Frank (D-Mass.), then head of the powerful House Financial Services Committee, don't blame the White House for the failure of cramdown. But others certainly do. "Their behavior did not well serve the country," says Rep. Zoe Lofgren (D-Calif.). It was "extremely disappointing."

When cramdown failed, Bair felt the complicated, weak incentives in HAMP doomed that program to failure: "I think Treasury wanted a press release. I think [Treasury Secretary]

Tim Geithner and [then Obama economic advisor] Larry Summers wanted to be able to tell the president that they were doing something on loan mods."

"I Got All Dressed Up"

Ramos's foreclosure made just as little sense to her as Wilshire's actions had. Suddenly, a company named Deutsche Bank was suing her. "This lawsuit that has been filed against me was *very shocking* since, I do *not* know who the plaintiffs are, or ever heard of them," she wrote in a handwritten note to the judge. "I have been paying thousands of dollars to another company 'Wilshire Credit Corp' (which never returns my calls, or acts upon paperwork they request from me)."

The full name of the plaintiff was "Deutsche Bank National Trust Company as Trustee for the MLMI Trust Series 2007-MLN1." For Ramos, it might as well have been another language. When Merrill Lynch assembled her security, it had hired Deutsche Bank, a massive German bank with a large U.S. presence, to be the trustee. The trustee's job was to channel payments from the servicer to the investors and act as the investors' representative. That meant Deutsche Bank appeared on foreclosure suits as the plaintiff, even though it was the servicer, Wilshire, that had chosen to foreclose and hired attorneys to pursue it.

Ramos tried to get an attorney but found they were either too expensive or said they couldn't help her. The Florida Bar ran a project to provide borrowers with free legal help, but it was only for people who hadn't been sued by their lenders yet, they informed her in a letter.

Fighting foreclosure alone has been the norm for homeowners during the crisis. Although many jurisdictions don't track the number of unrepresented homeowners, it's clearly the overwhelming majority of cases, according to a Brennan Center for

Justice report. In New Jersey, for instance, 93 percent of foreclosure cases in 2010 had no attorney on record.

Ramos did her best to represent herself. One legal-services organization directed her to another county's courthouse, where a "self-help" area was set aside for borrowers who wanted to contest their foreclosures. No attorneys were there to help, but the court did provide information about the process and sample forms. She drove three hours and then carefully followed the model they had there for filing an "answer" to the motion to foreclose. In the three-page document she later filed with the court, she laid out her case in numbered paragraphs. She was a victim of predatory lending, she alleged. And since she'd learned during her long hours of research online that Mortgage Lenders Network had gone out of business shortly after her mortgage went through, she alleged there was no way that Deutsche Bank or anybody else could have recently acquired ownership of it.

For her court hearing, she bought a matching skirt and top at a secondhand store. "I got all dressed up, because I didn't want to look like a ragamuffin." She even donned heels, a throwback to her department store days. She arrived at the courthouse nervous but ready to plead her case. But her hearing had been rescheduled, she learned, though no one had told her. She didn't know what it meant. "I thought maybe they went through my records and evidence, and that's why it was canceled." At the very least, it meant she'd have a few more months in her home.

Three and a half months later, she received a notice that her case was back on. Her hearing would be in ten days. In response, she filed a five-page "Motion to Dismiss with Prejudice" and attached about a hundred pages of everything she thought was relevant: news articles and court filings about Mortgage Lenders Network, letters from Wilshire and her e-mails to the governor and FBI about the misstatement of her income on her loan application. No one could mistake it for a filing by a lawyer, but she thought it was enough to show something was wrong. "I thought the court system would at least question it."

Her hearing, of which there is no transcript because the Citrus County courts don't transcribe foreclosure hearings, didn't last long. Ramos arrived with her neighbor, Dave Shea, but they say a court officer wouldn't let him in. She found herself in front of Citrus County Judge Carol Falvey, who was sitting by herself at the end of a long table. Wilshire's attorney was on the speakerphone. "I instantly felt intimidated," Ramos recalls.

At one point, Ramos objected that Deutsche Bank hadn't shown it owned the loan. The voice on the phone said the company had filed papers showing it had proper standing to sue. Ramos had never received them. She remembers the judge saying the attorneys should send her those documents. The voice agreed. Nevertheless, the judge signed a judgment of foreclosure.

Ramos' home would be sold. None of the accusations she'd made in her filings had been directly addressed, either in a written response from Wilshire's lawyers or in the judge's order. "It was like I'd never filed the paper," she says. The whole hearing had lasted a few minutes.

An Address and a GPS

She emerged stunned and confused. She and Shea decided to see those documents themselves. The clerk's office was just downstairs, after all. They pulled her case file, a folder of about 200 pages, roughly half of which were Ramos's own submissions. What they found in the other documents was bewildering.

In October, Wilshire's lawyers had filed what they called the "Original Assignment of Mortgage." But the document purported to transfer her mortgage from a lender called Mortgage Lender's Acceptance Corp. to the Deutsche Bank trust. Her lender had been Mortgage Lenders Network. Who was Mortgage Lender's Acceptance Corp.?

The document gave an address in nearby Ocala. They decided to go check it out.

Following the directions from a GPS device, they found themselves at an office park. There was nothing like a Mortgage Lender's Acceptance Corp. to be found. Hoping to find the building's manager, they called the number on a sign advertising space for lease. "We get the guy who's been the manager of that building for five years," Shea says. He told them no business by that name had ever been there. Convinced they'd found still more fraud, the pair decided to go immediately to the authorities.

"We walked right in the front door of the State Attorney General's office," recalls Shea. Attorneys from the office spoke to them in the lobby for about twenty minutes. "I was hoping they would stop the fraud," says Ramos, but instead they asked her to send a written complaint. She says she did so but never heard back. Theresa Edwards, a former assistant attorney general in Florida, says the office was inundated with such complaints.

The assignment is unquestionably an error. Mortgage Lender's Acceptance Corp., to start with, was not her lender and never had any connection to her actual lender, Mortgage Lenders Network. The assignment even has an error in how the wrong company's name is written; the apostrophe is misplaced, presenting the name as *Lender's* instead of *Lenders'*. A company called Mortgage Lenders' Acceptance Corp. was once active in Florida, according to an incorporation filing, but not since the late 1990s.

Two parties are responsible for the mistake. The first is Wilshire, which employed the woman who signed the document. The other is the law firm working on Wilshire's behalf, Smith, Hiatt & Diaz, a large Florida firm that handles thousands of foreclosures a year—what critics would call a foreclosure mill. Generally, the servicer's attorneys prepare the assignments and send them to the servicer to be executed. Whoever actually entered in the wrong lender, Wilshire's employee signed off on it, and Smith, Hiatt & Diaz filed it with the court. Attorneys at Smith, Hiatt & Diaz did not respond to multiple calls and e-mails requesting comment.

That's who's responsible, narrowly defined. The real culprit, as with almost all servicing problems, is the bottom line. To save money, servicers usually do not document ownership of a mortgage until it's necessary to foreclose. Instead, servicers keep on file blanket authorizations for their employees to sign on behalf of the lenders whose loans they handle. As a result, a single servicing employee might sign hundreds of documents in a day on behalf of a dozen or more different lenders. Often, that low-level employee will sign as a vice president of this or that bank.

The process has produced laughable errors, transferring the mortgage to "Bogus Assignee" or dating a document "9/9/9999." "People just aren't paying attention," says Edwards, the former Florida assistant attorney general who now defends borrowers from foreclosure. "They're running them through so quickly they make mistakes."

While working with the attorney general's office in 2010, Edwards and a colleague cataloged examples of the industry's documentation practices in a presentation for county officials titled "Unfair, Deceptive, and Unconscionable Acts in Foreclosure Cases."[1]

At some servicers or companies working on their behalf, employees forged the signatures of other employees. The most famous of these is "Linda Green," an actual employee of DocX, a company that specialized in document production. Her name, with a signature obviously penned by many different hands, adorns tens of thousands of documents filed across the United States. Green and other former employees of DocX, which was shut down in 2010, told *60 Minutes* that management instructed them to sign on Green's behalf. Last year, one of the servicers that had hired DocX sued the company in a Texas court, alleging that more than 30,000 documents had been improperly executed.

The servicer, American Home Mortgage Servicing, claimed it had been ignorant of what DocX termed "surrogate signing" and is suing for damages. Lender Processing Services, DocX's parent company, does not dispute that its employees were forging signatures but said the company had gone back to fix the affected assignments and is contesting the suit.

While servicers say employees shouldn't sign another person's name, the servicers insist there's nothing wrong with their employees signing on behalf of other companies as long as proper authorization has been granted.

But in some cases, servicers have filed documents without any authorization. Internal documents obtained by ProPublica show that the nation's fifth-largest servicer, GMAC Mortgage, did just that. GMAC, a subsidiary of Ally Financial, wanted to pursue foreclosure against a New York homeowner, but the original lender had gone out of business.

"The problem is we do not have signing authority," Jeffrey Stephan, the head of GMAC's "Document Execution" team, wrote in an e-mail. Stephan went ahead and signed a document purporting to be an officer of the defunct lender anyway. A GMAC spokeswoman acknowledged Stephan didn't have authority to sign the document and said the company was planning to pursue foreclosure on the loan after it resolved the problem.

The MERS Mirage

What is shocking about Ramos's case—the false transfer of her mortgage from a defunct company that had never been connected to her loan—is that it is anything but unusual. Hers and thousands of similar cases could be written off as errors, shoddy and outrageous, perhaps, but mostly unintentional. But alongside those errors was something else entirely: the mortgage-servicing industry deliberately avoided publicly documenting ownership of loans. Indeed, the industry had created a sophisticated strategy to avoid filing legal documentation of who actually owns a mortgage.

The strategy involves a kind of shell company, one that exists to avoid government fees and allow gigantic financial institutions to toss mortgages to one another as easily as if they were baseballs. It is a system that takes the once public and legal record of ownership—who the homeowner owes money to—and embeds it inside a private company.

The document that transferred Ramos's mortgage to Deutsche Bank is signed by a woman purporting to be an "Assistant Secretary" of "Mortgage Electronic Registration Systems, Inc. as nominee for Mortgage Lender's Acceptance Corp.," a seemingly hopeless trail of abstractions. But Mortgage Electronic Registration Systems, or MERS, is an industry creation. When lenders record a mortgage or assignment, they have to pay a fee to a county office. To avoid billions in fees and make it easier to transfer mortgages, the industry launched MERS in the 1990s.

MERS does two things. Its computer system keeps track of loans. But, more important, MERS poses as the true lender in public records. If a mortgage states that MERS is the lender's "nominee," then MERS can take its place—at least on paper. In the county clerk's office, the mortgage is registered not to Mortgage Lenders Network or Merrill Lynch or Deutsche Bank or any other institution that actually lends money to a homeowner, but to MERS. And any change in real ownership of the mortgage, such as when Mortgage Lenders Network sold Ramos's mortgage to Merrill Lynch, is recorded only inside MERS, not in public records. With MERS, no matter how many times a loan is bought and sold, there's usually no need to file anything else or pay any extra fees—until it's time to foreclose.

The system currently contains roughly half of the nation's active mortgages, or about 30 million.

Even though MERS has only a few dozen employees, the company has authorized at least 8,000 people at hundreds of other companies—typically servicers but also law firms and other companies—to sign as officers of the company. That's how Ramos's assignment came to be signed by a Wilshire employee in Oregon purporting to be an "Assistant Secretary" of Virginia-based MERS.

MERS spokeswoman Janis Smith said the Wilshire employee had been properly appointed as a MERS officer.

Maybe, but a number of municipalities have sued MERS, seeking to recoup lost fees and charging the company with fraud. The latest and biggest suit, in early February, came from the New York attorney general, who charged MERS and three major banks, including Bank of America, of widespread document fraud. New York's suit charges that the industry's use of MERS to facilitate foreclosures has led to filing "false and deceptive" documents.

MERS says the system is legal and that it will fight the suit.

The involvement of MERS explains why Ramos and Shea didn't find any lender at the office park. The address listed for Ramos's lender—the no-longer-operating-in-Florida Mortgage Lenders' Acceptance Corp.—was actually MERS's registered Florida address at the time. Maintained by a separate corporate-services company, the address existed merely to satisfy state law and receive mail. In trying to find an actual lender at the address, Ramos had been chasing shadows.

"You Feel Powerless to Help"

On the morning of April 13, 2009, Sheila Ramos waited at home to hear whether her last chance to avoid foreclosure had been successful. This time, she had her own lawyer, who was at that moment arguing her case to the judge. Ramos was hopeful. After all, how could a judge give away her home on the basis of the phony paperwork she had uncovered?

That couldn't stand. Finally, they'd have to deal with her. They'd have to acknowledge her loan was fraudulent in the first place. After a year of fighting and complaining to every authority she could think of, she would finally be heard.

Just finding an attorney to represent her had been an ordeal. One she'd contacted told her he couldn't help but suggested Janet Varnell, a prominent consumer-advocate attorney in central Florida, so Ramos gave her a try.

Varnell was hesitant. An experienced litigator, she'd never handled a foreclosure case. The Florida Bar, however, had been pushing attorneys to take cases no matter their experience in the area because of the overwhelming need in the state. Legal-aid organizations couldn't keep up. Varnell, who runs a practice with her husband, felt a responsibility to try it.

"Despite never having done a day of foreclosure defense in my life, I knew better than the average attorney what to do," she says.

And Ramos had a strong case, Varnell thought. Not only was Ramos a victim of predatory lending, she thought, but the documents used to foreclose on her were clearly flawed. "There's someone on every corner in Florida who's in desperate need of help, so you don't just go running around offering help to people who don't have substantial claims," she says.

Varnell not only took the case for free but paid the fifty-dollar fee to reopen the case. About two weeks before Ramos's home was scheduled to be sold, Varnell submitted a motion to cancel the sale, overturn the judgment, and dismiss the foreclosure suit altogether.

At the center of her argument was the faulty assignment. Typical of the servicer's last-minute rush to collect the documents necessary to foreclose, the assignment was actually dated a day after Smith, Hiatt & Diaz, Wilshire's law firm, filed suit against Ramos. The original complaint had asserted that "Deutsche Bank National Trust Company as Trustee for the MLMI Trust Series 2007-MLN1" was the holder of the note and mortgage but offered no documentation to support that. Instead, all that had been attached was a copy of the note and mortgage made out to Mortgage Lenders Network, the original lender. The assignment, dated the next day and filed months later, couldn't fix that problem, she argued. It only made matters worse that the assignment was itself obviously flawed, confusing things further by referring to the wrong lender.

The early signs for Ramos were good. Smith, Hiatt & Diaz responded to the motion by immediately moving to cancel the upcoming sale. A hearing was quickly scheduled. Varnell would have Judge Falvey's ear for a fifteen-minute phone call.

Falvey wasn't impressed. Again, because the county does not transcribe foreclosure hearings, there's no transcript, but Varnell remembers the judge being dismissive of the flaws in the mortgage's documents. The foreclosing party appeared to have the note and mortgage, and that was good enough for her.

When asked about the ruling, Falvey's assistant said the judge doesn't comment on individual cases.

Ramos was crushed, and so was Varnell. "Frankly, it came as a shock," the lawyer recalls. "I remember crying when I knew the judge was not going to give us our day in court . . . crying more for myself because you feel powerless to help."

In the wake of the legal defeat, Varnell struck a deal with the attorney from Smith, Hiatt & Diaz: If Varnell did not appeal Falvey's ruling, Wilshire would indefinitely postpone the foreclose sale and evaluate Ramos for a modification.

Knowing what she knows now, Varnell wrestles with this decision. It was a kind of capitulation but a realistic one, she thinks. At the time, in early 2009, few Florida state court decisions clearly established that the lender needed to clearly establish ownership of the note and mortgage in order to foreclose. "The law was not really well advanced at the time," she says.

Since then, a number of similar cases have made their way to the appellate level. In late 2011, Florida's Fourth District Court of Appeal overturned two district decisions because, as in

Ramos's case, the lender hadn't executed an assignment before the complaint.

"If I had been in this situation today," says Varnell, "I probably would have gone on and filed the appeal, and I feel I would have won."

Since losing Ramos's case, Varnell has represented more than a dozen other homeowners and had much more success, even getting some of the foreclosure suits thrown out.

From the perspective of the mortgage industry, borrowers are just finding a "technical legal argument to get out of paying your mortgage" by seizing on flawed documents, said Tom Deutsch, executive director of the American Securitization Forum, which counts the country's biggest banks among its members. When mortgages like Ramos's were sold to Wall Street banks like Merrill Lynch, agreements clearly laid out the transfers, he says, and there's no "role for the court there to look any farther than that clear chain of title."

Many judges haven't agreed, sometimes dealing the banks high-profile defeats, as the Massachusetts Supreme Court did in early 2011.

"They're basically saying, 'Don't hold us to the rules because we're really doing the right thing; just trust us,'" says Edwards.

About a week after Ramos's hearing, on April 20, 2009, Wilshire signed a contract with the Treasury Department to join HAMP. As part of its general agreement to follow HAMP's rules, Wilshire would be required to review all eligible loans for modifications. Loans in foreclosure like Ramos's were explicitly defined as eligible. If Ramos did get a modification through the program, her monthly payments would be cut almost in half.

A Constant Churning

HAMP was just ramping up. The Obama administration's foreclosure-prevention program relied almost entirely on servicers—and inside those companies, employees were scrambling.

Wilshire hired Justin Gersey as the HAMP project manager to oversee the company's implementation of the government's program. The government's plan to overhaul the servicing business in a matter of months was unrealistic, he says, especially for servicers larger than Wilshire. "That's just ridiculous that they could expect somebody to turn something around that quickly."

While hundreds of thousands of borrowers were calling, desperate for help, servicers were taking a triage approach to the new program, he says, deciding which guidelines to implement first and which ones to postpone. The Treasury Department was developing the program as it was being implemented, so it issued new rules and clarifications every so often. "It was this constant churning of things," says Gersey.

The large servicers were "all basically operating on giant, mainframe systems that are probably twenty years old," the legacy of years of cost-cutting, says Steven Horne, who worked as an advisor to Fannie Mae in 2007 and now runs Wingspan Portfolio Advisors, a company that specializes in handling troubled loans. That restricted their "ability to be nimble and adjust quickly to monthly changes in HAMP," he says. "And then retrain a staff of 10,000? Very, very difficult."

In fact, in the first several months of the program, the biggest challenge was just getting someone, anyone, at the servicers to pick up the phone. According to government data, borrowers complained about this basic problem more than any other.

Making matters worse was the continuing surge in delinquencies because of the ever-increasing unemployment rate. Overall, more borrowers fell behind in 2009 than during any other year of the crisis. In January of that year, about 4.3 million homeowners were two or more months behind. By December, more than 6 million were.

The Treasury Department exacerbated the problem by requiring borrowers to send in a stack of documents to prove their income, say current and former servicing employees. Servicers were already prone to losing borrowers' documents. That the

Treasury required servicers to collect borrowers' signed tax returns in addition to proof of income such as pay stubs and a written statement of hardship didn't help. The requirement was later changed so that homeowners just had to send in a signed form authorizing the servicer to request the return from the IRS.

But critics such as Horne think getting tax returns was unnecessary: "I find it deeply ironic that these loans are being underwritten ten times more stringently for a modification than they were for the original extension of credit," he says.

The voluminous document requirements were put in place to ensure that the homeowners who received help were deserving. HAMP would not "rescue the unscrupulous or irresponsible by throwing good taxpayer money after bad loans," Obama said when announcing the program. "It will not reward folks who bought homes they knew from the beginning they would never be able to afford."

Critics see a double standard. "In a nanosecond, we gave over $125 billion to nine big banks, with very few effective controls on the money," says Bair, the former FDIC chairman, referring to the Treasury's first use of TARP funds in October 2008. "But when we started talking about helping borrowers, then all of the sudden we had to be very careful about political pushback."

All these factors—unprepared, understaffed servicers; evolving and detailed government rules and document requirements; and the explosion in delinquencies—created a catastrophe. Administration officials had touted the program as a way to ensure that millions of homeowners could be efficiently and rationally considered for modifications. Instead, chaos reigned.

"We Have a Faxing Problem"

When HAMP was launched, Chris Wyatt was an employee at a company similar to Wilshire: Litton Loan Servicing, another small subprime servicer bought by a Wall Street bank, in this case Goldman Sachs. As at Wilshire, there was constant pressure to keep costs low.

HAMP initially seemed attractive for the servicer, he says, because of the taxpayer subsidies it offered, such as the $1,000 that government officials guessed might be enough. Litton deliberately delayed dealing with some delinquent homeowners until the program was launched, Wyatt recalls, in order to put them into HAMP modifications and collect the incentive payments.

In the first few months of its participation in the program, Litton put tens of thousands of homeowners into trial modifications. That was easy, because nothing had to be documented. Under the agreements, if the borrower made the lowered payments for the three-month trial period, they'd receive permanent modifications.

The hard part was for Litton to collect the borrowers' papers and crunch the numbers to verify the terms of the permanent modifications. That, he says, "turned out to be a total disaster."

Wyatt led Litton's "Executive Response Team," which was charged with handling customer complaints. Litton employees, overwhelmed and undertrained, frequently made basic errors when calculating a homeowner's income, he says. HAMP guidelines often weren't followed, because Litton was "way understaffed" and couldn't keep up, he recalls. But the worst part was the way Litton dealt with homeowners' documents, he says.

When homeowners faxed their documents, they didn't go to Litton, Wyatt says. They went to India, where a low-cost company scanned and filed the documents—but often misfiled or lost them. Wyatt says Litton routinely denied modifications because homeowners had not sent their documents when, in fact, they had.

In a process internally referred to as a "denial sweep," Litton's computers would automatically generate denial letters for every homeowner who, according to Litton's records, hadn't sent their documents. But untold numbers of those documents had been lost on another continent. Wyatt complained about the practice in multiple meetings with senior management, he says, but managers were chiefly worried about reducing the overwhelming backlog.

In general, Wyatt recalls, Litton was much more careful about granting modifications than denying them. Yes, HAMP gave financial incentives for each modification Litton and other servicers made, but modifications also meant closer scrutiny from the program's auditors.

As of the end of 2010, fewer than 12 percent of the borrowers who'd applied for a HAMP modification with Litton were granted one. The vast majority of those denials, Wyatt says, were not legitimate. Goldman Sachs's emphasis on maximizing profits rather than preventing foreclosures is typical of the servicing industry, he says, particularly the larger banks.

"They could have addressed the crisis way earlier. Had companies changed their philosophy and said, 'You know what? We're not going to beef up our collections staff; we're going to beef up our loss-mitigation staff.' Had they done that and come up with loan-modification scenarios that were reasonable and put people into more affordable payments early on, we wouldn't be where we are now."

A spokesman for Goldman Sachs said the company disagreed with Wyatt's account but offered no specifics.

At Bank of America, by far the country's largest servicer, an employee who works in one of the bank's many call centers finds the process as mystifying as do the borrowers to whom he speaks every day.

The employee says homeowners have been regularly routed to him after being rejected from HAMP for unclear reasons. Sometimes it's news to them they'd been denied at all.

He says he's learned not to put any stock in those previous denials—the income information in Bank of America's system entered by some other employee in another department is often incorrect. The best he can do, he says, is to persuade the homeowner to start over with him.

Of course, homeowners are typically weary after months of mistakes, denials, and lost documents. A little more than a year after HAMP was launched, *ProPublica* surveyed almost 400 homeowners. The average respondent had been seeking a modification for more than a year, sent in the same documents six times, and spent several hours each month on the effort. So when the Bank of America employee asked such homeowners to start all over again, well, it took some coaxing.

"I would say to them, 'Listen, I've gotta get some documents.' They'd be like, 'Oh no, please don't ask me for documents.' I'm like, 'Listen, I know what you've been through. We all know we have a faxing problem here. Just resend them. I'll look for them in three days,'" he says. If they weren't in his system, he'd ask the homeowner to resend them, he says. Three days later, he'd look again. "Usually by the third time, I'd get it."

Why does this employee wait three full days to look for a fax instead of just walking over to the machine? Because Bank of America, like Litton, uses a company in India to scan and file documents that borrowers send. Those papers get lost all the time, he says.

"The whole documentation-collection thing has got to be purposely not funded. Like, I can't get a fax. I work for a huge bank that has tons of money, and you're telling me that I can't get a fax?"

The disorganization provides numerous opportunities for borrowers to be denied a modification. And because it's so much easier to decline than approve a modification, many employees have taken advantage of those opportunities. As he recalls one of his colleagues putting it to him, “I’m in the declining business.”

Bank of America did not respond to questions about the employee’s account.

The Wave Hits Prime Borrowers

As the economy collapsed, hundreds of thousands of Americans lost their jobs, and, suddenly, it wasn’t just subprime borrowers like Ramos whose homes were in jeopardy but homeowners with prime mortgages, those given to borrowers with good credit. Today, nearly twice as many prime as subprime borrowers face foreclosure.

Thomas Sanderson of Chicago was among the hundreds of thousands of prime borrowers calling his servicer in the first months of 2009. A civil engineer who ran his own consultancy, he has a college degree and far more financial and legal sophistication than Ramos. But the recession dealt a mortal blow to his business, and he’d fallen a couple payments behind before he found another job.

Modifying Sanderson’s loan should have been an easy call, saving investors far more than a foreclosure would cost them. After all, he had a new job and could make his monthly payments again. He just couldn’t catch up on the back payments, he says.

But instead of helping Sanderson avoid foreclosure, Chase pushed him into it. A bank employee told him to make payments on a HAMP “trial” modification, but when the lower payments made him fall even further behind, Chase launched a foreclosure suit. In the end, it took almost two years and more than 200 conversations with Chase employees, he says, before he finally won an elusive modification. He has pages of notes detailing his talks with Eric, Dustin, Cathy, Leanne, Lucille, Angela, and on and on. He was successful, he says, only because he played hardball.

After Chase's lawyers filed suit against him, an assignment was executed transferring his mortgage from his original lender to the 2004 security into which his loan had been bundled. It was signed by a notary and two employees of Lender Processing Services purporting to be vice presidents of MERS.

Through a listserv for borrowers facing foreclosure, he found others with the same signatories who were investigating their paperwork. One man had sent off to get the notary's application from the state of Minnesota, and offered to share it with Sanderson. When Sanderson put the application, which bore the notary's signature, side by side with his assignment, he found the signatures bore no resemblance to one another, raising the question of whether the notary's signature had been forged. That all three signatories were employees of Lender Processing Services, the parent company of DocX, only increased his suspicions.

A spokeswoman for Lender Processing Services declined to comment on the documents.

Nevada's attorney general recently filed suit against Lender Processing Services, alleging widespread document fraud, among other things. The company says the charges are untrue but is in settlement talks with the attorney general.

In the twentieth month of his quest for a loan modification, and after yet another denial, Sanderson finally lost his patience. For most of that time, he'd been making payments, though sometimes Chase had rejected them. He'd also been paying his second mortgage, a smaller monthly sum that was also with Chase. He threatened to stop paying both, he recalls. He told a Chase employee he'd fight it out in court.

"I was like, 'Screw you guys. I'll stop paying and drag this out forever and live for free,'" he says. He mentioned the suspicious mortgage assignment and problems with the note. "Boom! Right after that, they sent me a permanent modification."

The modification, which he signed and has been paying since, set his payments to about what he'd been paying before he fell behind. Like the overwhelming majority of modifications since the launch of HAMP, his was achieved outside the program.

Christine Holevas, a spokeswoman for Chase, didn't respond to Sanderson's experience other than to say the company was "pleased we were able to provide the borrower with a modification" and that recently Chase had significantly reduced its backlog of customer complaints.

HAMP's False Hopes

Under HAMP regulations, Ramos should have been automatically considered for the program. And of course, Wilshire's attorneys had pledged she'd be reviewed. But Ramos and Varnell, her attorney, heard nothing from the company. Meanwhile, Varnell wasn't optimistic about her prospects for a modification even if she was reviewed.

Since the summer when Wilshire had first launched foreclosure proceedings, Ramos's brother had passed away, leaving the family with less income. That and Ramos's past dealings with Wilshire didn't give much reason for hope.

Indeed, in Ramos's security, very few homeowners had won modifications. Every month since the security was issued in 2007, its trustee, Deutsche Bank, has issued reports for the investors. Those reports do not show a single modification until September 2010. By that time, a year and a half after HAMP's launch, more than a third of the loans in the security had already been foreclosed on.

Simon, the spokesman for Bank of America, argues that the reports were likely inaccurate. "Wilshire was very active in modifications and other workout programs from the start of the economic crisis and well before the introduction of HAMP," he says. "The apparent lack of modifications in the securitization pool may be a reflection of how they were reported [to Deutsche

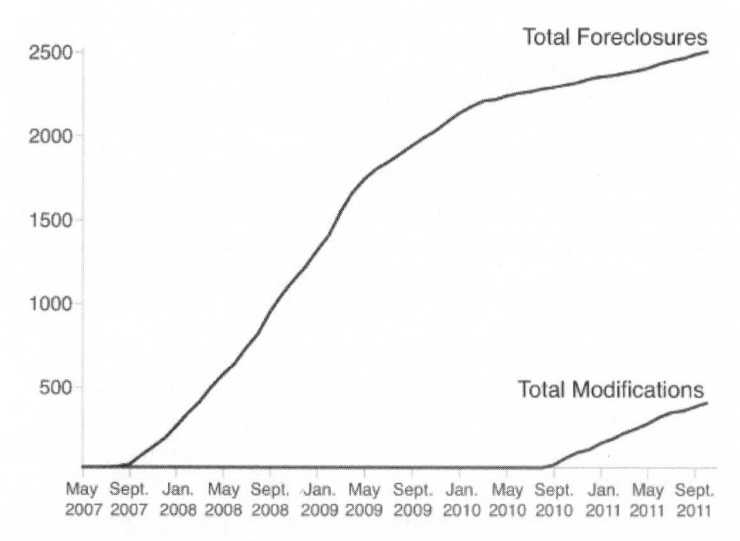

Foreclosures and Modifications in the Security That Includes Ramos's Mortgage
Sources: Deutsche Bank trust reports, ProPublica analysis.

Bank]," he said. "Wilshire may not have specifically flagged them as 'modifications.'"

(Bank of America acquired Wilshire when it bought Merrill Lynch in late 2008. In early 2010, it sold Wilshire to IBM but retained servicing for all the loans that Wilshire had been handling.)

There's not much evidence that Wilshire really was "very active in modifications." A recent analysis by Amherst Securities, a firm that provides research on mortgage-backed securities, showed that Wilshire had been the stingiest of all the major subprime servicers on granting modifications. The analysis found a similar tendency at Bank of America's other subsidiaries, which all ranked at the bottom of a list of nineteen servicers. Bank of America declined to respond to questions about its servicers' low rate of modifications.

Some homeowners have sued Wilshire, alleging it ignored HAMP's rules. In Florida, a married couple in the same security as Ramos endured a similar ordeal. Wilshire had led the couple to believe they were being evaluated for HAMP but pursued foreclosure anyway, according to their appeal of the foreclosure judgment. They also allege that Bank of America, which assumed servicing for the security in 2010 from Wilshire, was no better and sought to sell the house while they were still waiting for an answer to their modification application.

Their appeal centers on the servicers' false promises and a flawed mortgage assignment similar to Ramos's. In this couple's assignment, the lender appears to be accurately named, but, as with Ramos's, the assignment was executed after Wilshire launched the foreclosure suit. The couple's attorney, Daniel Rock, argues that the late assignment means the plaintiff (Deutsche Bank National Trust Company, As Trustee for The MLMI Trust Series 2007-MLN1) never had standing to sue, so the foreclosure should be thrown out. He adds that the couple isn't looking to get a free house, just a modification. "For goodness' sake, it's just silly not to take these people. They're well off enough to cover the debt service."

Bank of America's Simon says the company doesn't comment on pending litigation.

Overall, HAMP has fallen well short of the administration's goal of helping 3 to 4 million homeowners. As of January 2012, 951,319 homeowners had received modifications under the program, while more than 2.5 million had been rejected.

Administration officials have argued that, by and large, most of those rejected simply didn't qualify for the program. The main culprit is widespread unemployment, they say; HAMP had been designed in response to the subprime crisis and its unaffordable loans, not to help prime borrowers reeling from job losses. Under this theory, most people simply didn't make enough to afford even modified payments.

The underlying assumption, of course, is that servicers have been correctly denying applicants—despite the widespread outcry from homeowners and housing counselors about wrongful denials. Indeed, according to the Treasury's own numbers, the most common reason servicers have cited for rejecting homeowners is that they failed to send in all of their documents. Given servicers' notorious tendency to lose papers, there's reason to think many of those denials were illegitimate.

Oversight of the program has been astonishingly lax. When servicers signed contracts with the Treasury to participate in the program, they agreed to submit to inspections by government auditors. In 2010, through the Freedom of Information Act, *ProPublica* sought the audits for ten of the largest servicers in the program. After stonewalling the request for more than a year, the Treasury finally agreed to release the audits for only one servicer, GMAC, the fifth-largest, because the company had explicitly consented to their release. The other companies refused, and the Treasury continues to withhold audits of those servicers.

The documents showed that GMAC hadn't undergone a major audit until more than a year into the program. When an audit report was finally completed, it found that GMAC had seriously mishandled many loan modifications, miscalculating homeowner income in more than 80 percent of audited cases, for example.

Yet GMAC suffered no penalty. GMAC itself said it hasn't reversed a single foreclosure as a result of a government audit.

Treasury has sent mixed messages about its ability to penalize banks over the course of the program, threatening "monetary penalties and sanctions" in late 2009 and then saying it lacked the power to enforce such penalties. Throughout, Treasury has reacted to rule violations by requesting that servicers make improvements. Treasury finally departed from its cooperative approach in the summer of 2011, more than two years after HAMP's launch, when it withheld incentive payments from three of the top ten servicers. (GMAC was not among them.) The companies would not receive the public subsidies for completing modifications until they made certain changes. By March 2012, all of the withheld subsidies had been released.

Nearly three years after the introduction of HAMP and several months after federal regulators required the major banks to improve their operations, any improvements seem meager. Servicers now must provide a "single point of contact" model, meaning that borrowers, instead of having to call an 800 number and never reaching the same person twice, must have one person in charge of their application.

The current Bank of America employee says he's supposed to be the borrower's source of information, but he frequently finds himself searching for answers his managers can't provide. He and his colleagues could use a "single point of contact" themselves at Bank of America to get answers, he says. "We are absolutely clueless." Training was inadequate, and a new computer system spits out tasks for him to complete that he often doesn't understand. "All we do is talk to the customer and give them excuses all day."

"I Gave It My Biggest Fight"

In June 2009, Ramos finally decided to give up and move out. Wilshire could seek again to sell the home at any time, Varnell told her. Ramos was also haunted by what it actually looked like to be kicked out of your home.

That February, she'd been startled to see several of her neighbors' belongings lined up along the curb. The Pillas, who lived just two houses down from Ramos, had been evicted that day and were trying to keep hold of what they could without a moving truck. "A lot of people came by thinking it was garbage," said Vito Pilla, sixty-three, a disabled Vietnam vet who's been fighting throat cancer for several years and lived in the house with his wife and teenage triplet boys.

The couple had fallen behind when his wife injured her back around the same time that their mortgage payments had jumped. Pilla knew he was facing foreclosure but thought it might be delayed because he was still in communication with his servicer, Wells Fargo. A Wells spokeswoman says the servicer had made "multiple attempts to help" but that "we were unable to find an option to keep the borrowers in the home."

What the family hadn't managed to get out of the house was put out near the street. "A little at a time is what we did during the day," Pilla says. Forced to choose what to save, they prioritized family heirlooms.

Ramos remembers salvaging wedding pictures from among the piles of possessions to make sure the Pillas kept them. "We didn't want to go through that," Ramos says. The only way to be sure they'd avoid it was to move first. "All these people was depending on me, and I gave it my biggest fight to save that home, and I couldn't."

Fortunately, Ramos had somewhere to go. Her longtime partner, Dave Backus, owned a plot of land on Hawaii's Big Island. It was way up in the north, a rural area far from any resorts and beaches. Ramos had planned on eventually selling her Florida home and using the proceeds to build a home there and retire, but now it would have to serve as is. With no structure on the property, they'd have to pitch tents.

Even so, it was clearly the best option for the family, says Stacey O'Rourke, a child welfare services counselor with the nonprofit Devereux who worked on the case. Ramos had approached the organization, which is licensed by Florida's Department of Children and Families, for help. "We try to keep children in their homes," O'Rourke says. But if Ramos had lost the house and stayed in Florida, she says, "The kids would have ended up in foster care." Since Ramos had adequately cared for the children for several years and "wanted so bad to keep these kids," it was a no-brainer to keep them together.

The problem was getting Sheila, her mother, and all three children to Hawaii.

O'Rourke put together a fundraising effort that included an article in the *Citrus County Chronicle*: "Grandmother, family lose home." It's something O'Rourke says she hadn't done before and hasn't done since. "It was a desperate situation that called for desperate measures." O'Rourke says she raised about $1,800.

With Backus covering the plane tickets, the funds helped get new tires and gas for the car to drive first to Alabama, where they put their most valued possessions in storage, and then to Atlanta, where their flight departed.

On the first night of their new life, Backus, lit by flashlight, mowed a patch of land to pitch a tent. They had running water but little else. They cooked on a camping stove and kept their perishables in coolers. To shower, they warmed water over the fire pit and then hauled a bucket back into the woods, where they'd rigged a makeshift shower on a tree. Everyone shared the one outhouse they'd built in the woods.

Over the past two and a half years, they've built the campsite into a full-fledged settlement. Several large tents built of tarps, canvas, bungee straps, rope, wood, and metal poles are spread over one corner of their twenty-acre plot. There's a kitchen tent, what might be called the master-bedroom tent about twenty yards away, and a few others where the children and Ramos's mother sleep. Backus is a capable builder, and now everyone has access to a real shower and a flush toilet.

Near the end of their first year, they finally got electricity. Now they have a washer, dryer, and refrigerator. Ramos and Backus make frequent trips to the local dump to look for discarded or donated items to salvage.

The kitchen, with its sink, hanging pots and pans, and oven, seems like any other kitchen except for the lack of walls. The hilly plot overlooks the ocean, and on a nice day—and most days there are nice—you can understand why Ramos would say, "I don't know if I'd want to go back to the house at this point." The family has even been joined by a cousin of Ramos's, a retired federal employee who lives there with her husband, because what's left of her retirement wasn't enough to live comfortably elsewhere.

Four months after Ramos left Florida, Wilshire's attorneys again sought to foreclose on the home. Together with the various foreclosure and late fees, the interest that had been accruing since Ramos made her last payment in early 2008 added up to a debt of $314,000—about $52,000 more than the original loan. While the home had been appraised at $403,000 in late 2006 when the loan was made, it was worth nowhere near that when it was put up for auction in December 2009. As a result, Wilshire chose instead to take possession of the home and sell it later.

The next month, it was listed for $204,900. It stayed on the market for six months until it finally sold for $171,500.

The security's investors bore the loss, not the servicer, which recouped all fees and expenses.

A subsequent report to investors listed the realized loss from Ramos's mortgage as $167,430, 64 percent of the original loan.

Epilogue

In the fall of 2010, three years into the foreclosure crisis, federal and state law-enforcement agencies and banking regulators finally cracked down on banks. Servicers had admitted that they'd filed tens of thousands of false affidavits to courts in foreclosure cases across the country. Employees had sworn they'd personally examined borrowers' information when they really hadn't.

The revelation prompted investigations beyond just robo-signing, as the practice was dubbed. Suddenly, longstanding servicer abuses and problems, which had been allowed to endure without serious consequences, were getting new scrutiny.

In February, a coalition of forty-nine state attorneys general and the federal government announced a $25 billion settlement with the five biggest mortgage servicers. Along with widespread problems with foreclosure documentation, investigators had found a raft of servicer abuses, including charging bogus fees, improperly denying modification requests, and giving false information to borrowers.

Still, the outcome from the settlement is mainly forward-looking. The banks agreed to follow a new set of rules for homeowners applying for modifications in 2012 and beyond. This time, violations would be punished, law officials said. "If people are eligible for a loan modification, the banks won't screw up those decisions anymore," said Iowa attorney general Tom Miller.

For homeowners like Ramos who've already lost their homes, of course, the new rules come too late. The settlement will offer them a small sum, about $2,000 on average, as compensation.

Separately, federal banking regulators are overseeing a massive "Independent Foreclosure Review." The review covers homeowners who were in the foreclosure process at any time in 2009 or 2010. Accordingly, both homeowners like Sanderson who didn't lose their homes and those like Ramos who did will be eligible—about 4.3 million in all.

To conduct the reviews, the banks have hired outside consultants, which in turn have hired hundreds of temporary employees to do the work. That's angered some members of Congress, who noted that job postings for the temp spots call for some foreclosure- or mortgage-servicing experience but little else. For the banks, the review and settlement are a way to put the foreclosure crisis behind them.

When we sent Bank of America a list of twenty-six questions about Ramos's case, the spokesman Simon declined to respond point by point. Bank of America believes Wilshire appropriately handled her loan, he wrote, but "we are suggesting that Ms. Ramos and others who raise similar concerns consider applying for the new government-mandated and -monitored independent foreclosure review. We believe this will be a more productive, fair, conclusive and efficient pursuit for everyone than continuous give-and-take around pointed questioning and speculation inherent in the reporting process."

For Ramos, the review is likely to be the last word on her foreclosure. She plans to submit the "Request for Review Form," on which she'll argue that Wilshire mishandled her account in a number of ways, didn't appropriately review her for a modification, and filed faulty documents to foreclose on her. A temporary employee of Promontory Financial Group, the consultant hired by Bank of America, will likely be the one to review her claims against Wilshire's file. Eventually, probably sometime in 2013, Ramos will receive a letter. It will inform her of the exact dollar amount of the "financial injury" she suffered through the process, and if the number is above zero, a check will be included.

The decision will be final.

Olga Pierce and Karen Weise contributed reporting to this story.

Note

1. Edwards and a colleague, June Clarkson, were forced to resign their positions in May 2011, a few months after a newly elected attorney general, Pam Bondi, took office. Critics alleged the move was meant to quash the duo's foreclosure-fraud investigations. Top officials hired by Bondi said the pair was fired for performance issues. In response, Edwards and Clarkson have pointed to a positive performance review from their direct supervisor. A state inspector general report cleared Bondi of wrongdoing.

Part II

Bad Medicine

Fortune

Fortune's Mina Kime chillingly describes the dire consequences when a West Chester, Pa., medical-device maker ignored a warning from the company's regulatory staffer and didn't wait for approval before marketing to surgeons a cement meant to be injected in the spine. What occurred is a classic example of malfeasance by an insular corporation run by a reclusive and autocratic Swiss multibillionaire. The case offers a rare, sometimes disturbing glimpse inside the shrouded world of medical devices, where surgeons will sometimes turn for advice during operations to twenty-something sales representatives. In the end, there were needless deaths for some and near-misses for others, criminal and civil charges, settlements and prison time, though not for the Swiss billionaire.

Mina Kimes

3. Bad to the Bone: A Medical Horror Story

On November 16, 2011, Georgia Baddley, a seventy-year-old woman living near Salt Lake City, received a shocking call from a special agent at the U.S. Department of Health and Human Services. The agent told her that the government had come across new information about her mother's death.

Baddley was speechless. Eight years before, her eighty-three-year-old mother, Barbara Marcelino, had unexpectedly died during spine surgery. At the time, Baddley didn't question what had happened; surgery was always risky for a woman of that age. She was horrified when the agent told her that the surgeon had injected bone cement into her mother's spine and that the product—which was not approved for that use—may have played a role in her death.

The agent explained that the government had filed criminal charges against the maker of the cement, a company called Synthes, and four of its executives. After hanging up the phone, Baddley sat in stunned silence. "I was taken aback," she says. "I had no idea that anything like that had happened."

Most people have never heard of Synthes, a medical device maker headquartered in West Chester, Pa. But the company became part of one of the most recognizable names in health care in June when Johnson & Johnson completed the purchase of it for nearly $20 billion—the largest acquisition in J&J's history. Market watchers cheered the deal, which will expand the company's stable of high-margin orthopedic products. J&J, which has endured a series of reputation-sullying recalls and lawsuits in recent years, specifically cited Synthes's "culture" and "values" as evidence of its appeal, even as former Synthes executives awaited sentencing on charges of grievous conduct.

In 2009 the U.S. attorney in Philadelphia accused the company of running illegal clinical trials—essentially, experimenting on humans. Between 2002 and 2004, Synthes had tested a product called Norian XR, a cement that has a unique capacity to turn into bone when injected into the human skeleton. The Food and Drug Administration explicitly told Synthes not to promote Norian for certain spine surgeries, but the company pushed forward anyway. At least five patients who had Norian injected into their spines died on the operating-room table. One was Barbara Marcelino.

The indictment of Synthes and its executives shook the health-care industry. What occurred is a classic example of corporate malfeasance, but set inside an insular corporation run by a reclusive and autocratic Swiss multibillionaire, the provider of the largest individual gift in the history of Harvard University. The case offers a rare, sometimes disturbing glimpse inside the shrouded world of medical devices, where surgeons occasionally turn for advice during operations to twenty-something sales representatives.

Most of all, this is a story about a company that repeatedly ignored evidence of potential lethal consequences. Interviews with more than twenty former employees and surgeons involved in the Norian project, hundreds of pages of court transcripts, and company documents submitted in the case reveal that Synthes not only disregarded multiple warnings that it was flouting the rules but also brushed off scientists' cautions that the cement could cause fatal blood clots.

The Department of Justice targeted four high-ranking executives, all of whom pleaded guilty to a misdemeanor under an unusual provision of health-care law called the Responsible Corporate Officer Doctrine. They accepted responsibility for the company's crime of running unauthorized clinical trials and for engaging in off-label marketing, or promoting products for unapproved uses, without conceding that they were involved in the crime. At the time, no executive had ever gone to prison for such a charge. (Lawyers for the four executives declined to make their clients available for interviews or to comment on the facts of the case.)

Off-label marketing is so common among drug and device makers that it's often dismissed as the equivalent of driving slightly over the speed limit. During the past decade, pharmaceutical behemoths such as Merck, Pfizer, Abbott Labs, and GlaxoSmithKline have paid billions in fines to settle charges that they engaged in off-label drug promotion. Yet cases continue to happen, in part because the potential profits often exceed the fines.

But this wasn't the typical off-label marketing case. Nor was it typical of trials for medical devices or drugs. Patients sometimes die during such clinical trials—but only after being advised of the risks and then granting their consent. In hiding the unapproved status of the cement, prosecutors argued, Synthes denied patients the right to choose whether they wanted to be test subjects.

For the Justice Department, the Synthes case posed an unprecedented opportunity. It could finally hold individual businessmen accountable for their actions. Mary Crawley, the assistant U.S. attorney who led the prosecution, urged the court to send the executives to jail for their "venal crime." The "callous disregard of patient safety," she argued, "warrants the highest sentence the law will allow."

• • •

Synthes is based about twenty-five miles west of Philadelphia, but its roots lie in Switzerland. In 1958 four Swiss surgeons founded a research organization devoted to their belief—controversial at the time—that broken bones could be better fixed internally with implants. They developed products, branded with the name "Synthes," that they licensed to a pair of Swiss manufacturers.

In the 1970s one of the founding surgeons bought an airplane from an enigmatic Swiss businessman named Hansjörg Wyss (pronounced hans-yerg vees). The son of a mechanical-calculator salesman, Wyss boasted a worldly résumé. He had worked in Turkey, Pakistan, and the Philippines, and had graduated from Harvard Business School. When he met the surgeon, he was working for a chemical company and selling planes on the side. Wyss struck a deal to become head of Synthes's U.S. operation.

Wyss later became CEO of the entire company and over the next thirty years built it into an industry giant that specializes in making plates and screws to stabilize broken bones. Along the way he became a multibillionaire, splitting his time in the United States among homes in Pennsylvania, Martha's Vineyard, Massachusetts, and Tucson. He was CEO until 2007 and remained chairman of the company, which has 12,000 employees, until it became part of J&J (where it's now in the renamed DePuy Synthes division). Last year Synthes generated $4 billion in sales. Until the J&J acquisition, Wyss and his family owned nearly 50 percent of Synthes's shares.

Wyss, seventy-six, shuns the limelight. Unassuming, with wavy gray hair and owlish glasses, he often wore baggy corduroys to work and drove an old Volvo for years. Wyss has generally shied away from the press, telling a Swiss newspaper in a rare interview last year, "Nobody knows me, and I hope that it stays like this." In a phone interview with *Fortune*, Wyss declined to comment on the central issues in this article but did address several smaller points. A Synthes spokesperson declined to discuss the Norian case.

Wyss donates heavily to liberal-leaning nonprofits and in 2008 gave $125 million to Harvard to fund a biological-engineering institute. An avid hiker and outdoor enthusiast, he has poured millions of dollars into preserving land in the Rocky Mountain states, a region he fell in love with as a student.

Former Synthes employees portray Wyss as an intimidating, hands-on leader. Nisra Thongpreda, the manager first assigned to the Norian project, would testify before a grand jury that "for somebody who is at his level and his level of success, I would say he has a surprising amount of contact with what's going on." (Her grand jury testimony, like other such testimony mentioned in this article, was excerpted in a public court filing; she did not respond to requests for comment.) Several former Synthes staffers recall meetings where Wyss probed the minutiae of their projects. "It would feel like he wasn't paying attention," says a former employee. "Then, all of a sudden, he'd turn and raise a question that was far in the weeds—maybe the single dollar amount of something you proposed."

Wyss's level of control could verge past micromanagement. Several former employees say he wouldn't let the company provide Internet access in the mid-2000s; workers who wanted to go online had to sign in to a single computer in front of everyone. Maria Maccecchini, who was president of biomaterials at Synthes for eight months in 2004, says the CEO was fixated on the brand of toilet paper used in company restrooms, the color of the desks, and the shape of the plates in the cafeteria (he insisted that they be square).

One former employee recalls how, as he was walking into Synthes's headquarters on a fall day, he saw Wyss hunched over in the foyer. The CEO was picking up leaves off the floor, one by one, and then putting them outside.

• • •

In the late 1990s a fledgling biotech company called Norian popped up on Wyss's radar. The startup, based in Cupertino, Calif., had developed a calcium-phosphate-based cement, also called Norian, with almost miraculous qualities. When implanted in the skeleton, the cement not only fills cracks but also gradually transforms itself into actual human bone.

Synthes bought the company in 1999 for about $50 million. At that point Norian had already obtained FDA approval to market two versions: Norian SRS, for use in the arm, and Norian CRS, for use in the skull.

There was a third potential application for the cement—one that Synthes executives hoped could be extremely lucrative—and it's this use that would eventually prove disastrous: filling fractures in the spine. In the 1990s specialists were increasingly touting the benefits of a procedure called a vertebroplasty. To perform the surgery—typically done to treat vertebral compression fractures, or VCFs, a common side effect of osteoporosis—surgeons inject cement into the spine. At the time, the procedure was performed with acrylic cement, which contained a material used to build aquariums. Norian, with its unique properties, seemed like a superior alternative.

When Synthes acquired Norian, the company did not yet have permission to sell it for use in the spine. As is true any time a company wants to market a high-risk medical device (and under FDA rules, the cement was considered a device) for a new purpose, Synthes would have to convince regulators that the new use was safe and effective.

The government's response was discouraging. An FDA representative told Synthes in a conference call that it would "almost definitely" need to pursue a path that typically necessitates clinical trials, according to minutes of the call. To do that, the company would have to obtain an Investigational Device Exemption, or IDE, from the FDA. (In FDA jargon, the "exemption" grants the manufacturer the right to conduct human tests.) Then Synthes would have to persuade a large number of patients to undergo experimental treatment and conduct a lengthy and expensive clinical study.

Instead of preparing a clinical study, Synthes made the first of a series of fateful choices, deciding to launch right into market research. In February 2000, Wyss announced at an all-hands meeting that there would be a strong push for vertebroplasty, according to factual findings by the judge in the criminal case. In March, employees in Synthes's spine division began interviewing spine surgeons about Norian. Their report, which was shared with executives, pointed out that Americans suffer more than 500,000 VCFs each year and that the "market potential" was "considerable." It concluded, "There is excitement about using Norian for vertebroplasties."

Whispers of the project began spreading, prompting the first—but not the last—alarm within Synthes. A strait-laced regulatory staffer named Michael Sharp was appalled when he learned, in a chance conversation, about the plan to promote Norian. Companies are explicitly barred from marketing products for uses that haven't been authorized by the FDA. Even mentioning unapproved uses to surgeons is prohibited.

Sharp fired off an e-mail to Tom Higgins, the president of Synthes Spine, and Richard Bohner, vice president of operations at Synthes, expressing his concern that the company was testing Norian without going through the proper channels. "Regulatory is unaware that this is even being considered," he wrote.

Higgins met with Sharp. The regulatory staffer says he made it clear that Synthes employees shouldn't discuss Norian with spine surgeons. Higgins assured him, Sharp recalls, that the company wasn't going to promote the product for use in the spine. "At that point," says Sharp, "I thought the issue was entirely put to bed."

But the project didn't die there. In February 2001 a surgeon in Santa Monica used Norian to perform two procedures on elderly patients with vertebral compression fractures. In both cases, according to company documents, the patients experienced rapid drops in blood pressure shortly after the surgeon injected the cement, and an anesthesiologist had to administer drugs to keep them from dying.

When Sharp learned about the surgeries, he e-mailed Bohner again. Bohner alerted his boss, Michael Huggins, the head of Synthes's North American division, who sent a cautionary message to the sales force about the dangers of off-label marketing. Prosecutors would later dismiss Huggins's e-mail as "anything but strongly worded" and "confusing at best."

Despite the warnings, the vertebroplasty project rolled on. Sharp left the company for reasons, he says, having nothing to do with Norian. In April 2001, Higgins organized a focus group in Cupertino with surgeons who were interested in using Norian to treat VCFs. The doctors discussed the operations that had gone wrong in Santa Monica, according to minutes of the meeting. Dr. Sohail Mirza, a surgeon at the University of Washington, suggested that Norian could be causing problems if it entered the bloodstream. The spine contains multiple blood vessels, and any leakage into them could send cement to the lungs and heart, causing a fatal clot. Mirza said it was critical that Synthes conduct an animal study before using Norian in human patients. The company agreed to fund a small study.

Meanwhile, Synthes's top brass was scheduled to meet with Wyss in November to decide whether to proceed with plans to sell Norian for use in the spine. A few weeks before the meeting, Higgins asked a regulatory employee to mock up a clinical trial for using Norian in vertebroplasty. The staffer estimated it would take three years and cost about $1 million. He told Higgins that Synthes needed government approval to test Norian on people—a fact that was common knowledge, according to prosecutors and several former Synthes employees.

That November, Huggins, Higgins, and their colleagues met with Hansjörg Wyss in Tucson. It was judgment day for the vertebroplasty project. The attendees discussed the prospect of doing a clinical study, according to the meeting's minutes. Then Higgins asked whether Synthes should get an IDE and conduct trials.

The answer, according to the minutes, was no: "Decision made not to pursue an IDE study, but to get a few sites to perform 60–80 procedures and help them publish their clinical results." No explanation was mentioned. Synthes wasn't taking the onerous—but expected—route of getting an IDE. Instead, it would get a few doctors to do the procedure on their own, which the company hoped would popularize the product. It was, prosecutors later alleged, an end run.

The implications of the minutes are clear. But their passive construction raises a question. "Decision made"—by whom? Nisra Thongpreda, the manager in charge of Norian, later told a grand jury that Wyss had made the call. (Wyss declined to comment.) Prosecutors, who never charged her, asked how she knew it was the CEO. "Because I was there at the meeting," Thongpreda said. She later added, "Tom Higgins asked Mr. Wyss . . . about the IDE study and Mr. Wyss said no."

The prosecutor pressed for more. "Was that about it—just no?"

"Just no," said Thongpreda.

• • •

Former employees describe Synthes as highly regimented—the kind of place where employees do what they're told. "Everybody's just a sort of a worker bee," says one former staffer. Wyss was known for handpicking young executives, typically men who had gone to top-notch schools, and guiding their careers. Several former employees say Huggins and Higgins, who had attended, respectively, Wharton and Harvard, belonged to that group. "He picked these guys and cultivated them," says a former Synthes manager. "They were all fiercely loyal."

They also knew, former staffers say, that the man everyone called "Mr. Wyss" didn't tolerate dissent. Several recall a story, well known at Synthes, about the CEO attending a meeting at a Marriott hotel. Wyss asked a hotel employee for a banana. When the worker ignored his request, Wyss was "boiling," says a former employee who was in the room. Days later the company announced that henceforth Synthes employees could not stay at Marriott hotels. (Wyss says he banned the chain because it didn't donate the leftover food from Synthes's meeting to a homeless shelter.)

Wyss had rejected clinical trials. But there was a less-demanding form of regulatory approval, a process intended for modifications of permitted devices. Synthes applied for this type of approval and sure enough, in December 2001, the FDA blessed the use of Norian in the spine. But there was a crucial caveat. The FDA said that Norian could not be mixed with another substance before it was injected into the spine—which is precisely what vertebroplasties require. (Defense attorneys would later assert that the FDA's language was confusing.)

The general clearance effectively prohibited Synthes from promoting Norian for vertebroplasties—but did give it a foot in the door to spine surgeons' operating rooms. It's almost as if, to use a benign analogy, Synthes bought nosebleed tickets to a football game and then tried to sneak into the VIP section.

In the spring of 2002, Thongpreda received an unsettling e-mail from Dr. Jens Chapman, an orthopedic surgeon at the University of Washington who was working, along with his colleague Mirza, on the animal study funded by Synthes. The early results were alarming. Chapman informed her that when Norian was injected into the bloodstream of a pig, "the entire pulmonary artery system had clotted off." As he put it, "We were expecting to kill the pig . . . but not suddenly and with a relatively small dose." (Chapman declined to comment; Mirza did not respond to requests to be interviewed.)

Over the next few weeks, according to prosecutors, top executives at Synthes held a series of meetings about Norian. On May 13, 2002, Huggins and Higgins met with Wyss and decided to proceed with their plan to informally test it for vertebroplasties. On May 22, Huggins and Higgins met again. This time there was "high concern about SRS in spine test market," according to a document assembled by an employee who didn't attend the meetings. On May 28, Huggins spoke with Wyss, and they "agree[d] to go ahead with Vertebroplasty Test Market."

Then, a couple of days later, the whole project almost blew up. One of Synthes's medical consultants at the time was an orthopedic surgeon named Ken Lambert. An old friend of Wyss, Lambert had been doing work for Synthes for decades, even briefly sitting on the company's board. One afternoon he was in Synthes's offices when he stumbled across a box of Norian. Lambert noticed that the shipping label was addressed to a spine surgeon. "I was starting to smell a rat, so I said, 'Let's open it up,'" he says. "And there it was: directions on how to mix it." Lambert called Huggins, who assured him he would look into the matter.

Huggins was shaken. On May 30, 2002, he e-mailed Higgins and Bohner and told them he had talked to Lambert and was having "second thoughts" about the plan to promote Norian. "We discussed about the need to perform a real study to test Norian," he wrote. "It seems Spine is bypassing the needed blocking and tackling without thinking this all the way through."

Huggins's apparent crisis of conscience caused a stir in the lower ranks. By then Thongpreda had transferred responsibility for the project to Josi Hamilton, a twenty-six-year-old product manager. Hamilton was rattled. She began assembling a timeline that would document the internal approvals, hoping it would protect her if she got into trouble.

For a moment it seemed as though Huggins might kill the vertebroplasty project. But then, without any sign of explanation in the record, he let the issue drop. An internal e-mail shows only that the executive met with Wyss a few days after expressing his doubts.

Lambert, meanwhile, was still spooked. On June 10, 2002, he sent a late-night e-mail to Thongpreda. "In my respectful opinion, giving SRS directly to a surgeon for him to use without any protocol [control] is not a controlled study; given the other issues I have mentioned, this action amounts to human experimentation whose only defense seems to be that it will be a small study," he wrote. He forwarded the e-mail to Huggins and Higgins, adding that the company could "suffer serious consequences" if it didn't conduct proper studies.

The next day Lambert forwarded the e-mail to his old friend Wyss. "Dear HJW," he wrote. "I'm never sure what information gets to your level but some things have happened recently that could have serious consequences. If you are aware of all of this, then the system works."

Lambert was the second person to explicitly caution the company against testing Norian for unapproved uses. But like Sharp's earlier warnings, Lambert's went unheeded. He says he didn't hear back from the CEO, and his phone calls went unanswered. Eventually, Lambert says, Wyss contacted him—to inform him that Synthes would not be renewing his contract. (Wyss says the contract ended for unrelated reasons.)

Two weeks later Jens Chapman and his colleague sent the final results of their study to Higgins. The first test involved mixing Norian with human blood in test tubes, then watching how quickly clots formed. The scientists noted that "a relatively small amount of Norian results in the formation of a very large volume of clot," which could block the flow of blood inside the heart or lungs.

The final word on the pig test was equally worrisome. The surgeons had injected Norian into a large vein leading to the animal's heart to simulate what would happen if the cement leaked during vertebroplasty. The pig's blood pressure plunged. When the scientists cut into it after its demise, they noted that volumes of blood clot containing Norian had amassed in its lungs. The animal had died in less than thirty seconds.

• • •

The FDA does not regulate doctors' activity; as a result, off-label prescribing is ubiquitous. A 2006 study in the *Archives of Internal Medicine* examined hundreds of millions of prescriptions and found that more than 20 percent were written for off-label use. "A surgeon can prescribe anything," says a former Synthes employee. "If he says, 'Let's put a bowling ball in your body,' he can do it." Physicians are quick to note that, because the FDA's approval process can be frustratingly slow, off-label drug and device usage is a crucial part of health care.

Surgeons regularly use devices in unapproved ways. The culture of orthopedic surgeons is particularly aggressive. Predominantly male, "orthopods" are the jocks of the surgical world. Sales representatives tell stories of doctors playing loud rock music in the operating room and throwing instruments at the wall when they get frustrated. Several surgeons tell *Fortune* they simply don't have time to pore over labels. Lambert offers a blunt appraisal: "'Off-label' is not at all a pejorative term—it's almost the opposite. Reading the label is for people who read labels."

Surgeons don't always listen to the FDA, but they do heed the young sales representatives who bring them devices and routinely watch them operate. "It sounds ridiculous, because here's a guy who went to medical school and did his residency, and he's listening to some guy in the back of the room," says one former Synthes salesperson. Another adds: "It's not uncommon to have a surgeon with a drill in his hand, about to drill a hole, looking over his shoulder at you saying, 'Is this right?'"

In the summer of 2002, Hamilton, the young Norian product manager (who had recently graduated from business school), began training spine surgeons to mix SRS with barium sulfate in order to perform vertebroplasties—an act explicitly prohibited by the label. During this preliminary trial, which Synthes employees called "test market phase 1," a select group of surgeons conducted several dozen surgeries using the mixture, SRS-R.

Hamilton later testified that she knew she was on thin ice. The FDA's warning was unambiguous: They weren't supposed to talk about mixing SRS. But whenever they brought up their concerns with their managers, they were assured that everything would be fine. Hamilton, who was later granted immunity from prosecution in exchange for her cooperation, explained that it was understood at Synthes's spine division that off-label marketing was the status quo: "This is the way that it's done. And it happens every day."

The SRS-R test market proceeded successfully. Dozens of surgeries went off without a hitch, and Synthes was ready to move on to phase 2. That September, Hamilton gave a presentation to several executives—including Wyss—about the vertebroplasty project. "Wyss inquired about the test-market setup and how surgeons, who are interested in the product, were to be trained," the minutes of the meeting stated.

That winter, employees in the regulatory division were tasked with getting the FDA to approve the mixed version of Norian, rechristened as Norian XR, for general use in the spine. It was a touchy subject. The FDA had recently issued a public notification that stressed the off-label nature of vertebroplasties. In December 2002 it approved the mixed version. But Synthes was still stymied: The FDA ordered it to include a warning on its label that said XR should not be used to treat vertebral compression fractures.

The fact that Synthes couldn't promote XR for its target market didn't seem to bother its executives. Higgins sent the vertebroplasty team a celebratory e-mail. "Let me take a moment to congratulate the four of you [on] getting XR approved," he wrote. "Very Well Done!"

Less than a month later Dr. Barton Sachs, a spine surgeon in Texas, used Norian to treat a VCF. His patient, a seventy-year-old Oklahoma native named Lois Eskind, said beforehand that she was in excruciating pain and that she'd "rather have surgery than live like this." Fifteen seconds after Sachs injected the cement into her spine, Eskind's blood pressure plummeted. As a Synthes sales representative looked on, Sachs attempted to resuscitate her for thirty minutes before she died. (Sachs declined to comment.)

Hamilton and Thongpreda called the doctor to find out what had happened. Sachs said he didn't know the cause of death; the family had not requested an autopsy. He didn't blame Norian, but he was concerned, according to minutes of the call: "He did the technique the way he was supposed to and the outcome was catastrophic."

Whenever a death or injury occurs that may implicate a medical device, the manufacturer is obligated to report what happened to the FDA. Synthes did not report Eskind's death. According to an internal document, the company's regulatory staffers decided that, because Sachs didn't conclusively blame Norian for his patient's death, they didn't have to send a report.

If Synthes staffers were disturbed by Eskind's death, they didn't show it. That month a group of employees met to discuss a sales plan for Norian. The document they put together predicted revenue of at least $20 million by 2005, with after-tax profit margins of 50 percent.

In mid-August, Hamilton and her team launched the next phase of its test market with a surgeon forum in San Diego. Spine doctors from around the country flew in (their travel expenses were paid for by Synthes, which also organized a dinner and golf outing). Hamilton handed out binders of information about Norian XR, her business cards tucked inside. Sachs delivered a keynote address. There was a training session where surgeons practiced injecting XR into the vertebrae of cadavers. "The takeaway from the course was that this stuff is safe, and it works, and there's very little downside risk," says one of the surgeons Synthes trained.

For the moment everything seemed to be going fine. The forum was a huge success. Several surgeries went smoothly. Then, on September 19, disaster struck again. Dr. Paul Nottingham, a surgeon based outside San Francisco, was operating on Ryoichi Kikuchi, an eighty-three-year-old prize-winning physicist. Shortly after Nottingham injected him with XR, Kikuchi's blood pressure sank. The doctor couldn't resuscitate him, and he died on the table.

Nottingham couldn't ascertain why his patient had died, and Kikuchi's family didn't request an autopsy. But unlike the previous surgeon to lose a patient, Nottingham was quick to point a finger at Norian, which had apparently leaked during the operation. When Hamilton called Nottingham to discuss what had happened, the surgeon erupted. "He claimed the sales consultant 'pushed' this product on him and was unclear as to its status on the market," she wrote in minutes of the call. This time Synthes did file a report to the FDA. But it was vague and left out key details.

Nottingham asserts that the company misrepresented the product to him. "Synthes is very much to blame for pushing a product that they didn't have the indications [i.e., approvals] for," he says, adding that he never used Norian again. "I used it once—that was enough."

Hamilton also called Nottingham's partner, Dr. Hieu Ball, to discuss what happened. Ball had more experience with Norian; according to prosecutors, he had assisted on one of the failed surgeries that took place in 2001 in Santa Monica. He had also performed five operations using Norian, Hamilton wrote. "Based on his own experience," she added, "he will continue to use XR."

In December 2003, John Walsh, who had just become head of regulatory affairs at Synthes Spine, signed off on Norian XR's technique guide, a brochure that was given to surgeons. The guide omitted the warning that the FDA had ordered Synthes to include on the label, which said that Norian shouldn't be used to treat VCFs.

It also included two "case examples"—real X-rays of anonymous patients who had had surgeries with Norian. One of the X-rays belonged to a forty-one-year-old male. The other came from a seventy-year-old female. The female, prosecutors later revealed, was Lois Eskind. Unbeknown to the surgeons who received the brochure, the case study came from a woman who had died after being injected with Synthes's product.

• • •

On January 21, 2004, Barbara Marcelino checked into a hospital near San Francisco for spine surgery. Her daughter, Georgia, called her that evening to see how she was doing. Georgia had wanted to fly out for the surgery from her home in Salt Lake City, but her mother insisted that she didn't have to because it was an "easy" procedure. "She said, 'I think this is going to help me a lot and make me feel a lot better,'" recalls Georgia.

Their conversation was light. Marcelino, an avid reader who enjoyed Proust, complained about the Stephen King novel she was reading. Petite, with soft white hair and a small, heart-shaped mouth, Marcelino fretted about spilling a glass of water in her hospital bed.

Her surgeon was Hieu Ball. At 10:30 that night, according to prosecutors, Ball started to operate. A Synthes sales representative—the same one who witnessed Kikuchi's death—was in the room. Ball injected the cement into Marcelino's spine at 11:10 p.m. Her blood pressure immediately plummeted. At 11:12, Ball attempted CPR. At 12:12 a.m., Marcelino was pronounced dead. An autopsy later revealed foreign material in the blood vessels in her lungs, though the results were inconclusive because of the prolonged CPR.

Ball declines to comment on why Marcelino died. He says he was unaware of Synthes's animal studies involving Norian and believes he used Norian in an approved manner. "We were using it based on the recommendation of the company." (Ball's lawyer adds that "of the 20–30 times he used Norian, there was only one instance of complication.")

When the company received news of Marcelino's death, Hamilton quickly drafted a letter to surgeons that stated, "Synthes is stopping the distribution and usage of Norian XR." Her letter was never sent. Instead, Walsh, the spine division's new regulatory chief, helped put together a different letter for surgeons. This version simply stated that "deaths have been reported." Norian, it said, should not be used to treat VCFs—but Synthes would "continue to explore new approaches to the treatment of vertebral compression fractures." The letter did not mention a recall, and Synthes continued to sell Norian.

Rumors about the deaths quickly spread at headquarters, and staffers began to panic. Then, on the morning of May 11, 2004, the project finally imploded. Capt. Joseph Despins, an FDA investigator, arrived at Synthes headquarters and announced that he had received a tip that the company had engaged in off-label marketing.

Over the next month, Despins conducted a series of interviews. Synthes's staffers denied almost everything. Bohner said he knew nothing about a vertebroplasty test market for SRS.

Hamilton disputed having encouraged surgeons to use Norian off-label. Huggins told Despins that he didn't recall what was discussed at meetings.

Despins didn't buy it. His 143-page inspection report concluded that the company had violated FDA rules. Synthes, he wrote, should have applied for an IDE before testing Norian. Despins accused the company of off-label marketing.

Around the same time, Chapman—the surgeon who had conducted the study in which a pig had died only seconds after being injected with Norian—came back into the picture. (It wouldn't be the last time.) The surgeon wrote a letter at Huggins's behest that defended the cement, according to prosecutors. They later pointed out that Chapman had recently been named to the Hansjörg Wyss chair at the University of Washington, which received a $2 million endowment from Synthes's CEO. The prosecutors concluded: "So we submit the letter should be taken with a grain of salt."

• • •

It took nearly five years of FDA proceedings, investigation, and grand-jury hearings before federal prosecutors were ready to move. By 2009 they were prepared to indict not only Synthes but also four individuals: Huggins, Higgins, Bohner, and Walsh. The executives' attorneys negotiated a deal in which the men would plead guilty to a misdemeanor under the Responsible Corporate Officer Doctrine. The U.S. Supreme Court has ruled that the Food, Drug, and Cosmetic Act allows prosecutors to charge individuals who lack actual knowledge of a crime simply because they are "standing in a responsible relation to a public danger."

When Synthes was charged, as noted earlier, the doctrine had never been used to send an individual to prison. Most people expected the four executives to receive fines, or possibly probation.

On June 16, 2009, the grand jury handed up an indictment against Synthes and the executives. It was a doozy. Norian, the company, was charged with fifty-two felony counts, including lying to the FDA and intent to defraud. Synthes, its corporate parent, was charged with forty-four misdemeanors. Though the U.S. attorney's office charged the four businessmen with just a single misdemeanor for their roles as "responsible corporate officers," it outlined in excruciating detail the history of the Norian XR test market and deaths. The U.S. attorney's office issued a press release peppered with lurid details, including the allegations that Synthes had performed "human experimentation."

The defense attorneys were furious. They believed they were the victims of a bait and switch. In their view, their clients had agreed to take general responsibility for their company's actions only to find themselves charged with a litany of misdeeds—without any need for the prosecutors to prove that the executives had committed those acts. There was no reason, they argued, that the judge should consider the prosecution's allegations in his sentencing decision.

The assistant U.S. attorney who prosecuted the case, Mary Crawley, disagreed. Just because the government didn't have to establish that the executives were involved in the crime didn't mean it couldn't do so if it wanted, she argued. In a filing, she wrote: "[The] four individuals seek to transform the responsible corporate officer doctrine from a sword intended to achieve maximum adherence to the U.S.' food and drug safety laws into a shield insulating the genuinely culpable parties from the consequences of their own intentional wrongdoing."

The war between Crawley and attorneys for the executives raged on for two years. Meanwhile, in October 2010, Synthes pleaded guilty, agreeing to pay $23 million in fines and divest Norian. In exchange, the Justice Department promised not to bring any new criminal charges against Synthes employees.

That included Wyss. He was not charged in the indictment, but he was mentioned. The prosecutors cited "Person 7" as making the initial decision not to pursue an IDE study. A key on the last page identified Person 7 as Synthes's "CEO and major shareholder." The U.S. attorney's office declined to comment on why it didn't charge Wyss, but the answer may be simple: The CEO's name appears multiple times in e-mails and meeting minutes, but only as a recipient and attendee. Wyss's name also turns up in documents less and less as events reached their peak.

Around the time of the guilty plea, Synthes was quietly exploring a sale. In late September 2010, Wyss met with top executives from Johnson & Johnson, including Alex Gorsky, then head of its medical devices unit and now its CEO. The company saw the opportunity to achieve dominance by buying one of the highest-margin players in a growing market. Seven months later, on April 27, 2011, J&J announced that it was buying Synthes for about $20 billion. (J&J declined to comment for this article.) The deal, which formally closed in June 2012, valued the Wyss family stake at about $10 billion.

• • •

On November 21, 2011, the four Synthes executives appeared for sentencing in a federal courthouse in Philadelphia. Huggins went first. His lawyer touted Huggins's devotion to his family and his community service. The judge, Legrome Davis, told Huggins to stand, and the packed room fell silent.

Huggins's conduct, the judge said, was "egregious"—so egregious that he was going to send him to prison for nine months. "I think that a lesser sentence would not speak to the harm that has been done here," Davis said. It was the first time in his twenty-five-year career, he continued, that he had sentenced someone above the federal guidelines, which suggested Huggins get no more than six months in jail.

"But I do it because it is necessary," he boomed. "Because what has occurred in this case, in terms of wrongfulness—it's eleven on a scale of ten." Davis denied Huggins's request that he be allowed to turn himself in later. Instead, as his wife and daughters watched, Huggins was placed in handcuffs and led directly into custody.

Davis sentenced the next executive, Higgins, to nine months. The third man to face the judge was Bohner. His lawyer, Brent Gurney, took a surprising tack when asked about Bohner's guilt. "There is another person who is not present in this process who may have a bearing in answering your question, Your Honor," he said. That person, he continued, was none other than the man who ran Synthes during the illegal clinical trials: Wyss.

It was Wyss, Gurney continued, who made the initial decision to test the bone cement without doing proper clinical trials. It was Wyss, he charged, who created a corporate culture where people could not "stand up and stop things that were wrong, especially when they were coming from the top." Gurney cited Synthes employees who told the grand jury that the chairman was "hands-on," "forceful," and an "800-pound gorilla" who refused to brook dissent.

Davis seemed unconvinced. Then, just as the judge was laying into the executives' "shameful behavior," the confrontation took a bizarre turn: Gurney suddenly collapsed, hitting his head on a table as he fell. For a moment he lay on the floor, bleeding. When he regained consciousness, the lawyer—who declined to discuss the episode—was taken to a hospital. The hearings continued, and the judge sentenced the fourth executive, John Walsh, to five months.

Gurney recovered and returned to court in December for his client's rescheduled hearing. This time he made no mention of Wyss, and Davis sentenced Bohner to eight months. Gurney asked if he could delay Bohner's sentence so that his client wouldn't have to spend the holidays in a detention center. Davis said no. "To me, jail is not a question of personal convenience to the defendant," he said. "In the scheme of things, it's an incredibly brief sentence." He sent Bohner straight to prison.

• • •

The jail sentences in the Synthes case stunned the industry, sparking fears of increased risk for executives. Some defense lawyers warn that the government's strategy could backfire. "Now that executives realize that they may be facing real jail time, they may be reluctant to plead guilty," says Adam Hoffinger, the attorney at Morrison & Foerster who represented Tom Higgins.

Government lawyers counter that prosecuting individuals is the only way to stop off-label marketing because companies have come to view fines as a cost of doing business. As a result, the Responsible Corporate Officer Doctrine, which was mostly dormant throughout the 1990s, is resurgent. In 2007 the government used it to pursue charges against three officials at Purdue Pharma. In 2011 the former CEO of KV Pharmaceutical was sentenced to thirty days in jail. The Justice Department used the Synthes case to send a message: The threat of incarceration is real.

As for the convicted former Synthes executives, Walsh was released from a Pennsylvania prison camp in late April after serving a five-month sentence. Huggins, Higgins, and Bohner were all released at the end of the summer.

Synthes itself suffered little from the Norian debacle. After settling with the government, the company sold the bone cement unit to Kensey Nash, a small manufacturer located just down the road, for $22 million (just $1 million less than its fine). Today J&J's DePuy Synthes unit is the product's exclusive distributor.

• • •

The civil litigation over Norian is far from over. The families of Barbara Marcelino and Ryoichi Kikuchi jointly sued Synthes, the four executives, and Wyss. Their lawyers, Greg Rueb and Joseph Motta, called the defendants' conduct "reprehensible, despicable, deceptive." Wyss's attorney has filed a motion to dismiss the suit, arguing that the families "failed to allege any specific facts indicating that Wyss had any personal involvement" in the purported crime.

Eskind's daughter, Eva Sloan, filed suit against Synthes in late July. "One of the most offensive things was the little piddly sentence they got for this," she says. "They could have gone to 7-Eleven and stolen a six-pack of beer and got more time." Like the Kikuchi and Baddley families, the Eskinds say they were kept in the dark about the circumstances of their relative's death for nearly a decade.

These disasters didn't put an end to the use of Norian in the spine. Three years ago, an article in the *New England Journal of Medicine* concluded that vertebroplasties are basically ineffective. But many spine surgeons still believe in the procedure.

In June of this year, another death came to light. A man from Enumclaw, Wash., named Russell Bryant filed a suit against Synthes alleging that his wife, Joan Bryant, had died after being injected with Norian. This lawsuit described events similar to the others, but with a troubling twist: Bryant's surgery took place on July 6, 2009—three weeks after the government had filed charges against Synthes. Even more shocking, one of the two surgeons named in the complaint was Jens Chapman, the same person who had studied Norian in the early 2000s and observed the rapid death of a pig injected with the cement. (Chapman's lawyer declined to comment.)

The complaint's version of the facts is as follows: Chapman first attempted surgery on June 29, 2009. After he started operating, Bryant began bleeding profusely and had to be transferred to the intensive-care unit. On July 6, Chapman tried again (according to a report filed by the company, a Synthes sales representative was in the operating room). After Chapman injected

Norian into Bryant's back, she experienced cardiovascular collapse and died.

Bryant's suit asserts that his wife, who was fifty-eight, was healthy when she went into surgery. She reported on a hospital questionnaire that she "felt full of life, felt calm and peaceful and felt happy all the time."

A few weeks after Bryant's death, two reports were submitted to the FDA. One described a fatal surgery that took place on July 6, 2009—Bryant's death, according to the complaint. The other report recounted a death that had occurred nearly two years earlier, on August 17, 2007. It stated that a woman injected with Norian had died during spine surgery; an autopsy found cement fragments in her lungs.

The belated timing of the second report caught the attention of Bryant's lawyer, Dan Hannula, who suspected that Chapman had submitted both notifications. With the help of an investigator, Hannula found a woman from Enumclaw whose operation and death matched the description in the report. Reba Golden died on Chapman's operating table on August 17, 2007, according to her daughter Cindy. She was sixty-seven. Until this summer, Cindy says, she had no idea that Norian might be implicated in her mother's death. She plans to sue.

Wall Street Journal

A *Wall Street Journal* team examines a drug epidemic that annually kills more than 15,000 Americans—and it's not the one we're spending $15 billion a year to fight. As Thomas Catan, Devlin Barrett, and Timothy W. Martin document, Americans are overdosing on prescription painkillers called opioids, "more than from heroin, cocaine, and all other illegal drugs combined." The dealers aren't shady Colombian drug lords but retail pharmacies. Some doctors sell prescriptions for profit while others view opioids as a legitimate tool for managing chronic pain. The rise in their use has made drug overdoses the leading cause of accidental death in the United States. The *WSJ* team meticulously tracks the problem through the life of a young woman who worked as a doctor's receptionist. In 2006, he prescribed an opioid for pain in her neck and her back, and by July 4, 2010, at age twenty-three, she was dead.

Thomas Catan, Devlin Barrett, and Timothy W. Martin

4. Prescription for Addiction

Jaclyn Kinkade, a twenty-three-year-old doctor's-office receptionist and occasional model, was a casualty of America's number-one drug menace when she overdosed and died, alone, in a tumbledown clapboard house in Dunnellon, Fla.

The drugs that killed her didn't come from the Colombian jungles or an Afghan poppy field. Two of the three drugs found in her system were sold to Ms. Kinkade, legally, at Walgreen Co. and CVS Caremark shops, the two biggest U.S. pharmacies. Both prescription drugs found in her body were made in the United States—the oxycodone in Elizabeth, N.J., by a company being acquired by generic-drug giant Watson Pharmaceuticals Inc., and the methadone in Hobart, N.Y., by Covidien Ltd., another major manufacturer. Every stage of their distribution was government-regulated. In addition, Ms. Kinkade had small amounts of methamphetamine in her system when she died.

The United States spends about $15 billion a year fighting illegal drugs, often on foreign soil. But America's deadliest drug epidemic begins and ends at home. More than 15,000 Americans now die annually after overdosing on prescription painkillers called opioids, according to the Centers for Disease Control and Prevention—more than from heroin, cocaine, and all other illegal drugs combined.

Rising opioid abuse means that drug overdoses are now the single largest cause of accidental death in America. They surpassed traffic accidents in 2009, the most recent CDC data available.

Paradoxically, the legality of prescription painkillers makes their abuse harder to tackle. There is no Pablo Escobar to capture or kill. Authorities must contend with an influential lobby of industry representatives and doctors who argue against more restrictions, saying they would harm legitimate patients. And lawmakers have been reluctant to have the federal government track Americans' prescriptions, leaving states to piece together a patchy, fragmented response.

Ms. Kinkade's final days, and the path of the drugs that killed her, were reconstructed from medical and prescription records, police files, and interviews. Many records were assembled by Ms. Kinkade's father and stepmother.

Shuffling through the documents at their living-room table, Bruce Kinkade, a garage-door salesman, and his wife, Ann, said they don't wish to absolve their daughter of responsibility. "We're not naive and want to say she was a perfect angel," said Ann Kinkade, Jaclyn's stepmother.

But the Kinkades say the companies and licensed professionals that supplied her with the drugs must also bear some responsibility. "Jackie didn't wake up one day and say, 'Hey, I'm going to be a drug addict today,'" Ann Kinkade said. "Jackie pretty much got sent there by a doctor, got hooked, and continued to go back."

There are few easy villains in prescription drug abuse. Companies, physicians, and addicts alike are all pieces in a complex puzzle. For some time, regulators have been cracking down on doctors who prescribe to addicts for profit. Now, federal and state officials are starting to move up the supply chain to pursue pharmacies and distributors.

On September 12, the Drug Enforcement Administration revoked the licenses of two Florida CVS stores, which it claims sold excessive amounts of oxycodone without ensuring the pills weren't diverted to the black market. CVS is fighting the DEA's order in administrative and federal courts.

Two days later, the agency served Walgreen with a suspension order halting sales of controlled substances from its Jupiter, Fla., distribution center, calling it an "imminent threat to public safety." The DEA's regulatory action alleges that the facility—the state's largest oxycodone distributor—"failed to maintain effective controls" of its narcotic painkillers.

Walgreen said it is working with regulators and has tightened its procedures. CVS said it was committed to working with regulators "to reduce prescription drug abuse and diversion while ensuring access to appropriate, effective pain medication for our patients who need them."

Participants in the drug-supply chain acknowledge the problems but point to others as the weak link. Doctors involved say pharmacies should be able to tell if patients are secretly using several physicians to obtain more drugs. Druggists say they can't second-guess a valid prescription. Manufacturers and distributors say they are simply delivering products ordered by healthcare professionals.

What makes this drug scourge different from previous ones, such as heroin in the 1970s and cocaine in the 1980s, is that everyone in the distribution chain is identifiable. The DEA itself controls the supply spigot by setting drug companies' production quotas for opioids like oxycodone and hydrocodone.

For years, opioids were reserved mainly for cancer or terminally ill patients because of fears over their safety and addictiveness. But over the past fifteen years, many doctors have come to view them as an essential tool to manage chronic pain. Around the same time, drug makers began marketing patented, time-release formulations of the drugs, making it a lucrative category.

Today, a growing number of doctors say the pendulum has swung too far, with powerful narcotics being dispensed for even relatively minor complaints. Last year, pharmacies dispensed more than $9 billion in prescription opioid painkillers, more than twice the amount a decade earlier, according to IMS Health, a research firm. The number of prescriptions has risen fourfold. The generic version of Vicodin, a blend of hydrocodone and acetaminophen, is now the most prescribed drug in the country.

Opioids come from the same narcotics family as heroin and can produce similar addictions, researchers say. "We're basically talking about heroin pills," said Andrew Kolodny, chairman of the psychiatry department at Maimonides Medical Center in New York.

Studies show that opioid addicts come from a surprisingly broad swath of the population: the middle-aged, the elderly, and, increasingly, young adults. Many U.S. veterans returning from Iraq and Afghanistan with physical and mental injuries are also becoming dependent on prescription painkillers, researchers say.

In recent decades, researchers have come to view addiction as a disease rather than just a personal failing. Some people are more predisposed to becoming addicted because of heredity, experience, and other factors that have yet to be fully understood. But some drugs are simply more addictive than others.

New research suggests that drugs like opioids cause long-lasting changes to the brain, rewiring some areas to crave more drugs while simultaneously damaging the parts that can control those cravings. The drugs can damage the brain's ability to feel pleasure, so regular users eventually need to take them not to get high or help with pain but just to feel normal. Avoiding unpleasant withdrawal symptoms ends up conditioning many drug users' daily lives.

One of the most confounding aspects of this latest epidemic is that it blurs the lines between legal and illegal drug use. Some people first take drugs from their family medicine cabinets to get high then go to doctors to get more. Others are originally prescribed the pills for legitimate reasons then buy them on the street once they're hooked.

Many, such as Ms. Kinkade, end up mixing legal and illegal drugs in ways that can prove lethal.

Ms. Kinkade was a lively, talkative woman with blond hair, a fear of caterpillars, and a pit-bull terrier, Bentley, that traveled everywhere with her.

She was first prescribed an opioid on October 27, 2006, by the doctor who employed her as a receptionist, prescription records show. According to medical records and an entry from her diary, she had been suffering back and neck pain. Thomas Suits, her employer, prescribed twenty pills of Endocet, a drug containing oxycodone. "I'd never taken opioids before," Ms. Kinkade wrote in a diary entry. "But I started the med routine and OMG I felt no pain."

Dr. Suits didn't recall prescribing the medication, said his wife, Irene Machel, a doctor who also works at the clinic. She declined to discuss the matter further.

Endo Health Solutions, which made the pills, declined to comment on Ms. Kinkade. "These types of stories are tragic and we obviously take them seriously," said Endo spokesman Blaine Davis. "Our responsibility, as a company that is very dedicated to the field of pain management, is to educate both physicians and patients about appropriate use."

Soon Ms. Kinkade was seeking more drugs. On January 5, 2007, she saw Bruce Kammerman, a family practitioner at a clinic in Stuart, Fla., and came away with a generic blend of oxycodone and acetaminophen. A scan taken a month later showed no problems with her spine, according to the medical report. Through his lawyer, Dr. Kammerman declined to say why he wrote the prescription. "That's a sad case," said his attorney, Lance Richard. "Maybe she didn't have justifiable pain but she certainly came in and made complaints about it. At some point the doctor just has to go on the patient's word."

Dr. Kammerman was arrested in July at a pain clinic in Vero Beach, Fla., charged with drug trafficking, racketeering, and illegally selling controlled substances. The DEA said in a news conference he was prescribing an average of 1,700 oxycodone tablets a day. Dr. Kammerman's lawyer said his client has done nothing wrong and pleaded not guilty.

Ms. Kinkade broke up with her boyfriend. She began missing work. One day she was found curled up under her desk, crying. "She always used to be clean-cut, nice makeup," said Susan Cochran, a former colleague. Then "she would come in in sweatpants and it was like: 'Who is this person?' "

Ms. Kinkade changed jobs to work at a radiologist's office. There, she had two other scans, in April and July 2008. Neither showed significant spine problems, according to the medical reports. Ms. Kinkade started seeking clinics that asked fewer questions. "Family practitioners hate writing narcotics," she wrote in her diary. "Nowadays—I'll just go str8 to pain docs."

During that period, she was prescribed large amounts of oxycodone, her records show, combined with antianxiety drugs and powerful muscle relaxants. Her parents grew increasingly alarmed. "Sometimes you'd be having a conversation with her and her head would just drop," Mr. Kinkade said. "And she'd say: 'Oh, I'm just tired; I was out late.' "

After reviewing her records, he said, "We estimated that at one point she was taking 13.4 pills per day, for nothing wrong with her."

In May 2009, Mr. Kinkade and his wife asked a judge to have their daughter forcibly admitted to drug treatment under a Florida law. Their request was initially denied because she wasn't a minor. Angered by their efforts, Ms. Kinkade moved out of their home and drove across the state to her biological mother's house. She crashed her car and was found wandering along the highway in a drug-induced daze, her parents said, searching for her pills.

Legal records show she was arrested several times for minor crimes such as possessing controlled drugs without a prescription and shoplifting small items, including makeup and cake topping. In each case, she was released and the charges dropped.

She started visiting a pain clinic in Tampa called Doctors Rx Us, where she was prescribed oxycodone, methadone, alprazolam, and gabapentin, an antiseizure medication, according to records her parents collected. Housed in a rundown strip mall, the clinic today is called Palm Medical Group after a name change in 2011, according to its state records.

Ms. Kinkade was prescribed the drugs by two physicians at Doctors Rx Us: Richard Smith and William Crumbley. Dr. Crumbley was arrested in December and charged with operating a nonregistered pain clinic at another location. He has pleaded not guilty.

Dr. Smith and the clinic declined repeated interview requests. A lawyer for Dr. Crumbley said he was innocent of any wrongdoing.

On May 3, 2010, Ms. Kinkade stopped at a CVS in Crystal River, Fla., and picked up a prescription written by Dr. Smith for ninety tablets of 10 mg methadone, along with ninety tablets of alprazolam, an antianxiety drug.

"Jaclyn Kinkade's death is a terrible tragedy that highlights the need for a comprehensive national effort to prevent prescription drug abuse," CVS said in a statement.

Information provided by the manufacturer suggests that the methadone dispensed to Ms. Kinkade was likely supplied to CVS by Cardinal Health Inc. Cardinal was the only distributor to have sold that particular drug to that CVS branch during that period, according to the manufacturer's records. CVS and Cardinal declined to comment.

Last year, the DEA launched a probe of the Florida-based operations of Cardinal Health and CVS Caremark. The agency alleged they dispensed "extremely large amounts" of oxycodone with signs that the drugs were "diverted from legitimate channels."

CVS said it has "responded to the DEA's concerns, including implementing enhancements to our policies and procedures for filling controlled substance prescriptions." Cardinal settled with the DEA in May, agreeing to suspend sales for two years at one of its key distribution facilities in Lakeland, Fla.

The methadone Ms. Kinkade picked up at the end of her life was made in Hobart, N.Y., by Mallinckrodt, a unit of health-care giant Covidien. "Any death from abuse or misuse of prescription drugs is tragic," Covidien said. "That's why we believe that, as a nation, ending the abuse, diversion and misuse of powerful pain medications is necessary to ensure adequate treatment of pain and access to that treatment for legitimate pain patients."

On May 10, 2010, Ms. Kinkade was stopped by police in Levy County, Fla., for having an expired registration. A drug-sniffing dog reacted to her car and she was arrested for possessing a generic form of Xanax without the correct prescription. This time, her parents let her sit in jail for a couple of weeks while they organized a place for her in a rehabilitation program. They bailed her out May 25 and enrolled her in drug treatment.

Over the next month, Ms. Kinkade went to the treatment program during the day and seemed to improve, her parents said. Then, the evening of June 24, she climbed out the window at her parents' house.

A few days later, on the other side of Florida, she met up with a boyfriend, according to a statement he later gave police. She returned to Doctors Rx Us, where Dr. Smith wrote a prescription for ninety tablets of 30 mg oxycodone, according to prescription records. It would be her last.

The next day, Ms. Kinkade filled the prescription at a Walgreens in Beverly Hills, Fla. The oxycodone would have come from Walgreen's Jupiter, Fla., distribution center, a company spokesman said. On September 14, the DEA barred that facility from selling controlled substances, alleging that it failed to maintain effective controls to stop large amounts of oxycodone from reaching the black market. "When [companies] choose to look the other way, patients suffer and drug dealers prosper," Mark Trouville, the DEA special agent in charge, said at the time. Walgreen said in a statement it is cooperating with the DEA.

The oxycodone came from the New Jersey plant of Actavis, a Swiss pharmaceutical company. In April, Actavis was bought by Watson Pharmaceutical in a $5.8 billion deal awaiting regulatory approval. An Actavis spokesman described Ms. Kinkade's situation as a "tragic occurrence" and called for discussion on "how to prevent such cases in the future." A Watson spokesman cautioned against action that would make it harder to treat legitimate patients. He said the company supported educating patients about the drugs' proper use.

The morning of July 4, Ms. Kinkade's boyfriend found her sitting cross-legged and slumped in his room at a white, low-slung house tucked behind a trailer park. The medical examiner said she died from a drug cocktail including oxycodone, methadone, and methamphetamine.

Ms. Kinkade's physical decline made such an impression on the detective who investigated the case that, two years later, he still recalls the scene. In the living room, he noticed a poster of Ms. Kinkade modeling for a biker magazine.

"Wow, she's a beautiful young lady," Detective Matthew Taylor remembered thinking. "When I actually saw her, it was as different as night and day."

Washington Post

The chilling tales of perverse incentives and tawdry ethics in the medical/pharmacological complex take another twist in Peter Whoriskey's devastating examination of the multi-billion-dollar market for anti-anemia drugs. For years, a trio of drugs made by two companies, Amgen and Johnson & Johnson had been star performers in the world of pharmaceutical blockbusters. But studies showed the drugs' benefits were often wildly overstated and their serious risks overlooked, even as deaths attributed to them began to pile up. Finally, Medicare released a report last year that said there was no evidence the drugs had any "clinical benefit," at all. The companies expressed regrets, but Whoriskey shows the fiasco was no accident. The companies had waged expensive lobbying campaigns to win approval for the drugs, dragged their feet on full testing, created incentives for doctors and hospitals to prescribe the largest doses possible, and steamrolled regulators who tried to stem the flow of drugs.

Peter Whoriskey

5. Anemia Drugs Made Billions, but at What Cost?

On the day Jim Lenox got his last injection, the frail fifty-four-year-old cancer patient was waiting to be discharged from the Baltimore Washington Medical Center. He'd put on his black leather coat. Then a nurse said he needed another dose of anemia drugs.

His wife, Sherry, thought that seemed odd, because his blood readings had been close to normal, but Lenox trusted the doctors. After the nurse pumped the drug into his left shoulder, the former repairman for Washington Gas said he felt good enough to play basketball.

The shots, which his cancer clinic had been billing at $2,500 a pop, were expensive.

Hours later, Lenox was dead.

For years, a trio of anemia drugs known as Epogen, Procrit, and Aranesp ranked among the best-selling prescription drugs in the United States, generating more than $8 billion a year for two companies, Amgen and Johnson & Johnson. Even compared with other pharmaceutical successes, they were superstars. For several years, Epogen ranked as the single costliest medicine under Medicare: U.S. taxpayers put up as much as $3 billion a year for the drugs.

The trouble, as a growing body of research has shown, is that for about two decades, the benefits of the drug—including "life satisfaction and happiness" according to the FDA-approved label—were wildly overstated, and potentially lethal side effects, such as cancer and strokes, were overlooked.

Last year, Medicare researchers issued an eighty-four-page study declaring that among most kidney patients, the original and largest market for the drugs, there was no solid evidence that they made people feel better, improved their survival, or had any "clinical benefit" besides elevating a statistic for red blood cell count.

It was a remarkable finding of futility: While drugmakers had seen billions in profits over twenty-two years, much of it from taxpayers, millions of patients had been subjected to dangerous doses that might have had little advantage.

How did this happen?

To answer the question, the *Washington Post* obtained the agreements between the drugmakers and the Food and Drug Administration, reviewed thousands of pages of transcripts and company reports, and relied on new academic research, some by doctors who once administered the drugs but now look askance at the drugmakers' original claims.

The multi-billion-dollar rise and fall of the anemia drugs illustrates how the economic incentives embedded in the U.S. health-care system can make it not only inefficient but also potentially deadly.

Through a well-funded research and lobbying campaign, Amgen won far-reaching approvals from the FDA. Both pharmaceutical companies conducted trials that missed the dangers and touted benefits that years later would be deemed unproven. The companies took more than a decade to fulfill their research commitments. And when bureaucrats tried to rein in the largest doses, a high-powered lobbying effort occurred until Congress forced the regulators to let the drugs flow.

But at the center of any explanation of the popularity of these drugs are the nation's doctors, clinics, and hospitals and the choices they made for patients.

Americans might like to think that doctors focus on only their health. But physicians and hospitals have to pay the bills, too, and, in some cases, the more they treat a patient, the more they earn. This was especially true in the case of the anemia drugs: The bigger the dose, the more they made.

Unlike medications that a patient picks up at the store, drugs administered by a physician, as these were, can yield a profit for doctors if there is a "spread"—a difference between the price they pay for the drug and the price they charge patients.

In this case, drugmakers worked diligently to make sure that doctors had an incentive to give large doses—that the spread was large. They offered discounts to practices that dispensed the drug in big volumes. They overfilled vials, adding as much as 25 percent extra, allowing doctors to further widen profit margins. Most critical, however, was the company's lobbying pressure, under which Congress and Medicare bureaucrats forged a system in which doctors and hospitals would be reimbursed more for the drug than they were paying for it.

The markup that doctors, clinics, and hospitals received on the drugs given to Medicare patients reached as high as 30 percent, according to the Medicare Payment Advisory Commission, a group that advises Congress. And the markup on doses given to patients covered by private insurance was even larger.

The incentives worked.

At the peak of the boom in 2007, more than 80 percent of 175,000 dialysis patients on Medicare were receiving the drug at levels beyond what the FDA now considers safe, according to federal statistics. Although other patients were receiving the drugs, the United States keeps closer records on dialysis patients.

"It was just so easy to do—you put this stuff in the patient's arm, and you made thousands of dollars," said Charles Bennett, endowed chair at the Medication Safety and Efficacy Center of Economic Excellence at the University of South Carolina and one of the critics of the use of the drug in cancer patients. "An oncologist could make anywhere from $100,000 to $300,000 a year from this alone. And all the while they were told that it was good for the patient."

Take, for example, the doses of Aranesp that Jim Lenox was given several times during his cancer treatment, though not the injection he received at the hospital, which was Procrit.

The insurance company reimbursed the clinic about $900 for each, according to his patient records. The clinic would have paid about $600 for a dose of that size, at average prices from that time, meaning a profit of roughly $300 per administration.

"Jim trusted the doctors," Sherry Lenox said.

The incentives drove remarkably high profits at Amgen—enough to elevate the small California firm into a Fortune 500 company. Its profit margin reached over 30 percent of sales, far higher than the industry average. As much as a third of that was coming from reimbursements funded by U.S. taxpayers.

Daniel Coyne, a professor of medicine at Washington University who had been a paid speaker for Amgen, promoting the drug, called the case "a paradigm for the pharmaceutical industry."

Coyne said he became a critic after the drug's danger surfaced and the company continued to promote higher doses.

"Amgen can say they are very contrite," Coyne said. "They can say, 'Isn't it a shame that we didn't know.' But this isn't a shame for Amgen. They won. They made billions."

Amgen declined requests for interviews but responded to questions via e-mail. In a statement, the company said that as the understanding of the drugs has evolved, the company "quickly and responsibly communicated these new findings" and updated the product labeling fifteen times since its approval.

"Any assertion that Amgen misled the public about the risks and benefits . . . is a gross misstatement of the facts," the company said. "On the contrary, Amgen's primary concern is for patients."

As for the high reimbursement rates for the drugs, the company said it "has consistently advocated for appropriate access to vital therapies, and we routinely engage with policy-makers to share our views on key issues."

Johnson & Johnson similarly declined interview requests but said in a statement, "As our understanding of the risk-benefit profile of [the drugs] has evolved over time, we have worked closely with the FDA to ensure new and relevant information is included in labeling."

Emerging in the late eighties, the new anemia drugs were among the earliest blockbusters from the nascent biotech industry.

Anemia arises when the body produces too few red blood cells, which carry oxygen from the lungs to the rest of the body.

The drugs consisted of man-made versions of a natural hormone called erythropoietin, which stimulates the body to produce red blood cells.

The discovery, which grew out of research funded in part by the National Institutes of Health, gave doctors an entirely new "natural" way of treating anemia. The previous method consisted of giving patients transfusions of red blood cells, a cumbersome process that can take as long as four hours.

To get the new man-made hormone approved, Amgen submitted the results of a key clinical trial of patients on dialysis. Because they, and other patients with kidney disease, frequently suffer from anemia, they would become the core market for the drugs.

That trial established that, indeed, the drug stimulated the production of red blood cells. Patients given the drug showed fewer signs of anemia—their hematocrit, or percentage of red blood cells as a percentage of blood, rose significantly.

The researchers also examined the evidence in the trials for signs of harmful side effects.

"The risks associated with [the] therapy are minimal," Amgen wrote to the FDA.

The first two drugs of the trio, Epogen and Procrit, were approved by the agency in June 1989 for patients with kidney disease. Amgen made both; Procrit was licensed by Johnson & Johnson. Amgen's Aranesp would be approved in 2001.

For a narrow portion of those patients—dialysis patients with anemia so severe they needed occasional blood transfusions—the drugs, if used in limited amounts, did offer a critical benefit, one that doctors say amounted to a revolution in treatment. Patients with severe anemia said it could restore their vitality. The new drugs allowed them to avoid the risks of transfusions, which can carry diseases and raise future complications for transplant patients.

The trouble would arise as the drugmakers won FDA approval for vastly expanded uses, pushing it in larger doses, for milder anemia and for patients with a wider array of illnesses. Very quickly, the market included nearly all dialysis patients, not just the roughly 16 percent who required blood transfusions. The size of average doses would more than triple. And over the next five years, the FDA would approve it to treat anemia in patients with cancer and AIDS, as well as those getting hip and knee surgery.

The key to their marketing was the claim that the drugs at higher doses could make patients feel better. By 1994, the drug's label, approved by the FDA, advertised a range of benefits: "statistically significant improvements for . . . health, sex life, well-being, psychological effect, life satisfaction, and happiness."

Those claims, withdrawn thirteen years later because they did not meet new FDA standards for proof, would be the basis of television and print advertising campaigns, pitched to people with potentially fatal illnesses.

The drugs, according to one, offered "Strength for Life."

But while ads touted the drugs' virtues, some at the FDA had raised safety concerns. To address them, the drugmakers agreed to conduct two key safety studies.

The first was supposed to evaluate the drug's "safety profile" and enrolled 2,100 patients. Scientists affiliated with Amgen published "interim" results in 1991 and 1993.

But the full safety results of the study were never published, and in later lists of safety investigations by the FDA and Amgen, there appears to be no reference to this study.

It's not clear from the agency's records how seriously anyone was taking the results, anyway. Amgen filed a "clinical study report" with the agency in 1995, and the company says its research commitment was fulfilled then. But the FDA did not deem the study completed until March 2004, almost fifteen years after the company agreed to conduct it.

Neither Amgen nor the FDA would release a copy of the study report.

An FDA spokesman explained that the original report had been "misfiled" and that the agency has instituted tracking procedures to prevent that from happening.

A company spokesman said the report's findings were consistent with what was known of the risks at the time.

The second promise of a safety report would arise as the drugs were being approved for cancer patients. In 1993, the companies agreed to conduct a study of whether the drugs might have "stimulatory effects" on tumor growth.

That year, Johnson & Johnson started a study of patients with small-cell lung cancer.

It was supposed to have 400 patients.

Eleven years later, the company said it was having difficulty recruiting them, having enrolled only 224. That meant it would be harder to reach statistically significant conclusions. Moreover, the FDA noted that in about 17 percent of the cases, data were missing.

With FDA approval, Johnson & Johnson halted the study, never finding evidence of clear dangers. But as Medicare researchers would later remark, the patients taking the drugs appeared more likely to die than those taking the placebo.

Amgen scientists agreed that the trial results favored the survival of the placebo group but wrote to the FDA that there still wasn't enough information.

"The data are sparse," they wrote to the FDA.

With the abandonment of that trial in 2004, the drugmakers committed to doing another study, which was supposed to be completed by 2008, according to an FDA letter to Amgen.

It still has not been completed.

It has been enlarged, Amgen officials said, and is not expected to be finished until 2017—nearly twenty-five years after the drug was approved for use in cancer patients.

Amgen noted that the company "has sponsored and conducted many of the studies that have enhanced the understanding of [the drugs], including the discovery of new adverse events."

One of the first questions facing regulators and doctors was a simple one: How much of this drug should be used?

Huge profits rested on the answer.

Doctors measure anemia by gauging a person's hematocrit, the red blood cell percentage. In a healthy person, the hematocrit is about 40 percent or higher.

Before the new drugs, doctors might give a person a blood transfusion if their hematocrit dropped below 25 percent. The transfusion would raise them up to about 30 percent hematocrit but not all the way to "normal" levels.

With the advent of the drugs, which were easier than transfusions, doctors and drugmakers began to propose boosting a patient's hematocrit all the way up to "normal" levels. Should patients who were just slightly anemic—and not just the sliver of transfusion-dependent patients—be given the drug to make them "normal"?

Funded by Amgen, the Normal Hematocrit Trial sought to explore the possibilities of raising the treatment target. It drew in more than 1,200 patients who were on dialysis and had a history of heart trouble. It was one of the largest trials to have been done on the drugs at the time.

About half the patients received enough Epogen to boost their hematocrit up to normal levels of about 42 percent; the other half received only enough to get them to 30 percent, the level typically achieved with transfusion.

Three years after the study began, the trial was halted. Patients in the "normal" higher-dose group were dying or having heart attacks at a higher rate than those in the lower-dose, lower-hematocrit group.

It was an indication that the drugs could be deadly. But what could have been a clear warning turned murky as it was presented to the public.

After the termination of the trial, the FDA added a summary of the results to the Epogen label, but it didn't limit the recommended dosing levels, which the agency had recently expanded.

The reason for the "increased mortality" at the higher doses "is unknown," the label said.

Then, when the results were reported in the *New England Journal of Medicine* in 1998, key information was glossed over or omitted.

Of the eight authors of the journal article, four were employees of Amgen; two others had served as consultants to the firm. This was disclosed in the article.

The authors did recommend that, when using the drugs in patients with heart problems, hematocrit levels should not be boosted all the way to normal. But the researchers sounded a skeptical note about the danger.

The rate of death was higher in the higher-dose group, the paper acknowledged, but "not significantly."

"A higher . . . dose was not associated with higher mortality," it said.

But, as it turns out, there was a statistically significant sign of danger—at least as the FDA now reports the study's results.

Moreover, while the article suggested there were quality-of-life benefits to higher hematocrit levels, it left out the fact that no such difference was detected between patients in the higher-dose and lower-dose groups.

Neither of these issues would have become public if not for Coyne, who filed a Freedom of Information Act request with the FDA asking for the actual results of the trial.

It took the agency three and a half years to respond to his request.

"These are very, very significant discrepancies," Coyne said.

The four authors of the paper who were not employed by Amgen defended the article and said that "at no time was the intent of the original [article] to mislead anyone," according to a letter made available to the *Post*, by doctors Anatole Besarab, W. Kline Bolton, Allen R. Nissenson, and Steven Schwab.

The omission of the quality-of-life finding was a "victim of editing," the letter said. Similarly, the authors said they used a different statistical technique, one they considered more appropriate, to determine that the danger signal fell short of significance following input from the journal editors and a statistician. A *New England Journal of Medicine* spokesperson said the 1998 article was accurate.

If there was a clear warning sign, however, it appears to have been lost.

Three years after the edited results of the Normal Hematocrit Trial appeared in the *New England Journal of Medicine*, the first listed author, Besarab, then of the West Virginia University School of Medicine, cowrote an article recommending high dosage levels. It also said that patients in the trial's high-dose group had seen "significant improvements" in quality of life.

"Should the Hematocrit Be Normalized . . . ?" it asked. "Yes!"

Similarly, in a 1999 paper, Bolton asked whether raising hematocrit to normal levels with the drug might be the "Viagra" of the field.

Across the country, the dosages continued to rise.

To understand the financial incentives at play as physicians tried to determine how much of the drug to prescribe, consider how much money a small change in FDA policy meant to the drugmakers.

When the agency first approved the drug, it recommended boosting a patient's hematocrit up to 33 percent but no more; a few years later, after Amgen's suggestion, it expanded the target range up to 36 percent.

That might not sound like a big difference, but the change had huge financial implications. As hematocrits rise, more of the drug is required to get it to rise again. An average dialysis patient dosed to reach the higher level consumes about 40 percent more of the drug, a jump that would push the amount consumed from $7,000 to $10,000 annually.

Amgen advanced the idea at hospitals around the country that patients should get their hematocrits raised. The sales pitch was that higher hematocrit meant a better quality of life.

"They'd bring lunch in, or they'd have presentations at conferences, and they'd always have the same message: A little was good, more is better," said Steven Bander, formerly chief medical officer with Gambro, one of the nation's largest dialysis chains. "They would quote all these studies about quality of life. They never talked about the negative data."

The pitch worked: The average dose for the drugs more than doubled in the early to mid-nineties.

In a statement, Amgen said it "carefully trains its sales representatives on the importance of communicating the safe use of our medicines and responsible marketing" and alerted doctors directly.

But the company also had another key advocate within many of the nation's hospitals and clinics.

The most commonly used dosing guidelines that doctors in the field used were issued by a group organized by the National Kidney Foundation, which says it has measures in place to manage conflicts of interest. But Amgen was the "founding and principal sponsor" of the guidelines. Moreover, in 2006, of the sixteen members of the foundation's panel that created the new dosing guidelines, ten reported receiving consulting fees, speaking fees or research funds from Amgen or Johnson & Johnson's subsidiary, Ortho Biotech.

It recommended doses at the high end of the FDA target recommendations.

But the enthusiasm for higher doses would go much further than that.

After a sharp rise in spending in the mid-nineties, the bureaucrats instituted a rule: No longer would Medicare cover expenses for the drugs when the patient significantly exceeded the FDA recommended level. Moreover, physicians could no longer apply for exceptions to the limits.

These restrictions provoked a protest—from doctors, dialysis clinics, and the drug companies.

Amgen, which already had a sizable in-house lobbying effort, turned to powerful outside help. It spent $2.4 million on lobbyists that year, according to OpenSecrets.org. Among the Amgen representatives were Haley Barbour, the former chairman of the Republican National Committee, and C. Boyden Gray, formerly White House counsel to George H. W. Bush.

But it was then-senator Arlen Specter (D-Pa.) who led the charge against the new policy. During a hearing, he angrily questioned Nancy-Ann Min DeParle, the director of the Health Care Financing Administration, which had implemented the policy. As chairman of the subcommittee overseeing the agency's budget, Specter could command more than the usual deference.

"There is a fury out there in the medical community as to what you are doing," Specter, then a Republican, told DeParle.

Specter wanted Medicare to cover enough Epogen for patients to reach a hematocrit of 37.5; that change could have raised by 20 percent the amount of Epogen that doctors could freely prescribe in an average patient, adding a cost of $2,000 or more. Moreover, he indicated that if doctors wanted to go higher, they should be able to do so as long as they submitted a written justification.

Specter wanted to know: Who were the bureaucrats to question how doctors prescribe medicine?

"Ms. DeParle, what is your level of expertise in this field? What is your background and training?" Specter asked.

"I am a lawyer, sir," she replied, according to a transcript.

"So there is no special level of expertise that you have to make this kind of an evaluation?" Specter, a lawyer, wanted to know.

Medical experts on her staff believed that Epogen was being overused, she said. Thousands of patients, after all, showed dosing levels greater than the FDA recommendation.

But within months, the Medicare bureaucrats had not only backed off the restriction but agreed to Specter's higher limit.

On the day the agency raised the maximum level, Amgen shares spiked 6 percent.

Specter received $7,000 in campaign contributions that election cycle from the Amgen political action committee and $2,000 from the Johnson & Johnson PAC.

Specter did not return phone calls or an e-mail requesting comment.

DeParle declined to comment.

The doses kept rising.

By 2006, about half of all dialysis patients were getting so much of the drugs that their hematocrits were rising beyond the FDA-recommended ceiling of 36 percent. More than 80 percent were getting more than the level now deemed advisable.

Amgen defended the higher doses, saying that it was difficult for doctors to precisely target hematocrit levels.

"Physicians are not necessarily acting inappropriately when patients' [hematocrit] temporarily exceed the FDA label target range," the company said in a statement at the time.

The industry's success at beating back attacks by the Medicare bureaucrats to rein in costs would be repeated again and again.

It wasn't just the drugmakers who were advocating for the drugs, either. On Capitol Hill, the nation's dialysis clinics, which were receiving as much as 25 percent of their revenue from using the drugs, were sometimes a key ally of the drugmakers.

One of the nation's largest dialysis chains, in fact, in 2004 offered bonuses to its chief medical officer if he blocked efforts to reform the payment system. According to a financial filing, Charles J. McAllister, chief medical officer of DaVita, the dialysis company, was to receive a $200,000 bonus if the rules for the drugs' use being considered by regulators were dropped or delayed. He was to receive an additional $100,000 if the then-new legislation, known as the Medicare Modernization Act, didn't cut into the company's revenue.

The Medicare proposal was "deeply flawed," DaVita spokesman Skip Thurman said in a recent statement, because it limited dosing levels "without regard to the patient."

At times, the companies would even enlist the patients to lobby on their behalf.

For example, in what may have been the drugmakers' largest lobbying push, the companies sought to undo a Medicare proposal in May 2007 to restrict the use of the drugs in cancer patients.

The company spent millions trying to turn back this effort, including developing a website, Protectcancerpatients.org, that solicited testimonials from patients and instructed them on how to contact officials. Johnson & Johnson set up a similar one called Voiceforcancerpatients.com.

Amgen lobbying expenditures and political efforts jumped that year. The company ranked as the largest contributor to the campaign of House Speaker Nancy Pelosi (D-Calif.), which got $42,050.

Amid the campaign, Reps. Anna G. Eshoo (D-Calif.) and Mike Rogers (R-Mich.) drafted a letter to Medicare, signed by a majority in both houses, warning that the proposed Medicare limits on the drugs could have a "broad range of unintended health consequences."

Contacted recently, Eshoo and Rogers indicated that the decision to use the drugs should be determined by doctors and patients, not the federal government.

"As a cancer survivor myself, I know every drug has risks," Rogers said in a statement. "The federal government should not be in the business of dictating the practice of medicine."

But among the most frequently lobbied issues appears to have been prices and doses, according to lobbyist disclosures.

For years, the profit margin for health-care providers—the "spread" between what they paid for the drugs and what Medicare paid in reimbursement—led the Office of the Inspector General to issue at least seven reports recommending either that the reimbursement price be reduced or the incentives changed. The Government Accountability Office and the Medicare Payment Advisory Commission made similar recommendations. At least a couple of times during the Clinton administration, the president's proposed budget called for changing the incentives. But the measures didn't make it through.

Instead, for years, the profit margins remained wide. As late as 2009, dialysis clinics were getting a markup of 9 to 17 percent on the drugs, according to an inspector general's audit.

Eventually, however, there was no lobby that could overcome the steady drumbeat of health warnings that came from researchers.

For years, a small Bethesda-based nonprofit think tank, the Medical Technology and Practice Patterns Institute, had been publishing studies that challenged the conventional enthusiasm for the drug and the government policies that it said promoted their overuse. Then in November 2006, a study published in the *New England Journal of Medicine* reported that kidney patients targeted for higher doses were linked to higher risks of hospitalization, strokes, and death. In December, a group of Danish researchers said that it had stopped a trial of Aranesp in cancer patients because of an increase in deaths and tumor growths. And that was just the beginning of the bad news, which Amgen didn't seem particularly eager to share.

After the Danish research, the company waited three months before informing the public and did so only after the *Cancer Letter*, a newsletter, reported the findings. Analysts at the time asked chief executive Kevin Sharer why there had not been a prompt disclosure.

"Perfection says we should have done that," he said.

Then the FDA cracked down: The drugs' use was ruled out in cancer patients considered curable, it was ruled out in patients considered just slightly anemic, maximum recommended doses were lowered, and the agency told doctors in many cases to use the smallest amount possible to avoid a blood transfusion.

The agency also began to look askance at the alleged benefits, for which the evidence, in retrospect, seemed flimsy. There was no solid proof, under revised FDA guidelines for such measures, that use of the drugs leads to "statistically significant" improvements in happiness and other benefits, the agency said. Those quality-of-life claims, once so critical to the drug's adoption, were removed from the label.

But it wasn't just safety concerns that cut into sales. Shifting economic incentives depressed them, too.

Last year, nearly two decades after the Office of the Inspector General first suggested it, the economic incentives to use more of the drugs on patients in dialysis disappeared. Medicare added the drugs to a system known as "bundling," under which a health-care provider is allowed a certain amount of money per dialysis patient, rather than more money for each dose.

The effects were immediate, suggesting again that health is not the only factor that doctors weigh in treating patients. After a quarterly sales plunge in April, Amgen chief operating officer and president Robert Bradway blamed the drop on the new payment scheme.

The lower doses were "driven by changes in the market arising from bundling," he said.

In the first year of the new policy, sales of Epogen, the drug most affected by the rule, dropped 20 percent.

Although companies that sell dangerous drugs often pay a price in court, no major class-action lawsuits have been mounted, at least in part because the patients taking the drugs were already ill, attorneys said.

Amgen has been hit with whistleblower lawsuits alleging that the company engaged in illegal sales tactics, including the charge from several states that the company overfilled vials to provide an illegal kickback to doctors and hospitals. The company has denied that allegation, saying the overfill is common industry practice to ensure that doctors and nurses can withdraw a full dose from a vial. The company has set aside $780 million to settle the lawsuits, and says it has reached an agreement in principle to resolve the claims.

For those who have lost relatives who had been given the drugs, only doubts remain: What killed their loved ones—the disease or the drugs they took to treat it?

Jim Lenox, who had been fighting cancer off and on for six years, had been given the drugs multiple times, his insurance records show. It is impossible to know with certainty whether these drugs caused or hastened his death, doctors said, but they raised his risks. In a study now cited in a black-box warning on the drug label, the drugs decreased the survival of patients with the same type of cancer.

Sherry Lenox, fifty-eight, a waitress at a chain restaurant, still keeps a box of his medical records, wondering if, at some point, what happened will become clear. The night after the hospital visit in January 2008, he came home to a gathering of children and grandchildren. The hospital did not respond to requests for comment.

Shortly afterward, he collapsed, bleeding from his nose and mouth. Sherry Lenox tried to revive him. He was dead within minutes. His death certificate lists his cause of death as cancer.

"These days, when I think about him, I think a lot about the good things—what a great guy he was, our family," she said.

That's why Sherry Lenox, who has turned up at FDA meetings to confront physicians and drug company officials, presses them with a question: "Would you give big doses of these drugs to your loved ones?"

She said she has never gotten an answer.

Part III

Big Business

BusinessWeek

Ever since 1998, when Bryan Burrough and John Heylar published *Barbarians at the Gate*, business-journalism editors have had an insatiable appetite for merger stories: how deals were negotiated, what hotels hosted the last-minute negotiations, which vintages were downed when the vital documents were finally signed. But all those stories tend to end just when the really hard work begins: most mergers fail because mergers are hard. Drake Bennett's journey inside the mechanics of the United-Continental merger is fascinating because it starts with the merger a done deal and then looks at the multitude of tiny decisions that need to be made to make it succeed in practice. It turns out that something called brew-basket depth is crucial.

Drake Bennett

6. Making the World's Largest Airline Fly

Last July, fourteen months after United and Continental Airlines announced they were combining to form the largest carrier in the world, the merged airline took one of the thousands of steps required to integrate its fleet: It harmonized the coffee. Just as each carrier had its own logo, slogan, and peerage of frequent-flier status levels, each served its own blend of joe. Continental's coffee was from a company called Fresh Brew, United's was from Starbucks.

"The new United," as the merged airline called itself, had to choose. With one food-service supply chain, it made no sense to maintain two coffee contracts. And buying from one source offered the possibility of bigger volume discounts, exactly the sort of savings that United and Continental executives had hoped to create with the merger. The coffee question represented a tiny aspect of the problem of running an airline, but the quantities were huge: last year the new United sent enough coffee into the sky to brew 62 million cups.

The vice president in charge of food services at United is a slim, chipper woman named Sandra Pineau-Boddison. She considers herself a coffee enthusiast "only if you count mochas as true coffee." Still, Pineau-Boddison did not take United's coffee decision lightly. For months the issue dominated the meetings of the beverage committee, a fourteen-member panel drawn from procurement, flight operations, finance, food services, and marketing. United's head chef, a burly, bearded Irishman named Gerry McLoughlin, sat in. The committee solicited bids, then came up with twelve different blends to try. Members tasted them blind, and, in an affront to Pineau-Boddison's sweet tooth, tasted them black.

By mid-2011 there was a front-runner: a lighter roast Fresh Brew blend called Journeys. It was cheaper than the old United's Starbucks, and it did better in the taste tests. When colleagues outside the beverage committee were asked to weigh in, they concurred. The new United's chief executive officer, Jeff Smisek, dropped by the food services floor for a cup and signed off on it. Journeys was served at a meeting of the company officers to general approval. Just to be sure, food services took the new blend on the road, to Washington Dulles, Chicago O'Hare, Denver, Los Angeles, and San Francisco, asking flight attendants to try it. Out of the 1,100 who did, all but eight approved. "We thought this was a home run," says Pineau-Boddison.

On July 1 the new United introduced its new coffee. Fliers on the "legacy United" fleet, accustomed to Starbucks, let out a collective yowl of protest. Pineau-Boddison had expected some resistance—Starbucks, after all, is a popular brand—but this was something else. Flight attendants reported a barrage of complaints. Pineau-Boddison received angry e-mails from customers, as did Smisek. The coffee, fliers complained, was watery.

The beverage committee launched an inquiry. The coffee itself, they discovered, was only part of the problem. Airplane coffee is made from small, premeasured "pillow packs" that sit in a brew basket drawer at the top of the galley coffee machine. When the drawer is closed, boiling water flows through the pillow into the pot below. The old United brew baskets, the committee discovered, sit a quarter of an inch lower than Continental's, leaving a space for water to leak around the pillow pack. That fugitive water was diluting the coffee—in fact, the old

United had installed the deeper brew baskets for that very purpose, after passengers complained that their Starbucks was too strong. And so, by the end of the year, the beverage committee found itself back where it had started, trying out new pillow packs.

That's coffee. Not a matter of life or death, or even on-time arrival. It's not a question that requires federal regulatory approval or a union vote. Nor is it an issue that has anything to do with the core service of an airline, which is flying people from one place to another.

• • •

The past decade has seen a wave of consolidation among airlines: US Airways and America West merged, so did Delta and Northwest, Southwest and AirTran, and Air France and KLM. In the past few weeks, US Airways and Delta have expressed interest in each other while independently eyeing American Airlines, now in Chapter 11.

All this amalgamating may be a good thing for the airlines. It could wring redundancies out of the system and, done right, bring order and discipline to an industry that since its deregulation in 1978 has been prone to destabilizing price wars and chronic overexpansion. (It's also likely to raise fares, at least on some routes.) In buying Continental, United promised Wall Street $1.2 billion in new revenue and cost savings.

Still, combining airlines is tremendously difficult, largely because of the enormous number of things two airlines may do differently. At the new United, a few major decisions were made before the merger itself as preconditions imposed by one side or the other: naming Continental CEO Smisek the head of the new company, calling it United, and headquartering it in Chicago. The company has spent the time since then trying to work out everything else.

In conference rooms in the glossily renovated United Building in downtown Chicago and in United's offices in the Willis (formerly Sears) Tower a few blocks away, Continental employees transplanted from Houston are working alongside their new United colleagues, spending months debating questions such as whether to board flights back to front, as most airlines do, or window, middle, then aisle, as legacy United did; whether miniature ponies will be allowed, as they were on Continental, to travel in the cabin as service animals (they will); whether Jet Skis are allowed as baggage (no); what information to print on the boarding pass; what direction dog crates should face when loaded into the cargo hold (backwards, as at legacy United, so spooked dogs don't recoil and tip the crate off the conveyor belt); whether to require baggage handlers to wear steel-toed shoes (no official decision yet); what shape the plastic cups for cold beverages should be (wider than the old United cups but skinnier than the old Continental ones); whether unaccompanied minors should be identified by a bracelet or a button (bracelet); whether to have a first-class cabin like United or just business class like Continental (the former); and whether, in the first-class cabin, to serve nuts in a bag or heated in a ramekin (ramekin).

Like the coffee fiasco, even simple-seeming choices grow comically intricate when they involve commercial air travel, with its constant balancing of safety, cost, space, style, reliability, convenience, speed, and comfort. Last year, United had thirty-three teams working on integration, and in the fourth quarter alone spent $170 million on everything from technology training to severance to repainting airplanes.

"Merging two airlines is unlike merging any other businesses because it's such a complex business, and we are so heavily regulated," says Smisek, sitting surrounded by scale models of jetliners in his office in the United Building, with a view of the Chicago River and the office towers to the north. "There's huge technology issues, fleet issues, facilities issues, people issues. It also takes several years, which I think is surprising to a lot of people."

With United and Continental, the cultural complications are particularly sharp. Over the past decade and a half, Continental has built a reputation as a carrier that made its employees happy and catered to customers. At premerger United, relations between workers and management were openly hostile, poisoned by the battles of a recent bankruptcy. Among workers at the new airline there is hope but also palpable impatience about the pace of the process. The company has yet to reach joint agreements with any of the unions representing the newly consolidated workforce. The new United management, however, sees the merger as a rare opportunity. Despite recent signs of financial health among airlines, industry margins remain thin, squeezed by oil prices, a heavily unionized workforce, price-sensitive customers, and a supremely perishable product. (Once a plane leaves the gate, an unsold seat is never going to be sold.) Merging two large airlines into the world's largest carrier buys some breathing room. It also provides a chance to step back, reexamine how things are done, and try to get them right.

• • •

If you want to blame someone when your United flight is canceled, blame Jim DeYoung. He oversees the consolidated network operations center, a NASA-style command room in Elk Grove Township on the outskirts of Chicago. Here, 170 staffers monitor information from the entire fleet, keeping track of speeds, altitudes, departure times, and scheduled and estimated arrival times. The network operations center determines when a plane should speed up, when it should slow down, when it should be rerouted. Day to day, the ops center is the airline's brain. When I visited DeYoung in mid-January, it was snowing hard in Chicago, and he had just canceled 235 flights in and out of O'Hare.

For the past year and a half, DeYoung has had a second job, which is to merge Continental's operations center in Houston with United's in Elk Grove. "We decided that we were going to treat this, at least in my division, in a similar manner as an O'Hare snowstorm," he says. "It's a daunting task to integrate these while the airline's moving, and we can't just stop the airline."

Among the questions that preoccupy DeYoung and the ops center's integration teams is the speedup-slowdown calculation. Every airline has a different algorithm to determine when a plane will go faster to make up for a late departure, and when, to the disappointment of its passengers, it will not. Flying faster burns more fuel, and fuel costs money; United burned 3.3 billion gallons of jet fuel last year at a cost of about $25,000 a minute. But being late costs money, too: Customers who miss connections have to be rebooked and sometimes put up in hotels; flight crews have to be paid for the extra time; and ground crews sit idle while they're on the clock. The speedup-slowdown algorithm crunches all of those factors and tells the ops center when the cost of being late outweighs the cost of speed. While DeYoung won't get into specifics—he says these are trade secrets—United's and Continental's algorithms didn't always agree. One of the ops center's integration teams is working on a system that marries elements of both.

The team's biggest headache in the merger, however, has been combining flight information systems. Along with labor negotiations, information technology tends to be the thorniest part of an airline merger. Integrating IT dogged the 2005 America West–US Airways consolidation: When the new airline combined its reservation-and-ticketing programs in March 2007, the new system couldn't communicate with airport kiosks, and snarls at ticket counters led to days of missed flights, delays, and angry customers. Flight information systems—as opposed to passenger information systems—present a different, more frightening, challenge. If data were to be corrupted in the switchover from two flight information systems to one, the airline could find itself without vital information about its flights—their destination or arrival times, their flight numbers, or locations. It would be like the lights going out in the middle of a juggling act.

DeYoung takes an almost ghoulish pleasure in describing the stakes. "You're nodding your head," he tells me, "and I'm thinking I'm not imparting just how bad this could have gone." His eyes widen: "There's just so much information."

Last August the ops center's functional integration team (its "FIT team"; each department at the new company had one) decided that legacy United's flight information system, Unimatic, would be better able to handle the size of the merged airline's fleet than Continental's. At that, a second team, made up of computer technicians and ops center managers, began drawing up an exhaustive list of tests and contingency plans to ensure that the data could be combined without causing a catastrophe. DeYoung insisted that the airline's emergency operations center be fully staffed for the data cutover—a measure legacy United had last taken in April 2010, when the Icelandic volcano Eyjafjallajökull grounded European flights for weeks.

For their final test in late October, the transition team had an empty Continental 737 fly from Houston to El Paso and back just to make sure the ops center could track it. The team had the pilots pretend to have a mechanical problem and return to the gate. That showed up in the system. Then it had the pilots change the flight number and reroute the plane to Austin to see if that showed up. It did. Encouraged by the dress rehearsal, DeYoung set a date for the transition.

On November 2, just after midnight, a time when there would be relatively few flights in the air, technicians took Unimatic offline. With a couple of mouse clicks, they started flowing

Continental's data into it. For the next hour, as the technicians updated and tested the software, the Elk Grove ops center tracked United's flights manually. That would become impossible when air traffic rose to daytime levels, and DeYoung had laid plans for a mass cancellation the next morning in case the system wasn't up and running. At 1:23 a.m. Central Time, the entire ops center was on its feet, everyone's eyes on the aircraft tracking screens as Unimatic went back online. There were a few small glitches—planes that had crossed the international dateline during the outage had an extra twenty-four hours added to their arrival time—but otherwise everything worked. Elk Grove broke into applause.

Integrating the flight information system was vital for the merger to clear its biggest regulatory hurdle: getting a single operating certificate from the Federal Aviation Administration. By the time the certificate was awarded on November 30, more than 500 employees had worked on the process, paring 440 manuals—governing everything that takes place before, during, and after a flight—down to 260.

Among those protocols was the wing-walker question: Continental had required two baggage handlers to walk beneath an airplane's wings to help guide it into the gate upon arrival. Legacy United went without wing walkers, preferring to have the handlers already at the wheels of baggage tractors. As part of the single-operating-certificate process, a team of airport operations people had to resolve the discrepancy. Looking into it, they found that wing walkers don't actually make planes less likely to run into things and that having workers poised to unload bags shaved ninety seconds off the process. And yet the new United went with wing walkers—it heightened the perception of safety, the airport operations team decided, and that was enough.

The last major piece of IT is the passenger information system, which is still split between two databases. As Smisek sees it, that means he's still running two separate airlines as far as customers are concerned. "If I've got a United ticket and I go to what I believe to be a United agent and it happens to be a Continental agent, the poor Continental agent can't even see me on the computer," he says. "Or I take a Continental plane and park it at a United gate, the agent can't handle the passengers, either coming off the airplane or coming onto the airplane. We have two different websites with two different loyalty programs." Swipe your card at a United kiosk, and you have to wait while the machine pings both systems to find you.

Sometime in the first week of March—it's a sign of the company's apprehension about the move that it declines to be specific—that will change. Throughout the new United, everyone is talking about a single passenger service system—PSS, they call it—in somewhat apocalyptic tones, the way IT consultants once invoked Y2K.

As with the flight system, there are technical issues—the company isn't eager to repeat US Airways' debacle—but there's also a human factor. The new United is adopting Continental's passenger services system, a Hewlett-Packard program called Shares. According to Martin Hand, United's senior vice president for customer experience, the program is more flexible than legacy United's program, Apollo. Shares is easier, among other things, to customize, so it can ask travelers whether they'd like to purchase an upgrade or extra legroom. But Shares is also less intuitive than Apollo, and United veterans are struggling to learn it. According to Smisek, all the dry runs have gone well; just after New Year's Day, legacy United agents handled all the Continental flights at LAX.

Still, there's some trepidation among the agents. "It's a little challenging at the moment. We just get this on-the-job training a couple hours here and there," says Traci Pierce, a customer service agent at O'Hare who was with the old United for twenty years before the merger. "I'm not nervous or scared yet, but probably, the day of, I'll be like, 'Oh God, I hope I can do this.' "

• • •

Once the airline solves that puzzle, it will face an even more complicated one: the demands of the people who work for it. The merger-related issue that will dominate the next year at United is negotiations with the unions—in particular over how to reconcile the two seniority scales that determine who gets to fly where and work when and how much everyone gets paid. And the uniforms. By the end of the year, United has promised new ones. The topic comes up often in conversations with employees. There are safety issues, like the steel-toed shoes, and some workers are impatient because they're putting off replacing their old uniforms. Many, however, have strictly sartorial concerns.

Warren S. Moore is an O'Hare customer service agent who came from the Continental side—a tall, amiable man with a slow stride who spends much of his time these days training his new colleagues on Shares. He's been happy with the merger; it's given him a lot of new people to get to know. But he does worry about the new uniforms. "I like the fact that Continental has three different types of shirts and a few different types of ties that you can wear as part of your uniform, where United only has the one," he says. "Because that gives me a different appearance every day, and that's important to me. Whereas the young ladies get to wear sweaters and jackets; they have quite a bit of apparel to distinguish their uniform."

Everyone at United is hoping this is the year the labor situation gets sorted out, but hopes in the airline business can be long deferred. Six and a half years after its merger with America West, US Airways still hasn't gotten unified contracts for pilots, and it announced a tentative pact with flight attendants only late last month. Delta, whose 2008 merger with Northwest is seen by many in the industry as exemplary, is only now beginning to merge much of its workforce after the National Mediation Board late last year rejected complaints from three unions that the airline interfered in their elections.

At the new United, management and labor have their own explanations for the delay: Airline negotiators say they had to wait for the unions to have elections and sort out their internal differences. Some of the unions, however, say the carrier has repeatedly dawdled in responding to demands and offers. "The emphasis has been on paint jobs and Presidents Clubs and not on the operational side," says Jay Pierce, head of the Continental pilots' union. Still, as he puts it, "I am bullish on 2012. I think we'll tie up all the contractual issues."

Considering how much attention the labor pacts have gotten, it's a surprise to find out that there's near-universal agreement—among management, labor, and industry analysts—that the airline doesn't really need the pacts to capture most of the gains of the merger. Other than mixing and matching flight crews, there's little that the lack of joint accords prevents them from doing. "Let's take the worst example ever, which is America West and US Air," says Robert McAdoo, a former airline executive and now an analyst at Avondale Partners. "They still haven't gotten their labor seniority thing put together, and they just had their best fourth quarter ever."

For the company, however, the point of getting the contracts merged is as much a social issue as a financial one. Before the new United can feel like one entity to consumers, it has to feel like one entity to its employees. Ultimately, that's the most difficult part of a merger—combining cultures. And with United and Continental, there's work to do. Once the nation's preeminent domestic carrier, United had still not fully recovered from its 2002 bankruptcy when it merged with Continental: Layoffs and salary and spending cuts had caused a sharp rise in customer service complaints and poisoned relations between unions and management. The low point may have been in 2008, when United pilots caused hundreds of flight cancellations by calling in sick in record numbers during the peak summer travel season. Then-CEO Glenn Tilton accused the union of conducting a "sick-out" to protest layoffs, and the company won a restraining order against the union in federal court.

Continental has been a far happier place. Like every other airline, it's had to contend with September 11, high fuel prices, and the 2008 recession. It has managed, however, to retain the gung-ho culture that still-beloved former CEO Gordon Bethune brought to the airline in the mid-1990s. During Bethune's tenure and after he stepped down in 2004, Continental regularly topped industry customer satisfaction surveys and was a stalwart on Fortune's list of the country's one hundred best employers.

Traci Pierce, the United gate agent, is optimistic. Over her two decades at United, she watched customer service and worker autonomy decline in tandem. When she first started, gate agents were able to hold flights for connecting passengers at their discretion. Gradually, the airline took that away, moving to a rigid cutoff. At the new United, she says, "We have the authority to say, we're going to hold for these people because we're still going to make it on time to our destination." The airline is also getting back to having two agents per gate where legacy United, in many cases, had scaled down to one. "I want to see it get back to the way it used to be where I was proud to work for United, not embarrassed," she says.

On March 1, United will launch its new new coffee. Again, it's a Fresh Brew blend, Kova, but a medium roast rather than a light roast. And it will come in a slightly larger pillow pack—2.5 ounces rather than 2.25—to ensure a stronger brew. Pineau-Boddison considered replacing the old United brew baskets, but she thinks the new coffee will be a faster fix. Asked whether this just means coffee drinkers on legacy Continental planes will be complaining that their coffee is too strong, she points out that this time the airline tested the coffee inflight, in legacy United and Continental planes. The response has been good. Still, she is holding her breath. "I got an e-mail from someone recently that said, 'It's not rocket science,'" she says, "and I thought, no, it's a little bit of rocket science."

With Mary Jane Credeur

The New Yorker

That ExxonMobil has become the finance arm of the Republican Party and, unusually in the current environment, gives 90 percent of its political support to a single party, is the result of a singular corporate culture developed over the company's century-long history. Steve Coll takes us inside one of the world's most formidable political operations. It exists in an ideological bubble in which in-house lobbyists strategize with Republican lawmakers then issue anti-environmental-regulatory arguments in carefully crafted press releases and bland, Power Point–laden speeches. But when Democrats take power, the machine has to adapt.

Steve Coll

7. Gusher

In late February, President Obama proposed, not for the first time, that Congress end four billion dollars' worth of subsidies for oil and gas companies. "They can either stand up for the oil companies, or they can stand up for the American people," the president declared during one of his weekly radio addresses not long afterward. He seemed to be signaling that he will be running for president this year, as he did four years ago, in open opposition to the American oil industry: "These are the same oil companies that have been making record profits off the money you spend at the pump. . . . It's outrageous. It's inexcusable."

The president's policies toward the oil industry are not easy to categorize. He has backed oil and natural-gas alternatives such as solar power and wind power and also the development of electric cars. Yet he has encouraged new domestic oil production as well. "We are drilling more," he declared in Oklahoma last month, standing before a huge stack of copper pipeline segments. "Anyone who says that we're somehow suppressing domestic oil production isn't paying attention."

The president's actions—attacking oil-company profits while proposing more oil drilling—can be best understood as political responses to rising gasoline prices. The average price of a gallon has risen by more than 15 percent since January, and congressional Republicans have repeatedly attacked the president for not doing enough to keep prices down. Between 2010 and 2011, overall spending on gasoline in the United States rose by 25 percent; the percentage of household income that Americans spend on gas has tripled since the late 1990s. The president has acknowledged that there is no way that the expansion of drilling can affect gasoline prices anytime soon—it takes a long time to add to the supply, and, in any event, gas prices are tied to the global oil price, which is determined by factors such as turmoil in the Middle East and Chinese consumption rates. But, by calling for more drilling, Obama can say that he is taking action. By lambasting the oil companies, he can suggest that he is not at fault.

The contest between the Democrats and Big Oil this year will be reciprocal, and Big Oil will be led by ExxonMobil, by far the largest and most profitable oil corporation headquartered in the United States. In recent election cycles, the corporation has directed more of its political-action-committee spending to Republicans than any other of the largest American public corporations. About 90 percent of ExxonMobil's PAC giving during the 2010 election cycle went to Republicans. An even higher percentage has gone to them this year, according to databases maintained by the Center for Responsive Politics. Among the other large shareholder-owned corporations that maintain active PACs, Walmart, General Electric, Bank of America, and Ford gave about half or more of their contributions to Democrats during the 2010 cycle. Even Dow Chemical, historically wary of Democratic politicians because of environmental and regulatory issues, directed about half of its PAC contributions to Democrats in the last cycle. Chevron and ConocoPhillips, the second- and third-largest American oil companies, gave to Democrats at twice the rate of ExxonMobil.

The evolution of the country's biggest and most powerful oil company into a finance arm of the Republican Party is a story of both energy economics and style. ExxonMobil describes itself as a nonideological corporation, yet it has developed an algorithmic formula for political spending and lobbying that has reinforced its alignment with Republican candidates in ways that Democrats could hardly see as anything but antagonistic. Over the past six years, the company has tried to adapt to the revival of the Democratic Party, but it has struggled to do so, in large part because of its own rigid internal culture.

• • •

ExxonMobil was created by a hostile act of the United States government. In 1911, the Supreme Court ordered the dismemberment of the Standard Oil monopoly, founded by John D. Rockefeller. Some of its executives, judging by the skepticism they express toward Washington, seem not to have got over the initial breakup. ExxonMobil's chairman and chief executive, Rex Tillerson, who is active in the Boy Scouts of America, told the magazine *Scouting* recently that his favorite book is *Atlas Shrugged*, Ayn Rand's dystopian 1957 novel, a touchstone for libertarians. The company has a culture of secrecy—with nondisclosure agreements and internal security that can make it seem like an intelligence agency. Company executives deflect press coverage; they sometimes withhold cooperation from congressional investigators, if the letter of the law allows; and when they speak in public, they typically read out sanitized, carefully edited speeches or PowerPoint slides.

On March 23, 1989, the Exxon *Valdez*, an oil tanker, ran aground on a reef in Alaska's Prince William Sound. The captain had been drinking, and he left the bridge shortly before midnight, in violation of company policies. His crew members became confused, attempted to turn the ship, and lost track of their position altogether. At a few minutes past twelve, there was a terrible sound. "Vessel aground. We're fucked," the chief mate called out.

The *Valdez* dumped more than 200,000 barrels of oil into the water. Soon, the pleading black eyes of oil-soaked sea otters became the symbols of a broad wildlife massacre. The *Valdez* disaster became a catalyst for reforms at ExxonMobil that still influence every aspect of its operations, including its approach to politics and lobbying. Almost since its founding, the company has emphasized procedure and orthodoxy. But after the wreck Exxon's executives placed extraordinary emphasis on uniform, scientific, idiot-proof, automated systems of safety, management, finance, and business analysis.

Some of the reforms made the company resemble a cult. ExxonMobil departments worldwide organized regular safety meetings and competitions. Workers were awarded prizes for insuring that office clerks did not leave file drawers open, lest someone bump into them. Failing to turn off a coffee pot might draw a written reprimand. Cars had to be backed into parking spaces, so that in case of an emergency the driver could see clearly while speeding away. Group safety confessionals covered conduct beyond the workplace and included discussions of the correct use of a ladder while cleaning gutters at home and the danger of getting too much sun on a beach vacation. Employees stood up and shared stories of "near-misses" with personal accidents, as in a twelve-step recovery program. One manager who had been at the company for twenty-eight years recalled listening to a colleague confess that while cutting the grass in his yard he had mishandled his lawnmower, causing an object to fly out of it and strike his leg.

The atmosphere within ExxonMobil's offices is one of studied formality; the corporate aesthetic suggests a Four Seasons hotel without many guests. At industry meetings, the ExxonMobil participants can usually be identified easily: the women in charcoal pants suits and the men in dark suits and white shirts, with short and proper haircuts. "They encouraged you to get married," a former employee recalled. Such values were "not just a lot of lip service," another longtime executive said. "J. D. Rockefeller went to church every Sunday and his employees better by God go to church on Sunday or they were not good employees."

According to interviews with current and former ExxonMobil managers and lobbyists, the corporation's political spending largely reflects the free-market outlook of its senior executives; virtually all of them joined the company out of college or graduate school and stayed on for life. ExxonMobil has engineered its free-market creed into a ranking and evaluation process, the "key vote system," for directing PAC contributions. The corporation's public-affairs analysts identify important votes in Congress that affect ExxonMobil's business interests; politicians are then rated on the basis of these votes. The corporation's heavy spending on Republicans is the outcome of objective analysis, an executive involved in political strategy said. "We are a business-oriented PAC," he told me. "Now, when you apply that litmus, our PAC is rightly criticized—that we tend to give more money to Republicans than to Democrats—but it is a result of the approach we take, and not a desired result."

Exxon's annual revenues of more than four hundred billion dollars are about the same as the gross domestic product of Norway. Since the 1950s, Exxon has always been in the top five on the annual Fortune 500 list. (In 1999, Exxon merged with Mobil, reuniting two Standard Oil descendants and forming the largest non-state-owned oil corporation in the world.) During the past decade, as global oil prices have risen, ExxonMobil's profits have smashed records. It functions as a corporate state within the American state—constructing its own foreign, economic, and human-rights policies—and its executives are self-conscious about their sovereignty. Its business model—drilling holes in the ground all over the world and maintaining oil and gas wells profitably for up to forty years at a stretch—means that the political and economic time horizons for its corporate strategies extend much farther than those of almost any government. Lee Raymond, Tillerson's predecessor, once remarked, "We see governments come and go."

• • •

ExxonMobil's headquarters are in Irving, Texas, on a placid campus near the Dallas–Fort Worth airport. Its Washington office is in a pink granite-and-concrete office building on K Street. A turret, topped by an American flag, distinguishes the building from the bland, conforming architecture of the capital's lobbying corridor. Inside ExxonMobil's suite, the furniture is dark cherry. Oil paintings of American landscapes line the walls; antique Mobil oilcans and signs for Esso decorate the shelves of conference rooms.

In 2005, Dan Nelson, a six-foot-eight former marine officer who served in Vietnam, took charge of the Washington office. ExxonMobil has long relied mainly on career employees, not outside lobbyists. Last year, of the thirteen million dollars it disclosed that it spent on lobbying in Washington, only about 20 percent went to outside consultants or influence-peddling firms. "I think we did it in-house so we could get it done right," Joseph A. Gillan, who worked on environmental issues in the ExxonMobil office early in the Bush administration, said.

During the Bush years, the corporation's Washington strategists informally divided the capital's officeholders into four tiers, in descending order of sympathy for ExxonMobil's agenda. There were those who represented the oil patch—senators and congressmen from Texas, Louisiana, Oklahoma, New Mexico, and Wyoming. This group included, after 2000, President George W. Bush and Vice President Dick Cheney. The second tier consisted of free-market Republicans who didn't particularly understand the oil-and-gas industry but who generally supported ExxonMobil's positions. The third tier consisted of Democrats or liberal Republicans who regularly voted against ExxonMobil's interests but who were open to discussion and might be persuaded to vote the industry's way. From 2001 to 2009, when Hillary Clinton served in the Senate, she fell into this category. Tier four was "the enemy," as some of the military veterans in the K Street office occasionally put it. These were Democrats and environmental activists who, ExxonMobil's executives believed, wanted to disenfranchise the corporation and use its unpopularity to galvanize liberal constituents and funders—senators such as Charles Schumer, of New York, and Dick Durbin, of Illinois.

Kenneth P. Cohen, ExxonMobil's vice president for public and government affairs, has overseen the corporation's political-action committee for more than a decade. Cohen, who has worked at ExxonMobil since 1977, is a mild-looking man of modest height with a thick head of graying hair. His operating manual for political strategy is a dark binder that is kept on a shelf in his second-floor office at the Irving headquarters. The first page carries the title "Public Policy Issues." A list of about two dozen subjects follows, from climate change to government subsidies for gasoline alternatives such as ethanol. For each policy area, the notebook contains a summary of ExxonMobil's lobbying position, which the corporation's public-affairs teams support worldwide, often using common language and PowerPoint slides. The notebook also provides a guide for judging American politicians.

During both the Bush and the Obama administrations, ExxonMobil has concentrated its efforts in Washington on preventing certain tax and regulatory bills from being enacted, such as Obama's proposal, this winter, to strip away industry tax advantages. The corporation has invested mainly in a blocking strategy, focusing its PAC donations on Republicans who can try to assure that no damaging laws go through. "Whoever's in power in the House has almost dictatorial power," a Washington consultant who has worked on oil-industry issues says. "If you control what's going on in the House, you have huge influence over the final" legislation, as well as over the budgets and spending mandates that shape regulation.

In the past decade, the leading recipient of ExxonMobil PAC contributions has been Representative Joe Barton, a Republican from Texas, who has held senior positions on the House Energy and Commerce Committee, where most legislation affecting the oil industry originates. Anne Northup, a former Republican congresswoman from Kentucky who now serves on the Consumer Product Safety Commission, received the second-largest amount of campaign money. ExxonMobil's ten leading campaign-contribution recipients in that decade were all House Republicans, according to research done by the journalist Ann O'Hanlon.

ExxonMobil's political-action committee has not made contributions to recent presidential campaigns, but its top executives have made it abundantly clear that they prefer Republicans in the White House. After President Bush won reelection, the company donated a quarter of a million dollars to help fund the celebrations for his second inaugural.

• • •

"We need a conversation with Democrats," Dan Nelson told his colleagues in the ExxonMobil office on K Street as the 2006 election neared. The company's Washington analysts could see that the Democrats were gaining momentum, and the corporation's unpopularity created a risk that Congress might enact a windfall tax or costly climate regulation. Leading Democratic election strategists were well aware of ExxonMobil's investments in the Republican Party, and they openly criticized the corporation. "There is no question there is a new phase of scrutiny for Exxon," Schumer, who was then chairing the Democratic Party's Senate Campaign Committee, said.

Normally, one of the easiest ways to open a conversation with a member of Congress is to donate to his or her reelection committee. The problem was that ExxonMobil made almost all of its contribution decisions on the mathematical analysis of the key vote system. Neither Obama (when he was in the Senate, after 2004) nor other leading Democrats heading for leadership positions in Congress or considering a presidential run in 2008 scored very well. During the Bush administration's second term, not a single Democrat in Congress scored above 50 percent. In the view of the system's internal critics, it failed to distinguish adequately between truly key votes and routine party-line votes, and this skewed the numbers against Democrats. ExxonMobil lobbyists maintained strong ties with some Democrats from industrial states, like the Michigan congressman John Dingell, and with other party members from Southern or conservative Western states who voted like Republicans on energy and tax issues. But the corporation's Washington office was not well prepared for a House of Representatives ruled by Nancy Pelosi or influenced by the environmentalist Henry Waxman, both from California.

ExxonMobil's most influential Democrat was Theresa Fariello, who had joined the corporation from the Clinton administration's Department of Energy in 2001. According to Alan Jeffers, an ExxonMobil spokesman, she was valuable because of "her skills and experience gained from leading ExxonMobil's global issues management process." A committed supporter of Hillary Clinton, she helped arrange a few consultancies and retainer contracts with lobbyists in Washington who were closely connected to Democrats. One such lobbyist was David Leiter, who had worked as the chief of staff for Senator John Kerry during the nineties. (Starting in 2006, Leiter's lobbying firm, ML

Strategies, has received about $25,000 a month from ExxonMobil.) Dan Nelson also brought on Louis Finkel, who had worked for years for a Democratic congressman from Tennessee, Bart Gordon. Still, in the K Street office, Democrats were seen at times as a mysterious species requiring specialized anthropological insights.

• • •

On November 7, 2006, the Democratic Party took control of the House. A few weeks later, Ken Cohen flew to Washington. On a chilly afternoon in early December, he traveled west on Interstate 66 to Warrenton, Virginia, in the foothills of the Blue Ridge Mountains. He turned in to the secluded grounds of the Airlie Center, a retreat facility for government and business leaders. Cohen had scheduled a private, three-day Opinion Leader Dialogue between ExxonMobil executives and environmental and corporate-responsibility activists, with whom he planned to test out some of ExxonMobil's strategies for dealing with an ascendant Democratic majority.

The ExxonMobil executives had invited fourteen guests, including two senior energy-policy analysts from the Brookings Institution, a human-rights activist at Freedom House, climate-policy specialists, a business-ethics professor, and a specialist in socially responsible investing. During the cocktail hour, one of the guests, who worked for an environmental nonprofit, mentioned to Cohen the brutal hours she spent at her job. "He was shocked," she recalled. He seemed to think that "people who worked in environmental groups in Washington had cushy lives."

Another participant recalled thinking of her hosts, "These were clearly thoughtful, smart, articulate people—they just lived in a totally different world than we live in." ExxonMobil had recently awarded its retiring chief executive, Lee Raymond, a compensation package worth four hundred million dollars. At the retreat, in an effort to suggest that the package was not as rich as that number might suggest, some of the ExxonMobil executives tried to explain the differences between pension benefits, stock options, and restricted stock. "You know you can't win on that message, right?" the participant says she remembers thinking as she listened. "You're talking to people who can't even take the Acela train to New York."

The next morning, the group assembled in a conference room around tables arranged in a hollow square. The agenda included two "dialogue sessions" on climate change and a third on corporate transparency and human rights. Cohen shared some of his internal surveys about ExxonMobil's reputation. In one, 47 percent approved of its overall corporate citizenship, but only 24 percent approved of its environmental stewardship.

The corporation's notoriously bad reputation on climate issues was almost certainly a factor in its lagging environmental marks. In the 1990s and through the first Bush term, ExxonMobil funded free-market research and communications groups that attacked the emerging science documenting global warming. The Union of Concerned Scientists, Greenpeace, and other environmental and public-advocacy groups exposed the corporation's investments in climate-change skeptics and accused executives of adapting science-smearing strategies similar to those employed by the tobacco industry, which long tried to downplay the dangers of smoking. Cohen had been involved in some of the controversial funding decisions, but after Tillerson became chairman, early in 2006, ExxonMobil reviewed and eventually halted its support for the more polarizing groups. It also experimented with new language and lobbying positions about the causes of and risks posed by global warming.

During the dialogue, according to Leslie H. Lowe, one of the participants, who was at that time the director of the energy-and-environment program at the Interfaith Center on Corporate

Responsibility, "They were really dancing around the question of certainty" about the risks of global warming and the evidence that man-made activity such as oil and gas use contributed. The group talked about setting a new tax on gasoline as a way to contain greenhouse-gas emissions.

"If you tax gasoline, people will be hurt," Cohen said. He argued that, even if the tax's proceeds were rebated to needy drivers, they would be forced to take the rebates and go out and buy gas with them.

The participants on both sides were trying "to be ever so polite," Lowe recalled. That night at dinner, she found herself sitting with an ExxonMobil executive. In what she hoped was an unthreatening tone, she asked, referring to climate policy, "Look, you're a science-based organization. How can you not accept the science that is basically confirmed by most mainstream thinkers?"

In response, the executive talked about the inherent uncertainties in weather modeling and forecasting.

Lowe listened, and then asked, "What are you going to say to your grandkids when they say, 'Grandpa, why did you fuck up the planet?' "

The executive, Lowe recalls, just chuckled good-naturedly.

• • •

Of all the candidates who started running for president in 2007, none spoke more often or more pointedly about ExxonMobil than Barack Obama. He criticized the corporation's profits and contrasted its wealth with the struggles of middle-class families. His campaign sought to link Senator John McCain to the pro-oil policies of Vice President Cheney, a former chief executive of the oil-services corporation Halliburton. By the summer of 2008, 62 percent of Americans surveyed had an unfavorable view of Cheney. "President Bush, he had an energy policy," Obama declared. "He turned to Dick Cheney and he said, 'Cheney, go take care of this.' . . . McCain has taken a page out of the Cheney playbook."

Off the campaign trail, Obama's views about energy and climate policy were subtle. He studied the issues and learned the nuances of automobile mileage standards, international oil markets, and clean-coal technologies, and how different forms of energy production contribute to global warming. But his strategists knew that to many independent voters and disillusioned Republicans the idea of an ExxonMobil-Cheney complex represented all that had gone wrong in the Bush years: the Iraq war and the rise in American economic insecurity. And so Obama salted his campaign speeches with ExxonMobil references even when they were gratuitous. "It's not going to be easy to have a sensible energy policy in this country," he said at one primary debate. "ExxonMobil made eleven billion dollars last quarter. They're not going to give up those profits easily."

The highest average retail price for a gallon of gasoline in American history—just over four dollars—was recorded in July 2008. Obama seized upon ExxonMobil's unprecedented profits at the time, about ten billion dollars per quarter. When McCain announced a plan to reform corporate taxes, Obama's researchers figured out how much of the benefits would go to ExxonMobil. "At a time when we're fighting two wars, when millions of Americans can't afford their medical bills or their tuition bills, when we're paying more than four dollars a gallon for gas, the man who rails against government spending wants to spend $1.2 billion on a tax break for ExxonMobil," Obama declared. "That isn't just irresponsible. It's outrageous!"

That summer, the Bush administration and the McCain campaign studied polls showing that many Americans favored new offshore oil drilling as a strategy to reduce high gasoline prices. The White House and McCain's strategists coordinated announcements to promote more domestic exploration in ocean waters;

this inspired chants of "Drill, baby, drill!" at Republican campaign rallies. Obama promptly linked McCain's offshore-drilling plan to ExxonMobil's profits and denounced it as merely an "oil-company wish list."

More than his profit bashing, however, Obama's climate and alternative-energy policies on the campaign trail got the attention of ExxonMobil's public-affairs executives and the K Street lobbyists. Obama pledged to impose a price on carbon-based fuels such as gasoline and to make large new investments in wind power and solar power. "We must end the age of oil," Obama declared. By the fall, the ExxonMobil executive involved in political strategy recalled, the corporation had been scolded by name so many times that "we felt like a candidate." He added, "We clearly knew that we were not electable."

• • •

ExxonMobil's initial response to Obama's ascendancy was to engage with Democrats and search for common ground on climate policy. Shortly before Election Day, Ken Cohen organized a meeting in Connecticut with about a hundred of ExxonMobil's public-affairs and media-relations specialists. He invited Bennett Freeman, a former Clinton administration official who had worked as a consultant on corporate-responsibility issues. Freeman had periodically addressed ExxonMobil's political team over the years, offering the perspective of a respectful Democratic critic.

Freeman praised the ExxonMobil managers for progress that he felt they had made in protecting human rights in violence-prone areas overseas where the company drilled for oil, such as Nigeria, and also for working to combat corruption in oil-producing countries. Then he turned to climate change.

"Look," he said. "You were in the late nineteenth century. With Tillerson, you've come a long way, but you're still in the late twentieth century. This is the twenty-first century, and on climate change you need to change your tone and change your substance."

He urged ExxonMobil to support legislation designed to control greenhouse-gas emissions, which would be introduced in Congress in 2009, no matter who was elected. "You need to get behind" some legislative approach aimed at "meeting carbon-reduction goals," he said. "On alternative energy—whatever technological capability you have, whatever is most viable, you have to get on it and do it. This is a carbon-constrained future you're looking at." Cohen and other executives took notes.

• • •

Around the time of Obama's inauguration, Tillerson replaced Dan Nelson, the retired marine, with Theresa Fariello, the former Clinton administration official, as head of the Washington office. ExxonMobil bought billboard space in the Washington Nationals' new baseball stadium on the Anacostia River and in the nearby Metro and put up ads depicting ethnically diverse ExxonMobil scientists and engineers surrounded by photographs of molecules and other visual images associated with scientific research. As the deep recession of 2009 descended, ExxonMobil also began to emphasize publicly the oil industry's role in job creation.

Ken Cohen told ExxonMobil's Management Committee that the strategy was working. In ExxonMobil's own public-opinion polling, its approval ratings soared during 2009, from about 30 percent the year before to about 50 percent. The polls showed that the reputations of all the big oil companies—ExxonMobil, BP, Chevron, and Shell—were starting to recover. Some of the improved ratings surely derived from retail gasoline prices, which plunged during 2009, because of the shrinking economy, but the advertising also seemed to be having an impact.

ExxonMobil's executives concluded that Democrats in Obama's Washington "don't want B.S. They don't want greenwashing. . . . We are prepared to disagree and hopefully we can think about it in a way that's mutually respectful." But ExxonMobil was constrained by the fact that most of its Democratic Party connections were tied to the failed presidential campaign of Hillary Clinton. Its principal Democratic lobbyist, David Leiter, was married to Tamera Luzzatto, who had been Hillary Clinton's Senate chief of staff during the campaign. The Clinton universe was in general more corporate-friendly and closer to Fortune 500 executive suites than the Obama campaign. ExxonMobil's executives said that they had felt as welcome in the Clinton White House as they did later in the Bush White House. Obama's campaign had received support from Hollywood and Wall Street, and he attracted allies at large technology companies such as Google, but he did not have broad connections to the largest industrial corporations.

After Obama named Clinton his secretary of state, ExxonMobil decided to invest in the Clinton Global Initiative, an enterprise conceived by Bill Clinton that channels corporate donations to humanitarian causes in the world's poorest countries. ExxonMobil owns oil fields and produces oil in a number of countries in Africa, and it has been involved in charitable and development work there. Yet even the relationship with the Clinton organization proved awkward at times.

On the morning of September 23, 2009, Rex Tillerson arrived at the Sheraton on Seventh Avenue in New York to participate in a plenary session at the Global Initiative's annual conference. The session was entitled "Investing in Girls and Women." It took place in a ballroom decorated in purple and red, with large television screens to help the audience see celebrities like Matt Damon and Bono; delegates sat with name tags dangling around their necks. Diane Sawyer came onstage to moderate. Next to her were Edna Adan, the founder of a maternity hospital in Somaliland; Melanne Verveer, the U.S. ambassador-at-large for global women's issues (and a neighbor of Dan Nelson); and Zainab Salbi, an Iraqi-born activist who had started a network called Women for Women International. Also on the panel were Tillerson and Lloyd Blankfein, the CEO of Goldman Sachs. The atmosphere suggested the laying on of liberal hands to cleanse two sinful multinational corporations.

Tillerson, who has a rich Texas accent, talked about initiatives to support girls and women in some of the poor countries where the corporation extracted oil. ExxonMobil, he said, was interested in exploring, on behalf of impoverished women: "What are the technologies . . . that will provide them capabilities to undertake their activities in a more effective and efficient way?"

Sawyer, Adan, Verveer, and Salbi fell into an intense discussion of female genital cutting. Adan said it was essential to "educate the men and the fathers to take a decision and stand and not just pass it off, and say 'This is a woman's problem.' " Salbi leaned across Tillerson to make another point; he shifted uncomfortably. He was not asked to offer an opinion.

Sawyer then asked him, "What is the responsibility of a multinational corporation to make the world better through charitable activity? Is it a tithe of 10 percent? How much?"

"Ultimately, this is our shareholders' money we're spending," Tillerson said. "So it's not my money to tithe. It's not the corporation's. It's our shareholders'."

• • •

ExxonMobil's initial efforts to reach out to the Obama administration gave way, during 2009 and 2010, to a succession of legislative and policy battles in which the corporation and the new president found themselves on opposite sides. Tillerson sought meetings with Treasury and White House officials to explain ExxonMobil's views on energy markets, domestic drilling, climate legislation, and the recession. On one occasion, Tillerson joined a group of chief executives at dinner with Obama. In general, however, wary administration officials saw no reason to favor ExxonMobil with access. There was little basis for trust on either side. ExxonMobil lobbying sessions with Obama's team at the Treasury Department or the Department of Energy could be stiff, with Fariello and other lobbyists enunciating ExxonMobil's advocacy positions, sometimes just by reading from notes and prepared materials. During the first three years of Obama's presidency, the corporation spent more than fifty-two million dollars on lobbying in Washington, about 50 percent more per year than during the Bush presidency.

The most important challenge that ExxonMobil faced was the climate bill, known as "cap-and-trade," which Obama and congressional Democrats introduced early in 2009. The House of Representatives passed a version of the law in June and moved it to the Senate, where the most difficult negotiations were expected. The proposed law would have established a new regulatory system under which polluting corporations could buy and sell permits to emit greenhouse gases, under an overall "cap" that would seek to reduce the rate of global warming.

ExxonMobil denounced the cap-and-trade system as unwieldy and bureaucratic. It did, however, announce that it would support a straight "carbon tax," which would create incentives for reductions in coal and oil use.

The proposal was a major policy shift for the corporation, which had come to it after years of isolated, deliberative policy analysis. But there was little support for the idea among Democrats. They knew that Republicans—many of whom had signed pledges never to raise taxes—wouldn't go for it. And they had determined that cap-and-trade was the climate-change policy they would try to pass. Exxon's support for a carbon tax would have been welcome in, say, the early nineties, when Al Gore was pushing the idea. But the debate had moved on.

Tillerson's support for a carbon tax marked the first time that any ExxonMobil chief executive had advocated responding to the threat of global warming by raising the cost of oil and gas production. But, because ExxonMobil ardently opposed Obama's cap-and-trade bill from the start, it managed to leave the impression, as a senior Obama adviser put it, that it sought to "follow a track that was quite different from the other majors—being firmly fixed in the 'Fuck you, no apologies, oil-is-here-to-stay' mode."

The story of how Obama's climate bill died in the Senate during 2010 involves many politicians, industry interest groups, and corporations. Ultimately, it was probably hurt most by the high unemployment rate, which made moderate Democrats and Republicans fret more about imposing new costs on the economy.

Throughout the lobbying scrum, ExxonMobil persisted with its lonely argument for a carbon tax. Its lobbyists left behind in congressional offices PowerPoint presentations documenting a private Hart Research Associates poll, "Energy and Climate Change Policy," showing that Americans preferred Tillerson's straight carbon-tax idea to cap-and-trade, especially when the differences between the two approaches were explained. But Tillerson had tied the corporation's lobbyists to a proposal that was irrelevant to the practical discussions then taking place on climate policy.

ExxonMobil's strategy in Washington was vindicated during Obama's first term: not only did cap-and-trade die but the windfall taxes on oil companies proposed by Obama during the campaign failed, too. When Republicans took back the House in the 2010 midterm elections, ExxonMobil's lobbyists no longer had reason to fear that Obama or congressional Democrats could upend their industry with climate or tax laws.

• • •

All of ExxonMobil's business strategies remain oriented toward the very long run. With little sign that climate legislation can be revived successfully, the most important issue during the next presidential term likely will be the regulation of hydraulic fracturing, or "fracking," drilling for unconventional gas trapped in shale rocks and other formations, an issue that will shape the corporation's business prospects in the United States for a generation or more. Obama and Mitt Romney, the most likely Republican nominee, disagree over oil-and-gas regulations, and this has reinforced ExxonMobil's alignment with the Republican Party. Exxon's interest in the matter increased substantially in 2010, when it bought America's leading unconventional-gas producer, XTO Energy.

Obama and his advisers have announced support for expanded domestic production of natural gas, including from unconventional gas beds, but environmentalists have raised concerns that fracking techniques might damage water supplies or cause other environmental problems, such as inducing earthquakes, particularly if regulation is left to the states, which often don't have sufficient expertise. The EPA has been investigating the practice. ExxonMobil strongly argues that regulation is better left to states and local communities. Mitt Romney, meanwhile, has pledged to deregulate the oil-and-gas industry—and to get the EPA out of the industry's way. He has complained that Obama's approach has unnecessarily limited domestic oil and gas production. "I want regulators to see businesses and enterprises of all kinds as their friends, and to encourage them, and move them along," Romney said while campaigning in Mississippi.

In recent weeks, Tillerson has been speaking out, too, against greater regulation. "You can be afraid of a lot of things that you don't understand," Tillerson told an industry conference in Houston in March. He pledged to bring forward "facts" and to encourage a "science-based discussion." In an interview with the *Wall Street Journal*, he expressed his impatience with the layers of regulation his company faces. "There are a thousand ways you can be told 'no' in this country." In January, Tillerson and Ken Cohen gave twenty-five hundred dollars each, the maximum for individual contributions, to Romney's presidential campaign.

• • •

Tillerson and Obama appear to share at least one understanding about energy policy and the 2012 campaign: they are both aware that the partisan and media-amplified war over where to place the blame for rising gasoline prices is largely a phony one.

Global oil prices, and therefore gasoline prices, have been increasing this year for geopolitical reasons: for example, the economic sanctions imposed on Iran, accompanied by threats of war, which have caused speculators to bet on a possible oil-supply disruption. Obama may have spooked the oil markets by suggesting that, if necessary, he might wage war on Iran to prevent that country from acquiring nuclear weapons. But Israel has been the main source of such threats, and Obama has chided those engaged in "loose talk" about war. Over all, short of trying to avoid war in the Middle East, there is not much that any president of the United States can do to determine the price of gasoline. In theory, he could seek temporary tax rebates for drivers or attempt to flood world oil markets by selling off the country's strategic petroleum reserve, which is intended to protect the American economy from oil-supply disruptions caused by war or natural disaster. But these would be temporary and expensive measures that would not alter the global factors that drive oil prices or the price volatility exacerbated by waves of speculative money flowing onto electronic oil-futures exchanges. In late March, Fatih Birol, the chief economist of the International Energy Agency, an intergovernmental forum, warned that high oil prices now posed a greater risk to the world economy than even Europe's sovereign-debt crisis.

ExxonMobil and other large oil corporations do not have much influence over the changing retail price of gasoline, either. Big oil companies make the vast majority of their profits by finding oil and gas, pumping it out, and selling it wholesale. ExxonMobil can neither control prices at the pump nor make high profits there.

This year, Obama has been saying that, during his time in the White House, American oil imports have fallen to their lowest level in years. The United States reduced oil imports by a million barrels a day, or about 10 percent, in 2011. "Last year, we relied less on foreign oil than in any of the last sixteen years," Obama said in his State of the Union speech in January. This is in some respects a perverse boast: oil imports have dropped primarily because of the recession and the weak recovery. However, rising domestic production of unconventional oil in places such as North Dakota, along with energy-efficiency drives supported by the administration, are also factors, and they could lead to a further decline in imports even as the economy picks up.

The president has acknowledged that there is no cheap or quick way to change America's gasoline economy or to relieve drivers from their vulnerability to price spikes. Producing and using alternative transportation fuels on a large scale across the United States, Obama has noted, is a "problem that may not be solved in one year or one term or even one decade."

That happens to be ExxonMobil's view as well. Earlier this year, the corporation published an annual forecast of global energy demand to the year 2040. Its latest analytical models, developed with the same rigor as the key-vote system, take into account all of the electric-car dreams of the Obama administration, as well as the promotion of solar power and wind power in the United States, Europe, and elsewhere. The models forecast that worldwide gasoline consumption for use in cars may well decline in the next three decades. Truck, airplane, and ship fuel consumption, however, will increase by 60 percent, mainly in fast-growing poor countries. Decades from now, oil, gas, and coal, ExxonMobil's analysts predicted, "will continue to be the most widely used fuels."

Part IV

Bad Business

New York Times

In an extraordinary piece of investigative reporting, David Barstow uncovers how Wal-Mart paid tens of millions of dollars in bribes to officials in Mexico and then attempted to cover up its crimes. Implicating the company's vice chairman and top executive, Eduardo Castro-Wright, in the systematic bribes and its former CEO Lee Scott in the cover-up, the piece sliced ten billion dollars off Wal-Mart's market value in a single day, resulted in Castro-Wright's resignation, and sparked a federal Foreign Corrupt Practices Act probe. Marvel at the sprawling, complicated reporting here and how Barstow turns it into a compelling story about corruption at the world's biggest private employer.

David Barstow

8. Vast Mexico Bribery Case Hushed Up by Wal-Mart After Top-Level Struggle

In September 2005, a senior Wal-Mart lawyer received an alarming e-mail from a former executive at the company's largest foreign subsidiary, Wal-Mart de Mexico. In the e-mail and follow-up conversations, the former executive described how Wal-Mart de Mexico had orchestrated a campaign of bribery to win market dominance. In its rush to build stores, he said, the company had paid bribes to obtain permits in virtually every corner of the country.

The former executive gave names, dates, and bribe amounts. He knew so much, he explained, because for years he had been the lawyer in charge of obtaining construction permits for Wal-Mart de Mexico.

Wal-Mart dispatched investigators to Mexico City, and within days they unearthed evidence of widespread bribery. They found a paper trail of hundreds of suspect payments totaling more than $24 million. They also found documents showing that Wal-Mart de Mexico's top executives not only knew about the payments, but had taken steps to conceal them from Wal-Mart's headquarters in Bentonville, Ark. In a confidential report to his superiors, Wal-Mart's lead investigator, a former FBI special agent, summed up their initial findings this way: "There is reasonable suspicion to believe that Mexican and USA laws have been violated."

The lead investigator recommended that Wal-Mart expand the investigation.

Instead, an examination by the *New York Times* found, Wal-Mart's leaders shut it down.

Neither American nor Mexican law enforcement officials were notified. None of Wal-Mart de Mexico's leaders were disciplined. Indeed, its chief executive, Eduardo Castro-Wright, identified by the former executive as the driving force behind years of bribery, was promoted to vice chairman of Wal-Mart in 2008. Until this article, the allegations and Wal-Mart's investigation had never been publicly disclosed.

But the *Times* examination uncovered a prolonged struggle at the highest levels of Wal-Mart, a struggle that pitted the company's much publicized commitment to the highest moral and ethical standards against its relentless pursuit of growth.

Under fire from labor critics, worried about press leaks, and facing a sagging stock price, Wal-Mart's leaders recognized that the allegations could have devastating consequences, documents and interviews show. Wal-Mart de Mexico was the company's brightest success story, pitched to investors as a model for future growth. (Today, one in five Wal-Mart stores is in Mexico.) Confronted with evidence of corruption in Mexico, top Wal-Mart executives focused more on damage control than on rooting out wrongdoing.

In one meeting where the bribery case was discussed, H. Lee Scott Jr., then Wal-Mart's chief executive, rebuked internal investigators for being overly aggressive. Days later, records show, Wal-Mart's top lawyer arranged to ship the internal investigators' files on the case to Mexico City. Primary responsibility for the investigation was then given to the general counsel of Wal-

Mart de Mexico—a remarkable choice since the same general counsel was alleged to have authorized bribes.

The general counsel promptly exonerated his fellow Wal-Mart de Mexico executives.

When Wal-Mart's director of corporate investigations—a former top FBI official—read the general counsel's report, his appraisal was scathing. "Truly lacking," he wrote in an e-mail to his boss.

The report was nonetheless accepted by Wal-Mart's leaders as the last word on the matter.

In December, after learning of the *Times* reporting in Mexico, Wal-Mart informed the Justice Department that it had begun an internal investigation into possible violations of the Foreign Corrupt Practices Act, a federal law that makes it a crime for American corporations and their subsidiaries to bribe foreign officials. Wal-Mart said the company had learned of possible problems with how it obtained permits, but stressed that the issues were limited to "discrete" cases.

"We do not believe that these matters will have a material adverse effect on our business," the company said in a filing with the Securities and Exchange Commission.

But the *Times* examination found credible evidence that bribery played a persistent and significant role in Wal-Mart's rapid growth in Mexico, where Wal-Mart now employs 209,000 people, making it the country's largest private employer.

A Wal-Mart spokesman confirmed that the company's Mexico operations—and its handling of the 2005 case—were now a major focus of its inquiry.

"If these allegations are true, it is not a reflection of who we are or what we stand for," the spokesman, David W. Tovar, said. "We are deeply concerned by these allegations and are working aggressively to determine what happened."

In the meantime, Mr. Tovar said, Wal-Mart is taking steps in Mexico to strengthen compliance with the Foreign Corrupt

Practices Act. "We do not and will not tolerate noncompliance with FCPA anywhere or at any level of the company," he said.

The *Times* laid out this article's findings to Wal-Mart weeks ago. The company said it shared the findings with many of the executives named here, including Mr. Scott, now on Wal-Mart's board, and Mr. Castro-Wright, who is retiring in July. Both men declined to comment, Mr. Tovar said.

The *Times* obtained hundreds of internal company documents tracing the evolution of Wal-Mart's 2005 Mexico investigation. The documents show Wal-Mart's leadership immediately recognized the seriousness of the allegations. Working in secrecy, a small group of executives, including several current members of Wal-Mart's senior management, kept close tabs on the inquiry.

Michael T. Duke, Wal-Mart's current chief executive, was also kept informed. At the time, Mr. Duke had just been put in charge of Wal-Mart International, making him responsible for all foreign subsidiaries. "You'll want to read this," a top Wal-Mart lawyer wrote in an October 15, 2005, e-mail to Mr. Duke that gave a detailed description of the former executive's allegations.

The *Times* examination included more than fifteen hours of interviews with the former executive, Sergio Cicero Zapata, who resigned from Wal-Mart de Mexico in 2004 after nearly a decade in the company's real estate department.

In the interviews, Mr. Cicero recounted how he had helped organize years of payoffs. He described personally dispatching two trusted outside lawyers to deliver envelopes of cash to government officials. They targeted mayors and city council members, obscure urban planners, low-level bureaucrats who issued permits—anyone with the power to thwart Wal-Mart's growth. The bribes, he said, bought zoning approvals, reductions in environmental impact fees, and the allegiance of neighborhood leaders.

He called it working "the dark side of the moon."

The *Times* also reviewed thousands of government documents related to permit requests for stores across Mexico. The examination found many instances where permits were given within weeks or even days of Wal-Mart de Mexico's payments to the two lawyers. Again and again, the *Times* found, legal and bureaucratic obstacles melted away after payments were made.

The *Times* conducted extensive interviews with participants in Wal-Mart's investigation. They spoke on the condition that they not be identified discussing matters Wal-Mart has long shielded. These people said the investigation left little doubt Mr. Cicero's allegations were credible. ("Not even a close call," one person said.)

But, they said, the more investigators corroborated his assertions, the more resistance they encountered inside Wal-Mart. Some of it came from powerful executives implicated in the corruption, records and interviews show. Other top executives voiced concern about the possible legal and reputational harm.

In the end, people involved in the investigation said, Wal-Mart's leaders found a bloodlessly bureaucratic way to bury the matter. But in handing the investigation off to one of its main targets, they disregarded the advice of one of Wal-Mart's top lawyers, the same lawyer first contacted by Mr. Cicero.

"The wisdom of assigning any investigative role to management of the business unit being investigated escapes me," Maritza I. Munich, then general counsel of Wal-Mart International, wrote in an e-mail to top Wal-Mart executives.

The investigation, she urged, should be completed using "professional, independent investigative resources."

The Allegations Emerge

On September 21, 2005, Mr. Cicero sent an e-mail to Ms. Munich telling her he had information about "irregularities" authorized "by the highest levels" at Wal-Mart de Mexico. "I hope to meet you soon," he wrote.

Ms. Munich was familiar with the challenges of avoiding corruption in Latin America. Before joining Wal-Mart in 2003, she had spent twelve years in Mexico and elsewhere in Latin America as a lawyer for Procter & Gamble.

At Wal-Mart in 2004, she pushed the board to adopt a strict anticorruption policy that prohibited all employees from "offering anything of value to a government official on behalf of Wal-Mart." It required every employee to report the first sign of corruption, and it bound Wal-Mart's agents to the same exacting standards.

Ms. Munich reacted quickly to Mr. Cicero's e-mail. Within days, she hired Juan Francisco Torres-Landa, a prominent Harvard-trained lawyer in Mexico City, to debrief Mr. Cicero. The two men met three times in October 2005, with Ms. Munich flying in from Bentonville for the third debriefing.

During hours of questioning, Mr. Torres-Landa's notes show, Mr. Cicero described how Wal-Mart de Mexico had perfected the art of bribery then hidden it all with fraudulent accounting. Mr. Cicero implicated many of Wal-Mart de Mexico's leaders, including its board chairman, its general counsel, its chief auditor, and its top real-estate executive.

But the person most responsible, he told Mr. Torres-Landa, was the company's ambitious chief executive, Eduardo Castro-Wright, a native of Ecuador who was recruited from Honeywell in 2001 to become Wal-Mart's chief operating officer in Mexico.

Mr. Cicero said that while bribes were occasionally paid before Mr. Castro-Wright's arrival, their use soared after Mr. Castro-Wright ascended to the top job in 2002. Mr. Cicero described how Wal-Mart de Mexico's leaders had set "very aggressive growth goals," which required opening new stores "in record times." Wal-Mart de Mexico executives, he said, were under pressure to do "whatever was necessary" to obtain permits.

In an interview with the *Times*, Mr. Cicero said Mr. Castro-Wright had encouraged the payments for a specific strategic purpose. The idea, he said, was to build hundreds of new stores so fast that competitors would not have time to react. Bribes, he explained, accelerated growth. They got zoning maps changed. They made environmental objections vanish. Permits that typically took months to process magically materialized in days. "What we were buying was time," he said.

Wal-Mart de Mexico's stunning growth made Mr. Castro-Wright a rising star in Bentonville. In early 2005, when he was promoted to a senior position in the United States, Mr. Duke would cite his "outstanding results" in Mexico.

Mr. Cicero's allegations were all the more startling because he implicated himself. He spent hours explaining to Mr. Torres-Landa the mechanics of how he had helped funnel bribes through trusted fixers, known as "*gestores*."

Gestores (pronounced hes-TORE-ehs) are a fixture in Mexico's byzantine bureaucracies, and some are entirely legitimate. Ordinary citizens routinely pay *gestores* to stand in line for them at the driver's license office. Companies hire them as quasi lobbyists to get things done as painlessly as possible.

But often *gestores* play starring roles in Mexico's endless loop of public corruption scandals. They operate in the shadows, dangling payoffs to officials of every rank. It was this type of *gestor* that Wal-Mart de Mexico deployed, Mr. Cicero said.

Mr. Cicero told Mr. Torres-Landa it was his job to recruit the *gestores*. He worked closely with them, sharing strategies on whom to bribe. He also approved Wal-Mart de Mexico's payments to the *gestores*. Each payment covered the bribe and the *gestor*'s fee, typically 6 percent of the bribe.

It was all carefully monitored through a system of secret codes known only to a handful of Wal-Mart de Mexico executives.

The *gestores* submitted invoices with brief, vaguely worded descriptions of their services. But the real story, Mr. Cicero said, was told in codes written on the invoices. The codes identified the specific "irregular act" performed, Mr. Cicero explained to Mr. Torres-Landa. One code, for example, indicated a bribe to speed up a permit. Others described bribes to obtain confidential information or eliminate fines.

Each month, Mr. Castro-Wright and other top Wal-Mart de Mexico executives "received a detailed schedule of all of the payments performed," he said, according to the lawyer's notes. Wal-Mart de Mexico then "purified" the bribes in accounting records as simple legal fees.

They also took care to keep Bentonville in the dark. "Dirty clothes are washed at home," Mr. Cicero said.

Mr. Torres-Landa explored Mr. Cicero's motives for coming forward.

Mr. Cicero said he resigned in September 2004 because he felt underappreciated. He described the "pressure and stress" of participating in years of corruption, of contending with "greedy" officials who jacked up bribe demands.

As he told the *Times*, "I thought I deserved a medal at least."

The breaking point came in early 2004, when he was passed over for the job of general counsel of Wal-Mart de Mexico. This snub, Mr. Torres-Landa wrote, "generated significant anger with respect to the lack of recognition for his work." Mr. Cicero said he began to assemble a record of bribes he had helped orchestrate to "protect him in case of any complaint or investigation," Mr. Torres-Landa wrote.

"We did not detect on his part any express statement about wishing to sell the information," the lawyer added.

According to people involved in Wal-Mart's investigation, Mr. Cicero's account of criminality at the top of Wal-Mart's most important foreign subsidiary was impossible to dismiss. He had clearly been in a position to witness the events he described. Nor was this the first indication of corruption at Wal-Mart de Mexico under Mr. Castro-Wright. A confidential investigation, conducted for Wal-Mart in 2003 by Kroll Inc., a leading investigation firm, discovered that Wal-Mart de Mexico had systematically increased its sales by helping favored high-volume customers evade sales taxes.

A draft of Kroll's report, obtained by the *Times*, concluded that top Wal-Mart de Mexico executives had failed to enforce their own anticorruption policies, ignored internal audits that raised red flags, and even disregarded local press accounts asserting that Wal-Mart de Mexico was "carrying out a tax fraud." (The company ultimately paid $34.3 million in back taxes.)

Wal-Mart then asked Kroll to evaluate Wal-Mart de Mexico's internal audit and antifraud units. Kroll wrote another report that branded the units "ineffective." Many employees accused of wrongdoing were not even questioned; some "received a promotion shortly after the suspicions of fraudulent activities had surfaced."

None of these findings, though, had slowed Mr. Castro-Wright's rise.

Just days before Mr. Cicero's first debriefing, Mr. Castro-Wright was promoted again. He was put in charge of all Wal-Mart stores in the United States, one of the most prominent jobs in the company. He also joined Wal-Mart's executive committee, the company's inner sanctum of leadership.

The Initial Response

Ms. Munich sent detailed memos describing Mr. Cicero's debriefings to Wal-Mart's senior management. These executives, records show, included Thomas A. Mars, Wal-Mart's general counsel and a former director of the Arkansas State Police; Thomas D. Hyde, Wal-Mart's executive vice president and corporate secretary; Michael Fung, Wal-Mart's top internal auditor;

Craig Herkert, the chief executive for Wal-Mart's operations in Latin America; and Lee Stucky, a confidant of Lee Scott's and chief administrative officer of Wal-Mart International.

Wal-Mart typically hired outside law firms to lead internal investigations into allegations of significant wrongdoing. It did so earlier in 2005, for example, when Thomas M. Coughlin, then vice chairman of Wal-Mart, was accused of padding his expense accounts and misappropriating Wal-Mart gift cards.

At first, Wal-Mart took the same approach with Mr. Cicero's allegations. It turned to Willkie Farr & Gallagher, a law firm with extensive experience in Foreign Corrupt Practices Act cases.

The firm's "investigation work plan" called for tracing all payments to anyone who had helped Wal-Mart de Mexico obtain permits for the previous five years. The firm said it would scrutinize "any and all payments" to government officials and interview every person who might know about payoffs, including "implicated members" of Wal-Mart de Mexico's board.

In short, Willkie Farr recommended the kind of independent, spare-no-expense investigation major corporations routinely undertake when confronted with allegations of serious wrongdoing by top executives.

Wal-Mart's leaders rejected this approach. Instead, records show, they decided Wal-Mart's lawyers would supervise a far more limited "preliminary inquiry" by in-house investigators.

The inquiry, a confidential memo explained, would take two weeks, not the four months Willkie Farr proposed. Rather than examining years of permits, the team would look at a few specific stores. Interviews would be done "only when absolutely essential to establishing the bona fides" of Mr. Cicero. However, if the inquiry found a "likelihood" that laws had been violated, the company would then consider conducting a "full investigation."

The decision gave Wal-Mart's senior management direct control over the investigation. It also meant new responsibility for the company's tiny and troubled Corporate Investigations unit.

The unit was ill-equipped to take on a major corruption investigation, let alone one in Mexico. It had fewer than seventy employees, and most were assigned to chasing shoplifting rings and corrupt vendors. Just four people were specifically dedicated to investigating corporate fraud, a number Joseph R. Lewis, Wal-Mart's director of corporate investigations, described in a confidential memo as "wholly inadequate for an organization the size of Wal-Mart."

But Mr. Lewis and his boss, Kenneth H. Senser, vice president for global security, aviation, and travel, were working to strengthen the unit. Months before Mr. Cicero surfaced, they won approval to hire four "special investigators" who, according to their job descriptions, would be assigned the "most significant and complex fraud matters." Mr. Scott, the chief executive, also agreed that Corporate Investigations would handle all allegations of misconduct by senior executives.

And yet in the fall of 2005, as Wal-Mart began to grapple with Mr. Cicero's allegations, two cases called into question Corporate Investigations' independence and role.

In October, Wal-Mart's vice chairman, John B. Menzer, intervened in an internal investigation into a senior vice president who reported to him. According to internal records, Mr. Menzer told Mr. Senser he did not want Corporate Investigations to handle the case "due to concerns about the impact such an investigation would have." One of the senior vice president's subordinates, he said, "would be better suited to conduct this inquiry." Soon after, records show, the subordinate cleared his boss.

The other case involved the president of Wal-Mart Puerto Rico. A whistle-blower had accused the president and other executives of mistreating employees. Although Corporate Investigations was supposed to investigate all allegations against senior executives, the president had instead assigned an underling to look into the complaints—but to steer clear of those against him.

Ms. Munich objected. In an e-mail to Wal-Mart executives, she complained that the investigation was "at the direction of the same company officer who is the target of several of the allegations."

"We are in need of clear guidelines about how to handle these issues going forward," she warned.

The Inquiry Begins

Ronald Halter, one of Wal-Mart's new "special investigators," was assigned to lead the preliminary inquiry into Mr. Cicero's allegations. Mr. Halter had been with Wal-Mart only a few months, but he was a seasoned criminal investigator. He had spent twenty-one years in the FBI, and he spoke Spanish.

He also had help. Bob Ainley, a senior auditor, was sent to Mexico along with several Spanish-speaking auditors.

On November 12, 2005, Mr. Halter's team got to work at Wal-Mart de Mexico's corporate headquarters in Mexico City. The team gained access to a database of Wal-Mart de Mexico payments and began searching the payment description field for the word "*gestoria*."

By day's end, they had found 441 *gestor* payments. Each was a potential bribe, and yet they had searched back only to 2003.

Mr. Cicero had said his main *gestores* were Pablo Alegria Con Alonso and Jose Manuel Aguirre Juarez, obscure Mexico City lawyers with small practices who were friends of his from law school.

Sure enough, Mr. Halter's team found that nearly half the payments were to Mr. Alegria and Mr. Aguirre. These two lawyers alone, records showed, had received $8.5 million in payments. Records showed Wal-Mart de Mexico routinely paid its *gestores* tens of thousands of dollars per permit. (In interviews, both lawyers declined to discuss the corruption allegations, citing confidentiality agreements with Wal-Mart.)

"One very interesting postscript," Mr. Halter wrote in an e-mail to his boss, Mr. Lewis. "All payments to these individuals and all large sums of $ paid out of this account stopped abruptly in 2005." Mr. Halter said the "only thing we can find" that changed was that Mr. Castro-Wright left Wal-Mart de Mexico for the United States.

Mr. Halter's team confirmed detail after detail from Mr. Cicero's debriefings. Mr. Cicero had given specifics—names, dates, bribe amounts—for several new stores. In almost every case, investigators found documents confirming major elements of his account. And just as Mr. Cicero had described, investigators found mysterious codes at the bottom of invoices from the *gestores*.

"The documentation didn't look anything like what you would find in legitimate billing records from a legitimate law firm," a person involved in the investigation said in an interview.

Mr. Lewis sent a terse progress report to his boss, Mr. Senser: "FYI. It is not looking good."

Hours later, Mr. Halter's team found clear confirmation that Mr. Castro-Wright and other top executives at Wal-Mart de Mexico were well aware of the *gestor* payments.

In March 2004, the team discovered, the executives had been sent an internal Wal-Mart de Mexico audit that raised red flags about the *gestor* payments. The audit documented how Wal-Mart de Mexico's two primary *gestores* had been paid millions to make "facilitating payments" for new store permits all over Mexico.

The audit did not delve into how the money had been used to "facilitate" permits. But it showed the payments rising rapidly, roughly in line with Wal-Mart de Mexico's accelerating growth. The audit recommended notifying Bentonville of the payments.

The recommendation, records showed, was removed by Wal-Mart de Mexico's chief auditor, whom Mr. Cicero had identified as one of the executives who knew about the bribes. The author of the *gestor* audit, meanwhile, "was fired not long after the audit was completed," Mr. Halter wrote.

Mr. Ainley arranged to meet the fired auditor at his hotel. The auditor described other examples of Wal-Mart de Mexico's leaders withholding from Bentonville information about suspect payments to government officials.

The auditor singled out José Luis Rodríguezmacedo Rivera, the general counsel of Wal-Mart de Mexico.

Mr. Rodríguezmacedo, he said, took "significant information out" of an audit of Wal-Mart de Mexico's compliance with the Foreign Corrupt Practices Act. The original audit had described how Wal-Mart de Mexico gave gift cards to government officials in towns where it was building stores. "These were only given out until the construction was complete," Mr. Ainley wrote. "At which time the payments ceased."

These details were scrubbed from the final version sent to Bentonville.

Investigators were struck by Mr. Castro-Wright's response to the *gestor* audit. It had been shown to him immediately, Wal-Mart de Mexico's chief auditor had told them. Yet rather than expressing alarm, he had appeared worried about becoming too dependent on too few *gestores*. In an e-mail, Mr. Rodríguezmacedo told Mr. Cicero to write up a plan to "diversify" the *gestores* used to "facilitate" permits.

"Eduardo Castro wants us to implement this plan as soon as possible," he wrote.

Mr. Cicero did as directed. The plan, which authorized paying *gestores* up to $280,000 to "facilitate" a single permit, was approved with a minor change. Mr. Rodríguezmacedo did not want the plan to mention "*gestores*." He wanted them called "external service providers."

Mr. Halter's team made one last discovery—a finding that suggested the corruption might be far more extensive than even Mr. Cicero had described.

In going through Wal-Mart de Mexico's database of payments, investigators noticed the company was making hefty "contributions" and "donations" directly to governments all over Mexico—nearly $16 million in all since 2003.

"Some of the payments descriptions indicate that the donation is being made for the issuance of a license," Mr. Ainley wrote in one report back to Bentonville.

They also found a document in which a Wal-Mart de Mexico real-estate executive had openly acknowledged that "these payments were performed to facilitate obtaining the licenses or permits" for new stores. Sometimes, Mr. Cicero told the *Times*, donations were used hand-in-hand with *gestor* payments to get permits.

Deflecting Blame

When Mr. Halter's team was ready to interview executives at Wal-Mart de Mexico, the first target was Mr. Rodríguezmacedo.

Before joining Wal-Mart de Mexico in January 2004, Mr. Rodríguezmacedo had been a lawyer for Citigroup in Mexico. Urbane and smooth, with impeccable English, he quickly won fans in Bentonville. When Wal-Mart invited executives from its foreign subsidiaries for several days of discussion about the fine points of the Foreign Corrupt Practices Act, Mr. Rodríguezmacedo was asked to lead one of the sessions.

It was called "Overcoming Challenges in Government Dealings."

Yet Mr. Cicero had identified him as a participant in the bribery scheme. In his debriefings, Mr. Cicero described how Mr. Rodríguezmacedo had passed along specific payoff instructions from Mr. Castro-Wright. In an interview with the *Times*, Mr. Cicero said he and Mr. Rodríguezmacedo had discussed the use of *gestores* shortly after Mr. Rodríguezmacedo was hired. "He said, 'Don't worry. Keep it on its way.'"

Mr. Rodríguezmacedo declined to comment; on Friday Wal-Mart disclosed that he had been reassigned and is no longer Wal-Mart de Mexico's general counsel.

Mr. Halter's team hoped Mr. Rodríguezmacedo would shed light on how two outside lawyers came to be paid $8.5 million to "facilitate" permits. Mr. Rodríguezmacedo responded with evasive hostility, records and interviews show. When investigators asked him for the *gestores*' billing records, he said he did not have time to track them down. They got similar receptions from other executives.

Only after investigators complained to higher authorities were the executives more forthcoming. Led by Mr. Rodríguez-macedo, they responded with an attack on Mr. Cicero's credibility.

The *gestor* audit, they told investigators, had raised doubts about Mr. Cicero, since he had approved most of the payments. They began to suspect he was somehow benefiting, so they asked Kroll to investigate. It was then, they asserted, that Kroll discovered Mr. Cicero's wife was a law partner of one of the *gestores.*

Mr. Cicero was fired, they said, because he had failed to disclose that fact. They produced a copy of a "preliminary" report from Kroll and e-mails showing the undisclosed conflict had been reported to Bentonville.

Based on this behavior, Mr. Rodríguezmacedo argued, the *gestor* payments were in all likelihood a "ruse" by Mr. Cicero to defraud Wal-Mart de Mexico. Mr. Cicero and the *gestores*, he contended, probably kept every last peso of the "facilitating payments."

Simply put, bribes could not have been paid if the money was stolen first.

It was an argument that gave Wal-Mart ample justification to end the inquiry. But investigators were skeptical, records and interviews show.

Even if Mr. Rodríguezmacedo's account were true, it did not explain why Wal-Mart de Mexico's executives had authorized *gestor* payments in the first place, or why they made "donations" to get permits, or why they rewrote audits to keep Bentonville in the dark.

Investigators also wondered why a trained lawyer who had gotten away with stealing a small fortune from Wal-Mart would now deliberately draw the company's full attention by implicating himself in a series of fictional bribes. And if Wal-Mart de Mexico's executives truly believed they had been victimized, why hadn't they taken legal action against Mr. Cicero, much less reported the "theft" to Bentonville?

There was another problem: Documents contradicted most of the executives' assertions about Mr. Cicero.

Records showed Mr. Cicero had not been fired, but had resigned with severance benefits and a $25,000 bonus. In fact, in a 2004 e-mail to Ms. Munich, Mr. Rodríguezmacedo himself described how he had "negotiated" Mr. Cicero's "departure." The same e-mail said Mr. Cicero had not even been confronted about the supposed undisclosed conflict involving his wife. (Mr. Cicero flatly denied that his wife had ever worked with either *gestor.*) The e-mail also assured Ms. Munich there was no hint of financial wrongdoing. "We see it merely as an undisclosed conflict of interest," Mr. Rodríguezmacedo wrote.

There were other discrepancies.

Mr. Rodríguezmacedo said the company had stopped using *gestores* after Mr. Cicero's departure. Yet even as Mr. Cicero was being debriefed in October 2005, Wal-Mart de Mexico real-estate executives made a request to pay a *gestor* $14,000 to get a construction permit, records showed.

The persistent questions and document requests from Mr. Halter's team provoked a backlash from Wal-Mart de Mexico's executives. After a week of work, records and interviews show,

Mr. Halter and other members of the team were summoned by Eduardo F. Solórzano Morales, then chief executive of Wal-Mart de Mexico.

Mr. Solórzano angrily chastised the investigators for being too secretive and accusatory. He took offense that his executives were being told at the start of interviews that they had the right not to answer questions—as if they were being read their rights.

"It was like, 'You shut up. I'm going to talk,'" a person said of Mr. Solórzano. "It was, 'This is my home, my backyard. You are out of here.'"

Mr. Lewis viewed the complaints as an effort to sidetrack his investigators. "I find this ludicrous and a copout for the larger concerns about what has been going on," he wrote.

Nevertheless, Mr. Herkert, the chief executive for Latin America, was notified about the complaints. Three days later, he and his boss, Mr. Duke, flew to Mexico City. The trip had been long planned—Mr. Duke toured several stores—but they also reassured Wal-Mart de Mexico's unhappy executives.

They arrived just as the investigators wrapped up their work and left.

A Push to Dig Deeper

Wal-Mart's leaders had agreed to consider a full investigation if the preliminary inquiry found Mr. Cicero's allegations credible.

Back in Bentonville, Mr. Halter and Mr. Ainley wrote confidential reports to Wal-Mart's top executives in December 2005 laying out all the evidence that corroborated Mr. Cicero—the hundreds of *gestor* payments, the mystery codes, the rewritten audits, the evasive responses from Wal-Mart de Mexico executives, the donations for permits, the evidence *gestores* were still being used.

"There is reasonable suspicion," Mr. Halter concluded, "to believe that Mexican and USA laws have been violated." There was simply "no defendable explanation" for the millions of dollars in *gestor* payments, he wrote.

Mr. Halter submitted an "action plan" for a deeper investigation that would plumb the depths of corruption and culpability at Wal-Mart de Mexico.

Among other things, he urged "that all efforts be concentrated on the reconstruction of Cicero's computer history."

Mr. Cicero, meanwhile, was still offering help. In November, when Mr. Halter's team was in Mexico, Mr. Cicero offered his services as a paid consultant. In December, he wrote to Ms. Munich. He volunteered to share specifics on still more stores, and he promised to show her documents. "I hope you visit again," he wrote.

Mr. Halter proposed a thorough investigation of the two main *gestores*. He had not tried to interview them in Mexico for fear of his safety. ("I do not want to expose myself on what I consider to be an unrealistic attempt to get Mexican lawyers to admit to criminal activity," he had explained to his bosses.) Now Mr. Halter wanted Wal-Mart to hire private investigators to interview and monitor both *gestores*.

He also envisioned a round of adversarial interviews with Wal-Mart de Mexico's senior executives. He and his investigators argued that it was time to take the politically sensitive step of questioning Mr. Castro-Wright about his role in the *gestor* payments.

By January 2006, the case had reached a critical juncture. Wal-Mart's leaders were again weighing whether to approve a full investigation that would inevitably focus on a star executive already being publicly discussed as a potential successor to Mr. Scott.

Wal-Mart's ethics policy offered clear direction. "Never cover up or ignore an ethics problem," the policy states. And some who were involved in the investigation argued that it was time to take a stand against signs of rising corruption in Wal-Mart's global operations. Each year the company received hundreds of internal reports of bribery and fraud, records showed. In Asia alone, there had been ninety reports of bribery just in the previous eighteen months.

The situation was bad enough that Wal-Mart's top procurement executives were summoned to Bentonville that winter for a dressing down. Mr. Menzer, Wal-Mart's vice chairman, warned them that corruption was creating an unacceptable risk, particularly given the government's stepped-up enforcement of the Foreign Corrupt Practices Act. "Times have changed," he said.

As if to underscore the problem, Wal-Mart's leaders were confronted with new corruption allegations at Wal-Mart de Mexico even as they pondered Mr. Halter's action plan. In January, Mr. Scott, Mr. Duke, and Wal-Mart's chairman, S. Robson Walton, received an anonymous e-mail saying Wal-Mart de Mexico's top real-estate executives were receiving kickbacks from construction companies. "Please you must do something," the e-mail implored.

Yet at the same time, records and interviews show, there were misgivings about the budding reach and power of Corporate Investigations.

In less than a year, Mr. Lewis's beefed-up team had doubled its caseload, to roughly 400 cases a year. Some executives grumbled that Mr. Lewis acted as if he still worked for the FBI, where he had once supervised major investigations. They accused him and his investigators of being overbearing, disruptive, and naive about the moral ambiguities of doing business abroad. They argued that Corporate Investigations should focus more on quietly "neutralizing" problems than on turning corrupt employees over to law enforcement.

Wal-Mart's leaders had just witnessed the downside of that approach: in early 2005, the company went to the FBI with evidence that the disgraced former vice chairman, Mr. Coughlin, had embezzled hundreds of thousands of dollars. The decision produced months of embarrassing publicity, especially when Mr. Coughlin claimed he had used the money to pay off union spies for Wal-Mart.

Meanwhile, Wal-Mart de Mexico executives were continuing to complain to Bentonville about the investigation. The protests "just never let up," a person involved in the case said.

Another person familiar with the thinking of those overseeing the investigation said Wal-Mart would have reacted "like a chicken on a June bug" had the allegations concerned the United States. But some executives saw Mexico as a country where bribery was embedded in the business culture. It simply did not merit the same response.

"It's a Mexican issue; it's better to let it be a Mexican response," the person said, describing the thinking of Wal-Mart executives.

In the midst of this debate, Ms. Munich submitted her resignation, effective February 1, 2006. In one of her final acts, she drafted a memo that argued for expanding the Mexico investigation and giving equal respect to Mexican and United States laws.

"The bribery of government officials," she noted dryly, "is a criminal offense in Mexico."

She also warned against allowing implicated executives to interfere with the investigation. Wal-Mart de Mexico's executives had already tried to insert themselves in the case. Just before Christmas, records show, Mr. Solórzano, the Wal-Mart de Mexico chief executive, held a video conference with Mr. Mars, Mr. Senser, and Mr. Stucky to discuss his team's "hypothesis" that Mr. Cicero had stolen *gestor* payments.

"Given the serious nature of the allegations, and the need to preserve the integrity of the investigation," Ms. Munich wrote, "it would seem more prudent to develop a follow-up plan of action, independent of Walmex management participation."

The Chief Weighs In

Mr. Scott called a meeting for February 3, 2006, to discuss revamping Wal-Mart's internal investigations and to resolve the question of what to do about Mr. Cicero's allegations.

In the days before the meeting, records show, Mr. Senser ordered his staff to compile data showing the effectiveness of Corporate Investigations. He assembled statistics showing that the unit had referred relatively few cases to law enforcement agencies. He circulated copies of an e-mail in which Mr. Rodríguezmacedo said he had been treated "very respectfully and cordially" by Mr. Senser's investigators.

Along with Mr. Scott, the meeting included Mr. Hyde, Mr. Mars, and Mr. Stucky, records show. The meeting brought the grievances against Corporate Investigations into the open. Mr. Senser described the complaints in Mr. Lewis's performance evaluation, completed shortly after the meeting. Wal-Mart's leaders viewed Mr. Lewis's investigators as "overly aggressive," he wrote. They did not care for Mr. Lewis's "law enforcement approach" and the fact that Mr. Scott convened a meeting to express these concerns only underscored "the importance placed on these topics by senior executives."

By meeting's end, Mr. Senser had been ordered to work with Mr. Mars and others to develop a "modified protocol" for internal investigations.

Mr. Scott said he wanted it done fast, and within twenty-four hours Mr. Senser produced a new protocol, a highly bureaucratic process that gave senior Wal-Mart executives—including executives at the business units being investigated—more control over internal investigations. The policy included multiple "case reviews." It also required senior executives to conduct a "cost-benefit analysis" before signing off on a full-blown investigation.

Under the new protocol, Mr. Lewis and his team would only investigate "significant" allegations, like those involving potential crimes or top executives. Lesser allegations would be left to the affected business unit to investigate.

"This captures it, I think," Mr. Hyde wrote when Mr. Senser sent him the new protocol.

Four days after Mr. Scott's meeting, with the new protocol drafted, Wal-Mart's leaders began to transfer control of the bribery investigation to one of its earliest targets, Mr. Rodríguezmacedo.

Mr. Mars first sent Mr. Halter's report to Mr. Rodríguezmacedo. Then he arranged to ship Mr. Halter's investigative files to him as well. In an e-mail, he sought Mr. Senser's advice on how to send the files in "a secure manner."

Mr. Senser recommended FedEx. "There is very good control on those shipments, and while governments do compromise them if they are looking for something in particular, there is no reason for them to think that this shipment is out of the ordinary," he wrote.

"The key," he added, "is being careful about how you communicate the details of the shipment to José Luis." He advised Mr. Mars to use encrypted e-mail.

Wal-Mart's spokesman, Mr. Tovar, said the company could not discuss Mr. Scott's meeting or the decision to transfer the case to Mr. Rodríguezmacedo. "At this point," he said, "we don't have a full explanation of what happened. Unfortunately, we realize that until the investigation is concluded, there will be some unanswered questions."

Wal-Mart's leaders, however, had clear guidance about the propriety of letting a target of an investigation run it.

On the same day Mr. Senser was putting the finishing touches on the new investigations protocol, Wal-Mart's ethics office sent him a booklet of "best practices" for internal investigations. It had been put together by lawyers and executives who supervised investigations at Fortune 500 companies.

"Investigations should be conducted by individuals who do not have any vested interest in the potential outcomes of the investigation," it said.

The transfer appeared to violate even the "modified protocol" for investigations. Under the new protocol, Corporate Investigations was still supposed to handle "significant" allegations—including those involving potential crimes and senior executives. When Mr. Senser asked his deputies to list all investigations that met this threshold, they came up with thirty-one cases.

At the top of the list: Mexico.

After the meeting with Mr. Scott, Mr. Senser had told Mr. Lewis in his performance evaluation that his "highest priority" should be to eliminate "the perceptions that investigators are being too aggressive." He wanted Mr. Lewis to "earn the trust of" his "clients"—Wal-Mart's leaders. He wanted him to head off "adversarial interactions."

Mr. Senser now applied the same advice to himself.

Even as Mr. Halter's files were being shipped to Mr. Rodríguezmacedo, Mr. Stucky made plans to fly to Mexico with other executives involved in the bribery investigation. The trip, he wrote, was "for the purpose of re-establishing activities related to the certain compliance matters we've been discussing." Mr. Stucky invited Mr. Senser along.

"It is better if we do not make this trip to Mexico City," Mr. Senser replied. His investigators, he wrote, would simply be "a resource" if needed.

Ten days after Mr. Stucky flew to Mexico, an article about Wal-Mart appeared in the *Times*. It focused on "the increasingly important role of one man: Eduardo Castro-Wright." The article said Mr. Castro-Wright was a "popular figure" inside Wal-Mart because he made Wal-Mart de Mexico one of the company's "most profitable units."

Wall Street analysts, it said, viewed him as a "very strong candidate" to succeed Mr. Scott.

Case Closed

For those who had investigated Mr. Cicero's allegations, the preliminary inquiry had been just that—preliminary. In memos and meetings, they had argued that their findings clearly justified a full-blown investigation. Mr. Castro-Wright's precise role had yet to be determined. Mr. Halter had never been permitted to question him, nor had Mr. Castro-Wright's computer files been examined, records and interviews show.

At the very least, a complete investigation would take months.

Mr. Rodríguezmacedo, the man now in charge, saw it differently. He wrapped up the case in a few weeks, with little additional investigation.

"There is no evidence or clear indication," his report concluded, "of bribes paid to Mexican government authorities with the purpose of wrongfully securing any licenses or permits."

That conclusion, his report explained, was largely based on the denials of his fellow executives. Not one "mentioned having ordered or given bribes to government authorities," he wrote.

His report, six pages long, neglected to note that he had been implicated in the same criminal conduct.

That was not the only omission. While his report conceded that Wal-Mart de Mexico executives had authorized years of payments to *gestores*, it never explained what these executives expected the *gestores* to do with the millions of dollars they received to "facilitate" permits.

He was also silent on the evidence that Wal-Mart de Mexico had doled out donations to get permits. Nor did he address evidence that he and other executives had suppressed or rewritten audits that would have alerted Bentonville to improper payments.

Instead, the bulk of Mr. Rodríguezmacedo's report attacked the integrity of his accuser.

Mr. Cicero, he wrote, made Wal-Mart de Mexico's executives think they would "run the risk of having permits denied if the *gestores* were not used." But this was merely a ruse: In all likelihood, he argued, Wal-Mart de Mexico paid millions for "services never rendered." The *gestores* simply pocketed the money, he suggested, and Mr. Cicero "may have benefited," too.

But he offered no direct proof. Indeed, as his report made clear, it was less an allegation than a hypothesis built on two highly circumstantial pillars.

First, he said he had consulted with Jesús Zamora-Pierce, a "prestigious independent counsel" who had written books on fraud. Mr. Zamora, he wrote, "feels the conduct displayed by Sergio Cicero is typical of someone engaging in fraud. It is not uncommon in Mexico for lawyers to recommend the use of *gestores* to facilitate permit obtainment, when in reality it is nothing more than a means of engaging in fraud."

Second, he said he had done a statistical analysis that found Wal-Mart de Mexico won permits even faster after Mr. Cicero left. The validity of his analysis was impossible to assess; he did not include his statistics in the report.

In building a case against Mr. Cicero, Mr. Rodríguezmacedo's report included several false statements. He described Mr. Cicero's "dismissal" when records showed he had resigned. He also wrote that Kroll's investigation of Mr. Cicero concluded that he "had a considerable increase in his standard of living during the time in which payments were made to the *gestores*." Kroll's report made no such assertion, people involved in the investigation said.

His report promised a series of corrective steps aimed at putting the entire matter to rest. Wal-Mart de Mexico would no longer use *gestores*. There would be a renewed commitment to Wal-Mart's anticorruption policy. He did not recommend any disciplinary action against his colleagues.

There was, however, one person he hoped to punish. Wal-Mart de Mexico, he wrote, would scour Mr. Cicero's records and determine "if any legal action may be taken against him."

Mr. Rodríguezmacedo submitted a draft of his report to Bentonville. In an e-mail, Mr. Lewis told his superiors that he found the report "lacking." It was not clear what evidence supported the report's conclusions, he wrote. "More importantly," he wrote, "if one agrees that Sergio defrauded the company and I am one of them, the question becomes, how was he able to get away with almost $10 million and why was nothing done after it was discovered?"

Mr. Rodríguezmacedo responded by adding a paragraph to the end of his report: They had decided not to pursue "criminal actions" against Mr. Cicero because "we did not have strong case."

"At the risk of being cynical," Mr. Lewis wrote in response, "that report is exactly the same as the previous which I indicated was truly lacking."

But it was enough for Wal-Mart. Mr. Rodríguezmacedo was told by executives in Bentonville on May 10, 2006, to put his report "into final form, thus concluding this investigation."

No one told Mr. Cicero. All he knew was that after months of e-mails, phone calls, and meetings, Wal-Mart's interest seemed to suddenly fade. His phone calls and e-mails went unanswered.

"I thought nobody cares about this," he said. "So I left it behind."

Alejandra Xanic von Bertrab and James C. McKinley Jr. contributed reporting from Mexico City.

Reuters

In some of the finest corporate reporting of the year, Reuters investigates Chesapeake Energy and its CEO, Aubrey McClendon, the riverboat gambler behind the recent rise of natural gas in the United States. This piece exposes Chesapeake's plotting to collude with its top rival to drive down prices for drilling rights in Michigan. Primary documents that one antitrust official calls a "smoking H-bomb" show McClendon offering to "smoke a peace pipe" to keep prices down and divvying up counties to avoid a bidding war. Days after this story appeared, the Justice Department and state authorities announced investigations.

Brian Grow,
Joshua Schneyer,
and Janet Roberts

9. Chesapeake and Rival Plotted to Suppress Land Prices

In e-mails between Chesapeake and Encana Corp, Canada's largest natural-gas company, the rivals repeatedly discussed how to avoid bidding against each other in a public land auction in Michigan two years ago and in at least nine prospective deals with private landowners here.

In one e-mail, dated June 16, 2010, CEO Aubry McClendon told a Chesapeake deputy that it was time "to smoke a peace pipe" with Encana "if we are bidding each other up." The Chesapeake vice president responded that he had contacted Encana "to discuss how they want to handle the entities we are both working to avoid us bidding each other up in the interim." McClendon replied: "Thanks."

That exchange—and at least a dozen other e-mails reviewed by Reuters—could provide evidence that the two companies violated federal and state laws by seeking to keep land prices down, antitrust lawyers said.

"The famous phrase is a 'smoking gun.' That's a smoking H-bomb," said Harry First, a former antitrust lawyer for the Department of Justice. "When the talk is explicitly about getting together to avoid bidding each other up, it's a red flag for collusion, bid-rigging, market allocation."

The revelation of the discussions between Encana and Chesapeake, the second-largest natural-gas producer in the United States, comes at a time when McClendon already is under fire.

The company's board stripped him of his chairmanship after Reuters reported that he took out more than $1.3 billion in personal loans from a firm that also finances Chesapeake. The IRS and the Securities and Exchange Commission have launched inquiries.

Stiff Penalties

The talks to suppress land prices could prove even more damaging—for McClendon, Chesapeake, Encana, and other top executives with both companies.

Private industry cartels are forbidden in the United States, where price-fixing between competitors is illegal under the Sherman Antitrust Act. Violations carry stiff penalties. Companies can be fined up to $100 million and individuals up to $1 million for each offense. Jail sentences—which are rare—can be as long as ten years, and collusion among competitors can lead to prosecution or fines for mail and wire fraud. Victims of bid-rigging can also seek triple the amount of damages.

Chesapeake and Encana say they discussed forming a joint venture in Michigan but opted against it. Typically, such partnerships can defray the steep costs of shale development, which include amassing thousands of acres of land and drilling dozens of wells.

In response to detailed questions from Reuters, Encana said it was undertaking an internal investigation, saying it "is committed to conducting its business in an ethical and legal way." It acknowledged that its U.S. branch "discussed, but did not go forward with, a joint venture with Chesapeake Energy" but added that it "cannot specifically address the questions posed at this time."

Chesapeake spokesman Jim Gipson also said there had been discussions with Encana about "forming an 'area of mutual interest' joint venture" in Michigan. But he said "no such agreement was reached between the parties. . . . Nor did Encana and Chesapeake make any joint bids."

Antitrust lawyers said the fact that the companies discussed a formal joint venture wouldn't dispel legal concerns.

"Nothing in the documents suggests any benefit to the joint venture other than making the price fall," said Darren Bush, a former attorney in the Antitrust Division of the Department of Justice and a law professor at the University of Houston. "If it has no other purpose, then it's just a shell and doesn't change the liability for illegal conduct."

Land Rush

The discussions about how to team up in Michigan apparently began in early June 2010, when Chesapeake and Encana were competing fiercely to acquire land in the Collingwood Shale formation in Northern Michigan.

The shale formation is a layer of oil- and gas-rich rock lying thousands of feet below the rolling hills, cherry groves, and family farms of northern Michigan. It extends from beneath the dunes on Lake Michigan and Lake Huron's shorelines to the center of the mitten-shaped state.

In 2010, the region was at the forefront of America's shale boom—a buying frenzy made possible by the innovative drilling technology known as hydraulic fracturing, or "fracking." The technique has fueled the largest U.S. land grab since the Gold Rush of the 1850s—and Chesapeake and Encana are among the biggest players nationwide.

Chesapeake's McClendon has been the single most acquisitive buyer. In the last ten years, his company has amassed more than fifteen million acres of land in the United States—an area about the size of West Virginia. Encana has leased 2.5 million acres. In Michigan alone, the two companies combined hold more than 975,000 acres of land—an area about the size of Rhode Island.

At a May 2010 auction of public land run by Michigan's Department of Natural Resources, Chesapeake and Encana had been the dominant buyers. Through intermediary bidders, the two giants spent almost $165 million combined—93 percent of the record $178 million taken in by the state—to acquire more than 84,000 acres of land. Chesapeake alone spent $138 million, according to a Reuters review of state data. Firms bid an average of $1,413 per acre for the right to extract oil and gas from the state-owned land.

Meanwhile, private landowners—aware that major energy companies were paying top dollar to lease property—sought competing bids from rival drillers. Some landowners were being offered more than $3,000 per acre in June 2010, documents reviewed by Reuters show.

Top executives from Chesapeake and Encana were growing weary of the rapidly escalating prices. In early June, Chesapeake vice president Doug Jacobson reached out to Encana to discuss what the e-mails characterized as an "area of mutual interest" in Michigan—regions where the two companies would have the option to share mineral leases equally after they were purchased.

A Common Practice

Area-of-mutual interest agreements are common in the oil industry. They allow drillers to share in the risks and rewards of developing an energy play. But they aren't meant to allow the discussion of strategies to divide territory or avoid competitive bidding, say oil and gas industry attorneys.

In subsequent months, the e-mails show, top officials discussed ways to prevent land prices from escalating. The solution they proposed: dividing up Michigan counties and private landowners between them.

From June 6 to June 15, 2010, the two companies swapped proposals. In many of the e-mails, officials refer to the companies by their three-letter stock abbreviations: CHK for Chesapeake and ECA for Encana.

On June 6, Chesapeake vice president Jacobson sent an e-mail with the subject line "CHK/ECA—MI" to Encana vice president John Schopp. It was copied to McClendon and to Jeff Wojahn, Encana's U.S. president. "Our proposal is pretty simple, but hopefully should be effective for us both," Jacobson wrote.

He outlined a strategy that included swapping land already leased in Michigan and dividing up counties and private landowners where new leases might be secured.

Both Chesapeake and Encana "will have the option of acquiring 50% of the acreage acquired by the other" within the area of mutual interest "on the same terms as the initial acquiring party," Jacobson wrote.

Jacobson added that "the parties will work together to decide the best way to make a deal with Merit," a Dallas-based energy company that owned more than 200,000 acres of land in Michigan. Chesapeake, he wrote, "has met with them twice to date. They will be tough and expensive."

Merit declined to comment.

"Hail Mary Pass"

On June 15, Jacobson reiterated Chesapeake's desire to strike a deal with Encana. In an e-mail to Schopp, the Encana vice president, Jacobson suggested they discuss plans to split up where, and from whom, each company would lease land in Michigan. The reason, the e-mail shows, was to ensure each company could acquire more land without bidding against the other.

"Also, when you are back in the saddle, I'd like to visit with you about the implications of the impact of our competition on acreage prices and whether or not the sooner we do this the better shot we have of keeping acreage prices from continuing to push up," Jacobson wrote to Schopp.

Two minutes later, Jacobson forwarded that e-mail to Chesapeake CEO McClendon and three other Chesapeake executives, documents show. The next day, McClendon sent his "peace pipe" e-mail to Jacobson—an e-mail that former Justice Department attorney First said could be "government exhibit No. 1" in an antitrust case.

"It's what the prosecutor puts up in a PowerPoint presentation for the grand jury," said First, now a professor at New York University. "It would take a Hail Mary pass to defend that."

To be sure, the documents reviewed by Reuters don't provide a complete picture of what went on between the two companies. One unanswered question is whether Chesapeake and Encana consummated any collusive agreements—a condition that might be necessary to convince a jury that the companies broke the law.

One internal Chesapeake document indicates McClendon may have backed away from what a company memo characterized as a "joint-bid strategy" relating to a Michigan state land auction in October. The e-mails also don't make clear what became of efforts between the companies to decide which of them would handle the bidding for land held by private owners.

But in the weeks after the discussions began, Chesapeake and Encana sharply cut the prices they were offering for land in Michigan, and average lease prices plunged in areas that had previously been hotly contested. At the time, the two companies were by far the largest lease buyers in the state.

"Coincidence?"

Chesapeake did some of its buying through contractor David McGuire, who secured Michigan leases on the company's behalf. In a July 16 e-mail to Chesapeake executives, McGuire reported that both companies had cut the maximum per-acre amount they were bidding by 50 percent. In the e-mail, McGuire asked the executives whether this was a "coincidence?" In response, Chesapeake's Jacobson didn't address the question directly. Instead, he told McGuire to pare back further lease buying.

Other documents show that in July Chesapeake put on hold more than a dozen deals it had been negotiating with large private land owners. The documents show that both Encana and Chesapeake simultaneously stopped negotiating with one land owner, Walter Zaremba, and both withdrew offers for his land.

"We suspected collusion when Encana called and said the deal was off, and Chesapeake lost interest at the same time," Zaremba said after Reuters showed him several of the e-mails, none of which he had previously seen. He was already in litigation with Encana, claiming that it reneged on a deal for about 20,000 acres he owns. "Sure as hell something happened because things don't just break down like that overnight."

Oil and gas industry lawyers said the cooperation plan outlined in the e-mails under the auspices of an "area of mutual interest" isn't how joint ventures are meant to be handled.

"These agreements are not a way in which companies divide up territory together or avoid sellers playing them off each other," said Bruce Kramer, an expert on oil and gas law.

Chesapeake and Encana have never publicly disclosed any joint venture, and oil-and-gas-industry analysts consider them fierce rivals. Each holds major land positions in several of the same shale-rich states. Their competitive streaks make the behind-the-scenes communications all the more striking.

At least a dozen e-mails between top-level executives of the two firms address themes that competitors are warned not to discuss with each other, according to antitrust guidelines set by the American Petroleum Institute, the leading U.S. oil-industry trade group.

To avoid potentially illegal behavior when competitors meet at an industry conference, for instance, the trade group warns against discussing any number of topics, most of which Chesapeake and Encana covered in the e-mails reviewed by Reuters.

Among the subjects the institute says competitors should avoid: sharing confidential or proprietary information; discussing agreements, either explicit or implicit, on pricing; company purchasing, merger or divestment plans; market allocation and development plans; inventories or costs. "Any discussion regarding potential energy or economic scenarios that may arise must be limited to generalities," the guidelines say.

"Bid Rotation"

Attempts at price-fixing by rival corporations are typically difficult to prove in court. That's because competitors rarely commit collusive agreements to writing.

Top Chesapeake and Encana executives, however, spelled out their ideas in great detail, the e-mails show, from the beginning of June 2010 through that October.

"This looks like a great start," Encana's Schopp replied June 7 to Chesapeake's Jacobson's proposal to divide bidding responsibilities. "A few suggestions that would maximize our effectiveness."

Among his recommendations was that the companies split owners into two groups; Chesapeake would handle negotiations with one and Encana with the other. That way, the two wouldn't bid against one another. Also copied on the June 7 e-mail from Schopp: Encana CEO Randy Eresman.

About one week later, June 15, at 6:51 a.m., McClendon himself weighed in. He copied Encana's U.S. president Wojahn and Eresman. Referring to one company that owned mineral leases on more than 30,000 Michigan acres, McClendon wrote that it "looks like Northstar wants us to bid against each other next week, let's discuss who should handle that one—thanks."

NorthStar is an energy company based in Traverse City, Mich. The company declined to comment.

Another note about NorthStar appeared in a June 16 Chesapeake summary of Michigan land deals. It said that McClendon "does not want to complete [*sic*] with Encana on this deal if CHK is interested."

"We call that bid rotation," a violation of antitrust law in which participants in a transaction select who will be the winner in advance of bidding, said Herbert Hovenkamp, a law professor and antitrust expert at the University of Iowa.

Later on June 16, Jacobson asked Schopp how soon he thought Encana could craft a formal deal to work together. Chesapeake, he added, was largely amenable to the "county split."

That's when Jacobson urged quick action to keep "acreage prices from continuing to push up."

Dividing Michigan

Perhaps the most sophisticated plan the two companies forged was developing a bidding strategy for the auction of state land in Michigan on October 26, 2010.

Bidding at the state's May 2010 auction had been vigorous and contested. That helped the state raise a record $178 million from the sale of more than 118,000 acres, according to a review of state auction data by Reuters. At that auction, 83 percent of the more than 1,200 winning bids had competitive offers.

Five months later, at the October auction, the bidding and the results proved remarkably different and far less lucrative. It raised just $9.7 million from the leasing of about 274,000 acres—more than twice the acreage sold in May but almost $170 million less in revenue.

The average winning bid in October was $46, the Reuters analysis shows. In May, it had been $1,413. Most of the winning bids in October were for the minimum price set by the state: $13 per acre.

One possible reason for the dreary auction results in October is that prices for natural gas had fallen significantly, about 20 percent.

Another possible reason, according to documents reviewed by Reuters: Two of the largest buyers in October—Chesapeake and Encana—had been discussing how to avoid bidding against the other.

On October 14—a dozen days before the state auction—Kurt S. Froistad, a land executive with Encana, e-mailed Gary Dunlap, Chesapeake's vice president of land. The subject line: "Michigan State Lease Sale."

Froistad told Dunlap he was "working on a draft agreement for the sale, but wanted to identify Encana's suggested contract lands and bidding responsibilities so you can take a look."

The suggested split shows Encana as the "bidder" at the auction for state land in Charlevoix, Cheboygan, Kalkaska, and Crawford Counties. Chesapeake would be the "bidder" in Emmet, Presque Isle, Roscommon, Missaukee, and Grand Traverse counties, according to the e-mail.

Chiefs in the Loop

Over the next three days, Chesapeake executives designed maps outlining the proposed split of bidding at the state auction, according to e-mails.

McClendon and Wojahn, president of Encana's U.S. unit, were aware of the proposed auction bidding strategy. "Understand our teams are working on a cooperative approach to state leasing, that's good I think. Anything else out there encouraging to talk about?" McClendon wrote in an e-mail to Wojahn on October 17.

"We haven't arrived at a strategy yet but as we approach the sale we will be happy to have a fulsome technical discussion," Wojahn replied on October 18.

A day later, Chesapeake drew up a particularly detailed map. It projected how the county split could allow each firm to end up with almost exactly 134,000 "oil acres" after the auction. Oil-rich shale is much more valuable, since crude trades at a massive premium to natural gas.

On October 20, Wojahn sent McClendon an update: "From what I understand (Encana's) John Schopp has been leading the charge on working with your team on arranging a bidding strategy. I have a meeting with John planned on Friday and a review with Randy Monday." Randy is Randy Eresman, Encana's CEO.

McClendon appears to have decided to back away from the auction plan proposed by Froistad. A summary of Chesapeake's new ventures, sent in an e-mail on October 23, notes that, as a result of a meeting with McClendon, staff members should inform Encana that Chesapeake had lost interest in the "joint-bid strategy."

In the end, Chesapeake and Encana did not acquire state land in the exact counties outlined in the proposals and in the maps Reuters reviewed. But an analysis of the auction results shows that neither company bought any land in the same county as the other. Earlier, at the May auction, bidders for Chesapeake and Encana had competed fiercely for tracts in several of the same counties.

Burden of Proof

Because the state does not keep a bid-by-bid record for parcels in which there was competition, it's unclear whether Chesapeake and Encana ever bid against each other in October.

But records do show that other companies bid against Chesapeake in just 10 percent of the 320 leases it purchased at the fall auction. That's in stark contrast to the Michigan state auction in May. Then, Chesapeake faced competing bids for every one of the more than 850 leases it secured.

Encana fared similarly in the fall auction. In October, only 27 percent of the 1,675 leases it purchased were contested. In the May auction, companies bid against Encana in each of its 70 successful offers.

Antitrust experts said that even though the plans discussed in the e-mails didn't play out exactly as envisioned, they nonetheless may have had the desired effect.

"In a situation where there is some level of collusion going on, it's hard to get agreement on everything. It's not easy to form cartels," said law professor First. "The fact that a cartel isn't perfectly effective doesn't mean it isn't harmful."

Chicago Tribune

When it comes to scare tactics and mendacity from Astroturf (or faux grassroots) organizations, a group that calls itself the Citizens for Fire Safety Institute exceeds most, and the *Chicago Tribune* deserves a huge amount of credit for uncovering the truth—and the lies. Americans are exposing themselves to enormous quantities of toxic chemicals every day thanks to the fire retardants pumped into couches and mattresses; the lie is that those fire retardants save lives while the truth is that they really just provide monster profits for three big companies, which go to great lengths to persuade lawmakers to keep the money flowing.

Patricia Callahan and
Sam Roe

10. Fear Fans Flames for Chemical Makers

Dr. David Heimbach knows how to tell a story.

Before California lawmakers last year, the noted burn surgeon drew gasps from the crowd as he described a seven-week-old baby girl who was burned in a fire started by a candle while she lay on a pillow that lacked flame-retardant chemicals.

"Now this is a tiny little person, no bigger than my Italian greyhound at home," said Heimbach, gesturing to approximate the baby's size. "Half of her body was severely burned. She ultimately died after about three weeks of pain and misery in the hospital."

Heimbach's passionate testimony about the baby's death made the long-term health concerns about flame retardants voiced by doctors, environmentalists, and even firefighters sound abstract and petty.

But there was a problem with his testimony: It wasn't true.

Records show there was no dangerous pillow or candle fire. The baby he described didn't exist.

Neither did the nine-week-old patient who Heimbach told California legislators died in a candle fire in 2009. Nor did the six-week-old patient who he told Alaska lawmakers was fatally burned in her crib in 2010.

Heimbach is not just a prominent burn doctor. He is a star witness for the manufacturers of flame retardants.

His testimony, the *Tribune* found, is part of a decades-long campaign of deception that has loaded the furniture and electronics in American homes with pounds of toxic chemicals linked to cancer, neurological deficits, developmental problems, and impaired fertility.

The tactics started with Big Tobacco, which wanted to shift focus away from cigarettes as the cause of fire deaths, and continued as chemical companies worked to preserve a lucrative market for their products, according to a *Tribune* review of thousands of government, scientific, and internal industry documents.

These powerful industries distorted science in ways that overstated the benefits of the chemicals, created a phony consumer watchdog group that stoked the public's fear of fire, and helped organize and steer an association of top fire officials that spent more than a decade campaigning for their cause.

Today, scientists know that some flame retardants escape from household products and settle in dust. That's why toddlers, who play on the floor and put things in their mouths, generally have far higher levels of these chemicals in their bodies than their parents.

Blood levels of certain widely used flame retardants doubled in adults every two to five years between 1970 and 2004. More recent studies show levels haven't declined in the United States even though some of the chemicals have been pulled from the market. A typical American baby is born with the highest recorded concentrations of flame retardants among infants in the world.

People might be willing to accept the health risks if the flame retardants packed into sofas and easy chairs worked as promised. But they don't.

The chemical industry often points to a government study from the 1980s as proof that flame retardants save lives. But the study's lead author, Vytenis Babrauskas, said in an interview that the industry has grossly distorted his findings and that the amount of retardants used in household furniture doesn't work.

"The fire just laughs at it," he said.

Other government scientists subsequently found that the flame retardants in household furniture don't protect consumers from fire in any meaningful way.

The U.S. Environmental Protection Agency, meanwhile, has allowed generation after generation of flame retardants onto the market and into American homes without thoroughly assessing the health risks. The EPA even promoted one chemical mixture as a safe, eco-friendly flame retardant despite grave concerns from its own scientists about potential hazards to humans and wildlife.

Since the 1970s manufacturers have repeatedly withdrawn flame retardants amid health concerns. Some have been banned by a United Nations treaty that seeks to eliminate the worst chemicals in the world.

Chemtura Corp. and Albemarle Corp., the two biggest U.S. manufacturers of flame retardants, say their products are safe and effective, arguing that they have been extensively evaluated by government agencies here and in Europe.

"Flame retardants provide an essential tool to enable manufacturers of products to meet the fire safety codes and standards necessary to protect life and property in a modern world," John Gustavsen, a Chemtura spokesman, said in a written statement.

His company, Gustavsen said, strongly disagrees with the main findings of the *Tribune*'s investigation.

Heimbach, the burn doctor, has regularly supported the industry's position that flame retardants save lives. But he now acknowledges the stories he told lawmakers about victims were not always factual.

He told the *Tribune* his testimony in California was "an anecdotal story rather than anything which I would say was absolutely true under oath, because I wasn't under oath."

Heimbach, a retired Seattle doctor and former president of the American Burn Association, also said his anecdotes were not about different children but about the same infant. But records and interviews show that the baby Heimbach said he had in mind when testifying didn't die as he described and that flame retardants were not a factor.

After the *Tribune* confronted chemical executives with Heimbach's questionable testimony, he offered, through his lawyer, another explanation for why his stories didn't add up: he intentionally changed the facts to protect patient privacy.

Yet the most crucial parts of his testimony—the cause of the fire and the lack of flame retardants—had nothing to do with privacy. Instead, they served to bolster the industry's argument that chemical retardants save lives.

In the last quarter-century, worldwide demand for flame retardants has skyrocketed to 3.4 billion pounds in 2009 from 526 million pounds in 1983, according to market research from the Freedonia Group, which projects demand will reach 4.4 billion pounds by 2014.

As evidence of the health risks associated with these chemicals piled up, the industry mounted a misleading campaign to fuel demand.

There is no better example of these deceptive tactics than the Citizens for Fire Safety Institute, the industry front group that sponsored Heimbach and his vivid testimony about burned babies.

Fear and Deception

In the website photo, five grinning children stand in front of a red-brick fire station that could be on any corner in America. They hold a hand-drawn banner that says "fire safety" with a heart dotting the letter "i."

Citizens for Fire Safety describes itself as a group of people with altruistic intentions: "A coalition of fire professionals, educators, community activists, burn centers, doctors, fire departments and industry leaders, united to ensure that our country is protected by the highest standards of fire safety."

Heimbach summoned that image when he told lawmakers that the organization was "made up of many people like me who have no particular interest in the chemical companies: numerous fire departments, numerous firefighters and many, many burn docs."

But public records demonstrate that Citizens for Fire Safety actually is a trade association for chemical companies. Its executive director, Grant Gillham, honed his political skills advising tobacco executives. And the group's efforts to influence fire-safety policies are guided by a mission to "promote common business interests of members involved with the chemical manufacturing industry," tax records show.

Its only sources of funding—about $17 million between 2008 and 2010—are "membership dues and assessments" and the interest that money earns.

The group has only three members: Albemarle, ICL Industrial Products, and Chemtura, according to records the organization filed with California lobbying regulators. Those three companies are the largest manufacturers of flame retardants and together control 40 percent of the world market for these chemicals, according to the Freedonia Group, a Cleveland-based research firm.

Citizens for Fire Safety has spent its money primarily on lobbying and political expenses, tax records show. Since federal law makes it nearly impossible for the EPA to ban toxic chemicals and Congress rarely steps in, state legislatures from Alaska to Vermont have become the sites of intense battles over flame retardants.

Many of the witnesses supporting flame retardants at these hearings were either paid directly by Citizens for Fire Safety or were members of groups that benefited financially from Citizens for Fire Safety's donations, according to tax documents and other records.

At the same time, Citizens for Fire Safety has portrayed its opposition as misguided, wealthy environmentalists. But its opponents include a diverse group of public health advocates as well as firefighters who are alarmed by studies showing some flame retardants can make smoke from fires even more toxic.

Matt Vinci, president of the Professional Fire Fighters of Vermont, faced what he called "dirty tactics" when he successfully lobbied for his state to ban one flame retardant chemical in 2009.

Particularly offensive to Vinci were letters Citizens for Fire Safety sent to Vermont fire chiefs saying the ban would "present an additional hazard for those of us in the fire safety profession." But the letter's author wasn't a firefighter; he was a California public relations consultant.

"Citizens for Fire Safety did everything they could to portray themselves as firefighters, as Vermont citizens for fire safety, when it really wasn't Vermont citizens for fire safety at all," Vinci said.

The group also has misrepresented itself in other ways. On its website, Citizens for Fire Safety said it had joined with the international firefighters' association, the American Burn Association, and a key federal agency "to conduct ongoing studies to ensure safe and effective fire prevention."

Both of those organizations and the federal agency, however, said that simply is not true.

"They are lying," said Jeff Zack, a spokesman for the International Association of Fire Fighters. "They aren't working with us on anything."

After inquiries from the *Tribune*, Citizens for Fire Safety deleted that passage from its website.

Gillham, the executive director, declined to comment. Albemarle, Chemtura, and ICL Industrial Products also declined to answer specific questions about the group.

Albemarle chief sustainability officer David Clary did say that his company has been transparent about its funding of Citizens for Fire Safety.

"We believe that this support for advocacy groups is critical to raise awareness of the importance of fire safety and give a voice to those who want to speak out on this important public issue," Clary said in a written statement.

Citizens for Fire Safety is the latest in a string of industry groups that have sprung up on different continents in the last fifteen years—casting doubt on health concerns, shooting down restrictions, and working to expand the market for flame retardants in furniture and electronics.

For example, the Bromine Science and Environmental Forum, based in Brussels, may sound like a neutral scientific body. But it was founded and funded by four chemical manufacturers, including Albemarle, to influence the debate about flame retardants made with bromine.

Albemarle's global director of product advocacy, Raymond Dawson, said in blunt testimony before Washington state lawmakers in 2007 that the forum is "a group dedicated to generating science in support of brominated flame retardants."

An official from Burson-Marsteller, the global public relations firm that helps run the organization, said the bromine group is not misleading anyone because regulators, scientists, and other stakeholders are well aware it represents industry.

The PR firm also helps run the Alliance for Consumer Fire Safety in Europe, which is funded by a trade association of flame retardant manufacturers. The alliance's director, Bob Graham, said the group's aim is to improve fire-safety standards for upholstered furniture sold in Europe.

The group's website taps into the public's fear of fire, touting an "interactive burn test tool" that allows visitors to choose a European country and watch a sofa from that nation being torched.

Next to a photo of an easy chair fully engulfed in flames, four words stand out in large capital letters: "ARE YOU SITTING COMFORTABLY?"

"Imagine a Child Crying"

The amount of flame retardants in a typical American home isn't measured in parts per billion or parts per million. It's measured in ounces and pounds.

A large couch can have up to two pounds in its foam cushions. The chemicals also are inside some highchairs, diaper-changing pads, and breast-feeding pillows. Recyclers turn chemically treated foam into the padding underneath carpets.

"When we're eating organic, we're avoiding very small amounts of pesticides," said Arlene Blum, a California chemist who has fought to limit flame retardants in household products. "Then we sit on our couch that can contain a pound of chemicals that's from the same family as banned pesticides like DDT."

These chemicals are ubiquitous not because federal rules demand it. In fact, scientists at the U.S. Consumer Product Safety Commission have determined that the flame retardants in household furniture aren't effective and some pose unnecessary health risks.

The chemicals are widely used because of an obscure rule adopted by California regulators in 1975. Back then, a state chemist devised an easy-to-replicate burn test that didn't require manufacturers to set furniture on fire, an expensive proposition.

The test calls for exposing raw foam to a candlelike flame for twelve seconds. The cheapest way to pass the test is to add flame retardants to the foam inside cushions.

But couches aren't made of foam alone. In a real fire, the upholstery fabric, typically not treated with flame retardants, burns first, and the flames grow big enough that they overwhelm even fire-retardant foam, scientists at two federal agencies have found.

Nevertheless, in the decades since that rule went into effect, lawyers have regularly argued that their burn-victim clients would have been spared if only their sofas had been made with California foam. Faced with the specter of these lawsuits—and the logistical challenge of producing separate products just for California—many manufacturers began using flame retardant foam across their product lines.

As a result, California has become the most critical battleground in recent years for advocates trying to reduce the prevalence of these chemicals in American homes.

Citizens for Fire Safety has successfully fought back with a powerful, and surprising, tactic: making flame retardants a racial issue.

The group and witnesses with ties to it have argued that impoverished, minority children would burn to death if flame retardants were removed from household products.

In 2009, for instance, members of the California State Assembly were considering a bill that would have made it unnecessary to add flame retardants to many baby products by excluding them from the state's flammability regulation.

Up to the microphone stepped Zyra McCloud, an African American community activist from Inglewood, Calif.

McCloud was president of a community group that listed Citizens for Fire Safety as a sponsor on its website and included photos of McCloud with Gillham, the executive director. She did not disclose this connection to the assembly, nor was she asked.

In a news release, Citizens for Fire Safety already had quoted McCloud saying that minority children, who constitute a disproportionate share of fire deaths, would bear the brunt of the "ill-conceived and unsafe legislation."

At the hearing, the committee chairwoman told both sides they were out of time for testimony, but McCloud pleaded with her to allow two elementary school students from her district to address lawmakers.

"We have spent all weekend long with the kids that have had family members and friends who have died in fires, and we are praying and appealing to you that you would at least allow the two boys to speak," she said.

One of the boys, a ten-year-old, read from a statement.

"I just want you to imagine a child crying for help in a burning building, dying, when there was a person who only had to vote to save their life," he said.

Citizens for Fire Safety prevailed. The bill later went down to defeat.

McCloud told the *Tribune*, "I've always been a person that's fought against things that would hurt children." She then asked for questions in writing but never answered them.

Nearly two years after that bill failed, one of the nation's top burn surgeons would also invoke the image of a dead child before California lawmakers on behalf of Citizens for Fire Safety.

"This Is Horrible"

When Dr. David Heimbach walked into the California Senate committee hearing last year, the stakes had never been higher for flame-retardant manufacturers.

Once again, senators were considering an overhaul of the state's flammability regulation—one that advocates believed would dramatically reduce the amount of flame retardants in American homes.

The bill would allow manufacturers to choose the existing candlelike flame test or a new one based on a smoldering cigarette, a far more common source of fires than candles. Manufacturers could pass the new test by using resistant fabrics rather than adding toxic chemicals to the foam inside.

To maintain the status quo—and avoid a hit to the bottom line—chemical makers needed to stress that fires started by candles were a serious threat.

Heimbach, Citizens for Fire Safety's star witness, did just that.

With Citizens for Fire Safety's Gillham watching from the audience, Heimbach not only passionately described the fatal burns a seven-week-old Alaska patient received lying on a pillow that lacked flame retardants, he also blamed the 2010 blaze on a candle.

In fact, he specifically said the baby's mother had placed a candle in the girl's crib.

Heimbach had told similar stories before, the *Tribune* found. In 2009, he told a California State Assembly committee that he had treated a nine-week-old girl who died that spring after a candle beside her crib turned over. "We had to split open her fingers because they were so charred," he testified.

In 2010, he told Alaska lawmakers about a six-week-old girl from Washington state who died that year after a dog knocked a candle onto her crib, which did not have a flame retardant mattress.

Heimbach's hospital in Seattle, Harborview Medical Center, declined to help the *Tribune* confirm his accounts. But records from the King County medical examiner's office show that no child matching Heimbach's descriptions has died in his hospital in the last sixteen years.

The only infant who came close in terms of age and date of death was Nancy Garcia-Diaz, a six-week-old who died in 2009 after a house fire in rural Washington.

In an interview, Heimbach said his anecdotes were all about the same baby—one who died at his hospital, though he didn't know the child's name. Contrary to his testimony, he said he had not taken care of the patient.

Told about Nancy, Heimbach said she was probably the baby he had in mind and e-mailed a *Tribune* reporter two photographs of a severely burned child, images that he said he had used in a presentation at a medical conference. Medical records and Nancy's mother confirmed those pictures were indeed of Nancy.

But Nancy didn't die in a fire caused by a candle, as Heimbach has repeatedly testified. Fire records obtained by the *Tribune* show the blaze was caused by an overloaded, overheated extension cord.

"There were no candles, no pets—just the misuse of extension cords," said Mike Makela, an investigator for the Snohomish County fire marshal's office.

In his testimony last year, Heimbach stated the baby was in a crib on a fire-retardant mattress and on a non-retardant pillow. The upper half of her body was burned, he said.

But public records show there was no crib—she was resting on a bed—and no pillow. And, Makela said, flame retardants played no role in the pattern of her burns.

Fire authorities, Heimbach said, "may know more about it than I do, but that was the information that I had."

Heimbach said he couldn't recall who gave him that information but that Citizens for Fire Safety did not help craft his statements. He said the group has paid for his travel to testify and for some of his time, though he would not give a dollar amount.

The details of his statements, he said, weren't as important as the principle. "The principle is that fire retardants will retard fires and will prevent burns," he said.

Later, Heimbach said through his attorney that federal rules prohibit him from disclosing information that would identify a patient. He said that when describing particular burn cases, he follows standard protocol under the rules by "de-identifying" patients—that is, changing or omitting identifying information to protect their privacy.

But in testimony at state hearings, Heimbach not only changed facts, he added new ones, such as candles starting deadly blazes and the lack of flame retardants—details that aided the chemical industry's position.

Nancy's mother, who asked that her name not be used, said she never granted Heimbach permission to use her daughter's photograph.

"Nancy's memory is sacred to us," she said. "My daughter deserves respect. She lived such a short time and she suffered a lot. This is horrible."

Heimbach was head of Harborview's burn center for twenty-five years; he also was a professor of surgery at the University of Washington until his retirement last year. He estimated he might have saved "hundreds if not thousands" of lives. In 2009, the Dalai Lama presented Heimbach an award for his pioneering care of burn victims around the world.

"I'm a well-meaning guy," Heimbach said. "I'm not in the pocket of industry."

When Heimbach testified last spring in California on the bill that could have significantly reduced the use of flame retardants, he didn't tell lawmakers he was altering facts about the burn victim. Only when asked by a senator did he reveal that Citizens for Fire Safety paid for his trip there.

When it came time to vote, the senators overwhelmingly sided with Heimbach and Citizens for Fire Safety, sticking with the furniture standard based on a candlelike flame.

Public health advocates had one last hope: Senators had seven days in which they could change their votes. As the advocates tried to persuade senators to reconsider, Citizens for Fire Safety put out a news alert that linked to a video called "Killer Couches!"

To the sounds of sinister music and crackling flames, a sofa made without flame retardants became an inferno. Then these words appeared: "Are You Sitting Comfortably?"

No senators changed their votes, and the bill was dead. The chemical companies had won again.

Tribune reporter Michael Hawthorne contributed to this report.

Part V

Media and Marketing

New York

There may be a business that's meaner and cattier than high-end fashion, but it's hard to think of many. Still, even the usual death-by-gossip of the New York fashion scene rises to a level *plus haute* when the competition pits houses headed by ex-husband and ex-wife. Meet the Burches. Christopher Burch is a fashion icon so wealthy he can wear red pajama bottoms to work. A few years ago, as Jessica Pressler brilliantly recounts, he helped his then-wife, Tory, launch a line hailed as the "next big thing" by none other than Oprah herself. They later split, and Tory, an ambitious publicist turned fashionista, began accusing her ex-husband of stealing her concepts. It was not long before the long fingernails came out and the two sides began a series of accusations and counter-accusations, not to mention character assassinations.

Jessica Pressler

11. His. Hers.

"Isn't it fun?" says Christopher Burch, stepping through the lime-lacquered doors of the Soho flagship of his new store, C. Wonder, and looking out at the candy-colored floor, where customers browse a vast array of merchandise to the songs of sixties girl group the Marvelettes. "This is my music," he says. "It's so me."

There's a note of paternal pride in his voice. As a venture capitalist and the head of J. Christopher Capital, Burch, who is fifty-eight, with white curly hair, crinkly eyes, and a Santa Claus demeanor, has had a hand in launching close to fifty brands, which have provided him with enough wealth that he feels comfortable spending a business day in a down vest, red pajama bottoms, and black velvet slippers. But C. Wonder is his baby, the first property in a long time that he feels is really his. "Look at this stitching," he marvels, running his hand across a rack of bright button-down blouses and preppy blazers before whirling off to the shoe area, where a huge tufted ottoman awaits suburban princesses who wish to try on the store's selection of loafers and colorful ballet flats. "See that quality?" he says, bending a ballet flat. "And look: It's on sale for thirty-nine dollars!"

In the home section, where light fixtures shaped like teapots dangle above a display of quirky crockery, Burch picks up a cow-shaped mug. "Now this little item, they didn't want," he says, referring to his creative team. "But I actually said, 'Look at all the moms who come in and want some coffee or Coke or whatever, and the kids want this,'" he says, caressing the cow's spots. "It's just fun. Isn't it so fun?"

A curly-haired salesgirl bounces over, her bracelets jangling. "Hey, Mr. B," she says, beaming.

"Hi, sweetie pie," Burch says, and they high-five.

"What do you think?" he asks her, as if genuinely wondering. "What do you think it is about this store?"

"I think it has really great energy," she replies and dutifully goes on about the adjustable music and lighting in the dressing rooms and the spontaneous dance parties the staff encourages customers to join in on, until finally she spins off to complete some task or other, perhaps with the help of cartoon birds.

The point is made: C. Wonder is fun. In fact, it's so fun, so warm and domestic and full of "Heart"—or "He-Art" as the letters embroidered on Burch's slippers spell out—you wouldn't expect it to be the subject of a vicious dispute. Especially not one between this friendly guy who bear-hugs his employees and his ex-wife, designer Tory Burch, a woman the *Times* recently described as "perfectly perfect." And yet this whimsical space has become a battleground where the Burches are fighting a decidedly unusual war over the brand—and life—they built together.

To Chris Burch, C. Wonder is the realization of a long-held dream to provide low-to-mid-price retail in a luxury setting. To Tory Burch, he might as well have erected a giant lacquered middle finger in the front window, directly facing the orange-lacquered doors of her eponymous store a few blocks away. "It's a rip-off. Tory knows it, and everyone knows it," says someone we will refer to as a Friend of Tory. "The interior is blatantly plagiarized. Then there's the snap bracelets. The wallets. The buttons . . ."

This is not merely a postmarital dispute between exes. Since their divorce in 2006, Chris and Tory Burch have continued to serve together on the board of what has become a billion-dollar company. Now, he also owns what looks, to some, like a competing brand. "There is some apparent customer confusion between the two brands," says board member Glen Senk. "And that's not good for anybody."

For now at C. Wonder, however, love is in the air. The store has just set up its windows for Valentine's Day, and Chris Burch points to a sign announcing that customers who find a love note in the store will receive 10 percent off. "See, that's kind of our vibe," he says. "I really just want to make women happy."

• • •

This instinct comes not just from the goodness of his He-Art. Catering to women also, as Chris Burch once remarked to a colleague, "makes a shit ton of money." He should know: He's been selling to them most of his life. Though he usually remains in the background, you may be familiar with some of his earlier work.

"I designed the first Christmas sweater," he tells me one evening, while sipping an iced tea in the bar at the Crosby Street Hotel. "They actually got pretty popular. Anyway."

Talking to Chris Burch is a kinetic experience—he's always doing things like photographing the whales on the backs of the chairs or showing you his mineral collection or saying, "Oh, can you write that down?" to the phalanx of loyal employees who attend to him with filial concern. He has a reputation for being cutthroat, but he doesn't think of himself like that. "I'm not a business guy," he says at the Crosby. "I'm a curious creative. And I love collaboration. Creativity, curiosity, and collaborations. Hey, can you write that down?"

This peripatetic personality made him a great investor but an easily distracted student growing up. On a semester abroad in England, he sweet-talked a Scottish factory into selling him a wholesale order of Shetland-wool sweaters with an eye toward selling them to WASPs in his hometown on the Philadelphia mainline. When the products arrived on the small side, he and his brother, Robert, drove around to colleges, selling to coeds instead. They sold out. Plus, his longtime friend George Corrigan says, "it was a great way to meet girls."

The brothers quickly ramped up their sweater game. They called their company Eagle's Eye, after their father's nickname, and got a post-office box to look official. Then came what Burch calls "probably the most exciting point in my life other than having children and all the other stuff."

In 1976, at a New York cocktail party celebrating the Bicentennial, he met a guy who told him about a factory in Hong Kong where they made things cheaper and faster than anybody. Burch placed an order for a huge number of sweaters, dirt cheap. Then he put an ad in *Glamour* and waited. On the eighth day, the postmaster told him he had mail. "And he had behind the desk two big white bags. Like, huge. I put them in the car and drove home to my parents' house, and I dumped the bags on the floor, and I'm not kidding you, there were probably a thousand checks for sweaters."

The Hong Kong connection enabled Eagle's Eye to increase production enough to start distributing nationally and to expand well beyond sweaters. The turtlenecks they festooned with strawberries and whales hit right in time for the preppy craze, and the business took off. Then: "I noticed a lot of our customers were turning into young moms," Burch says, "and Christmas was very much a family thing . . ."

Eagle's Eye opened a New York office in 1981, and on one of his trips there, Burch met his first wife, a fashion consultant named Susan Cole. They had three daughters and moved to a spacious home near his parents in the Philadelphia suburbs. Despite the failure of one of Chris's more esoteric innovations ("He wanted a sweater with a turkey on it that clucked," says Leslie Johnson, whom he hired as a designer), business thrived, and in

1989 Chris and Robert began selling their stake in Eagle's Eye (they ultimately made $60 million).

He bought a small apartment at the Pierre. By this time, Chris and Susan were having problems, and so he began spending more time in New York, ferreting out new business opportunities. "He'll talk to anybody," says Corrigan. "He gets his energy, his juice, from people." One of the people he met was Tory Robinson, a pretty blonde Vera Wang publicist who worked in his office building. Chris and Susan divorced, and in 1996 Chris and Tory were married. Their personalities couldn't have been more different: Chris was outspoken and disheveled, he once showed up at a dinner wearing his shoes on the wrong feet; Tory, thirteen years his junior, was far more polished. But they both had a certain steely ambition. "Chris wanted to be a player," says a friend of the couple, "and Tory is shrewd. She's as shrewd as they get."

During the Internet boom, he invested heavily in digital properties, made an enormous amount of money before the bubble popped, and parlayed his winnings into an eclectic assortment of businesses: cod farming, Voss water. She became one of the most photographed blondes on the charity circuit, standing out for her impeccable style and an I'm-not-taking-this-too-seriously smile. The couple had three children, all boys, and renovated the apartment at the Pierre, expanding it to include three suites and a hallway.

It was Tory Burch's idea to launch her own clothing line. At first, she wanted to revive Jax, the Beverly Hills boutique Jack and Sally Hanson started in the sixties for an elite clientele once described as "two-yacht housewives." Sally wasn't interested, so she began sketching her own designs. Her husband helped her raise the money—$10 million from outside investors and $2 million of their own. It was decided that Tory would be the face of the brand. In 2004, *Vogue* featured her and her now-9,000-square-foot apartment, decorated in "marmalade" and "peridot-green," in an elaborate spread heralding the launch of her boutique on Elizabeth Street. On opening day, New York's two-yacht housewives practically ransacked the store. Oprah hailed Tory Burch as the "Next Big Thing." Virtually overnight, she became a fashion icon.

From all outward appearances, Tory Burch was a model businesswoman, wife, and mother. "Before she leaves on a business trip, Tory writes notes to her kids and hides them around their spacious apartment," the *Palm Beach Post* reported breathlessly. But things weren't so perfectly perfect. While Tory Burch was developing her label, Chris Burch was working on a lower-priced line of his own, Winter & Miggs, which used the same factories to produce similar designs. People familiar with the line say Tory knew about it, that Chris had created Winter & Miggs as a hedge in case Tory Burch didn't succeed. But Friends of Tory say she only found out when visiting fashion editors commented to her about the line's similarities to hers and that she was livid.

Winter & Miggs never made its mark. But over the years, the same tension resurfaced. Chris Burch continued to push his wife to do lower-price items, and she continued to resist. "What Chris likes is selling to the masses," says a former employee. "His ex-wife is the opposite." Their personal relationship was suffering too—Tory was becoming increasingly impatient with her husband's eccentricities. Two years after the company launched, the couple separated, and Chris moved out of what had once been his bachelor pad. "Chris was pissed," says an FOT, adding, not unsympathetically, "He had reason to be."

Despite the tension, Chris Burch held onto his shares and stayed on the board of Tory Burch—the company was doing too well not to. Then Tory Burch started appearing in photographs with Lance Armstrong, and her ex-husband fell into a funk. A Friend of Chris recalls him saying that she was the love of his life. "He had kind of had this golden life. I hate to say it got the best of him. He just got, you know, caught off guard."

He developed serious health problems: first a herniated disk, then a rare disease that cost him the use of his right arm for months. In 2006, his mother died, and, soon after, his father collapsed from a heart attack while dancing at a country club.

There was a silver lining: The tragedies helped heal some of the animosity left over from their divorce. "You realize the pettiness has to stop," Tory said at the time. "Now we're putting the business and kids first."

• • •

"We're like *The Bucket List*, right, Billy?" asks Chris Burch, who is sitting in the front seat of the Escalade that is being maneuvered through Soho traffic by Bill Allen, his body man of twenty-one years.

"Yup, we're doing it," says Allen, who is a patient man, and not just because of traffic.

The bucket list seems to include world domination. J. Christopher Capital plans to roll out at least six new brands by 2013. There's C. Wonder, which Burch hopes will open 300 stores worldwide over the next six years; Electric Love Army, a clothing line he's developing with fashion publicist Kelly Cutrone; Poppin, an online office-supply company; and an as-yet-unnamed clothing company his daughters Alexandra ("Pookie") and Louisa ("Weezie") are working on together. The crown jewel of this empire will be "a two-floor, 40,000-square-foot department store that will be beyond your comprehension," he says, craning around to the back seat. "That's 99 Christopher."

"Number Nine Christopher," says Elissa Lumley, J. Christopher's director of communications.

"Right, right," he says. "I'm a little overwhelmed right now with brands."

Real estate is also a perennial interest. "I also bought an island," he says, although he doesn't want to get into specifics other than to say it's off the coast of Indonesia. ("I think it has like, indigenous people on it," Lumley says later at J. Christopher Capital's sprawling new offices on Twenty-fifth Street. "He's like, 'I'll give all those people jobs!' ")

The car pulls up to the Prince Street preview store of another of J. Christopher Capital's new brands: Monika Chiang, whose namesake may at least be partially responsible for Burch's new lease on life. He bolts to the back room, where Chiang—a tall, sultry thirty-seven-year-old in white jeans, Azzedine Alaïa boots, and a cashmere sweater that exposes a sliver of bisque-colored midriff—is shooting her fall look book.

"This is my girlfriend," he says, grabbing Chiang by the waist and planting a kiss on her cheek.

"*Hi-i-i-i*," she drawls.

Chiang, who sounds like she comes from California even though she was born in New York, met Burch at Dune, a club in the Hamptons that she managed during the summer of 2007.

"Tell the story," he suggests.

"He came in. He was trying to impress me. And I wouldn't have it, of course."

"She has a lot of style, as you can tell," says Burch. "And I walked up to her knowing quite well she wasn't in fashion and said, 'You're in fashion, aren't you?' And we actually dug each other."

The two now share a townhouse in the West Village when they aren't in Los Angeles, where Chiang's flagship recently opened, or in Miami, where Burch maintains a primary residence, or in Shanghai, where Chiang frequently joins Burch on his sourcing trips. That is where the idea for Monika Chiang the brand germinated: At his urging, she had some jewelry made for herself, and one thing led to another. "You never even asked me to do fashion, did you?" Burch asks.

"*Mmm-nnnn*," Chiang murmurs.

"I noticed she had a real edge," he says. Chiang had never designed clothing before, though she told reporters at the opening of her Los Angeles store that "I've had a lot of experience shopping." Her clothes, all leather and fur and high heels that could double as weapons, are as far from Tory Burch as you can get, though their stores on South Robertson Boulevard are just a few doors apart. This has not gone unnoticed by the FOTs. "It's almost like he's saying, 'I could put any girl, I could have anybody be the face of it, it doesn't matter,'" says one.

But this was nowhere near as infuriating as C. Wonder. In the weeks leading up to the grand opening, Tory Burch had heard so much about C. Wonder's likeness to her line that she and her company's president, Brigitte Kleine, decided to make the trip to Soho themselves. Even after being forewarned, they were shocked. Everything seemed familiar, from the buttons on the blouses to the *C* logo Chris had emblazoned on all of the items, which they could tell had been created by the same company that designed their double *T*.

"Tory must have wanted to puke when she went into that store," says a former employee. "I'm sure she was really hurt." The FOTs scoff at this notion. "Tory's beyond the point of being wounded by an ex-husband," says one. More like furious. Once again Chris had gone behind her back to create a lower-priced brand, and this time it looked like a direct competitor. "It is unclear whether this is an amicable homage or a hostile takeover," said the *Times* when C. Wonder opened. "I live in the neighborhood, and the resemblance stopped me in my tracks," says Susan Scafidi, a fashion lawyer and the head of the Fashion Law Institute at Fordham. "The physical décor and the packaging are like the packaging of a Tory Burch store."

To Tory Burch, the design and layout of C. Wonder seems like a deliberate attempt by her ex-husband to confuse the consumer into thinking the two brands are associated, à la Kate and Jack Spade. Chris Burch may have held back from using their shared last name, but by appointing himself the figurehead of C. Wonder, he'd all but guaranteed the association would be made in the business press. Which it was. In the weeks surrounding the opening, media coverage invariably noted C. Wonder was the brainchild of "Tory Burch's ex-husband," "the chairman of the board of Tory Burch," or "the man behind Tory Burch." Most galling to Tory was when Chris, in an interview about C. Wonder on Bloomberg television, referred to himself as "the founder of, and largest shareholder of," Tory Burch. (Chris and Tory are equal shareholders.) Ironically, the moment occurred in an interview about trademark infringement. "We are constantly having people . . . stealing our brand name, stealing our products, all over the world," he told the interviewer.

Everyone at the company knew Chris was fond of exaggeration—the Christmas sweater goes back at least as far as the fifties, by the way—but now FOTs felt he was inflating his role at Tory Burch to promote his competing brand. At the same time, they may be downplaying it. "He doesn't have a role," says an FOT, adding that beyond his initial investment, his involvement has been minimal. "That's bullshit," says a person with knowledge of both parties, pointing out that Chris's experience with factories in Asia made him instrumental to production. "Tory has done a brilliant job, but without Chris, it could not have been done. You can't deny that." Glen Senk offers a kind of middle ground. "Chris is a founder and a consultant," he says. "He has a million-and-one ideas, some of which the company has used and some of which the company hasn't used. There's a difference—and as a board member I can say this about myself—there's a difference between throwing out ideas and running a business."

Friends of Tory say Chris felt sidelined at the company and that may be one of his motivations in opening C. Wonder. "He's jealous," says one. "He thinks he didn't get enough recognition at Tory." A more impartial observer concurs: "The bottom line is he never got over Tory leaving him." But it's hard to imagine that such a massive retail operation, launched six years after a divorce, is motivated primarily by pique. Nor does it make sense that Chris Burch would undercut the company where he is co-chairman. If he's ripping his ex-wife off, he's ripping himself off, too.

Friends of Chris say he simply doesn't see the conflict—that to him the brand is genuinely reflective of the life he has lived. One of the rooms is modeled after a ski lodge he visited in Vail, they point out, another after an English townhouse he owned in the nineties. By this line of thinking, any physical resemblance to Tory Burch could be chalked up to years of living in a peridot-and-marmalade-colored apartment.

"I don't really get it," Kelly Cutrone says about the outrage coming from Tory Burch loyalists. "Did they trademark lacquer? Does Lilly Pulitzer start calling Tory and saying, 'Hey, you're doing a modernized version of what I used to do, please stop'? Does Yves Saint Laurent call and say, 'No, I'm the king of the tunic, I lived in Morocco'? Did the Knights of the Templars call off Christian Dior because he was using chain mail and that's they what wore in the Crusades?"

C. Wonder president Amy Shecter, a former Tory Burch executive, notes that the quantity of products the stores carry differentiates them from Tory Burch. "I mean, we have heart-shaped waffle-makers in our store," she says. "We have pigs that are docking stations." She starts to laugh. "They don't have heart-shaped waffle-makers! They don't have pig docking stations!"

This may not be enough for Tory Burch, who is serious about protecting the exclusivity of her brand. Last summer, a federal court awarded her company $164 million in a suit against online counterfeiters, believed to be the largest judgment ever awarded to a fashion company. A lawsuit against C. Wonder has almost certainly crossed her mind. Given Chris Burch's position on the board, the company could sue him for breach of fiduciary duty. It is already compiling photographs of C. Wonder products juxtaposed with Tory Burch products in a large binder—a kind of corporate burn book. But suing her ex-husband, the father of her children and the co-chairman of her own board, may be much more trouble than it's worth for Tory Burch. Since the beginning, she has kept the details of her business private, and a lawsuit of this kind would expose the inner workings of Tory Burch to everyone, including competitors who aren't relatives. The company would have to release minutes of its board meetings, for instance, at which Chris and Tory were both present—catnip to the fashion gossips who have followed her golden rise. "The family dynamic, or the former family dynamic, will absolutely rivet the consumer," says Scafidi.

For now, they're trying to deal with the problem quietly. Barclays Capital has been engaged to help sell off his shares, shopping them at a price that reportedly values the company at an aggressive $2 billion. Meanwhile, Tory Burch has been pressuring her ex-husband to reconceptualize C. Wonder. His daughters from his first marriage, who remain close with their stepmother, are also said to have asked him to make changes.

When I bring this up at the Crosby, Burch deflates like a helium balloon. "I don't want to talk about that stuff," he says so miserably that Elissa Lumley reaches out and rubs him on the shoulder. But then he brightens, insisting that he wishes Tory Burch well—both the person and the brand. "I'm so excited by the success of Tory," he tells me. "I'm so excited by the success of C. Wonder, of Monika Chiang, and of the brands I'll build in the future."

Speaking of: he's due to meet Monika at the movies. "I guess I'm just the luckiest guy alive," he says as he stands up. "That somehow I get to attract the most exciting entrepreneurs in the world, work with incredible women, and have amazing ex-wives."

It's a classic Chris Burch line: cheerful, odd, immodestly modest. The sort of thing that could drive an ex-wife crazy—or make a new partner giddy with anticipation. "Tory Burch was Tory Robinson when she met Chris Burch," Cutrone points out. "She was a publicist. Now she has a billion-dollar company. I don't know what the beef is. But I'm hoping he's able to continue his track record of turning publicists into billionaires, because I'm next in line."

San Francisco Weekly

Anyone with a sense of foreboding about the future of news in the age of search-engine optimization—writing about things that are already popular on Google in order to *also* become popular on Google—will feel no better, and probably a lot worse, after reading this profile of *Bleacher Report*. The sports "news" site relies on thousands of unpaid contributors writing opinion posts intended to tempt readers into a restless click. Its model is to crank out huge volumes of "content," regardless of merit, resulting in serious swamps of digital dreck (e.g., "Twenty-five Wardrobe Malfunctions in Sports," "The Twenty Biggest Criers in Sports," "Ten Possible Tiger Woods Porn Spin-offs: Mistress Edition"). Perhaps uniquely among journalistic entities, as Joe Eskenazi writes, *Bleacher Report* has a "blanket policy" forbidding its writers from actually seeking out and breaking news. On the other hand, it was bought by AOL for $200 million.

Joe Eskenazi

12. Top Five Ways *Bleacher Report* Rules the World!

Last year, sportswriter King Kaufman stepped up to the lectern at a symposium held on the Google campus. In a fourteen-year haul at Salon.com, Kaufman earned a reputation as one of the best and most cerebral sports journalists on the Internet. But his subject that day was his new job, improving the content quality at *Bleacher Report*—an outfit with a reputation almost directly opposite Kaufman's own.

The San Francisco–based site is an aggressively growing online giant, tapping the oceanic labor pool of thousands of unpaid sports fanatics typing on thousands of keyboards. Launched in 2008, *Bleacher Report* meteorically rose to become one of the nation's most popular websites and one of the three most-visited sports sites. Its dramatic success came via valuing site growth and pageviews over any semblance of journalistic "quality" or even readability. Operating a sports website on a supply-and-demand model turns out just as one would expect: High-trafficking *Bleacher Report* articles include "Twenty-Five Wardrobe Malfunctions in Sports," "The Twenty Biggest Criers in Sports," and "Ten Possible Tiger Woods Porn Spin-offs: Mistress Edition." The site quickly earned a rep for expertly employing the Google search engine to inundate the Web with horrible, lowest-common-denominator crap.

"A lot of what *Bleacher Report* has done has been lowest-common-denominator crap, and horrible," Kaufman admitted to the audience. His task was to alter this perception of the company. But this was not due to any sense of embarrassment or a late-night visit to the site's brass by the Ghost of Journalistic Standards Past. Like almost every move the company makes, this was a business decision. And a smart one.

"This was not a decision made by the CEO, who got tired of his friends saying at parties, 'Boy, *Bleacher Report* is terrible,'" Kaufman continued. "*Bleacher Report* reached a point where it couldn't make the next level of deal, where whatever company says 'We're not putting our logo next to yours because you're publishing crap.' Okay, that's the market speaking."

Several thousand miles away, *Bleacher Report*'s hiring of Kaufman and a platoon of professional writers—but continued reliance upon an unpaid cast of thousands—was interpreted differently. During a meeting in New York City, an executive at one of the nation's largest sports media companies quipped that *Bleacher Report*'s new strategy was akin to spritzing a little room deodorizer after leaving a steaming deposit in the toilet and failing to flush. An attendee recalls everyone laughing uproariously.

In August of this year, Turner Broadcasting announced it was quite willing to put its logo next to *Bleacher Report*'s, scooping up the website for a purported $200 million. *Bleacher Report* has joined the *Huffington Post* in the exclusive club of Web properties converting free, crowd-sourced content into nine-digit paydays. The transaction was not just a valuation, but a validation.

"Information has become more important than the source of information," says Michael Hall, director of new media for the New England Sports Network. In today's world, information is money—and few move information faster or more efficiently than *Bleacher Report* and its roughly 6,000 contributors. "They understand, probably better than any media outlet today, the exact value generated for them for every monthly unique visitor, every pageview served," continues Hall. "They understand that revenue impact better than anyone out there. Better than we do."

Every media entity questioning the wisdom of throwing down $200 million for *Bleacher Report*, notes Hall, is already co-opting the tricks mastered by *Bleacher Report*. "It's here to stay," he adds, "because it's what people want."

No one is laughing anymore.

• • •

There's no single narrative to encapsulate the ascent of *Bleacher Report*, a site that churns out around 800 articles a day penned by 2,000 "core contributors." The site is as polarizing as it is popular. And it is very popular. In August, some 14.2 million users visited it. Astronomical pageview numbers have translated into loads of advertising revenue—media reports peg the site as on pace to gross $30 million to $40 million this year.

It could be argued that *Bleacher Report*'s success is a twenty-first-century iteration of the American Dream. Four twenty-something sports nuts, friends since they attended the elite Menlo School in Atherton, quit their jobs in 2007 to found a sports website written by the fans, for the fans. In doing so, they harnessed the energy of the legions of sports enthusiasts who would have otherwise been yammering on call-in radio or laboring on obscure blogs and message boards and bundled the labor into a platform that could be backed by advertising dollars.

The site's deft use of search engine optimization (SEO)—the tweaking of content and coding to increase online visibility—propelled its unpaid, amateur writers' fare to the top of Google's search engine results, placing it on equal footing with original work created by established journalistic outlets. It's a rare sports-related Google search that doesn't feature a *Bleacher Report* article among the top results. And once readers click onto *Bleacher*

Report, they stick there—visitors are besieged with applications to subscribe to team-specific newsletters or mobile applications or drawn into click-happy slideshows, polls, or other user-engaging devices that rack up massive pageviews per visit (to date, a slideshow titled "The Twenty Most Boobtastic Athletes of All Time" has amassed 1.4 million views).

Every publication has produced its share of jarringly bad writing. Yet *Bleacher Report*, powered by thousands of hobbyists and publishing more stories in an hour than many sites produce in a year, has lapped the field. The following excerpts of raw copy were all retrieved from the 2011 diary of a bewildered *Bleacher Report* copy editor:

- "From 2001 to 2008, we all know that Matt Millen, the GM of the Detroit Lions, were the worst in NFL history. Much to the instability from the coaching staff were the constant drafting of players who obviously could not play. This slide show is but a simple look at how sad our drafting process was in that 8 year span."
- "An assessment over the last decade illustrates that last season was an irregularity, as many greenhorns fail to sustain success in their rookie campaigns. Despite this evidence, an affinity for adolescent ballplayers remains a universal affection among fantasy users. There are several arguments to explain why this empathy exists."
- "Beasley still gets his average of just over five rebounds per game, but the Timberwolves do not ask him to circumcise his game by staying in the blocks the way Miami did."

Not surprisingly, critics from traditional journalistic outlets continue to knock *Bleacher Report* as a dystopian wasteland where increasingly attention-challenged readers slog through troughs of half-cooked word-gruel, inexpertly mixed by novice chefs.

Whatever, grandpa.

After denigrating and downplaying the influence of the Internet for decades, many legacy media outlets now find themselves outmaneuvered by defter and Web-savvier entities like *Bleacher Report*, a young company engineered to conquer the Internet. In the days of yore, professional media outlets enjoyed a monopoly on information. Trained editors and writers served as gatekeepers deciding what stories people would read, and the system thrived on massive influxes of advertising dollars. That era has gone, and the Internet has flipped the script. In one sense, readers have never had it so good—the glut of material on the Web translates into more access to great writing than any prior era. The trick is sifting through the crap to find it. Most mainstream media outlets are unable or unwilling to compete with a site like *Bleacher Report*, which floods the Web with inexpensive user-generated content. They continue to wither while *Bleacher Report* amasses readers and advertisers alike.

But while critics' lamentations may be increasingly irrelevant, they're hardly unfounded. Perhaps uniquely among journalistic entities, *Bleacher Report* has a "blanket policy" forbidding its writers from seeking out and breaking news. A dictum on the site states: "While we don't doubt that some B/R writers have contacts they know and trust, a problem arises when we're asked to take a leap of faith that those sources are both legitimate and accurate." *Bleacher Report* is designed to engage in the far more lucrative practice of pouncing on news broken by others, deploying its legions of writers to craft articles—or better yet, multipage slideshows—linking to its own voluminous archives and supplanting original stories on the Google rankings. Breaking a story is no longer valuable: owning it is.

Bleacher Report declined to answer questions about this—or anything else. After weeks of entreaties to the site's publicity agency, we were informed that all of the higher-ups at both *Bleacher Report* and Turner we requested, by name, to interview were "unavailable at this time." (We did speak to several dozen current and former *Bleacher Report* writers and editors, many of whom requested anonymity due to fear of retribution.) *Bleacher Report*'s leaders, however, are often rather candid about the company's goals and values.

"Our approach is to really pay attention to what consumers are looking for. There is a notion of consumer demand that any company needs to be mindful of," *Bleacher Report* CEO Brian Grey told *SI.com*. "If you can pay attention to what people are looking for and use that intelligence to produce content that people are looking to consume, from our perspective, that's kind of where digital media is going."

Yet *Bleacher Report* does far more than just "pay attention."

• • •

One of the great ironies of *Bleacher Report* is that a site essentially founded on the mantra "for the fans" operates via an extremely regimented, top-down system. While nearly every major publication now has an SEO maven on board, *Bleacher Report* employs an entire analytics team to comb through reams of data, determining who wants to read what, and when, at an almost granular level. In this way, the site can determine the ideal times to post certain types of stories—thus meeting a demand that doesn't yet exist, but will.

Reverse-engineering content to fit a prewritten headline is a *Bleacher Report* staple. "The analytics team basically says, 'Hey, we think this is going to be trending, these eight to ten terms will be trending in the next couple of days,'" says a former editor for the site. "We say thank you, and we as editors come up with the headlines and pass those on to writers to write the content."

Methodically crafting a data-driven, SEO-friendly headline and then filling in whatever words justify it has been a smashing success for *Bleacher Report*. But it's a long way from any quaint notions of "journalism." This has been, however, standard practice for content farms such as Demand Media. Danny Sullivan, the editor of SearchEngineLand.com, notes that *Bleacher Report*'s CFO, Drew Atherton, held a similar position at Demand Media. Sullivan also mentions that Yahoo! analyzed its own search data and used it to reverse-engineer content. Prior to serving as *Bleacher Report*'s CEO, Grey held the top position at Yahoo! Sports.

The web version of this newspaper has on occasion dogpiled on breaking stories, and published the lists and slideshows commonly seen on the Web. And we have undoubtedly engaged in aggressive online practices in hopes of pushing our content and getting pageviews.

Bleacher Report, however, "is 'made-to-order news.' They'll make up whatever people search for," says Vivek Wadhwa, a researcher and tech columnist for *Bloomberg BusinessWeek* and the *Washington Post*. The triumph of *Bleacher Report*, he continues, is the natural outcome of gauging success and profitability based on Google-derived clicks. "This is custom-manufactured garbage. It is being mass-produced. This is a dumbing down of the Web."

And that leads to another great irony of *Bleacher Report*. A site laden with so much content even its own writers and editors decry as "stupid" is expertly run by some of the smartest executives on the Web. Transforming data into editorial directives, as Grey stated, "is kind of where digital media is going." *Bleacher Report* is already there.

• • •

The next David Halberstam, Bill Simmons, or A. J. Liebling may well be toiling as an unpaid, lower-level *Bleacher Report* contributor. But he or she will never rise up the site's chain of "reputation levels" without garnering pageviews—the currency of success at *Bleacher Report*. Writers are divided into six ranks ranging from "contributor" to "chief writer," with ascending subdivisions of each plateau (I, II, and III). Earning a promotion to "chief writer I" earns a writer a free *Bleacher Report* sweatshirt. He or she will also receive less tangible—but far more consequential—perks such as access to plum spots on the site or within team newsletters and mandated deference from copy editors.

Writers earn "medals" for high-trafficking or much-commented articles and "badges" based on monthly performance numbers. Along with a running pageview count, these plaudits are visually represented on a writer's profile page. Medals are delineated into seven "gem levels" based upon an article's popularity: bronze, silver, gold, platinum, sapphire, ruby, and diamond.

In the world of social media, steering contributors toward desired behaviors via virtual bling is called "gamification." It's not unlike visitors to an animal-centric website being allowed to spiff up their profiles with cute avatars—but only after they leave a requisite number of comments.

"Within the *Bleacher Report* community, [medals and badges] are a point of pride," says one writer. "It's hard not to feel like you're getting somewhere if you have a bunch of badges. It makes you want to work your way up to being an all-star journalist. But you're just working your way up to being an all-star *Bleacher Report* journalist."

A former editor at the site estimates that, even with continued editorial hiring, at least 90 percent of *Bleacher Report*'s gargantuan writing roster remains unpaid. Unable to earn actual crumbs, they compete for virtual crumbs. This is increasingly de rigueur for even established writers—and likely the only model today's young adults have ever known.

The ostensible goal of any enlistee is to ascend to the "featured columnist" position. A recruiting pitch on the site blares:

"Ever notice those credibility-enhancing 'Featured Columnist' icons in article bylines and on B/R Profile pages? Well . . . so has everyone else."

Featured columnists form the backbone of *Bleacher Report*, and some earn a monthly stipend many told us was in the ballpark of $600. This usually covers three assignments a week. These often require a major investment of time: "Predicting the Next Loss for Every Top Fifty College Football Team" may be an inane subject, but its sheer size likely makes it laborious.

The road to the promised land is paved with virtual sapphires and diamonds—and real pageviews and revenue generated for the organization. *Bleacher Report*'s higher-ups have provided neophyte writers a wealth of materials to help them thrive and thereby meet the site's bottom-line needs. The first lesson offered to students of "Bleacher Report U."—a self-guided new-media training curriculum—is to "key on a keyword." In short, write about the stuff people are searching for: "The Hot Keyword Database is an updated catalog of the web's most popular search terms—and your ability to incorporate these terms in your articles will be instrumental in your efforts to generate visitor traffic and maximize your exposure."

One of *Bleacher Report*'s top-five strategies for up-and-comers is to pen "hyperbolic headlines" and "always aim to either overstate or understate your position." As such, "NBA: LeBron James Signs with the Miami Heat," while accurate, is an unacceptable headline. The right take is "LeBron James Signing Makes the Miami Heat the Best Team in NBA History."

Finally, writers are urged to "cater to the masses." "For better or worse, readers love breezy sports-and-culture stories. If you really want to maximize your fanbase, your best bet is to give the people what they want." But, at the same time, don't forget to "beat against the mainstream." The exemplar of contrarian thinking offered within the site's curriculum is a *Bleacher Report* article titled "Why Tom Brady Is the Most Overrated Quarterback in NFL History."

This piece epitomizes much of what frustrates the site's detractors. The article's author, an affable nineteen-year-old college sophomore named Zayne Grantham, tells us he still thinks Brady is an overrated "system quarterback" who largely succeeds thanks to his team's capable defenses. (The New England Patriots advanced to the Super Bowl last year with the thirty-first-ranked defense in terms of passing and overall yardage in a thirty-two-team league.) But even Grantham doesn't believe Brady to be history's most overrated quarterback: "In hindsight, I may not have used that headline. I'll be one of the first to say he's one of the best quarterbacks we've ever seen."

And there you have it: Anyone baited into responding to these hyperbolic stories finds themselves debating a nonstarter argument with a teenager from Shreveport who doesn't even buy the premise of his own article.

But people do debate. They do comment. And they do read. That story has generated better than 14,000 pageviews and more than 440 comments—no "Twenty Most Boobtastic Athletes" tally, but not bad at all. "One of the goals is to get a lot of people to read your articles," Grantham explains. "That headline, by the nature of the words, brought in plenty of people."

Serving up red meat, sports-radio-style, is viewed as something of a necessary evil. One former writer recalls that, upon joining *Bleacher Report*, he rationalized, "You have to put out of your mind that they're obsessed with pageviews until you rise high enough to say, 'Now I can start focusing on quality.'"

He was promoted to featured columnist—but was disappointed to learn his new job largely consisted of providing copy for his editors' prewritten headlines. And these are often slideshows, several paragraphs of text woven around a photo or video and repeated fifty times. "When they started paying me, I began doing 95 percent slideshows," says former featured columnist Jeff Shull, who spent four years writing for *Bleacher Report*. "I did 496 articles, so probably over 400 of them are slideshows."

Even *Bleacher Report*'s "lead writers"—established and respected Web authors hired in the last year as part of the ostensible drive for quality and paid five-figure salaries—say they too are assigned prewritten headlines. "It's exactly the kinds of things *Bleacher Report* has become famous and infamous for, the things serious sports fans roll their eyes at: slideshows, top five this, top ten that," says one prominent writer. The prewritten headlines, adds another high-level writer, are "asserting why someone is the best player when he's not; why the obviously best player isn't really the best; why somebody is going to take over in the next year when it's implausible he would—basically, asserting something that's unlikely, giving it a good hook, and getting someone to click on it."

That's the technique generations of bloviating sports scribes have used to stir the pot. But Bleacher Report's lead writers didn't think this is what they were being brought in to do. "Why pay me lots of money to dumb down my content?" asks one. "They could have used unpaid people to do this."

This way, however, *Bleacher Report* doubles its pleasure by enjoying the cachet of employing high-end writers while raking in the hits from low-end material. "They can have it both ways," says one prominent writer. "An unsophisticated sports fan clicks on the story and it validates what he thinks. A sophisticated fan is so angry at the dumb headline, he can't help but hate-click on it." When this writer questioned the length of an assignment, he was told that it was determined by "our computer model."

It's a model that's computing well for *Bleacher Report*, if not every writer. "I started out being worried that joining up with *Bleacher Report* would make other people think I'm a fraud and a hack," says one high-level writer. "Now I'm worried I have become that fraud and hack."

And if he leaves, there is an army of writers ready to replace him.

• • •

Readers don't just visit *Bleacher Report*. They're funneled right into the site's revenue streams. "I know people who loathe *Bleacher Report* but are heavy users of its newsletter or app," says Ben Koo, the CEO of Bloguin, a network of sports blogs. "The inbox is the new social network for content companies."

Visitors to the site are aggressively pestered to sign up for team-specific newsletters or the Team Stream mobile app—which updates fans in real-time with articles about their chosen team pulled from around the web. *Bleacher Report* has established a direct, regular line of communication with millions of highly specified ad targets—and will continue to do so even if, in the future, the site is unable to lean so heavily on Google. "People undervalue the app and newsletters," continues Koo. "I think it's worth a quarter of Turner's acquisition price."

The site's Web dominance is woven into its very fabric. Online marketer and SEO expert Hugo Guzman points out that *Bleacher Report*'s "site architecture lends itself to SEO. They built a site to facilitate search engines spidering through and picking up all the different article pages and category pages." This, he notes, is a marked contrast to the legacy media sites that break the stories *Bleacher Report* goes on to dominate. Many of the nation's most prominent journalistic outlets are "on website platforms that were not built with SEO in mind. They were built when that was not even a factor." News sites were constructed to display stories. *Bleacher Report* is built to disperse them.

Guzman rattles off the "best practices" technical elements that have enabled *Bleacher Report*'s ascent: "Internal linking architecture!" "Metadata!" "Server-side elements!" He pauses and laughs. "I can guarantee you that there are other publications out there that have frameworks on par with *Bleacher Report*'s," he says. "So, ultimately, what's their biggest differentiator? Free content!" *Bleacher Report*'s volunteer army generates scads of material—and the money the site doesn't spend on writers is spent to move the company where it wants to go.

It couldn't get there, however, without addressing the pitfalls of crowdsourcing and lowest-common-denominator crap Kaufman mentioned to Google. So, in the last two years, the site has worked to rehabilitate its image: Would-be writers must gain admittance via a process that rejects seventeen out of every twenty applicants. Lead writers and knowledgeable featured columnists have been added to the roster, and many of the site's early contributors have been bounced. "A few years ago I couldn't look at their site without my eyes bleeding and my head pounding," says veteran sports journalist Kevin Blackistone. These days, "That doesn't happen with the same frequency." It's hard to argue *Bleacher Report* hasn't improved—but it's impossible to say it hasn't improved its curb appeal. This is what enabled its acquisition by Turner—and what may enable the amalgamated entity to strip the "Worldwide Leader in Sports" mantle from ESPN.

Turner, unlike ESPN, Fox Sports, or Comcast, lacked a major sports Web destination. Now it owns the no. 3 sports website in the realm. And with a hulking new digital platform on which to sell ads, Turner has a new method of making money. This would provide a leg up in bidding for whatever comes next. "By expanding their set of assets, it allows Turner to go after things, and, perhaps, successfully obtain things they couldn't otherwise," says Ed Desser, president of Desser Sports Media.

Before this deal, Desser continues, *Bleacher Report* was "just another aggregator of customer-created content." But now? The wave of the future. No media outlet can ignore the allures of crowdsourcing—or dismiss out of hand the rewards of reverse-engineering content.

"There was a time when the traditional media viewed new media as not up to their standards. But that time has passed," Desser notes. "Tastes change. Look at TV. Think about how much stuff would never have been on thirty years ago: vulgar language, sexual situations, eating bugs. It's all out there now. We're a long way from Ozzie and Harriet."

Or, as *Bleacher Report* puts it, "If you really want to maximize your fanbase, your best bet is to give the people what they want."

In an era when those who have more get more, when so many have been forced to recalibrate their expectations, it's hard not to see *Bleacher Report* as epitomizing more than just sportswriting on the Internet. Those on the top have profited handsomely. For the folks whose work powers the site, however, *Bleacher Report* is often the best opportunity they can find and a springboard to diminished dreams.

Drew Laskey is an occasional writer and onetime copyediting intern for *Bleacher Report*—and a full-time North Carolina basketball fanatic. He is now a copy editor for *Journatic*, an outfit recently popped on *This American Life* for using fake bylines to obscure that many of its articles were penned in foreign countries by nonnative English speakers paid a pittance. Laskey says the articles he copyedits at *Journatic*, incidentally, are "much cleaner through and through" than those at *Bleacher Report*.

He still remains an unabashed fan of the site. "If you take *Bleacher Report* seriously and you have the talent and the ability to learn and take constructive criticism, *Bleacher Report* can pay off for you," he says. "I've seen it pay off. People have gone on to other websites." He hopes it'll propel him to an internship writing for *InsideCarolina.com*. This unpaid position would "be my dream job. To have a payment attached to it would be surreal. It's something I can't even fathom."

Bleacher Report alum Lukas Hardonk is one of those writers who've gone on to paying gigs elsewhere. He's now the managing editor of the *Maple Leafs Central* blog and a contributing editor of *TheHockeyWriters.com*. "As bad a rap as *Bleacher Report* gets, it's really tremendous what they did for me," he says. Hardonk wrote three years for the site but found there were only so many slideshows in his system. By 2011, he realized he'd outgrown *Bleacher Report*. Still, "they kickstarted my career."

It'll be interesting to see where that career goes after the seventeen-year-old finishes his senior year of high school.

The New Yorker

While the future of digital journalism may not look all that rosy, the old print world isn't always such a terribly pretty sight either. Ken Auletta takes us to India—one of the few places on earth where newspapers still thrive—for a peek inside the newspaper empire of the Jain brothers, Samir and Vineet. Their company owns, among other entities, the *Times of India,* the largest circulation English-language newspaper in the world. Their profit margins are fat, but their business model relies on dubious journalistic ethics. Why simply run stories about movie stars and their films, for instance, when you can charge the studios for them?

Ken Auletta

13. Why India's Newspaper Industry Is Thriving

The square that borders the Dadar Railway Station is the largest of sixty-five newspaper-delivery depots in Mumbai. At four a.m., forty trucks and vans packed with newspapers and magazines have parked and slid open their back doors; the trash-strewn streets are otherwise deserted, and the loudest noise comes from the cawing of crows. During the next few hours, 231,000 newspapers will be unloaded, half of them published by Bennett, Coleman & Company, Ltd., India's dominant media conglomerate. Venders cluster around the back of each truck, handing up wads of rupees to the driver in exchange for their daily stacks of newspapers and magazines. Afterward, with helpers, they sit on the sidewalk inserting supplements and sorting the stacks into neat bundles. Then they pass the bundles to deliverymen—there are some 8,300 in Mumbai—who pack as many papers as they can onto motorbikes, rickshaws, bicycles, and shoulders and set out to slip them one by one under or beside the doors of the city's residents.

India is one of the few places on earth where newspapers still thrive. In the United States in the past five years newspaper-advertising revenues have plunged by fifty percent, to 24 billion dollars, according to the Newspaper Association of America, and net-profit margins now average 5 percent. In India, which has a population of a billion two hundred million, newspaper circulation and advertising are rising. There are an estimated 80,000 individual newspapers, 85 percent of which are printed in one of India's twenty-two official regional languages, and the circulation of English-language newspapers is expanding by about 1.5 percent annually. Many non-English newspapers are growing three times as fast, as about twenty million more Indians become literate each year. But, because English-language papers attract an upscale readership, they draw 70 percent of the available ad dollars.

The *Times of India* has a daily circulation of four million three hundred thousand, the largest of any English-language newspaper in the world. The *Economic Times* is the world's second most widely read English-language business newspaper, after the *Wall Street Journal*. Both are owned by B.C.C.L., along with eleven other newspapers, eighteen magazines, two satellite news channels, an English-language movie channel, a Bollywood news-and-life-style channel, a radio network, Internet sites, and outdoor billboards. The company generates annual revenues of a billion and a half dollars, a paltry sum compared with an organization like News Corp., which produces thirty-three billion. But the pretax profit margin of B.C.C.L.'s newspapers is a remarkable 25 to 30 percent. The company commands half of all English-language print advertising, half of English-language-newspaper readers, a third of TV news-channel ads, and almost a quarter of all radio and Web ads. It is the largest outdoor advertising company in India. The company has no debt.

One reason that Indian newspapers thrive is the absence of digital competition. Less than 10 percent of the population has access to the Internet, and, with two-thirds of the population surviving on less than two dollars per day, expensive smartphones and tablets aren't about to replace print media as the news-reading platform of choice. Also, Indian papers are cheap, costing between five and ten cents daily. There are few newsstands in

India—only five percent of papers are sold over the counter—and home delivery is free, paid for by the publishers. The actual price of each paper is even lower, because of what Indians call raddi, their recycling program. Subscribers save their newspapers, which are picked up by raddiwallahs each month; the customer receives about ten cents per pound, and the raddiwallahs sell the bundles back to the paper companies to be recycled.

The success of Indian papers, especially the *Times of India*, is also a product of their content and the unorthodox philosophy behind it. B.C.C.L. is a family-owned business, run by Samir Jain, the vice chairman, and his brother, Vineet Jain, the managing director. "Both of us think out of the box," Vineet told me on a recent afternoon. "We don't go by the traditional way of doing business." His company's dominance can be explained simply, he added, though its methods are not taught in most Western journalism schools. "We are not in the newspaper business, we are in the advertising business," he said. With newspapers sold so cheaply and generating little circulation revenue, newspapers depend more on ad revenue, he said, and, "if 90 percent of your revenues come from advertising, you're in the advertising business."

Jain sat behind a small wooden desk in an office the size of a large closet; the windows were covered by white shades, drawn against June's monsoon rains. At forty-six, Jain looked professorial, in dark slacks and a pale-blue dress shirt, black-framed eyeglasses, and short, parted hair that has begun to turn gray. "Earlier, the newspapers were written more for the intellectual elites," he said. "It was too serious at some point. It was not relevant to our readers."

Jain picked up a copy of the *Times of India* from his desk. The front page of the paper displays not six or seven stories but ten or eleven, plus a jumble of small boxes containing disparate news items, with no large photographs or design elements to provide a sense of neatness and symmetry. Jain flipped through the front section, which featured a mixture of national, local, and international news: a monsoon alert, graft charges against a presidential hopeful, a Mumbai train collision, and a story about the Taliban's praise for India's refusal to get militarily involved in Afghanistan. Investigative stories are rare. The *Times of India* sees itself not as an agenda setter but as a bulletin board, a mirror to what happened yesterday. The first section had many ads, and there were several advertising supplements.

The paper's innovations begin in its eight-page second section, which is titled the Bombay Times but is known in-house as Page Three. The section brims with color pictures of seductive women and muscular men, along with stories of Bollywood stars, handsome cricket pros, and international celebrities. The lead story that day described how aspiring actors, including a sultry Saiyami Kher, "are keen to start their innings in Bollywood." Jain explained that, like the surrounding stories, it was written by members of the reporting staff and paid for by the celebrities or their publicists. Most of the section was filled with ads or with stories that were ads; a similar section appears in each city in which the Times is published. An internal company report in June lauded the strategy as "so important that today nearly all Bollywood movie releases pay for promotional coverage ahead of movie releases, and actors/actresses pay to develop their brand through coverage in the paper." Tucked under the section's masthead, four words in small type inform the reader that the contents are an "advertorial, entertainment promotional feature." Jain insisted that this meets the transparency test. "It's on my masthead," he said. "It says 'advertorial' clearly. All newspapers in the world do advertorials." But in the Jains' newspapers the advertorials are written by staff reporters, and a reader needs a magnifying glass to be alerted.

Jain got the idea for this section several years ago, after reading an interview with Richard Branson, the owner of the Virgin Group, in which Branson remarked that the reason he parachutes from airplanes and performs similar stunts is that, with this free publicity, he annually saves his company tens of millions of dollars in advertising. "When I read it, I said, 'Oh, my God, eureka—I'm stupid!'" Jain said. "Why these guys are not advertising in my paper is because I'm giving them free P.R." If a Bollywood studio or a car company sponsored a fashion show, the show won't be ignored by the paper, Jain said, but the name of the studio or the company won't appear. "They are promoting a brand," Jain said. "Pay me for it." The Jains call this ad-sales initiative Medianet, and Jain contends that it is more honest than what existed before, when reporters were slipped envelopes with cash or accepted favors in exchange for positive coverage. Why shouldn't the paper, instead of the reporters, collect the bounty? Medianet generates about 4 percent of the company's revenues, a sum that is expected to double within a few years.

Another innovation, conceived by his brother Samir, is referred to as "private treaties" or "brand capital." Under this program, the newspaper offers a deal to smaller companies: it accepts ads in exchange for equity in a company. B.C.C.L. insists on one-third cash as a down payment and accepts real-estate ownership in lieu of equity; the resulting ads appear throughout the paper. The company has a stake in more than 350 companies, and this accounts for up to 15 percent of its ad revenues.

In the United States, several years ago, editors of the *New York Times* and the *Wall Street Journal* debated whether readers would be served, or journalism harmed, if the business department sold discreet ads that appeared on the papers' front pages. At the *Times of India*, or the Times Group, as the company is often called, the business side need not ask permission. The entire front page might be sold as an ad, for $450,000. Or two-thirds of it might be sold, or half, or a wraparound banner might be attached to the page; or the front-page ad might be followed by another, on page 2, with the normal page 1 buried inside the paper on page 3. For a hefty fee, the *Times of India* will even change the name on its masthead to, say, Wakudoki India (as it did on June 21), a play on a Toyota ad campaign that claims that the car "makes your heart go waku-doki." Samir and Vineet Jain make no pretense that what they do is a public calling. Rather than worry about editorial independence and the wall between the newsroom and the sales department, they propose that one secret to a thriving newspaper business lies in dismantling that wall.

• • •

Samir Jain may be one of the more unusual media executives in the world; certainly, he is one of the least visible. He has never granted an interview and made only a brief appearance, two decades ago, in a chapter on the Indian press, in Nicholas Coleridge's book *Paper Tigers*. Indian news-service photographers are under standing orders to snap his picture, but they rarely succeed, because he attends few public functions. His wife, Meera, with whom he had an arranged marriage when he was twenty-seven, is said to have no interest in the business and keeps an even lower profile. I met Samir two years ago, during one of his trips to the United States to speak with people in the media. He told me about the unusual ad-sales strategies he had implemented and of his newspapers' vibrant growth. If I visited India, I asked, would he talk with me about his business? He said that he would.

He didn't. Although Vineet and *Times* executives generously cooperated, Samir declined to meet. "The reason he probably doesn't give interviews is because he doesn't want the fame,"

Vineet told me. "It doesn't drive him. He doesn't want to be covered in newspapers and talked about. He'd rather be humble." The brothers are both press-shy. "On a rational basis, they believe we should not explain to our competitors what we are doing," Ravi Dhariwal, the company's CEO, said. "They will follow us eventually."

Samir Jain is fifty-eight, but he looks older, his once stark-black hair now gray. He follows a strict vegetarian diet and has a slim frame and face; his clothes tend toward the baggy, his buttoned shirt collars loose. He often speaks in parables. Namita Gokhale, a well-connected novelist who codirects the Jaipur Literature Festival, once sat next to Jain at a dinner. Jain told Gokhale, "I think history doesn't exist, and if I were prime minister I would ban the study of history." Gokhale devilishly responded, "What I'll do is give you two tight slaps and a kick, and if you can't remember it I'll agree there's no history!" Jain politely smiled, turned away, and ignored her the rest of the evening.

Jain spends about half the year at the company's offices in New Delhi and Mumbai and divides the rest between international travel and spiritual retreats, particularly in the holy city of Haridwar, a six-hour drive north of New Delhi, where he has a home. Here he and fellow-congregants wash away their sins in the River Ganges, do yoga, meditate, and chant.

Inside the company, an aura has enveloped Jain; when he enters a room, executives rise. They know not to interrupt him during his daily nap at 3 p.m. or when he is engaged with his "spiritual family." They groan when they are invited to an event at his house, knowing they will not be served alcohol. But he is not a forbidding figure; he always invites visiting *Times* executives to board at his home, sharing family meals. "The first filter he uses in any decision is 'Will this be spiritually OK? Will I be able to go to my guru?'" Dhariwal told me with admiration. "He discusses a lot with his guru, I think. And if his guru doesn't bless it, I think he just drops it."

• • •

The *Times of India* has belonged to the Jain family for more than sixty years. It was started in 1838, by British owners, then swallowed five decades later by a joint British holding company, Bennett, Coleman & Company. Not until 1946, a year before India won its independence from Britain, did an Indian, Ramkrishna Dalmia, purchase the paper and the holding company. An ardent nationalist, Dalmia was a champion of the independence movement. He was also a man of many whims. He fathered eighteen children with six wives, three of whom lived concurrently in separate homes. Dalmia was more interested in politics than in newspapers, and he entrusted the company to his son-in-law Shanti Prasad Jain, the grandfather of Samir and Vineet Jain. Under India's first prime minister, Jawaharlal Nehru, Dalmia was prosecuted for embezzlement and fraud. When he was released after two years in prison, in 1964, his son-in-law and daughter rebuffed his efforts to resume command of the company, creating a rift between the Dalmias and the Jains.

Shanti Prasad's son, Ashok Jain, took over in the 1960s; in 1975, Ashok's eldest son, Samir, joined the company as a junior executive, after receiving a university degree from St. Stephen's College, in New Delhi. During the next seven years, Samir concentrated on the media business, while his father focused on running the more than ten companies that made up the nonpublishing parts of B.C.C.L., including cement, jute, and textile businesses. By the late eighties, as vice chairman, Samir had assumed command of the company. In the nineties, his father, pursued by government charges of fraud and seeking medical treatment for a weak heart, left for the United States; Vineet joined Samir in 1993, as the deputy managing director, after graduating from the American College of Switzerland. Although the brothers confer on all points of the business, Samir concentrates on newspapers and broad strategy while Vineet focuses on television, radio, and the Internet. Company executives rarely address Samir by name, preferring instead to call him V.C.; they address Vineet as M.D.

When Samir Jain first took over, the various businesses of B.C.C.L. were in decline. With national literacy rising, he decided to gamble on newspapers. He led long strategy sessions. "His mind was very clear about what business we were in," Bhaskar Das, who became Samir's principal sales executive, told me. "We knew we were in the business of aggregating a quality audience. Before that, we just sold advertising space." Das, who joined the Times Group in 1980, is a member of the company's board of directors and now serves as president and principal secretary to Vineet. He is tall and lean, with a chiseled jaw and silver hair that falls to his shoulders, and wears designer glasses. "We are a derived business," Das said. "When the advertiser becomes successful, we are successful. The advertiser wants us to facilitate consumption."

Jain encouraged his executives to push back as he honed plans to forge a stronger business. "He's one of the most challenging and stimulating men I ever met," T. N. Ninan, a former editor of the *Economic Times*, who is usually a critic, said. "His mind is active. He reads people's motives very well." Jain recruited managers from consumer-product companies like PepsiCo and Unilever and invited them to attend editorial meetings. Credit cards, which, at the time, were hard to get in India, were secured for members of the sales team but not for the editorial team. This was Jain's way of downgrading elitist newspaper editors who might want to leave a mark on the paper, thereby constraining his ability to make business decisions. "Editors tended to be pompous fellows thundering from the pulpit, speaking in eighty-word sentences," Rahul Kansal, Jain's executive president and brand chief, told me. "They saw themselves as part of nation building, as part of a big dialogue. It did not connect too well with younger Indians."

Samir Jain pressed his executives to create a more youthful paper. Articles would be shorter, sentences snappier; there would be more sports, less politics, more Bollywood, more color, lower necklines, and few book reviews. "You can't write about Mahatma Gandhi's birthday for a fifteen-year-old," Das said. "You can give a passing reference for the grandfather." He added, "Everyone wants to feel young, think like the young. Youth is an aspirational band, not a demographic band. So if you make the paper youthful it satisfies everyone."

• • •

"Aspirational" is a word one hears often around the *Times* offices, as a way of characterizing the sunny outlook that the Jains say their readers want. "We keep saying the glass is half full, not half empty," Vineet said. Poverty, given that it's not a condition to which one aspires, receives scant coverage. In the early 1990s, Palagummi Sainath, now a rural-affairs editor at the *Hindu*, wrote several dozen newspaper reports on rural poverty as a freelancer at the *Times*. Later, when he spent four years living among the Dalit community, often described as the "untouchables," he didn't bother submitting the pieces he wrote about them to the *Times*. He recalls a *Times* editor once asking him why he was pitching a story on rural poverty: "How is this relevant to our readers?"

By the mid-nineties, the *Times* referred to itself, as Das did in his conversation with me, "not as a newspaper but as a brand," with target audiences that advertisers coveted. Although there is no absence of bleak news in the Times—railway accidents, terrorist attacks, bureaucracy, corruption"—our general take on life, and it comes back to our editorial philosophy, is one of optimism," Dhariwal told me. When a tsunami struck south India, the *Times* "tried hard to find some good stories there"—heroic rescues, families reunited. Recently, when Rajat Gupta, who was born in India, was convicted in New York of insider trading, the lead story on page 1 of the *Times* focused on the human dimension and was headlined "Jurors Were in Tears as They Held Gupta Guilty." Shekhar Gupta, the editor in chief of the *Indian Express*, a more hard-hitting paper, said that when he and Samir Jain encounter each other Jain usually hands him underlined copies of Hindu scripture and "affectionately" admonishes him that "my publication is too dark."

Little more than a decade after Samir Jain assumed control, the company had become the largest media corporation in India. "I would give all credit to my brother," Vineet Jain told me. The company also benefitted from a warmer economic climate; starting in 1991, India privatized many industries and reduced regulations. The government would continue to be the sole provider of news that aired on state radio; elsewhere, market forces were usually allowed to dominate the media.

Although the Jains were friendly to advertisers, they played hardball. "We tell advertisers that if you want to be in the *Times of India* you have to drop our Marathi competitors and take the ads to our Marathi paper," a senior executive, who asked not to be named, said. "We told advertisers that if you want the *Times of India* in Mumbai you drop the *Hindustan Times*." When the salmon-colored *Financial Times* prepared to expand into the Indian market, Samir Jain worried that it would undercut his salmon-colored *Economic Times*. So in 1993 he registered the term "Financial Times" as a trademark of his company and declared that if the British paper entered the country it would be violating his intellectual property. Two decades later, the case is still winding its way through the Indian court system.

Jain's artillery against existing competitors involved reducing newspaper prices. In 1994, when the top-selling paper in New

Delhi was the *Hindustan Times,* Jain slashed the price of the *Times of India* by a third, to one and a half rupees, or about three cents. He took care to build a bigger ad-sales force in advance because he knew that with lower circulation revenue the paper would need more ad income. By 1998, the *Hindustan Times* had slipped to second place in New Delhi. When Jain cut the price of the paper in Bangalore to a single rupee, Siddharth Varadarajan, one of his editors and the current editor in chief of the *Hindu,* told him, "This is predatory pricing." Jain responded, "Absolutely not. By lowering the price, I am expanding the number of readers." The gamble paid off: home subscriptions to the *Times* increased fivefold.

The inspiration for one of Samir Jain's more innovative pricing strategies was the zoo in Calcutta, his home town. As he walked by on a Monday, normally a slow day after a busy weekend, he was surprised to see a long line. To boost attendance, the zoo had lowered its admission price that day, he learned, which gave him an idea: one day a week, on Wednesdays, he would halve the price of the paper. Circulation rose, so Jain introduced "invitation pricing," lowering the price three days a week in certain locations. The strategies pioneered by Samir Jain at the *Times of India*—setting aggressive prices, employing focus groups to learn what readers crave, and, above all, treating advertisers as the primary customer—have since become standard in the industry. "His legacy is really making this business a profitable business," Sanjoy Narayan, the editor in chief of the *Hindustan Times,* conceded. "Before him the newspaper business was run almost like a nonprofit." He added, "He's been emulated by everyone else."

• • •

The Jain family is very close. With Samir's twenty-seven-year-old daughter, Trishla, and her husband, Satyan Gajwani, the brothers share a Gatsby-like home on three and a half acres in the exclusive New Delhi area off the Motilal Nehru Marg road. Their neighbors are billionaires, celebrities, and government officials, who live in "bungalows" hidden by high walls and tall, leafy jacaranda, acacia, gulmohar, and neem trees. A visitor to the Jain home is greeted at the dimly lit stone entrance by a statue of Ganesha, the elephant god, revered as the "remover of obstacles" and worshipped by many Hindus as the supreme deity. Inside are three living areas, with two separate kitchens, dining rooms, and living rooms. Samir's living room is more formal, with wooden floors covered with dark Persian rugs, walls adorned with centuries-old Indian and European paintings, and stained-glass windows. The rooms of Vineet and of Trishla and Gajwani are brighter and more modern. On the top floor, Trishla paints in a studio, seeking to insinuate into her paintings, collages, and sculptures text from the English literature she studied at Stanford.

The matriarch, Indu Jain, who holds the title of chairman, resides nearby, in the home in which the Jain brothers grew up. (Their father died, in 1999, of heart failure at a Cleveland hospital.) Indu has also embraced gurus, but Vineet has not. "She keeps pushing me to join," he told me. "Once in a while, to make her happy, I'll come. But I stay away from gurus. I'm not going to waste three hours listening to a discussion every day."

Close associates say that Samir's involvement with a guru and his ashram deepened after a series of family tragedies. A few years after his father's death, Samir's teenage son choked to death on a piece of food. The following year, his sister Nandita, who also worked at the company, died in a helicopter crash. "You never talk about death with Mr. Jain," a senior executive said. Not because he is uncaring, he added, but because Jain avoids the topic. The *Times* has adopted a similar stance. "We don't have many pictures of death," Vineet said. "We don't put death too much on the front page." As Samir's spirituality increased, his schedule became something of a mystery, even to fellow executives. Tom Glocer, the former CEO of Thomson Reuters, whose company had a joint television news venture with the *Times of India*, was impressed with the management of the company. Yet he had met Samir Jain only once. "Whenever we were supposed to have a meeting, I was told he was off to some shrine," Glocer said.

As Samir receded from view, Vineet assumed more responsibilities. In 2003, he helped launch Medianet, their venture to induce celebrities and brands to pay to have news written about them; two years later, he helped implement private treaties. He has also focused on transforming B.C.C.L. into a multimedia company, making investments in radio, television, and the Internet.

Because these businesses are mostly in Mumbai, Vineet spends more time in that city; he shares a house with his brother there, too. Although Vineet insisted that he and Samir do not determine content, he also said, "I am the content architect." He takes credit for the idea of running small, boxed editorials, under the rubric Times View, alongside some front-page stories, as a way of proposing a solution, he said, and because "the editorial page is only read by 5 percent of readers." He does not worry that including editorials with news stories might lead readers to think the news has been slanted to conform to either a commercial or a political interest. He extended the innovation to the *Economic Times* this year. When B.C.C.L. relaunched its twenty-four-hour satellite news channel, in 2006, Vineet spent weeks laboring over the name, finally settling on Times Now. He wanted talking heads to argue, not discuss. He wanted "a breathless nowness and immediacy, not leisurely features and analysis," according to *The Times of Media*, the company's official history. "It is about creating the illusion of breaking news, even if it is in fact news that's already been broken."

Vineet and Samir share a belief that government affairs and politics should not be the focus of their lives or of their newspapers. Even critics praise them for having no political agenda to advance their business. Hobnobbing with government leaders holds no interest for the Jains. When President Obama visited India, Vineet declined an invitation to a state dinner. "What will I do?" he said to me. "It's just meeting somebody, shaking hands. What's the point?" Besides, he added, "the closer I get to politicians, the more they'll interfere. It's a Catch-22. Politicians are no one's friends." If he befriended them, they'd call and complain about a story, or pressure him to run a different story. "You start getting calls every day. We don't get any calls. It's so easy," he said, smiling.

Vineet said that he is comfortable thinking of himself as the younger brother. "I think of one hundred small ideas, he thinks of three big ideas," he said. Sometimes Samir imparts fatherly advice: "He would say, 'Relax. Work less. Have a good balance. What are you chasing money for?'" But, Vineet said, "for me, it's not work. I love creating something. It's so much fun—I hardly take holidays. For me, this is a holiday." Unlike Samir, Vineet is divorced and was often seen in the company of beautiful women; people who don't know him sometimes mistake him for a playboy. "Samir is into God," an Indian publishing executive says. "Vineet is into women."

• • •

Although blurring business and editorial content has clearly worked well for the business side of the Jains' enterprises, critics are quick to point out what has been lost. "Samir Jain is the sharpest and most creative mind in media in the country," Shekhar Gupta, of the *Indian Express*, told me. But Gupta lamented the paid news and the private treaties and the power that the

Jains have granted advertisers. "The seed of the problem lies in the idea that you call focus groups, where you figure out what it is they like to read in a newspaper and then tailor the content accordingly," Gupta said. For standing by his principles, however, and not engaging in similar practices, Gupta has paid a price: the circulation of the *Express* has not risen above 300,000 in the past decade, and he admits to making only "modest" profits.

The poor quality of the journalism attracts the heaviest criticism. After graduating from the Columbia University School of Journalism and working for almost five years as a copy editor at the *Wall Street Journal*, Naresh Fernandes returned to India in 2002 as a news editor for the *Times*. "This wasn't the paper I had idolized all my life," he said one evening over a beer at the worn Press Club, in an area of Mumbai where reporters gather to drink. Rain pounded on a canvas roof. Fernandes recalled admonishing his reporters in a memo, "A quote is exactly what somebody said and the way he said it." A fellow editor dressed him down: "You're bringing American standards to the newspaper." Eight months later, Fernandes resigned.

Certain biases are baked into the coverage. The *Times* shows a greater interest in government corruption than in corporate corruption. In 2005, the Honda Motors plant in Gurgaon experienced an eight-month-long conflict between management and nonunionized workers over wages and work conditions, provoking violence and charges of police brutality. A doctoral study of the *Times* coverage by Vinod K. Jose, an editor at the magazine *The Caravan*, showed that the paper aired the concerns of Honda and the harm done to India's investment climate while largely ignoring the issues raised by workers. Ajit Balakrishnan, the founder of Rediff, an early and successful Indian portal and e-commerce site, sees the focus on government corruption as a dodge by the wealthier, English-speaking classes to avoid issues of real substance, like primary education and health care. The elites are "constantly living under fear that as democracy deepens, and people vote independently, their own role and comfortable place in society is eroding," Balakrishnan said. Critics claim that the company's paid news and private treaties skew its coverage and shield its newspaper advertisers from scrutiny. Vineet Jain calmly insisted that a wall does exist between sales and the newsroom, and that the paper does not give favorable coverage to the company's business partners. "Our editors don't know who we have," Jain said, although he later acknowledged that all private-treaty clients are listed on the company's website.

Aroon Purie, the CEO of the India Today Group, which includes dozens of magazines, four TV news channels, several radio stations and Web portals, and one newspaper, believes the Jains have granted too much power to advertisers. "They have set standards where advertisers can ask for anything," he told me. Brazen advertisers have said to him directly, "If the *Times of India* does it, why can't you do it?" He described interviewing *Times* reporters for jobs, "and they told me they couldn't write this story" because the subjects were private-treaty clients. His publications enter into barter deals with companies, Purie said, but "we don't say we won't write negatively about you."

In a 2010 interview with the magazine *Outlook*, Dhariwal, the company's CEO, said that each partner in a private treaty signs a contract that stipulates "that he will not get favorable editorial coverage." He added, "Give me one instance where our private-treaty investment has had favorable editorial mention, or a story has been suppressed."

The Hoot, a website devoted to media criticism, has pointed out one such instance. When an elevator operated by a construction company putting up a nineteen-story luxury apartment complex crashed in Bengaluru, killing two workers and injuring seven, the *Times* story did not include the name of the construction company, Sobha Developers, a private-treaty partner, "unlike all the other English and Kannada newspapers which explicitly did so," the site noted. "The third casualty in the accident" was "honest reporting and freedom of the press."

Palagummi Sainath, of the *Hindu*, offered an example of how the *Times* sometimes bends news to favor its advertisers. A full-page article, titled "Reaping Gold Through Bt Cotton," published on August 28, 2011, declared that Monsanto's genetically modified Bt cotton seeds have "led to a social and economic transformation of the villages." It appeared to be a news story, complete with a byline, but close inspection of the small print revealed that it was a "marketing feature," paid for by Monsanto. Reporting for the *Hindu*, Sainath noted that the advertisement had run "word for word" three years earlier as a news story in the Nagpur edition of the *Times*. And, he said, both the story and the ad were misleading: in fact, the Bt seeds did not grow cotton as promised; the land lay fallow, and farmers went bankrupt. Since 2003, more than thirty-three thousand farmers had committed suicide in the state of Maharashtra, including nine in the "model farming village" depicted in the story and the ad.

• • •

The business strategies embraced by the Jains have gradually permeated India's media industry. In 2010, a report by a subcommittee of India's Press Council, a toothless body largely composed of press potentates and politicians, found that the *Times*' Medianet had spurred an "epidemic" of paid news among newspapers and some of the more than five hundred television channels. "In the 1980s, after Samir Jain became the executive head of Bennett, Coleman Company Limited, publishers of the *Times of India* group of publications, the rules of the Indian media game began to change," the report concluded. They labeled many of the practices that followed as "extortionist," making clear that these were often criminal acts, as under-the-table payments were fraud, neither reported as income nor taxed. They recounted examples of local reporters selling ads to the same people they covered and receiving commissions on the sales and described a common practice in which many rural newspapers issued an unusual advertising rate card to political candidates. In a representative case, for $40,000, a candidate could arrange to have positive stories written about him for fifteen days; $30,000 bought ten days. Negative stories about one's opponent would cost extra. If a candidate paid nothing, the newspaper ignored him.

When the report was submitted to the Press Council, the thirty-member council initially declined to release it, worried that it would undermine the credibility of publishers. Then it published a small part of the report, expunging names and other specifics. "So the whole objective of naming and shaming was lost," Paranjoy Guha Thakurta, an independent journalist and one of the two authors of the report, told me. After more than a year, Thakurta and others finally managed to get the original report released in full. Even then, much of the Indian press had little to say about it. "In India, the print media doesn't write about itself," Sevanti Ninan, who has written for many Indian newspapers, and who, in 2001, founded the Hoot Web site, said. When it comes to self-criticism in the established press, Jonathan Shainin, an American-born editor at *The Caravan*, told me, it's "almost like an omerta."

Journalism in India can boast of many successes. The *Hindu* has twelve correspondents overseas, in addition to in-depth reporting on subjects like poverty. The *Hindu* and the *Express* reject paid news, as does the *Malayala Manorama*, a Malayalam-language paper, based in Kerala, which has the fourth-largest daily circulation in India. The *Times of India*'s New Delhi edition alone has a staff of 235. "I am a secret admirer of the *Times of India*," Krishna Prasad, one of the paper's fiercest critics and the editor in chief of *Outlook* acknowledged. "They are far less ideological than most newspapers in this country. On any given day, you get more variety, and on a big news day no one in this country covers the news in the three-hundred-and-sixty-degree fashion better than the *Times of India*. I think very few newspapers have the depth and breadth to match it."

Yet, by Western standards, the Indian press is not aggressive. Madhu Trehan, a Columbia School of Journalism graduate who was the founding editor of the magazine *India Today*, is an author and founder of Newslaundry, a website that seeks to critique the press. On her right shoulder is a small tattoo in blue ink: "OM?" It reminds her, she says, to "question everything." Trehan believes that Indian culture is hypocritically polite. "Harmony is more important than conflict," she said. "When children are honest, their father tells them they are being rude."

Darryl D'Monte, a Cambridge-educated editor and writer who once served in a senior editorial capacity at the *Times*, blames Samir Jain rather than culture for much of the industry's ethical weaknesses. "The *Times* has corrupted the entire face of Indian journalism, including television," he told me, noting that there is less international news, less coverage of the arts, less reporting on the many dire threats that India faces. Editors are preoccupied with what readers think they want to know about and with what advertisers want. "It's like a cancer that has spread," D'Monte said. "It is the most serious threat to journalism not only in this country but in the entire developing world."

• • •

One afternoon, Vineet Jain, sitting on a sofa in his home with a stack of work on the coffee table in front him, spoke of the challenges facing his company. He'd like to invest in more than three non-English newspapers; of the ten largest-selling newspapers in India, nine are published in regional languages. The *Times* ranks sixth in daily readership; the Hindi newspaper *Dainik Jagran* is first, with sixteen and a half million readers. Since there are fewer upscale readers than in the English-language press, advertising rates in regional-language papers are lower. But, because more copies are sold overall, there is more revenue.

Satyan Gajwani, Samir's son-in-law, entered the room, and Vineet invited him to join us at the dining-room table for a vegetarian lunch. Gajwani, twenty-seven and outgoing, had recently been promoted to supervisor of the company's digital businesses. He had met Trishla at Stanford, where he studied mathematical and computational sciences; his parents are from India, but he was born and raised in Miami. In 2007, as graduation neared, the couple planned to move to New York. After graduation, Samir took them to Maui for a week's vacation and talked to Gajwani about the family business. The couple moved into an apartment in the West Village. Trishla got a master's degree at Teachers College, and Gajwani went to work as an equity trader at Lehman Brothers. "He kept pitching me to move to India," Gajwani said. In December 2008, the couple moved into the Jain house in New Delhi. "I didn't know if I could live in India," Gajwani said, and he could not get engaged before he knew the answer. But his future father-in-law was persistent, treating him like a son, giving him a job and more and more responsibility at the company. The couple married in February 2011.

Vineet continued the strategic discussion, acknowledging that the company had come late to the television business. Because Samir is profoundly averse to debt, the company did not make a serious bid in 1992, when AsiaSat, a satellite service owned by Li Ka-shing, of Hong Kong, put a transponder up for sale in India. The prize went instead to Subhash Chandra, who went on to launch Zee Entertainment, and Zee's growth now exceeds that of the *Times*. Instead, the Jains own a twenty-four-hour news channel and a business channel, but these, and its English-movie and Bollywood channels, are niche businesses. They don't own a soap-opera channel that airs the kind of entertainment programming that attracts big audiences and advertising dollars. "We are always open to an acquisition," Vineet said. They have been in discussions with Sony, which owns a successful channel, in the hope of buying it or, perhaps, forming a partnership.

"In the long run, we might go public and use the funds to acquire TV stations," Vineet said. "We don't need money to grow publishing, but we do to grow television and Internet."

If the Jains do take their company public, the time to do so will be when their newspapers are expanding, so that investors will see B.C.C.L. as a growth stock. But that raises a question: How long before the Internet disrupts the newspaper industry in India? Vineet said that he believes newspapers in India will continue to grow for another fifteen years, abetted by expanding regional-language dailies. Today, the company's various sites—starting with its Yahoo-like IndiaTimes.com, which features health, travel, shopping, news, finance verticals, and e-mail—reach one-third of all Web users in India, with no pay walls. Quoting an April 2012, Comscore tally, Gajwani said that their digital ventures, which now employ 1,300 people, attract more unique visitors than any other Indian site.

Some in the Indian media believe that the Internet threat is more imminent. A case can be made that English-language newspapers in India are more vulnerable, which is the argument advanced by a senior editor at the *Times*. "Everyone who reads the *Times of India* is on the Net," he told me, and, with the price of smartphones steadily dropping, he expected the newspaper business to be disrupted more quickly. In fact, the editor said he believes that the "owners are deliberately underplaying the likely immediate impact of the Net, as they don't want advertisers and readers to go rushing off to the online edition." Gajwani agreed that the drop in the price of smartphones will spur additional online traffic, but he thinks that India's slow development of a 3G or 4G infrastructure to relay signals will stall the threat.

As servants brought glasses of sweet coconut water and sliced papaya, Vineet said that it was too confining to think of the *Times* as being in the journalism business. "If we say we're in the soap business, then you'll not do shampoo," he said. "If I say I am in the news business, then you won't do entertainment supplements. If you are editorially minded, you will make all the wrong decisions." It annoys him that so many newspapers in India have copied the *Times*' policy of exchanging ads for equity without openly admitting it. But he takes pride in having set the standard that most of the industry follows.

"Every competitor at first agitates over it, gets angry about it, and then quietly apes it," Krishna Prasad, the editor in chief of *Outlook* and the founder of *sans serif*, a media blog, told me. "Each player in the Indian market, whatever the language, is left with very few options And newspapers who say they are not doing it are basically lying." Prasad does not foresee any sort of awakening, in which Indian newspapers become more wary of the power wielded by advertisers and more receptive to the kinds of church-state ethical questions often posed in the West. "The toothpaste is out of the tube, and it can't be put back in," he said. "People have seen how sweet it is."

Los Angeles Times

This is the story of an elite group of flyers who paid hundreds of thousands of dollars in the eighties and nineties for the golden ticket of commercial airfare: an AAirpass for a lifetime of unlimited, free, first-class flights anywhere on the planet. Ken Bensinger reports on one man who flew round trip from Chicago to London sixteen times in less than a month and one who has racked up more than 30 million miles in the air. Another fell on hard times and started running a sort of airline within an airline, selling his companion seat to make ends meet. When American Airlines determines that the program is costing the company millions of dollars a year, it begins aggressively investigating its heaviest AAirpass users for fraud.

Ken Bensinger

14. The Frequent Fliers Who Flew Too Much

There are frequent fliers, and then there are people like Steven Rothstein and Jacques Vroom.

Both men bought tickets that gave them unlimited first-class travel for life on American Airlines. It was almost like owning a fleet of private jets.

Passes in hand, Rothstein and Vroom flew for business. They flew for pleasure. They flew just because they liked being on planes. They bypassed long lines, booked backup itineraries in case the weather turned, and never worried about cancellation fees. Flight crews memorized their names and favorite meals.

Each had paid American more than $350,000 for an unlimited AAirpass and a companion ticket that allowed them to take someone along on their adventures. Both agree it was the best purchase they ever made, one that completely redefined their lives.

In the 2009 film *Up in the Air*, the loyal American business traveler played by George Clooney was showered with attention after attaining 10 million frequent flier miles.

Rothstein and Vroom were not impressed.

"I can't even remember when I cracked 10 million," said Vroom, sixty-seven, a big, amiable Texan, who at last count had logged nearly four times as many. Rothstein, sixty-one, has notched more than 30 million miles.

But all the miles they and sixty-four other unlimited AAirpass holders racked up went far beyond what American had expected. As its finances began deteriorating a few years ago, the carrier took a hard look at the AAirpass program.

Heavy users, including Vroom and Rothstein, were costing it millions of dollars in revenue, the airline concluded.

The AAirpass system had rules. A special "revenue integrity unit" was assigned to find out whether any of these rules had been broken and whether the passes that were now such a drag on profits could be revoked.

Rothstein, Vroom, and other AAirpass holders had long been treated like royalty. Now they were targets of an investigation.

• • •

When American introduced the AAirpass in 1981, it saw a chance to raise millions of dollars for expansion at a time of record-high interest rates.

It was, and still is, offered in a variety of formats, including prepaid blocks of miles. But the marquee item was the lifetime unlimited AAirpass, which started at $250,000. Pass holders earned frequent flier miles on every trip and got lifetime memberships to the Admirals Club, American's VIP lounges. For an extra $150,000, they could buy a companion pass. Older fliers got discounts based on their age.

"We thought originally it would be something that firms would buy for top employees," said Bob Crandall, American's chairman and chief executive from 1985 to 1998. "It soon became apparent that the public was smarter than we were."

The unlimited passes were bought mostly by wealthy individuals, including baseball Hall of Famer Willie Mays, America's Cup skipper Dennis Conner, and computer magnate Michael Dell.

Mike Joyce of Chicago bought his in 1994 after winning a $4.25-million settlement after a car accident.

In one twenty-five-day span this year, Joyce flew round trip to London sixteen times, flights that would retail for more than $125,000. He didn't pay a dime.

"I love Rome, I love Sydney, I love Athens," Joyce said by phone from the Admirals Club at John F. Kennedy International Airport in New York. "I love Vegas and Frisco."

Rothstein had loved flying since his years at Brown University in Rhode Island, where he would buy a $99 weekend pass on Mohawk Air and fly to Buffalo, N.Y., just for a sandwich.

He bought his AAirpass in 1987 for his work in investment banking. After he added a companion pass two years later, it "kind of took hold of me," said Rothstein, a heavyset man with a kind smile.

He was airborne almost every other day. If a friend mentioned a new exhibit at the Louvre, Rothstein thought nothing of jetting from his Chicago home to San Francisco to pick her up and then fly to Paris together.

In July 2004, for example, Rothstein flew eighteen times, visiting Nova Scotia, New York, Miami, London, Los Angeles, Maine, Denver, and Fort Lauderdale, Fla., some of them several times over. The complexity of such itineraries would stump most travelers; happily for AAirpass holders, American provided elite agents able to solve the toughest booking puzzles.

They could help AAirpass customers make multiple reservations in case they missed a flight, or nab the last seat on the only plane leaving during a snowstorm. Some say agents even procured extra elbow room by booking an empty seat using a phony name on companion passes.

"I'd book it as Extra Lowe," said Peter Lowe, a motivational speaker from West Palm Beach, Fla. "They told me how to do it."

Vroom, a former mail-order catalog consultant, used his AAirpass to attend all his son's college football games in Maine. He built up so many frequent flier miles that he'd give them away, often to AIDS sufferers so they could visit family. Crew members knew him by name.

"There was one flight attendant, Pierre, who knew exactly what I wanted," Vroom said. "He'd bring me three salmon appetizers, no dessert and a glass of champagne, right after takeoff. I didn't even have to ask."

Creative uses seemed limitless. When bond broker Willard May of Round Rock, Texas, was forced into retirement after a run-in with federal securities regulators in the early 1990s, he turned to his trusty AAirpass to generate income. Using his companion ticket, he began shuttling a Dallas couple back and forth to Europe for $2,000 a month.

"For years, that was all the flying I did," said May, eighty-one. "It's how I got the bills paid."

In 1990, the airline raised the price of an unlimited AAirpass with companion to $600,000. In 1993, it was bumped to $1.01 million. In 1994, American stopped selling unlimited passes altogether.

Cable TV executive Leo Hindery Jr. bought a five-year AAirpass in 1991, with an option to upgrade to lifetime after three years. American later "asked me not to convert," he said. "They were gracious. They said the program had been discontinued and if I gave my pass back, they'd give me back my money."

Hindery declined, even rebuffing a personal appeal by American's Crandall (which the executive said he did not recall). To date, he has accumulated 11.5 million miles on a pass that cost him about $500,000, including an age discount and credit from his five-year pass.

"It was a lot of money at the time," Hindery said. "But once you get past that, you forget it."

In 2004, American offered the unlimited AAirpass one last time, in the Neiman-Marcus Christmas catalog. At $3 million, plus a companion pass for $2 million more, none sold.

• • •

Raised just miles from American's Fort Worth headquarters, Bridget Cade started in its reservations department in 1990. In 2007, she was promoted to the elite revenue integrity team, charged with rooting out passengers, travel agents, and others suspected of cheating the airline.

Her first big job was to investigate AAirpass users.

In September 2007, a pricing analyst reviewing international routes focused the airline's attention on how much the AAirpass program was costing, company e-mails show.

"We pay the taxes," a revenue management executive wrote in a subsequent e-mail. "We award AAdvantage miles, and we lose the seat every time they fly."

Cade was assigned to find out whether any AAirpass holders were violating the rules, starting with those who flew the most.

She pulled years of flight records for Rothstein and Vroom and calculated that each was costing American more than $1 million a year.

Rothstein, she found, would sometimes pick out strangers at the airport and give them surprise first-class upgrades with his companion pass. Once he flew a woman he'd just met in New Delhi to Chicago, a lift American later valued at nearly $7,500.

There was nothing in the AAirpass terms prohibiting that. But Cade considered the habit striking in light of something else she found. Rothstein made 3,009 reservations in less than four years, almost always booking two seats, but canceled 2,523 of them.

To Cade, this was evidence that Rothstein reserved flights he never intended to take. It also allowed him to hold seats until the last minute and offer them to strangers, she said later in court depositions, preventing American from selling them. Cade decided it was fraud and grounds for revocation.

On December 13, 2008, Rothstein and a companion checked in at Chicago O'Hare International Airport for a transatlantic flight. An American employee handed him a letter, which said his AAirpass had been terminated for "fraudulent behavior."

He apologized to his friend and filed suit in Illinois the following March.

Vroom's travel history told a different story, Cade found. Time and again, he booked trips with people he'd never flown with before, traveling round-trip to Japan or Europe without even staying overnight.

"We suspect he is selling his AAirpass companion tickets," Cade wrote in a February 2008 email. That, she later said, was against the rules.

She decided to try to catch him in the act.

Checking Vroom's bookings for first-timers, Cade came across Auyon Mukharji, a recent college graduate abroad on a music scholarship. He was scheduled to fly from London to Nashville with Vroom on July 30, 2008.

Working with airline security, Cade hatched a plan to confront Mukharji at London's Heathrow Airport, challenging him to admit he had paid Vroom.

"Mukharji appears to be naive, without financial wherewithal, and most probably very anxious to return 'home,'" American's head of global investigations wrote in an e-mail.

At check-in, American agents detained Mukharji and escorted him to a private office. A former New York police detective working in American security offered a free ticket to Nashville if he'd confess to giving Vroom money.

But Mukharji insisted he hadn't, and American ultimately released him and gave him a coach ticket home. He could not be reached for comment.

Vroom landed at Heathrow that morning. As he boarded American Flight 50 from Dallas/Fort Worth to London the evening before, security officers took note of the clothes he was wearing, down to the Crocs on his feet.

Inside Heathrow, Vroom headed for the VIP lounge, where an American employee handed him a letter and said he could never again fly on the airline.

Vroom was shocked, unable to believe that his golden ticket was gone. He told the airline he had met Mukharji through a friend and, because both had attended Williams College in Massachusetts, simply offered him a ride to the United States as a friendly gesture.

With Mukharji insisting he had not paid for his ticket, Cade and her team began tracking down other Vroom flight companions.

In one instance, an American security agent called Sam Mulroy, a Dallas personal trainer who had been set to fly with Vroom to Europe, and told him his trip had been canceled. The agent promised a first-class ticket if he admitted to paying Vroom, according to company e-mails and correspondence.

When Mulroy refused, American froze his frequent flier account, offering to release it in exchange for details of payments, the documents show. Mulroy complained to American and the Transportation Department that he was being "extorted [in] an effort to punish another customer." He did not respond to requests for comment.

Weeks later, American sued Vroom in Texas state court. Vroom countersued.

In discovery, company lawyers tracked down a Dallas woman who had cut Vroom a $2,800 check to fly her son to London. An elderly couple gave him $6,000 for a trip to Paris. And bank records showed more than $100,000 in checks to Vroom written by owners of a local jewelry store who frequently flew with Vroom.

Vroom admits to getting money from some flying companions, but says it was usually for his business advice and not payments for flights. Other times people insisted on paying him, he said.

Cade wasn't done. In early 2009, the phone rang at the home of Willard May, the former bond broker who openly sold his ticket when he was forced out of work. His AAirpass, too, had been yanked.

"I never tried to deceive American," said May, noting that the *Dallas Morning News* in 1993 published an article quoting him and an American official about the practice.

Still, May didn't make a fuss when the call came. He'd grown tired of flying.

• • •

These days, Vroom busies himself substitute teaching and hosting lectures in a custom-made cinder-block home in a hip Dallas neighborhood.

His lawyers say the seat-selling accusation is moot because Vroom's contract didn't prohibit it; American didn't ban the practice until three years after Vroom bought his pass.

Rothstein also denies committing fraud, saying his contract did not ban making multiple reservations. "It sure seems like the airline was looking for an excuse to be rid of my client," said Gary Soter, Rothstein's attorney.

Last summer, an Illinois federal judge ruled that Rothstein had violated the contract by booking empty seats under phony names, including Bag Rothstein. American had years earlier acknowledged that "airport personnel have become complacent" with the practice, court records show, and Soter planned to appeal. But that case and Vroom's were thrown into limbo when American's parent company, AMR Corp., filed for Chapter 11 bankruptcy protection in November.

American spokeswoman Mary Sanderson said the canceled passes are "very isolated and represent an extremely small percentage of our overall AAirpass accounts."

"We actively analyze all of our ticketing and program policies for any improper activity," she said. "If we determine that any activity has violated our policies or is fraudulent in nature, we take the actions we deem appropriate."

Cade investigated at least two other AAirpass holders, court records show, and concluded that both also had committed fraud. American declined to say why their passes had not been revoked.

Rothstein moved to New York in 2009 and works for a trading firm. His office is crammed with family photos and reminders of exotic locales he visited flying American. Among his possessions is a 1998 letter on company stationery from Bob Crandall, with whom Rothstein once flew on the supersonic Concorde.

"I am delighted that you've enjoyed your AAirpass investment," the executive wrote. "You can count on us to keep the company solid, and to honor the deal, far into the future."

Part VI

Big Think

Interfluidity

Steve Waldman has carved out a niche for himself as one of the most original economic thinkers online. His blog, *Interfluidity*, is always provocative, wonky, and host to extremely high-level discussions. Here, he develops a typically incisive theory of inequality, coming to the conclusion that unless and until we reduce it, we'll never reach full employment. Waldman doesn't pander to a broad audience, but if you put some effort into following his argument, he'll always repay you with insights you can find nowhere else.

Steve Randy Waldman

15. Trade-offs Between Inequality, Productivity, and Employment

I think there is a trade-off between inequality and full employment that becomes exacerbated as technological productivity improves. This is driven by the fact that the marginal benefit humans gain from current consumption declines much more rapidly than the benefit we get from retaining claims against an uncertain future.

Wealth is about insurance much more than it is about consumption. As consumers, our requirements are limited. But the curve balls the universe might throw at us are infinite. If you are very wealthy, there is real value in purchasing yet another apartment in yet another country through yet another hopefully-but-not-certainly-trustworthy native intermediary. There is value in squirreling funds away in yet another undocumented account, and not just from avoiding taxes. Revolutions, expropriations, pogroms, these things do happen. These are real risks. Even putting aside such dramatic events, the greater the level of consumption to which you have grown accustomed, the greater the threat of reversion to the mean, unless you plan and squirrel very carefully. Extreme levels of consumption are either the tip of an iceberg or a transient condition. Most of what it means to be wealthy is having insured yourself well.

An important but sad reason why our requirement for wealth-as-insurance is insatiable is because insurance is often a zero-sum game. Consider a libertarian *Titanic*, whose insufficient number of lifeboat seats will be auctioned to the highest bidder in the event of a catastrophe. On such a boat, a passenger's material needs might easily be satisfied—how many fancy meals and full-body spa massages can one endure in a day? But despite that, one could never be "rich enough." Even if one's wealth is millions of times more than would be required to satisfy every material whim for a lifetime of cruising, when the iceberg cometh, you must either be in a top wealth quantile or die a cold, salty death. The marginal consumption value of passenger wealth declines rapidly, but the marginal insurance value of an extra dollar remains high because it represents a material advantage in a fierce zero-sum competition. It is not enough to be wealthy; you must be much wealthier than most of your shipmates in order to rest easy. Some individuals may achieve a safe lead, but, in aggregate, demand for wealth will remain high even if every passenger is so rich their consumption desires are fully sated forever.

Our lives are much more like this cruise ship than most of us care to admit. No, we don't face the risk of drowning in the North Atlantic. But our habits and expectations are constantly under threat because the prerequisites to satisfying them may at any time become rationed by price. Just living in America you (or at least I) feel this palpably. So many of us are fighting for the right to live the kind of life we always thought was "normal." When there is a drought, the ability to eat what you want becomes rationed by price. If there is drought so terrible that there simply isn't enough for everyone, the right to live at all may be rationed by price, survival of the wealthiest. Whenever there is risk of overall scarcity, of systemic rather than idiosyncratic catastrophe, there is no possibility of positive-sum mutual-gain insurance. There is only a zero-sum competition for the right to be insured. The very rich live on the very same cruise ship as the very poor, and they understandably want to keep their lifeboat tickets.

If insurance were not so valuable, it would be perfectly possible to have very high levels of inequality and have full employment. The very rich might employ endless varieties of servants to cater to their tiniest whims. They'd get little value from the marginal new employee, but the money they'd lose by paying a salary would have very little value to them, so the new hire could be a good deal. But because of the not-so-diminishing insurance value of wealth, the value of hiring someone to scratch yet another trivial itch eventually declines below the insurance value of holding property or claims. There is a limit to how many people a rich person will employ, directly or indirectly.

In "middle-class" societies, wealth is widely distributed and most peoples' consumption desires are not nearly sated. We constantly trade off a potential loss of insurance against a gain from consumption, and consumption often wins because we have important, unsatisfied wants. So we employ one another to provide the goods and services we wish to consume. This leads to "full employment"—however many we are, we find ways to please our peers, for which they pay us. They in turn please us for pay. There is a circular flow of claims, accompanied by real activity we call "production."

In economically polarized societies, this dynamic breaks down. The very wealthy don't employ everybody because the marginal consumption value of a new hire falls below the insurance value of retaining wealth. The very poor consume, but only the most basic goods. In low productivity, highly polarized economies, we observe high-flying elites surrounded by populations improvising a subsistence. The wealthy retain their station by corruption, coercion, and extraction while the poor employ themselves and one another in order to satisfy these depredations and still survive. Unemployment is not a problem, exactly, but poverty is. (To be "unemployed" in such a society means not to be idle but to be laboring for an improvised subsistence rather than working for pay in the service of the elite.)

Idle unemployment is a problem in societies that are highly productive but very unequal. Here basic goods (food, clothing) can be produced efficiently by the wealthy via capital-intensive production processes. The poor do not employ one another because the necessities they require are produced and sold so cheaply by the rich. The rich are glad to sell to the poor, as long as the poor can come up with property or debt claims or other forms of insurance to offer as payment.[1] The rich produce and "get richer," but often they don't much *feel* richer. They feel like they are running in place, competing desperately to provide all the world's goods and services in order to match their neighbors' hoard of financial claims. However many claims they collectively earn, individually they remain locked in a zero-sum competition among peers that leaves most of them forever insecure.

It is the interaction of productivity and inequality that makes societies vulnerable to idle unemployment. The poor in technologically primitive societies hustle to live. In relatively equal, technologically advanced societies, people create plenty of demand for one another's services. But when productivity and inequality are combined, we get a highly productive elite that cannot provide adequate employment, and a mass of people who preserve more value by remaining idle and cutting consumption than by attempting low-productivity work. (See "rentism" in Peter Frase's amazing *Four Futures*.)

One explanation for our recent traumas is that "advanced economies" have cycled from middle-class to polarized societies. We had a kind of Wile E. Coyote moment in 2008, when, collectively, we could no longer deny that much of the debt the "middle class" was generating to fund purchases was, um, iffy. So long as the middle class could borrow, the "masses" could simultaneously pay high-productivity insiders for efficiently produced core goods and pay one another for yoga classes. If you didn't look at incomes or balance sheets but only at consumption, we appeared to have a growing middle-class economy.

But then it became impossible for ordinary people to fund their consumption by issuing debt, and it became necessary for people to actually pay down debt. The remaining income of the erstwhile middle class was increasingly devoted to efficiently produced basic goods and away from the marginal, lower-productivity services that enable full employment. This consumption shift has the effect of increasing inequality, so the dynamic feeds on itself.

We end up in a peculiar situation. There remains technological abundance: "we" are not in any real sense poorer. But, as Izabella Kaminska wonderfully points out, in a zero-sum contest for relative advantage among producers, abundance becomes a threat when it can no longer be sold for high-quality claims. Any alternative basis of distribution would undermine the relationship between previously amassed financial claims and useful wealth, and thereby threaten the pecking order over which wealthier people devote their lives to stressing and striving. From the perspective of those near the top of the pecking order, it is better and *it is fairer* that potential abundance be withheld than that old claims be destroyed or devalued. Even schemes that preserve the wealth ordering (like Steve Keen's "modern jubilee") are unfair, because they would collapse the relative distance between competitors and devalue the insurance embedded in some people's lead over others.

The zero-sum, positional nature of wealth-as-insurance is one of many reasons why there is no such thing as a "Pareto improvement." Macroeconomic interventions that would increase real output while condensing wealth dispersion undo the hard-won, "hard-earned" insurance advantage of the wealthy. As polities, we have to trade off extra consumption by the poor against a loss of insurance for the rich. There are costs and benefits, winners and losers. We face trade-offs between unequal distribution and full employment. If we want to maximize total output, we have to compress the wealth distribution. If inequality continues to grow (and we don't reinvent some means of fudging unpayable claims), both real output and employment will continue to fall as the poor can serve one another only inefficiently, and the rich won't deploy their capital to efficiently produce for nothing.

Distribution is the core of the problem we face. I'm tired of arguments about tools. Both monetary and fiscal policy can be used in ways that magnify or diminish existing dispersions of wealth. On the fiscal side, income-tax-rate reductions tend to magnify wealth and income dispersion while transfers or broadly targeted expenditures diminish it. On the monetary side, inflationary monetary policy diminishes dispersion by transferring wealth from creditors to debtors, while disinflationary policy has the opposite effect. Interventions that diminish wealth and income dispersion are the ones that contribute most directly to employment and total output. But they impose risks on current winners in the race for insurance.

Why did World War II, one of the most destructive events in the history of world, engender an era of near-full employment and broad-based prosperity both in the United States, where capital and infrastructure were mostly preserved, and in Europe, where resources were obliterated? People have lots of explanations, and I'm sure there's truth in many of them. But I think an underrated factor is the degree to which the war "reset" the inequalities that had developed over prior decades. Suddenly nearly everyone was poor in much of Europe. In the United States, income inequality declined during the war. Military pay and the GI Bill and rationing and war bonds helped shore up the broad public's balance sheet, reducing indebtedness and overall wealth dispersion. World War II was so large an event, organized and motivated by concerns so far from economic calculation, that squabbles between rich and poor, creditor and debtor, were put aside. The financial effect of the war, in terms of the distribution of claims in the United States, was not very different from what would occur under Keen's jubilee.

Although in a narrow sense, the very wealthy lost some insurance against zero-sum scarcities, the postwar boom made such scarcities less likely. It's not clear, on net (in the United States), that even the very wealthy were "losers." A priori, it would have been difficult to persuade wealthy people that a loss of relative advantage would be made up after the war by a gain in absolute circumstance for everyone. There is no guarantee, if we tried the jubilee without the gigantic war, that a rising tide would lift even shrinking yachts. But it might very well. That's a case I think we have to make, before some awful circumstance comes along to force our hand.

Note

1. It is interesting that even in very unequal, high productivity societies, one rarely sees the very poor reverting to low-tech, low-productivity craft production of goods the wealthy can manufacture efficiently. One way or another, the poor in these societies get the basic goods they need to survive, and they mostly don't do it by spinning their own yarn or employing one another to sew shirts. One might imagine that once people have no money or claims to offer, they'd be as cut off from manufactures as subsistence farmers in a low-productivity society. But that isn't so. Perhaps this is simply a matter of charity: rich people are human and manufactured goods are cheap and useful gifts. Perhaps it is just entropy: in a society that mass-produces goods, it would take a lot of work to prevent some degree of diffusion to the poor.

However, another way to think about it is that the poor collectively sell insurance against riot and revolution, which the rich are happy to pay for with modest quantities of efficiently produced goods. "Social insurance" is usually thought of as a safety net that protects the poor from risk. But in very polarized societies, transfer programs provide an insurance benefit to the rich by ensuring poorer people's dependence on production processes that only the rich know how to manage. This diminishes the probability the poor will agitate for change, via politics or other means. Inequality may be more stable in technologically advanced countries, where inexpensive goods substitute for the human capital that every third-world slum dweller acquires, the capacity and confidence to improvise and get by with next to nothing.

The New Republic

No one has mastered the art of the long takedown review quite like Evgeny Morozov. In taking on some new e-books published by the increasingly ubiquitous TED conference brand (*Hybrid Reality: Thriving in the Emerging Human-Technology Civilization,* by Parag Khanna and Ayesha Khanna; *The Demise of Guys: Why Boys Are Struggling and What We Can Do About It*, by Philip Zimbardo and Nikita Duncan; and *Smile: The Astonishing Powers of a Simple Act,* by Ron Gutman), Morozov argues that many of the shiny and exciting and easily digestible ideas propagated by TED are actually very dangerous. As he reveals the fallacies of the TED worldview, Morozov offers prose that is as precise as his target is muddled.

Evgeny Morozov

16. The Naked and the TED

I.

The new pamphlet—it would be too strong, and not only quantitatively, to call it a book—by Parag and Ayesha Khanna, the technobabbling power couple, gallops through so many esoteric themes and irrelevant factoids (did you know that "fifty-eight percent of millennials would rather give up their sense of smell than their mobile phone"?) that one might forgive the authors for never properly attending to their grandest, most persuasive, and almost certainly inadvertent argument. Only the rare reader would finish this piece of digito-futuristic nonsense unconvinced that technology is—to borrow a term of art from the philosopher Harry Frankfurt—bullshit. No, not technology itself; just much of today's discourse about technology, of which this little e-book is a succinct and mind-numbing example. At least TED Books—the publishing outlet of the hot and overheated TED Conference, which brought this hidden gem to the wider public—did not kill any trees in the publishing process.

It might seem odd that Parag Khanna would turn his attention to the world of technology. He established his reputation as a wannabe geopolitical theorist, something of a modern-day Kissinger, only wired and cool. For almost a decade he has been writing pompous and alarmist books and articles that herald a new era in international relations. He has also been circling the globe in a tireless effort to warn world leaders that democracy might be incompatible with globalization and capitalism. And that the West needs to be more like China and Singapore. And that America is running on borrowed time. And that a new Middle Ages are about to set in. ("When I look at the 21st century, I reverse the numbers around and I see the 12th century.") This is probing stuff.

All of these insights are expressed in linguistic constructions of such absurdity and superficiality ("a world of ever-shifting (d)alliances," "peer-to-peer micromanufacturing marketplace") that Niall Ferguson's "Chimerica" looks elegant and illuminating by comparison. Khanna must be a gifted schmoozer, too: the acknowledgments sections of his books are primary documents of contemporary name-dropping. Almost everyone he quotes can expect effusive praise. As I. F. Stone once said about Theodore White, "a writer who can be so universally admiring need never lunch alone."

Khanna's contempt for democracy and human rights aside, he is simply an intellectual impostor, emitting such lethal doses of banalities, inanities, and generalizations that his books ought to carry advisory notices. Take this precious piece of advice from his previous book—the modestly titled *How to Run the World*—which is quite representative of his work: "The world needs very few if any new global organizations. What it needs is far more fresh combinations of existing actors who *coordinate* better with one another." How this A-list networking would stop climate change, cyber-crime, or trade in exotic animals is never specified. Khanna does not really care about the details of policy. He is a manufacturer of abstract, meaningless slogans. He is, indeed, the most talented bullshit artist of his generation. And this confers upon him a certain anthropological interest.

The "technological" turn in Khanna's "thought" is hardly surprising. As he and others have discovered by now, one can continue fooling the public with slick ahistorical jeremiads on geopolitics by serving them with the coarse but tasty sauce that is the Cyber-Whig theory of history. The recipe is simple. Find some peculiar global trend—the more arcane, the better. Draw a straight line connecting it to the world of apps, electric cars, and Bay Area venture capital. Mention robots, Japan, and cyberwar. Use shiny slides that contain incomprehensible but impressive maps and visualizations. Stir well. Serve on multiple platforms. With their never-ending talk of Twitter revolutions and the like, techno-globalists such as Khanna have a bright future ahead of them.

In their TED book, the Khannas boldly declare that "mastery in the leading technology sectors of any era determines who leads in geoeconomics and dominates in geopolitics." Technology is all, the alpha and the omega. *How to Run the World*, which appeared last year, already contained strong hints about what would happen once he embraced the shiny world of technobabble with open arms (and, one presumes, open pockets). There we learned that "cloud computing—not big buildings and bloated bureaucracies—is the future of global governance," and, my favorite, "everyone who has a BlackBerry—or iPhone or Nexus One—can be their own ambassador." Of their own country of one, presumably.

Hybrid Reality contains few surprises. Khanna and his wife fashion themselves as successors to Alvin and Heidi Toffler, an earlier fast-talking tech-addled couple who thrived on selling cookie-cutter visions of the future one paperback, slogan, and consulting gig at a time. Today the Tofflers are best-known for inspiring some of Newt Gingrich's most outlandish ideas as well as for popularizing the term "information overload"—a phenomenon which, as numerous scholars have shown, was hardly specific to 1970 (which is when Alvin Toffler mentioned it in *Future Shock*) and is probably as old as books themselves. To embrace the Tofflers as intellectual role models is to make a damning admission: that one is far more interested in inventing half-clever buzzwords than in trying to understand the messy reality that those buzzwords purport to describe. In a recent article in *Foreign Policy* on the Tofflers, the Khannas are unusually candid about what it is they admire about them:

> Need we say more [about this prediction]? Even though it was written during the Carter administration, if you remove the dates from the passage above you have a template for most of today's editorial columns on the aftermath of the current financial meltdown. It's all here: the identity crisis of corporations, skyrocketing commodity prices, morally bankrupt economists, and currencies in flux and free-fall.

So the Tofflers have much to teach us about the origins or the consequences of the current financial crisis! This of course is laughable. The fact that, three decades later, their glib, abstract, and pretentious writings can still serve as a template for the likes of the Khannas says more about the state of public debate in America today than it does about the accuracy of Toffler-style futurism.

When the Khannas discuss the charms of their newly found profession in *Hybrid Reality*, the whole enterprise is revealed as a jargon-laden farce: "Futurism is a combination of long-term and long-tail, separating the trends from the trendy and the shocks from the shifts, and combining data, reportage, and scenarios." It doesn't sound like a very demanding job: "It helps to travel and be imaginative, but it is even more useful to observe children." And why all this effort? So that we can better predict the apocalypse. "Avoiding civilizational collapse will require harnessing technologies that help us decipher complexity, overcome decision overload, and produce comprehensive strategies." The Khannas have come to accomplish nothing less than the rescue of civilization.

• • •

Toffler worship and futuristic kitsch aside, what does *Hybrid Reality* actually argue? There are several disjointed arguments. First, that technology—"technology with a big 'T,'" as they call it—is supplanting economics and geopolitics as the leading driver of international relations. This means, among other things, that Washington deploys tools such as Flame and Stuxnet simply because it has the better technology—not because of a strategic and military analysis. It is a silly argument, but wrapped in tech-talk it sounds almost plausible.

For the Khannas, technology is an autonomous force with its own logic that does not bend under the wicked pressure of politics or capitalism or tribalism; all that we humans can do is find a way to harness its logic for our own purposes. Technology is the magic wand that lifts nations from poverty, cures diseases, redistributes power, and promises immortality to the human race. Nations, firms, and cities that develop the smartest and most flexible way of doing this are said to possess *Technik*—a German term with a substantial intellectual pedigree that, in the Khannas' hands, can mean just about anything—and a high "technology quotient."

Today, they believe, we are entering a new era, when humans will be so intricately dependent on technology that "human-technology coexistence has become human-technology coevolution." This is what the Khannas mean by the "Hybrid Age"—a "new sociotechnical era that is unfolding as technologies merge with each other and humans merge with technology." They proceed to outline its inevitable consequences. Designer babies? Check. Cloned humans? Check. Sex robots that "can be made to look like anyone you want"? Check. A paradise!

Any stretch of time that deserves a name of its own—an age, an era, an epoch—must have at least a few distinct characteristics that make it stand out from the past. The problem is that all the features that the Khannas invoke to emphasize the uniqueness of our era have long been claimed by other commentators for their own unique eras. The Khannas tell us that "technology no longer simply processes our instructions on a one-way street. Instead, it increasingly provides intelligent feedback." How is that different from Daniel Boorstin's bombastic pronouncement in 1977 that "the Republic of Technology where we will be living is a feedback world"? And the Khannas' admonition that "rather than view technology and humanity as two distinct domains, we must increasingly appreciate the dense sociotechnical nexus in which they constantly shape each other"—how is this different from what Ortega y Gasset wrote more eloquently in 1939: "Man without technology . . . is not man"?

The idea of hybridity that the Khannas assume to be their sexy and original insight has been with us for a long time—long before social media and biotechnology. While some dismiss such theorists of hybridity as Bruno Latour and Donna Haraway, who have questioned the epistemological foundations of the modern scientific enterprise, as being on the wrong side of the Science Wars, hybridity is by no means a postmodernist idea. Here is Daniel Callahan—a respected bioethicist who can hardly be accused of PoMo transgressions—writing in 1971: "We have to do away with a false and misleading dualism, one which abstracts man on the one hand and technology on the other, as if the two were quite separate kinds of realities. . . . Man is by nature a technological animal; to be human is to be technological. . . . When we speak of technology, this is another way of speaking about man himself in one of his manifestations."

For modern theorists of technology, hybridity is an ontological—not an emergent—property. They believe, to quote Callahan again, that "to be human is to be technological" and that it has always been thus. As it turns out, this seemingly innocent assumption about the world can have serious implications for how we think about politics, morality, and law. It inspired Latour's notion of "distributed agency"—in its crudest form, the idea that neither guns nor people kill people but rather a fleeting, one-off combination of the two. (The entity that shoots is a "gun-man.") This is not meant to suggest that people no longer have to go to jail for murder. It is only to point out that, if we really want to explain a particular act of shooting, we need to account for factors like the material design of the gun, the marketing considerations of its manufacturers, the severity of antigun laws, and so on.

The latest technologies might make us more aware of this hybridity—of the techno-human condition, if you will—but to speak of the Hybrid Age makes as much sense as to speak of the Nature Age: the fact that climate change makes us more aware of the air we breathe or the water we drink does not fundamentally alter the dynamics of our dependence on these resources. To posit that we are moving into the Hybrid Age is to assume that there was once a time—according to the Khannas, it was just a few years ago—when such hybridity was not the case, when man and technology trod their separate paths. It is to believe that human nature changed sometime last year or so. This, of course, is nonsense—even if it makes technology companies feel important. As the Dutch philosopher of technology Peter-Paul Verbeek puts it in his fine book *Moralizing Technology*, "We are as autonomous with regard to technology as we are with regard to language, oxygen, or gravity."

But still the Khannas roll dizzily along. "The Hybrid Age is the transition period between the Information Age and the moment of Singularity (when machines surpass human intelligence) that inventor Ray Kurzweil, author of *The Singularity Is Near*, estimates we may reach by 2040 (perhaps sooner). The Hybrid Age is a liminal phase in which we cross the threshold toward a new mode of arranging global society." These are end times. The Hybrid Age is the preparation for the apotheosis of the Singularity—a Singularity-lite of sorts. (Ayesha Khanna serves as a faculty adviser to Singularity University.) This periodization of history is just a marketing trick. Those who believe in Kurzweil's ugly and ridiculous thesis, which at TED conferences is probably the majority, have already grudgingly accepted the fact that a few unexciting decades will transpire before it comes to pass—and so the Khannas move in to claim these decades as their own, as their brand, while promising us that all the fun of the Singularity—who doesn't fancy uploading his soul to the cloud so that it can commingle with the soul of Steve Jobs?—will happen even sooner than we think.

As the Hybrid Age sets in, inaction is not an option. "You may continue to live your life without understanding the implications of the still-distant Singularity, but you should not underestimate how quickly we are accelerating into the Hybrid Age—nor delay in managing this transition yourself." Sinners, repent! The day of the Lord is nigh! And in case you wonder where you might turn for assistance in "managing this transition," the Khannas are there to help. They are eschatological consultants. They run a for-profit consulting firm "providing insight into the implications of emerging technologies" that bears the proud name of the Hybrid Reality Institute. So far the firm's main accomplishment seems to be convincing the TED Conference to print its verbose marketing brochure as a book. But perhaps this is what the Hybrid Age is all about: marketing masquerading as theory, charlatans masquerading as philosophers, a New Age cult masquerading as a university, business masquerading as redemption, slogans masquerading as truths.

• • •

This book is not just useless piffle about technology; it is also an endorsement of some rather noxious political ideas. Those already familiar with Parag Khanna's earlier celebrations of autocracies in Southeast Asia will not be surprised by some of the most outrageous paragraphs in his TED book. China is one of the Khannas' role models. They have the guts to write that "a decade from now we will look back at China's 12th Five-Year Plan as the seminal document of the early 21st century." Take your pick: Twelfth Five-Year Plan or Charter 08. Somehow the latter never gets a mention in this book. Perhaps it is not seminal enough, or it is insufficiently driven by technology. And what makes the Five-Year Plan so seminal? "It pledges $1.5 trillion in government support for seven 'strategic emerging industries,' including alternative energy, biotechnology, next-gen IT, high-end manufacturing equipment, and advanced materials." Would it really surprise anyone if in a few years some of that $1.5 trillion were to trickle down to the Hybrid Reality Institute?

The Khannas also heap praise on Singapore, "a seamlessly efficient cosmopolitan world capital of finance and, increasingly, innovation." Alas, they do not explain how Singapore has become so "seamlessly efficient." Perhaps this quotation from Lee Kuan Yew, its first long-time ruler—conveniently omitted by the Khannas—may shed some light: "Everytime anybody wants to start anything which will unwind or unravel this orderly, organized, sensible, rational society, and make it irrational and emotional, I put a stop to it without hesitation." The Khannas approvingly note that Singapore is "the leading role model in city-state *Technik* for entities from Abu Dhabi to Moscow to Kuala Lumpur." That all three aforementioned cities are situated in despicable authoritarian regimes—which might explain why they look up to Singapore—does not much trouble the Khannas. They recently announced that they are moving to Singapore. Good. The autocratic city and the apologists for autocracy deserve each other.

It only gets worse, as the Khannas proceed to profess their deep and inherently antidemocratic admiration for technocracy. That they can spit out the following passage without running any risk of being disinvited from respectable dinner parties and television shows is a sign of how well our debate about technology—a seemingly neutral and nonpolitical issue—conceals deeply political (and, in this case, outright authoritarian) tendencies:

> Using technology to deliberate on matters of national importance, deliver public services, and incorporate citizen feedback may ultimately be a truer form of direct participation than a system of indirect representation and infrequent elections. Democracy depends on the participation of crowds, but doesn't guarantee their wisdom. We cannot be afraid of technocracy when the alternative is the futile populism of Argentines, Hungarians, and Thais masquerading as democracy. It is precisely these nonfunctional democracies that are prime candidates to be superseded by better-designed technocracies—likely delivering more benefits to their citizens. . . . To the extent that China provides guidance for governance that Western democracies don't, it is in having "technocrats with term limits."

Things in Hungary are pretty bad, but to suggest that Hungarians would be better off with China-style governance is really reprehensible. And to imply that China's technocrats have term limits is outright offensive.

In the domestic American context, the Khannas also celebrate the infusion of "experts such as Tim O'Reilly and Craig Newmark [who] . . . stepped in to advise Washington on Gov 2.0 technologies such as open-data platforms." "Such citizen-technologists," we are told, "are crucial . . . to [improving] government efficiency." Once again, the technologists—and the technocratic agencies they are enlisted to support—are presented as objective, independent, and free of any ideological leanings. Nowhere do we learn that Tim O'Reilly runs a profitable corporation that might stand to benefit from the government's embrace of open-data platforms, or that Craig Newmark is a committed cyber-libertarian who used to worship Ayn Rand. Or that Jimmy Wales, who is advising the British government, is so enthralled with Rand and objectivism that he named his daughter after one of the characters in a Rand novel. Nor do the Khannas tell us that the public embrace of "open-data platforms" is often accompanied by an increase in government secrecy or a growing reluctance to fund public journalism. (Why fund the BBC if "citizen-investigators" can now be asked to do all the digging for free?) The pursuit of efficiency alone cannot guide public policy—this is why we have politics, but technocrats rarely want to hear such truths. And the Khannas cannot be trusted to tell them.

• • •

As is typical of today's anxiety-peddling futurology, the Khannas' favorite word is "increasingly," which is their way of saying that our unstable world is always changing and that only advanced thinkers such as themselves can guide us through this turbulence. In *Hybrid Reality*, everything is increasingly something else: gadgets are increasingly miraculous, technology is increasingly making its way into the human body, quiet moments are increasingly rare. This is a world in which pundits are increasingly using the word "increasingly" whenever they feel too lazy to look up the actual statistics, which, in the Khannas' case, increasingly means all the time.

What the Khannas' project illustrates so well is that the defining feature of today's techno-aggrandizing is its utter ignorance of all the techno-aggrandizing that has come before it. The fantasy of technology as an autonomous force is a century-old delusion that no serious contemporary theorist of technology would defend. The Khannas have no interest in intellectual history or in the state of contemporary thought about technology. They prefer to quote, almost at random, the likes of Oswald Spengler and Karl Jaspers instead. This strategy of invoking random Teutonic names and concepts might work on the unsophisticated crowds at Davos and TED, but to imagine that either Spengler or Jaspers have something interesting or original to tell us about cloning, e-books, or asteroid mining is foolish. "A new era requires a new vocabulary," the Khannas proclaim—only to embrace the terminology that was already in place by the end of the nineteenth century. They may be well funded, but they are not well educated.

Their promiscuous use of the word *Technik* exposes the shaky foundation of their enterprise—as well as of many popular discussions about technology, which inevitably gravitate toward the bullshit zone. To return to Harry Frankfurt, the key distinction between the liar and the bullshitter is that the former conceals "that he is attempting to lead us away from a correct apprehension of reality," whereas the latter conceals that he is not interested in reality at all. The bullshitter "does not care whether the things he says describe reality correctly. He just picks them out, or makes them up, to suit his purpose." To suggest that Parag and Ayesha Khanna—and numerous pundits before them—might be pursuing purposes other than describing—or improving—reality is almost self-evident. (A look at the website of the Hybrid Reality Institute would suffice.) The more interesting question here is why bullshit about technology, unlike other types of bullshit, is so hard to see for what it is.

It is here that the Khannas stand out. *Technik*, as they use this term, is something so expansive and nebulous that it can denote absolutely anything. *Technik* is the magic concept that allows the Khannas to make their most meaningless sentences look as if they actually carry some content. They use *Technik* as a synonym for innovation, design, engineering, science, mastery, capital, the economy, and a dozen other things. It is what fixes cities, reinvigorates social networking, and grants us immortality. *Technik* is every pundit's wet dream: a foreign word that confers an air of cosmopolitanism upon its utterer. It can be applied to solve virtually any problem, and it is so abstract that its purveyor can hardly be held accountable for its inaccuracies and inanities.

It is *Technik* that makes much of the Khannas' writing circular and simplistic. Take this highly confusing sentence: "Good *Technik* requires a combination of the attributes that deliver high human development, economic growth, political inclusiveness, and technology preparedness." Translation: "Good *Technik* requires *Technik*." As for the simplistic part, try this: "*Technik* unites the scientific and mechanical dimensions of technology (determinism) with a necessary concern for its effect on humans and society (constructivism)." If I read the Khannas correctly—and I cannot be sure, for they seem confused about the terms "determinism" or "constructivism," at least as those are used in the philosophy of technology—their novel interpretation of the old German term *Technik* proposes to reveal that technologies are material and technologies have effects. Is this insight so profound that it needed a high German word to explain it?

But the Khannas do not want to abandon the simpler term "technology," either, so they try to inflate it, too. Remember, "the Hybrid Age is the era when we renew our thinking about technology with a big 'T.'" Sticking to the notion of "technology with a big 'T'" yields insights such as this: "From the printing press to penicillin and now Twitter and genomics, technology ceaselessly demonstrates its transformative impact." The printing press and penicillin and Twitter and genomics do indeed have transformative effects, but to assume that they all matter in the same way—which is the inevitable result of lumping them under the rubric of "Technology," the one with its own rules, wants, and agendas—is as stupid as it is dangerous.

Perhaps, if one had to give a three-minute TED presentation about penicillin, Twitter, genomics, and the printing press—but why would anyone ever want to give such a talk?—a catch-all term such as "technology" might be of some help. But analytically it is useless, in the way that lumping Warhol, Chardin, hip-hop, Chaplin, Haydn, and science fiction under the term "arts" is useless. At such a level of generality every fool can sound brilliant. The unfortunate thing is that, while few people would grant any substance to an argument that identifies a common meaning in Warhol, Chardin, hip-hop, Chaplin, Haydn, and science fiction, we easily fall for grand theories that mysteriously connect humans and material artifacts to some grand narrative about the universe, be it the Singularity, Toffler's Third Wave, or the Hybrid Age. When, fifteen years ago, Leo Marx accused technology of being "a hazardous concept" for leading precisely to this kind of addled thinking, he was too polite. In the hands of skilled hustlers such as the Khannas, technology is itself a counterfeit concept, which does little but make complex ideas look deceptively simple. Much like Glenn Beck's magic blackboard, it connects everything to everything without saying anything significant about anything.

II.

I can surmise why the Khannas would have wanted to write this book, but it is not immediately obvious why TED Books would have wanted to publish it. I must disclose that I spoke at a TED Global Conference in Oxford in 2009, and I admit that my appearance there certainly helped to expose my argument to a much wider audience, for which I remain grateful. So I take no pleasure in declaring what has been obvious for some time: that TED is no longer a responsible curator of ideas "worth spreading." Instead it has become something ludicrous, and a little sinister.

Today TED is an insatiable kingpin of international meme laundering—a place where ideas, regardless of their quality, go to seek celebrity, to live in the form of videos, tweets, and now e-books. In the world of TED—or, to use their argot, in the TED "ecosystem"—books become talks, talks become memes, memes become projects, projects become talks, talks become books—and so it goes ad infinitum in the sizzling Stakhanovite cycle of memetics, until any shade of depth or nuance disappears into the virtual void. Richard Dawkins, the father of memetics, should be very proud. Perhaps he can explain how "ideas worth spreading" become "ideas no footnotes can support."

The Khannas' book is not the only piece of literary rubbish carrying the TED brand. Another recently published TED book called *The Demise of Guys: Why Boys Are Struggling and What We Can Do About It*—coauthored by Philip Zimbardo, of the Stanford Prison Experiment fame, is an apt example of what transpires when TED ideas happen to good people. One would think that a scholar as distinguished as Zimbardo would not need to set foot in Khanna-land, but, alas, his book brims with almost as many clichés and pseudo-daring pronouncements. Did you know that "in porn, male actors have enormous penises," and that "porn is not about romance"? The book's main premise is that the Internet and video games are rewiring the brains of "guys," much to the detriment of civilization. Read and be terrified, especially if you are a "guy," because "[guys'] brains are being catered to by porn on demand and by video games at a flick of the switch or a click of the mouse." This is almost as good as Allan Bloom's admonition in *The Closing of the American Mind* that Walkman headphones lead to parricide. The evidence presented is inconsistent and all over the map. As the science journalist Carl Zimmer has noted, *The Demise of Guys* gives a *Daily Mail* column as much credibility as a peer-reviewed paper. And a new TED book on the science of smiling—*Smile: The Astonishing Powers of a Simple Act*, by Ron Gutman—contains even more banality than the Khannas' little masterpiece of TED emptiness—a remarkable feat. There one may read, for example, that "under certain conditions, when men see women smile at them they interpret that as a sign that the women think they are attractive." This is what passes for advanced thinking.

When they launched their publishing venture, the TED organizers dismissed any concern that their books' slim size would be dumbing us down. "Actually, we suspect people reading TED Books will be trading up rather than down. They'll be reading a short, compelling book instead of browsing a magazine or doing crossword puzzles. Our goal is to make ideas accessible in a way that matches modern attention spans." But surely "modern attention spans" must be resisted, not celebrated. Brevity may be the soul of wit, or of lingerie, but it is not the soul of analysis. The TED ideal of thought is the ideal of the "takeaway"—the shrinkage of thought for people too busy to think. I don't know if the crossword puzzles are rewiring our brains—I hope TED knows its neuroscience, with all the neuroscientists on its stage—but anyone who is seriously considering reading *Hybrid Reality* or *Smile* should also entertain the option of playing Angry Birds or Fruit Ninja.

Parag Khanna's writings on geopolitics never amounted to much of anything even before his turn to technology, but it is instructive to see how his presentation has changed now that he has embedded himself in the TED firmament. Save for a hackneyed nod to the "world's chessboard," he now makes only cursory references to power structures and strategic alliances. Instead he strikes all the right chords to elicit approval from the TED crowd—musing on genetics, neuroscience, synthetic biology—all in order to inform us that "our ability to augment ourselves" is growing by the minute. As is customary in such discourse, no mention is made of the fact that the Human Genome Project, for all the hype it generated a decade ago, has not accomplished much. Likewise, MRI scans are celebrated as if they offered direct and immediate access to truth. ("Harnessing fMRI mental scans, companies . . . are gathering the 'unspoken truth.'") The Khannas' Japan—as packaged for TED consumption—is the land of cutting-edge technology: you would never know that 59 percent of Japanese homes still have (frequently used!) fax machines.

The Khannas are typical of the TED crowd in that they do not express much doubt about anything. Their pronouncements about political structures are as firm and arrogant as some scientists' pronouncements about the cognitive structures of the brain. Whatever problems lurk on the horizon are imagined primarily as problems of technology, which, given enough money, brain power, and nutritional supplements, someone in Silicon Valley should be in a position to solve. This is consistent with TED's adoption of a decidedly nonpolitical attitude, as became apparent in a recent kerfuffle over a short talk on inequality given by a venture capitalist—who else?—which TED refused to release for fear that it might offend too many rich people.

Since any meaningful discussion of politics is off limits at TED, the solutions advocated by TED's techno-humanitarians cannot go beyond the toolkit available to the scientist, the coder, and the engineer. This leaves Silicon Valley entrepreneurs positioned as TED's preferred redeemers. In TED world, tech entrepreneurs are in the business of solving the world's most pressing problems. This is what makes TED stand out from other globalist shindigs, and makes its intellectual performances increasingly irrelevant to genuine thought and serious action.

Another fine example of the TED mentality in the context of global affairs is *Abundance*, a new book cowritten by Peter Diamandis, the cofounder of the Singularity University. He is a TED regular and the person who blurbed Khanna's book as "an enormously important contribution to our thinking about how to create a better tomorrow." (Singularity may rid us of death, but it won't abolish backscratching.) Diamandis delivers an abundant list of pressing global problems accompanied by an equally abundant list of technologies that can fix them. Here, too, politics rarely gets a mention.

Given TED's disproportionate influence on a certain level of the global debate, it follows that the public at large also becomes more approving of technological solutions to problems that are not technological but political. Problems of climate change become problems of making production more efficient or finding ways to colonize other planets—not of reaching political agreement on how to limit production or consume in a more sustainable fashion. Problems of health care become problems of inadequate self-monitoring and data-sharing. Problems of ensuring one's privacy—which might otherwise get solved by pushing for new laws—become problems of inadequate tools for defending one's anonymity online or selling access to one's own data. (The Khannas are not alone in believing that "individuals [must] gain control over the value of their time, skills, data, and resources. We must be ruthless in earning from those who want our attention.")

It is in the developing world where the limitations of TED's techno-humanitarian mentality are most pronounced. In TED world, problems of aid and development are no longer seen as problems of weak and corrupt institutions; they are recast as problems of inadequate connectivity or an insufficiency of gadgets. According to the Khannas, "centuries of colonialism and decades of aid haven't lifted Africa's fortunes the way technology can." Hence the latest urge to bombard Africa with tablets and Kindles—even when an average African kid would find it impossible to repair a damaged Kindle. And the gadgets do drop from the sky—Nicholas Negroponte, having spectacularly failed in his One Laptop Per Child quest, now wants to drop his own tablets from helicopters, which would make it harder for the African savages to say "no" to MIT's (and TED's) civilization. This is *la mission civilatrice* 2.0.

It is hardly surprising that the Khannas' deep admiration of Singapore's technocratic authoritarianism is well received by the TEDdies—after all, they prefer to fix broken countries as if they are broken start-ups. That solving any of their favorite global problems would require political solutions—if only to ensure that nobody's rights and interests are violated or overlooked in the process— is not something that the TED elite, with its aversion to conventional instruments of power and its inebriated can-do attitude, likes to hear. Politics slows things down; but technology speeds things up. TED's techno-humanitarians—that brigade of what the Nigerian American writer Teju Cole has dubbed "The White Savior Industrial Complex"—would defer to China's "technocrats with term limits" and have them bulldoze entire villages in order to build another Foxconn plant rather than bother with the slow progress of political reform. The Khannas are on to something when they write that "the Hybrid Age . . . might also become a Pax Technologica," but there are pitifully few reasons to believe that a Pax Technologica would do much good for the world. Techno-humanitarianism is much more techno than humanitarian.

Part VII

Adventures in Finance

Bloomberg

Bloomberg's Wall Street reporter Max Abelson captured the angst Wall Streeters felt at losing the record pay and profits from the heady days before the financial collapse and becoming simply richer than almost everybody else. Facing a slump in revenue from investment banking and trading, Wall Street firms trimmed discretionary pay, leaving executives facing sharply reduced circumstances and speaking—perhaps not wisely—about the dreadfulness of having to choose whether to spend on the kids' private school tuition, a hoped-for summer house rental, or an upgrade on a 1,200-square-foot Brooklyn duplex. Out? Annual ski trips to Aspen and Tahoe and three-day trips to Ibiza for a bachelor's party. In? Clipping grocery coupons. Abelson's deft reporting weaves in a measure of sympathy for people adjusting to lowered expectations rather than simply caricaturing them.

Max Abelson

17. Wall Street Bonus Withdrawal Means Trading Aspen for Coupons

Andrew Schiff was sitting in a traffic jam in California this month after giving a speech at an investment conference about gold. He turned off the satellite radio, got out of the car and screamed a profanity.

"I'm not Zen at all, and when I'm freaking out about the situation, where I'm stuck like a rat in a trap on a highway with no way to get out, it's very hard," Schiff, director of marketing for broker-dealer Euro Pacific Capital Inc., said in an interview.

Schiff, forty-six, is facing another kind of jam this year: Paid a lower bonus, he said the $350,000 he earns, enough to put him in the country's top 1 percent by income, doesn't cover his family's private-school tuition; a Kent, Connecticut, summer rental; and the upgrade they would like from their 1,200-square-foot Brooklyn duplex.

"I feel stuck," Schiff said. "The New York that I wanted to have is still just beyond my reach."

The smaller bonus checks that hit accounts across the financial-services industry this month are making it difficult to maintain the lifestyles that Wall Street workers expect, according to interviews with bankers and their accountants, therapists, advisers, and headhunters.

"People who don't have money don't understand the stress," said Alan Dlugash, a partner at accounting firm Marks Paneth & Shron LLP in New York who specializes in financial planning for the wealthy. "Could you imagine what it's like to say I got three kids in private school, I have to think about pulling them out? How do you do that?"

Bonus Caps

Facing a slump in revenue from investment banking and trading, Wall Street firms have trimmed 2011 discretionary pay. At Goldman Sachs Group Inc. and Barclays Capital, the cuts were at least 25 percent. Morgan Stanley capped cash bonuses at $125,000, and Deutsche Bank AG increased the percentage of deferred pay.

Wall Street's cash bonus pool fell by 14 percent last year to $19.7 billion, the lowest since 2008, according to projections by New York state comptroller Thomas DiNapoli.

"It's a disaster," said Ilana Weinstein, chief executive officer of New York–based search firm IDW Group LLC. "The entire construct of compensation has changed."

Most people can only dream of Wall Street's shrinking paychecks. Median household income in 2010 was $49,445, according to the U.S. Census Bureau, lower than the previous year and less than 1 percent of Goldman Sachs CEO Lloyd Blankfein's $7 million restricted-stock bonus for 2011. The percentage of Americans living in poverty climbed to 15.1 percent, the highest in almost two decades.

House of Mirth

Comfortable New Yorkers assessing their discomforts is at least as old as Edith Wharton's 1905 novel *The House of Mirth*, whose heroine Lily Bart said "the only way not to think about money is to have a great deal of it."

Wall Street headhunter Daniel Arbeeny said his "income has gone down tremendously." On a recent Sunday, he drove to Fairway Market in the Red Hook section of Brooklyn to buy discounted salmon for $5.99 a pound.

"They have a circular that they leave in front of the buildings in our neighborhood," said Arbeeny, forty-nine, who lives in nearby Cobble Hill, namesake for a line of pebbled-leather Kate Spade handbags. "We sit there, and I look through all of them to find out where it's worth going."

$17,000 on Dogs

Executive-search veterans who work with hedge funds and banks make about $500,000 in good years, said Arbeeny, managing principal at New York–based CMF Partners LLC, declining to discuss specifics about his own income. He said he no longer goes on annual ski trips to Whistler, Tahoe, or Aspen.

He reads other supermarket circulars to find good prices for his favorite cereal, Wheat Chex.

"Wow, did I waste a lot of money," Arbeeny said.

Richard Scheiner, fifty-eight, a real-estate investor and hedge-fund manager, said most people on Wall Street don't save.

"When their means are cut, they're stuck," said Scheiner, whose New York–based hedge fund, Lane Gate Partners LLC, was down about 15 percent last year. "Not so much an issue for me and my wife because we've always saved."

Scheiner said he spends about $500 a month to park one of his two Audis in a garage and at least $7,500 a year each for memberships at the Trump National Golf Club in Westchester and a gun club in upstate New York. A labradoodle named Zelda and a rescued bichon frise, Duke, cost $17,000 a year, including food, health care, boarding, and a daily dog walker who charges $17 each per outing, he said.

"Crushing Setback"

Still, he sold two motorcycles he didn't use and called his Porsche 911 Carrera 4S Cabriolet "the Volkswagen of supercars." He and his wife have given more than $100,000 to a nonprofit she founded that promotes employment for people with Asperger syndrome, he said.

Scheiner pays $30,000 a year to be part of a New York–based peer-learning group for investors called Tiger 21. Founder Michael Sonnenfeldt said members, most with a net worth of at least $10 million, have been forced to "re-examine lots of assumptions about how grand their life would be."

While they aren't asking for sympathy, "at their level, in a different way but in the same way, the rug got pulled out," said Sonnenfeldt, fifty-six. "For many people of wealth, they've had a crushing setback as well."

He described a feeling of "malaise" and a "paralysis that does not allow one to believe that generally things are going to get better," listing geopolitical hot spots such as Iran and low interest rates that have been "artificially manipulated" by the Federal Reserve.

Poly Prep

The malaise is shared by Schiff, the New York–based marketing director for Euro Pacific Capital, where his brother is CEO. His family rents the lower duplex of a brownstone in Cobble Hill, where his two children share a room. His ten-year-old daughter is a student at $32,000-a-year Poly Prep Country Day School in Brooklyn. His son, seven, will apply in a few years.

"I can't imagine what I'm going to do," Schiff said. "I'm crammed into 1,200 square feet. I don't have a dishwasher. We do all our dishes by hand."

He wants 1,800 square feet—"a room for each kid, three bedrooms, maybe four," he said. "Imagine four bedrooms. You have the luxury of a guest room, how crazy is that?"

Vegas, Ibiza

The family rents a three-bedroom summer house in Connecticut and will go there again this year for one month instead of four. Schiff said he brings home less than $200,000 after taxes, health-insurance, and 401(k) contributions. The closing costs, renovation, and down payment on one of the $1.5 million seventeen-foot-wide row houses nearby, what he called "the low rung on the brownstone ladder," would consume "every dime" of the family's savings, he said.

"I wouldn't want to whine," Schiff said. "All I want is the stuff that I always thought, growing up, that successful parents had."

Hans Kullberg, twenty-seven, a trader at Wyckoff, New Jersey–based hedge fund Falcon Management Corp., who said he earns about $150,000 a year, is adjusting his sights, too.

After graduating from the Wharton School of the University of Pennsylvania in 2006, he spent a $10,000 signing bonus from Citigroup Inc. on a six-week trip to South America. He worked on an emerging-markets team at the bank that traded and marketed synthetic collateralized debt obligations.

Wet T-Shirt

His tastes for travel got "a little bit more lavish," he said. Kullberg, a triathlete, went to a bachelor party in Las Vegas in January after renting a four-bedroom ski cabin at Bear Mountain in

California as a Christmas gift to his parents. He went to Ibiza for another bachelor party in August, spending $3,000 on a three-day trip, including a fifteen-minute ride from the airport that cost a hundred dollars. In May he spent ten days in India.

Earlier this month, a friend invited him on a trip to Mardi Gras in New Orleans. The friend was going to be a judge in a wet T-shirt contest, Kullberg said. He turned down the offer.

It wouldn't have been "the most financially prudent thing to do," he said. "I'm not totally sure about what I'm going to get paid this year, how I'm going to be doing."

He thinks more about the long term, he said, and plans to buy a foreclosed two-bedroom house in Charlotte, North Carolina, for $50,000 next month.

M. Todd Henderson, a University of Chicago law professor who's teaching a seminar on executive compensation, said the suffering is relative and real. He wrote two years ago that his family was "just getting by" on more than $250,000 a year, setting off what he called a firestorm of criticism.

"Yes, terminal diseases are worse than getting the flu," he said. "But you suffer when you get the flu."

"Have to Cut"

Dlugash, the accountant, said he's spending more time talking with Wall Street clients about their expenses.

"You don't necessarily have to cut that—but if you don't cut that, then you've got to cut this," he said. "They say, 'But I can't.' And I say, 'But you must.' "

One banker who owes Dlugash $20,000 gained the accountant's sympathy despite his six-figure pay.

"If you're making $50,000 and your salary gets down to $40,000 and you have to cut, it's very severe to you," Dlugash said. "But it's no less severe to these other people with these big numbers."

A Wall Street executive who made ten times that amount and now has declining income along with a divorce, private-school tuitions, and elderly parents also suffers, he said.

"These people never dreamed they'd be making $500,000 a year," he said, "and dreamed even less that they'd be broke."

Dealbreaker

Certain things just can't be explained in the mass-market press, and the London Whale trade that caused billions of dollars in losses for JP Morgan is one of them. For one thing, JP Morgan refused to offer any details about what its trading desk did—and for another, what its trading desk did was so mind-bendingly complex that few journalists could even understand it, and none could explain it in a way that the average newspaper reader could comprehend. This is where the blogosphere comes in. Matt Levine, an equity-derivatives geek turned blogger, understands complex concepts and can talk about them in a conversational and even funny way. This stuff isn't easy. But for people who wanted to really get up to speed on a hugely important story, there was only one place to turn.

Matt Levine

18. The Tale of a Whale of a Fail

Hi! Would you like to talk about the London Whale? Sure you would. The amount of misunderstanding of our poor beleaguered beluga is staggering, so I figured we could try to embark on a voyage of discovery together. Maybe we'll figure it out. Along the way we'll talk a tiny bit about the Volcker Rule. I am going to try to talk very slowly and simplify things so if you are pretty financially sophisticated you could skip this post (I've linked to some better things to read at the end), or just get really angry at me in the comments. Also this post is terrifyingly long, sorry!

So. You are JPMorgan. People come to you and give you money because you are a bank, and they want you to hold on to their money for them. You pay them interest so you need to invest their money to earn interest—ideally you earn more than you pay so you can make money and pay bonuses and stuff. You invest that money, broadly speaking, by lending it to other people who want to do things with it. Some of those people are buying houses; some of them are running businesses. Those are the main ones. (Some are buying cars or educations; others are running countries or municipalities. Ignore that.)

Now a tangent, which is long but important. Some of the money that you lend to people running businesses, you actually lend to people running businesses—like, they come to you and

Treasury and CIO: Selected Income Statement and Balance Sheet Data

As of or for the three months ended March 31,			
(in millions)	**2012**	**2011**	**Change**
Securities gains[a]	$453	$102	344%
Investment securities portfolio (average)	361,601	313,319	15
Investment securities portfolio (ending)	374,588	328,013	14
Mortgage loans (average)	12,636	11,418	11
Mortgage loans (ending)	11,819	12,171	(3)

(a) Reflects repositioning of the Corporate investment securities portfolio
For further information on the investment securities portfolio, see Note 3 and Note 11 on pages 91–100 and 113–117, respectively, of this Form 10-Q. For further information on CIO VaR and the Firm's nontrading interest rate-sensitive revenue at risk, see the Market Risk Management section on pages 73–76 of this Form 10-Q.

ask you for a loan and you give it to them. Some of it you don't because you don't have enough good loans to make—not enough people come to you for loans because they're not building factories because Obama or whatever, or people do come to you for loans but it's for terrible things so you say no. So you have "excess deposits," deposits that you haven't loaned out, and you invest those. You invest those in securities—that is, loans that someone already made and packaged into bonds to be bought and sold on the market. Since you are by hypothesis JPMorgan, you do this investing of excess deposits through your Chief Investment Office, or CIO, which is staffed by cetaceans. You can tell how much of this investing JPMorgan does because they disclose it on page 33 of their Form 10-Q filed with the SEC yesterday:

Now these investments are absolutely 100 percent without any doubt whatsoever "proprietary" in the sense that you have bought them with money and hope for them to pay you back with interest, as opposed to hoping to sell them immediately to a customer. And there is a thing called the Volcker Rule intended to prohibit "proprietary" trading. So this portfolio violates the Volcker Rule, right? No, not at all. The Volcker Rule applies to proprietary positions held in the trading book and intended to be sold within sixty days. As a rough cut, it appears that the CIO positions are mostly longer-term, which is what you'd expect from a bank investing its deposits that would otherwise be put in three-to-seven-year corporate loans or thirty-year mortgages.[1]

Okay so now you're JPMorgan and you've got about $375 billion worth of securities in the CIO—alongside some $700 billion of loans (page 87 of the 10-Q), of which $115bn are in your commercial bank (lending to businesses—page 28), $70bn are in your investment bank (lending to bigger businesses—page 16), $240bn are in retail (basically mortgages and stuff—page 18), and $187bn are in card services and auto (credit cards, car loans, student loans—page 25). So you have $185bn of corporate loans, plus whatever chunk of that $375bn CIO position is corporate bonds, which seems to be about $60bn (page 92). And you have something called "lending-related commitments," meaning revolving credit commitments where you have agreed to lend companies money if they ask for it—that number is almost $1 trillion (page 51), presumably almost all corporate. Add to that the fact that your investment bank involves buying and selling lots of corporate bonds as a market-maker, and doing derivatives with corporations where they might owe you money (something like $100bn, page 51 again), and you get the sense that JPMorgan has a lot of exposure to corporate credit. Meaning that if corporations start going bankrupt, JPMorgan will lose a lot of money.

That's obvious—they're a bank, that's what happens to banks, they lend money and if the borrowers don't pay it back then they are sad. Here if none of their *corporate* borrowers (leaving aside governments, mortgage borrowers, etc.) pays them back a cent, they lose in round numbers $250 billion on loans, $100 billion on trading receivables, and up to $1 trillion more if those borrowers draw their revolvers before defaulting (as they are wont to do).

THAT WOULD BE TERRIBLE.

But here is another important thing to realize. If instead of defaulting, companies just Became Shakier Credits—that is, if the market decided that all those companies looked less *likely* to pay their debts—JPMorgan would, to a first approximation, be pretty okay. Because to some rough approximation JPMorgan doesn't care about the day-to-day swings in creditworthiness of their borrowers; they care about getting paid back at the end. Banks do a thing called "maturity transformation," meaning that in some loose sense their social *function* is to lend money to companies and then *wait* for it to be paid back, instead of just consigning those companies to borrowing afresh every day from fickle liquidity-hungry investors. This is reflected in their accounting: the loans are reflected on an accrual basis; that is, there is some loss reserve against them which can change as they get less likely to be repaid, but JPMorgan doesn't book a profit or loss every time the market value of those loans goes up or down. Similarly the CIO securities are for the most part "available-for-sale," meaning again that JPMorgan's *income* (for accounting) doesn't reflect changes in their value, unless and until they're sold for a profit or loss.

So now we have to get a little bit technical and we can't avoid it, I am sorry, but here we are, we'll hold hands and go slow and it will be okay. You want to hedge your risk that things will go horribly pear-shaped and lots of your borrowers don't pay you back. (You can handle some regular number of them not paying you back—you're a bank, that's your job—but if things are worse than expected and a lot of them go belly-up that's a problem for you.) One thing that you could do is just buy massive quantities of something called CDS, for "credit default swaps," which function to a first approximation like insurance on corporate debt and pay off if a particular corporation defaults. You could buy CDS on every company you lend to in the amounts that you lend, but (1) this would eat up all your profits and (2) you can't really, it doesn't trade for all of them. But you could instead buy CDS on an index—basically a contract that references 125 big companies, and if some of them default it pays off a little and if all of them default it pays off a lot. That won't exactly match your profile—why would you be lending to those 125 companies and no others?—but the idea here is that if things go horrible, they will go horrible across the board, and your payouts on the index will have some rough match with your losses on your lending. Just a rough match, not perfect.

So you could probably try to buy index CDS—sometimes this is called CDX, after a particular index that is traded a lot, think of it as standing for "Credit Default indeX" because in finance, true story, "index" starts with an "x"—on, what, $1.35 trillion of corporate exposure. But you won't do that for bunches of reasons. One is that there's not nearly enough of it—all of the index CDS in the world, combined, including investment-grade and high-yield debt, tranched and untranched, American and European and Australian, everything, adds up to about $11.2 trillion of "notional" (just the amount that is "insured"), and for you to get 12 percent of that seems pretty hard and for you to get the right 12 percent—the stuff that correlates with your risk—seems impossible. Another is that you would basically be spending all your profits from lending[2] on the CDS, so you'd have no money left over to do things like buy computers or rent office space or pay bonuses. A third is that, the way CDS works, it is accounted for on a mark-to-market basis, but remember that your loans are not (see two paragraphs ago). So if credit got *better*, you would have a creepy loss in your income statement because you would "lose money" on your CDS and not "make money" on your loans and securities. If you are a bank, "losing money" for accounting purposes is actually a big deal not only because people get mad at you and stuff but also because it affects how well capitalized you are—lose enough money, on a mark-to-market basis, and you could get shut down. (This, again, is part of why you don't take mark-to-market gains and losses on your loans.)

That is your problem—you want to hedge against a disaster, but you can't just buy insurance against anything bad happening. So what you do is you conceive of a trade that:

- pays you plenty of (real) money on a disaster, but
- doesn't cost you a lot of (real *or* fake/mark-to-market) money on a nondisaster, like regular market moves

What is that trade?

Well, it starts by buying credit protection on things that make you a lot of money if things go bad. What you're looking for here is a concept loosely called "leverage," which means loosely that you don't pay very much now but get a lot of money if things go bad very quickly. Think of it as: rather than pay for something that moves down a bit when credit improves a bit and up a bit when it worsens a bit, you're paying for something that moves down *a lot* when credit improves a bit and down a lot when it worsens a bit. Some types of protection that do that are:

- buying very short-dated credit protection, like a credit index set to expire in December 2012, so that if things get really bad really fast you are ready for it,
- buying protection on something called "tranches," which pay you relatively more for the next few defaults among the companies in the index, rather than paying you the same amount for all defaults in that index, and/or
- buying protection on high-yield indexes (junk bonds!), which are likely to go bankrupt faster if things get bad

It seems very likely that JPMorgan's CIO did some or all of the above. It is hard to know! There is a deep mystery—if you like mysteries (and derivatives!) you can read the links above, but the deepest part of the mystery is that when all the hedge funds were complaining to Bloomberg about how JPMorgan was *writing* lots of protection on CDX.IG.NA.9 (next paragraph), no one was complaining that they were *buying* the protections mentioned above. I have no solution to the mystery and neither, it appears, does anyone else outside of JPMorgan. [**Update: untrue! Meet me in the usual place.**[3]]

Okay anyway though, this hasn't solved any of your problems except maybe the size one (because you are buying lesser amounts of more intense protection). You are still paying money for protection, and you still lose money if credit improves. So you do the second half of this trade: you "write protection" (sell CDS) on the broad index. This is, again, very approximately like selling an insurance policy: you take in money now, and pay out some money if the companies in that index default. JPMorgan's CIO very clearly did exactly that, on an index called the CDX.IG.NA.9 10-year, which despite the name matures in 2017. Intuitively—though it doesn't quite work this way for curve trades so if you know about credit trading you'll want to skip the rest of this sentence—you need to sell *more* of this broad protection than you bought in the previous paragraph because what you bought in the previous paragraph was more intense than what you're selling, so that's why the whale sold so very much protection on this index.[4]

So what have you done? Something in outline like the following:

- You are getting money in on one end by selling protection and paying it out on the other by buying protection, so you are not paying out all of your profits.
- You have a position that is relatively neutral to credit market moves: if credit markets move up a bit, your big CDS-writing

trade moves up a bit (you make some money), and your smaller but more intense CDS-buying trade moves down a lot (which, multiplied by the smaller size, means you lose some money, and they sort of offset). This is called being "DV01 neutral" but don't worry about it. The point is that you don't have huge mark to market losses when markets go up or down regular amounts.

- You have a position that makes a lot of money on bigger moves. So if a bunch of companies go bankrupt your really intense trade pays off a lot, while your less intense trade doesn't cost that much. So in the really bad state of the world this is a good hedge for you. This is called being "long convexity" or "gap risk" but don't worry about it.

There is much complexity swept under the rug here but the concept is a bet something like this:

- Take 100 companies
- For each one that goes bankrupt, you pay me $2
- For the first five that go bankrupt, I'll pay you $1 each
- For the next five that go bankrupt, I'll pay you $3
- For the next ten that go bankrupt, I'll pay you $5
- If more than 20 go bankrupt, you don't get any more—I've paid you the max of $70.

You lose a bit but not a lot if things stay good, you break even if things go mediocre, and you do great if things are really bad. (But there's some horizon where if things are really really bad, more than thirty-five defaults, you start to lose again. This may or may not be a feature of JPMorgan's bets.)

It seems fairly certain that *in broad concept* this is what JPMorgan's Chief Investment Office was doing. But the above allows for lots of nuance. You want a hedge that is basically flat when things are basically okay, and pays out a lot when things are terrible. But define "flat," and "okay," and "a lot," and "terrible." These are hard judgments and are influenced by your expectations about the world. If you think that there are likely to be only two to three defaults, then the bet above looks like a real disaster hedge: it loses money in the expected case but pays off a lot if there are a staggering, unlikely twenty defaults. But if you think that there are likely to be thirty to forty defaults, then the bet above looks ridiculously optimistic—not a hedge at all, but rather something that loses money if things are at the bad end of expectations.

What seems, loosely, to have happened to the Whale is a combination of things. One is, he got more optimistic and so sold more protection—making the bet *relatively* more bullish, though not *absolutely* bullish. It is almost certainly—though who knows?—not correct to say, as everyone does, that Iksil was long $100 billion of corporate credit in his CDX book. It is certainly correct to say that the CIO was overall long credit—that's what it does! invest JPMorgan's money in credit instruments!—or that JPMorgan as a whole was long credit—it's a bank!—but the credit derivatives book probably was a hedge designed to hedge tail risk.

The second is, his model was wrong. At a bank, that little flow chart of the bet that I set out above gets programmed into a computer, and the computer knows your cash flows and what the expected value of them is based on market conditions. If the market is predicting seven defaults, the computer knows that, and knows that I will pay you $14 and you will pay me $11, and it will discount those cash flows and spit out a present value of the bet based on current market conditions. But it's hard to know what the market is predicting, and the actual bets were vastly more complicated than this, and so it turns out that the computer just got it wrong. Bad computer! Bad people who programmed it! Bad people who relied on it without checking! But these things happen; the surprise is that they happened at JPMorgan, which usually avoids them.

The third is, people figured out it was him, talked to Bloomberg, and started picking him off—making it more expensive for him to do his trades (in the sense that he showed mark-to-market losses). They did this on a bet that eventually he would have to unwind his position and they would make money. They did.

You can draw various lessons from this and I guess you have. There's the Volcker Rule, of course, and it's safe to say that everyone's suspicious about whether this is, or would be, or should be, allowed by the Volcker Rule as a "hedge." What does it hedge you ask? Well, the thing I described above in excruciating detail hedges JPMorgan's risk of a lot of corporate bankruptcies. Yes, you say, but what does Bruno Iksil's $100bn CDX long credit position hedge? Well, it hedges his short credit position. Which hedges JPMorgan's overall long credit position. OKAY, you say, and walk away in disgust to write a bigger Volcker Rule.

Hedging is hard because you can only try to hedge with things that you expect to be correlated in the world that might come about, and you don't really know what state of the world will actually occur or what will be correlated with what in that world. You win some you lose some, out of failure in foresight or model error or the other side of the trade trading against you.

What does that argue for? I don't think it argues anything at all about the Volcker Rule: banning hedging can't be a solution, and banning something that you call "portfolio hedging" doesn't fix bad models (or tell you what a "portfolio" is). Obviously this looks "prop" if you focus on one part of the trade, but that is as always in the eye of the beholder. Iksil didn't think he was betting on corporate credit improving; he thought he was adjusting his hedge to address current market conditions.

The more sensible response, if you want to prevent this sort of thing from blowing up the universe, is something like "stop doing sophisticated things" or at least "raise unsophisticated but large amounts of capital against your sophisticated things." Because obviously forcing JPMorgan to have capital equal to 20 percent of its non-risk-weighted assets would make it less likely that this would bring down JPMorgan. So, fine, that's probably right. But JPMorgan's Basel III capital (for what it's worth!) is down like twenty basis points on the loss, and there's no evidence at all that this brought down JPMorgan or did anything close to it. That's not much of an argument—many other banks are less well capitalized, and less well endowed with modeling skills, than JPMorgan, so if this did some small damage there it could do much larger damage elsewhere. On the other hand, there's at least a chance that JPMorgan is doing more sophisticated-cum-dangerous trades than other, less sophisticated banks *because it is more sophisticated*, and the reason that this screw-up happened at JPMorgan is that only JPMorgan dared to dream big enough to screw up this big.

Anyway. Here are some great things to read on Whaledemort if you are too smart to profit from the above:

- You have presumably already read Lisa Pollack, but if not *what are you doing here?*
- I don't really know what Felix Salmon is talking about here, but this is good, not only because he's nice to me
- Kid Dynamite will tell you a relevant story
- Peter Tchir does some relevant digging
- Sonic Charmer has some relevant things to say about the Volcker Rule
- Deus ex Macchiato is brief and sensible[5]

Notes

1. Without getting into it too much, it seems that the CIO portfolio and JPMorgan's available-for-sale securities match up in size and stated intent; see, for instance, page 92 of the Q for numbers and things like pages 48–49 for discussion of purpose etc.

2. And then some, since your revolvers are probably underpriced versus buying CDS.

3. Of course the person who knows is Lisa Pollack, who points out that hedge fund skew traders like to trade skew in the 10y because its maturity matches closely with liquid 5-year corporate CDS, so you can buy protection on the CDX and sell it on single names and make money. The 5y, which JPMorgan is hypothetically buying in huge size, does not present a useful skew trade because the other leg is very short-dated (under a year) and so can't be put on profitably. So hedge funds had no reason to complain about that. Alternatively, if your theory is not curve-trade flattener but buy protection on HY index and/or tranches, the absolute size there would be less and so would spark less complaining than the $100bn of protection written on the IG index.

4. Again: doesn't work for curve trades, where the DV01 on the 10-year is [oops, 5x] that on the near-expiry 5-year! So maybe it's not a pure curve trade, or if it is I can't really explain it. *This is the best explanation you're likely to find.* I'll stick with the stylized explanation in the text because it's stylized but I guess I find the curve-trade arguments, like, 70 percent persuasive. [Update: I'm coming around more to *arguments that this was buy-HY-write-IG* rather than a flattener but will basically remain agnostic.]

5. For the links embedded here in the online article, see http://dealbreaker.com/2012/05/the-tale-of-a-whale-of-a-fail/.

Reuters

Bethany McLean wonders how you can have fraud without fraudsters, writing about how the state and federal authorities who have sued Wall Street banks for fleecing customers can't seem to find any individual bankers to blame. The case in question here is particularly egregious: Bear Stearns pocketed refunds owed to its customers after knowingly selling them fraudulent mortgages. Yet almost half a decade after the financial crisis began, no executive on Wall Street has been held accountable. McLean, who made her name helping uncover the Enron fraud, asks why and uses the Bear Stearns case to examine possible reasons, none of which look good for the concept of justice.

Bethany McLean

19. Case Against Bear and JPMorgan Provides Little Cheer

Last week, New York attorney general Eric Schneiderman, who is the cochairman of the Residential Mortgage-Backed Securities Working Group—which President Obama formed earlier this year to investigate who was responsible for the misconduct that led to the financial crisis—filed a complaint against JPMorgan Chase.

The complaint, which seeks an unspecified amount in damages (but says that investors lost $22.5 billion), alleges widespread wrongdoing at Bear Stearns in the run-up to the financial crisis. JPMorgan Chase, of course, acquired Bear in 2008.

Apparently, this is just the beginning of a Schneiderman onslaught.

"We do expect this to be a matter of very significant liability, and there are others to come that will also reflect the same quantum of damages," Schneiderman said in an interview with Bloomberg Television. "We're looking at tens of billions of dollars, not just by one institution, but by quite a few."

The prevailing opinion seems to be, Yay! Someone is finally making, or at least trying to make, the banks pay for their sins. But while there is one big positive to the complaint, overall I don't think there's any reason to cheer.

Schneiderman's case clearly lays out the alleged bad behavior at the old Bear Stearns. Although Bear promised investors it was doing due diligence on the mortgages it purchased, it wasn't. Defendants "systematically failed to fully evaluate the loans, largely ignored the defects that their limited review did uncover, and kept investors in the dark about both the inadequacy of their review procedures and the defects in the underlying loans," alleges the complaint.

Even worse, Bear would make deals with the sellers of mortgages in which it would force them to make a payment for failed mortgages, but instead of taking the bad loan out of the trust, Bear would just keep the money—even though both Bear's lawyers and its accountants (this is truly stunning), according to Schneiderman's case, warned them that wasn't OK.

The complaint shows just how complicit the Bear bankers were in the proliferation of bad loans that almost took down the economy, and that alone makes it valuable. "He's finally telling the story so that people can understand the depth and magnitude of what went on," says Eliot Spitzer, who had Schneiderman's job after the dot-com bust.

But beyond that, there's not much to applaud. The biggest flaw is that Schneiderman decided not to name any individuals, a practice that is sadly all too common in financial fraud cases. The *New York Times* argued that it's a strength that the case doesn't focus on individuals and specifics and instead alleges a broad pattern of fraud. But naming names is powerful. Anonymity is weak, and that is amplified when the generalized wrongdoing allegedly occurred at a now-defunct bank. In addition, the lack of names is weird. How could the actions alleged in the complaint have been accomplished if real people didn't do them?

Schneiderman's office also brought charges under a specific New York State law called the Martin Act. The Martin Act doesn't require prosecutors to show that the defendants intended to commit fraud. This seems ridiculous. If Bear employees committed the acts detailed in the complaint, especially pocketing money that should have gone into investors' pockets, against the warnings of lawyers and accountants, how can they have intended anything other than fraud?

Which, of course, raises a few other questions. Chief among them: Why haven't Justice Department investigators brought criminal charges, and why hasn't the Securities and Exchange Commission even brought civil charges? Technically speaking, both are also members of the Residential Mortgage-Backed Securities Working Group, but both also have been conducting their own investigations since the crisis hit. The answer cannot be that Schneiderman discovered something new.

JPMorgan has complained that his suit relies on "recycled claims already made by private plaintiffs" and, well, it does. The notion that investment banks were knowingly putting bad loans into securitizations has been public knowledge since the fall of 2010. That was when executives from a company called Clayton Holdings, which was retained by many of the big banks to do due diligence on the mortgages they were buying, told the Financial Crisis Inquiry Commission that Wall Street knew that almost one-third of the mortgages they were securitizing didn't meet their own standards. Spitzer wrote a column for *Slate* calling the documents the "Rosetta stone" because he thought they provided such a clear road map for investigators. That's not all. Schneiderman's predecessor, Andrew Cuomo, actually entered into a cooperation agreement with Clayton back in 2008! Did it really take over four years to put together a complaint that doesn't even name real people?

As for the part about Bear pocketing money that should have gone to investors, that's been well known since at least early 2011, when Teri Buhl did an in-depth piece for the *Atlantic* on a lawsuit that bond insurer Ambac filed against JPMorgan in 2008, which was unsealed in early 2011. Buhl wrote that Bear traders were "pocketing cash that should have gone to securities holders." And the Ambac lawsuit named names!

In other words, everyone has had plenty of time.

So there are a couple of possibilities. One is that Justice and/or the SEC will follow up with their own charges now that Schneiderman has laid the groundwork. Maybe. But that doesn't make a lot of sense given the widespread availability of the information in his lawsuit and the length of time that has passed since the financial crisis. It's an old saw in legal circles that the more time goes by, the harder it is to file criminal charges. By now, it will feel strange if the Justice Department yanks four people who worked at the old Bear and in effect says: "You and only you are going to take the fall for the entire financial crisis!"

Another possibility is that those who say that federal agencies simply don't have the appetite to pursue the banks are right. Whether that's because they lack the resources and the political will, or because bringing criminal charges against individuals would inexorably lead up the chain to the institution, which would destroy it, and no one wants to see that happen, it doesn't much matter. If Schneiderman's lawsuit is the best we can manage under those constraints, then that's a tragedy.

A third possibility is that there's more nuance to what happened than Schneiderman's suit allows. (JPMorgan, for its part, has said it will contest the charges.) Some would still say that's all right, because if there are fifty shades of bad behavior, this is clearly one of them; so even if it's not the darkest, let's make the bankers pay up. The problem is that it's not the bankers who will pay. It's not the individuals who did these awful things, or former Bear Stearns executives who may have sanctioned it knowingly or unknowingly, or even current JPMorgan executives who will pay the big fine that will likely be the end result of all this. It's JPMorgan's current shareholders, which include mutual funds like indexers Vanguard and Wellington. In other words, we, the American investor class, are the ones who are going to pay. And if Schneiderman does indeed apply this same method to other banks, well, then we'll pay even more. I fail to understand why this is justice, or why this will do anything to dissuade bad behavior in the future.

I'm also bothered by what happened after Schneiderman filed his suit. First, JPMorgan Chase raised a stink, because in the minds of many JPMorgan executives, they performed a public service by purchasing Bear and have already paid enough for its misdeeds. Maybe it's not fair to blame Schneiderman's office for responding with a press release trumpeting the myriad ways in which JPMorgan Chase benefited from government assistance. But whether you love or hate the big banks, the alleged wrongdoing that happened at Bear has nothing to do with whether or not JPMorgan Chase benefited from government help. The punishment the bank should face for any misdeeds should be purely a matter of law, not public opinion about the bank bailout. Otherwise, we risk bastardizing the law.

Finally, I worry that this is all a classic "watch the birdie" exercise: Hey, folks, look over here at this facsimile of justice! Making the big banks pay somehow sure feels good, and if you don't look too closely, it may even distract you from the big questions. Namely, what should a financial institution that serves the needs of businesses and consumers—instead of one that uses us as fodder for its own profits and executive bonuses—look like? And how do we get from here to there? Instead, we're going to pay up, and in exchange, get business as usual. That's not a good deal.

Wall Street Journal

Because of his inflation-fighting credentials, Mario Draghi, the Italian president of the European Central Bank, was once described—approvingly—by the newspaper *Bild* as "rather German, even really Prussian." For inflation-wary Germans, that's the ultimate compliment. But as the Euro crisis unfolded, Draghi became persuaded that nothing could stabilize deteriorating European markets other than creating money to buy struggling countries' debt. The plan drew predictably stiff resistance from German officials, including the man who would become its biggest obstacle: Jens Weidmann. The forty-four-year-old president of the powerful Bundesbank viewed himself as a defender of the German bank's conservative monetary legacy. Drawing on interviews with high-level European sources, Brian Blackstone and Marcus Walker detail exactly how Draghi was able to do it.

Brian Blackstone and Marcus Walker

20. How ECB Chief Outflanked German Foe in Fight for Euro

As Mario Draghi watched euro-zone markets disintegrate in late July, he scribbled two sentences into the margin of an otherwise routine speech for London investors, changing the course of the three-year-old euro crisis.

"Within our mandate, the ECB is ready to do whatever it takes to preserve the euro," the European Central Bank president jotted. "And believe me, it will be enough."

The ECB had long resisted using its most powerful tool—its printing press—to save struggling European governments from the debt crisis. The Bundesbank, Germany's influential central bank, warned of dark consequences if the ECB tried that. Now Mr. Draghi, the ECB's Italian chief, was signaling that it would defy its biggest shareholder.

Investors' loss of confidence in the very survival of the euro convinced him there was no other option. Lenders were turning away from Spain and Italy, where a government insolvency could destroy the dream of European unity and rock the global economy.

By agreeing to create money to purchase struggling countries' debt without limit, the ECB has ushered in the decisive phase of Europe's battle to save the euro. If the ECB's resort to the printing press fails to stabilize markets and buy time for crisis-hit countries to recover, nothing else will, economists say.

Even if it works, the ECB will emerge a fundamentally different institution, having abandoned major planks of the economic orthodoxy that shaped its charter and first decade. A more activist central bank, while welcomed in most European countries, is already confronting deep skepticism in Germany, where fears are growing that it is sowing the seeds of inflation.

A loss of German support for the euro would call the currency's viability into question anew. The controversy over the ECB shows how the euro crisis is fueling tension among European nations. While many Germans fear a takeover of the currency union by Mediterranean countries, many southern Europeans feel that German obstinacy is prolonging the crisis.

This account of the ECB's momentous shift, based on interviews with numerous officials familiar with the events and with central players' thinking, shows how the cautious Mr. Draghi changed his mind about the bank's role and cultivated German political leaders to outmaneuver Bundesbank president Jens Weidmann, in a tactical struggle to redefine Europe's strategy against the crisis.

The battle lines were drawn immediately after Mr. Draghi's London speech on July 26.

Mr. Weidmann, sitting in his vast Bundesbank office with panoramic views of the Frankfurt skyline, was taken aback. Mr. Draghi soon called him from London to explain his remarks, arguing that markets had been betting on the breakup of the euro and that was unacceptable.

Mr. Weidmann countered that investors were betting against Italy and Spain because of flaws in their economies that only national politicians could fix. ECB bond buying would just take the heat off them.

"This is a political problem that in my view needs a political solution," Mr. Weidmann told the Italian, according to people familiar with the conversation.

For Mr. Weidmann, the ECB's gambit betrayed its founding principles, which were rooted in the traditions of the Bundesbank and the lessons of Europe's postwar history. Though only forty-four years old, Mr. Weidmann views himself as a defender of the German bank's legacy, against some nations' laxer monetary mores.

As a boy in the late 1970s, he learned the difference between the German mark and Europe's softer currencies during family vacations. On the mountainous Gargano peninsula in Italy's rustic southeast, he was struck by locals' use of *gettoni*, or tokens, in pay phones—because the value of lira coins was falling so fast that phone booths couldn't keep pace.

By his late teens, Mr. Weidmann said recently, he had "inhaled" the Bundesbank view: Central banks exist to defend a currency against politicians' cravings for easy money.

Germany's obsession with price stability is often said to stem from 1920s hyperinflation under the Weimar Republic. But for modern Germany's economic elite, it is rooted in a more recent experience: the postwar success of West Germany.

In Germans' collective memory, the Bundesbank's refusal to make politicians' life easy by printing money was critical. Though the Bundesbank briefly bought German bonds amid a recession in 1975, it soon stopped, and West Germany emerged with less inflation, debt, and unemployment than most other Western countries. "Not all Germans believe in God, but all believe in the Bundesbank," former European Commission president Jacques Delors once said.

During the troubled 1970s, Mr. Draghi was a doctoral student at the Massachusetts Institute of Technology, pondering why Italy was turning from a fast-growing economy into a financial mess.

When central banks buy bonds in large quantities, they pay for them with newly created money. Mr. Draghi concluded that Rome's habit of force-feeding its central bank with public debt was debasing the lira.

Mr. Draghi became one of Italy's most effective public officials in the 1990s, spearheading efforts to tame the budget deficit and qualify for euro membership. After a stint at Goldman Sachs, he became head of the Banca d'Italia in January 2006 at the age of fifty-eight.

Two weeks later, Germany's new chancellor, Angela Merkel, hired Mr. Weidmann, then a thirty-seven-year-old star analyst at the Bundesbank, to be her chief economics adviser. Mr. Weidmann became her most important aide during the global financial crisis and the euro-zone storm that followed.

In early 2011, Bundesbank president Axel Weber resigned after protesting a more limited ECB move to buy struggling euro nations' bonds. Mr. Weidmann got his job.

With Mr. Weber out of the picture, Mr. Draghi became the frontrunner for next ECB president—to the dismay of many Germans.

"Please not this Italian," wailed the tabloid *Bild*. "Mamma mia, for Italians, inflation is a way of life, like tomato sauce with pasta!"

Yet Mr. Draghi's credentials were strong. He presented himself to German media as a believer in the Bundesbank's anti-inflation orthodoxy, calling Germany "a model" for the rest of the continent. It worked. Ms. Merkel swung behind him. *Bild* declared him "rather German, even really Prussian."

The crisis, however, was taking a turn that would test Mr. Draghi's adherence to the German playbook.

By mid-2011 investors were fleeing Italian and Spanish bonds. Influential economists argued for a rethink of the ECB's role, saying what worked for Germany under the mark didn't necessarily work in a multinational currency union. They said only the ECB could prevent runs on countries, by promising to support their bonds, just as central banks backstop banks.

The ECB's Governing Council debated the argument that summer. Many of the national central-bank heads were sympathetic to it. Not Mr. Weidmann. Did central-bank officials know better than investors what a fair bond yield on governments' debt was, he asked. And was 7 percent really a calamity, or just unpleasant for finance ministers?

Afraid of a German backlash, the ECB bought Italian and Spanish bonds only halfheartedly, stressing that the buying was "limited" and "temporary." Bond investors weren't reassured. And then Italy, which had promised economic overhauls, reneged. The ECB, shaken by the experience, let struggling countries' borrowing costs rise again.

Mr. Draghi had stayed quiet during the debates. When he took over as president in November, he dashed hopes of more decisive bond buying. Instead, he launched a program to support banks with cheap loans.

The move brought a brief calm to bond markets. In early March, Mr. Draghi shelved what was left of the bond-buying program, after concluding it was ineffective. Mr. Weidmann thought he had won the argument.

The unraveling of euro-zone financial markets this summer forced Mr. Draghi to rethink.

Northern Europe's savings were steering clear of southern Europe's borrowers. So despite a wave of policy overhauls by new national leaders, Italian and Spanish borrowing costs were rising to unsustainable levels. As they rose, so did borrowing costs for the countries' small businesses, and they were gasping for affordable credit.

Political turmoil in Greece raised the odds of a euro exit that many feared would trigger bank runs across Europe's south. Companies around Europe made preparations for a breakup of the euro. Investors were increasingly pricing in catastrophe.

Mr. Draghi and allies on the ECB's executive board, especially Benoit Coeure of France and Jorg Asmussen of Germany, decided they needed a contingency plan. In late June, they and a few staff members began working in secret on a new bond-buying plan, one without the flaws of the previous effort.

This time, the ECB would help a government only if it signed on to strict policy conditions. Then, the bank would intervene without limit.

Mr. Draghi knew he would face blowback in Germany. A chorus of media, lawmakers, and economists there would accuse him of risking inflation, exceeding the ECB's mandate, and violating European treaties. He needed support from the highest level in Berlin.

Over months of calls and discreet visits to the chancellery, he had been building up a relationship of trust with Ms. Merkel and her veteran finance minister, Wolfgang Schauble. Mr. Draghi kept them informed of how his thinking was evolving.

Both Ms. Merkel and Mr. Schauble were dubious of bond buying. They worried it might not work and might remove the pressure on Italy and Spain to shrink deficits and ease rigid labor rules. But they also knew that euro-zone governments' bailout funds were too small and cumbersome to save Italy and Spain in case of a full-blown market run. Only the ECB could intervene quickly and massively.

For weeks, Mr. Draghi watched euro-breakup fears building in the thirty to forty financial indicators he studied daily. When he arrived in London on July 24, Spanish and Italian bond yields were spiking.

The ECB's plan wasn't yet ready. Mr. Draghi hadn't informed national central-bank chiefs. But, fearing a summer of chaos, he decided to vow publicly to do "whatever it takes."

Markets rejoiced at his July 26 speech. He knew the German backlash would begin the next day.

That evening, he phoned Mr. Schauble, who was vacationing on the sandy North Sea island of Sylt, and asked him to help publicly defend the ECB from German media fury.

Mr. Schauble, the German government's strongest believer in the euro and European unity, agreed, overriding finance-ministry officials who advised him not to comment on decisions of the central bank.

Mr. Draghi also called French president Francois Hollande and asked him to lobby Ms. Merkel for a joint Franco-German declaration of support. The chancellor, who was on a hiking vacation in the Alps, told Mr. Hollande she was comfortable with Mr. Draghi's move but wary of making a public statement on ECB matters. The two leaders' aides negotiated a wording.

The next morning, the Bundesbank launched its expected counteroffensive to Mr. Draghi's speech, attacking bond-buying as "problematic" and "not the most sensible" way to tackle the crisis.

But at lunchtime, Mr. Schauble issued a statement welcoming Mr. Draghi's promise to preserve the euro. Soon afterward, Ms. Merkel and Mr. Hollande declared their determination to do "everything" to defend the euro and called on "European institutions" as well as national governments to do their duty.

Berlin had broken with the Bundesbank. Mr. Draghi had the cover he wanted.

On August 1, a day before the ECB's Governing Council met to approve Mr. Draghi's plan, the Bundesbank website published an in-house interview with Mr. Weidmann in which he argued that his institution deserved special influence inside the ECB. "We are the largest and most important central bank in the Eurosystem and we have a greater say than many other central banks," he said.

But Mr. Weidmann lacked allies on the ECB's Governing Council. Over a dinner at ECB headquarters on August 1, the council members drew up a plan for bond buying. There was one big proviso: Before the ECB would buy their bonds, governments must ask other European countries for credit from the euro-zone bailout funds. That meant agreeing to policy conditions and intrusive monitoring.

At the next day's council meeting, Mr. Weidmann asked Mr. Draghi to make clear at a news conference that substantial differences remained within the ECB over bond buying.

Instead, Mr. Draghi said only Mr. Weidmann had reservations. That broke the ECB's tradition of not naming individual opponents of policy moves.

The German, watching on TV inside the Bundesbank's imposing headquarters, was annoyed. Had the Governing Council held a formal vote, he wouldn't have been alone, he felt. Mr. Draghi was going out of his way to isolate him.

But Mr. Weidmann also felt freer to criticize.

"Revolt of the Bundesbank," declared the cover of *Der Spiegel*, Germany's leading news magazine, later that month. In the interview inside, Mr. Weidmann warned that the ECB must focus "solely" on inflation, like the Bundesbank, or risk repeating the 1970s mistakes of the Banca d'Italia.

German media overwhelmingly sided with the Bundesbank. *Bild* claimed that Ms. Merkel had had to pressure Mr. Weidmann not to resign in protest. The Bundesbank denied the report, but many at the ECB believe the Bundesbank planted it to whip up anger in Germany.

Ms. Merkel, in further public statements, said the ECB was acting within its mandate.

Mr. Draghi pressed ahead. Investors were now convinced the ECB was serious. This time, Bundesbank hostility wouldn't hold it back.

The Bundesbank attacked again. It said Mr. Weidmann regarded bond purchases as "tantamount to financing governments by printing bank notes."

The statement exasperated other ECB governors, who felt the German was being extreme in his dissent while offering no alternative. In a rare rebuke of the hallowed Bundesbank by a

German politician, Mr. Schauble suggested in a newspaper interview that Mr. Weidmann was harming public trust in the ECB and should pipe down.

Mr. Weidmann isn't finished. Last month, in a speech in Frankfurt, he recruited the quintessential classic of German literature, Goethe's *Faust*, as an ally against the ECB.

In *Faust* part 2, Mr. Weidmann noted, the devil Mephisto tempts the Emperor into printing money to pay for public spending:

> Such paper notes, instead of pearls and gold,
> Are practical, you know how much you hold;
> No need to be a trader or a vendor,
> To lust for love and wine you can surrender.

In the play, Mr. Weidmann observed, a heady boom gives way to the collapse of the currency.

The markets, however, are listening to Mr. Draghi.

n+1

The Occupy Wall Street movement seems long ago and far away, but via a website called "Occupy the Boardroom" it left behind nearly 8,000 letters addressed to bank executives. The best were collected in *The Trouble Is the Banks*, edited by Mark Greif, Dayna Tortorici, Kathleen French, Emma Janaskie, and Nick Werle and published by the n+1 Foundation. In the letters "writers argue against the irresponsibility in Wall Street's pleas of helplessness: It's not me, it's the rules. It's my role. It's capitalism. If I weren't doing the wrong thing, somebody else would. The stockholders would have my head. The market will decide," as the editors' preface notes. In many of these frequently heartbreaking letters, the impact of the banks' decisions on the economic lives of ordinary Americans is poignantly and succinctly expressed.

Edited by Mark Greif, Dayna Tortorici, Kathleen French, Emma Janaskie, and Nick Werle

21. *From* The Trouble Is the Banks

Please Don't Harass My Father Any Further

Deena DeNaro

To: Lloyd H. Dean, Wells Fargo

Dear Lloyd,

In May 2007, I became the first person in my immediate family to get a degree, at age 38. I graduated owing more than $100,000 in private student loans. Payments were more than $1,100 per month. My 74-year-old retired father is the cosigner for most of these loans, but in September 2008, my dad lost $70,000 of his pension with the banks' collapse.

In December 2009, after just one year in the workforce, I was laid off due to cut-backs. For most of 2010, I wasn't able to find steady employment. In January 2011, I ran out of deferment with my private student loans. The banks began chasing my father as the cosigner. They have wrecked his line of credit and called in his home equity loan on which he never missed any payments.

In June 2011, my father saw a lawyer to try to get the payments reduced to something proportionate to his fixed income. In October 2011, he got word that the lawyer failed to get payments reduced enough. My dad wrote me a letter saying he had to sell his life insurance and rearrange his will to protect my sister and stepmom.

The letter arrived last Saturday.

He had a stroke on Sunday.

Now Wells Fargo is harassing him for payment of another student loan.

I am asking you to please suspend collection actions against my father until I have a job that will pay me enough to make the payments myself.

I always believed getting an education was the only way to succeed in life. Now I regret it every single day.

Sincerely,
Deena DeNaro
Durham, NC 27701

My Furnace Guy

Joel Roache

This week I had to call the gentleman who services my furnace. He is in his seventies, and it is hard for him to walk and even harder for him to climb up and down peoples' stairs. I asked him when he was going to retire. "Can't afford it!" he said. Forty years ago he bought into some kind of insurance deal and started paying $50. Not even pin money on Wall St., but he paid it every month for forty years, almost 500 months. At the end, because of systematic excessive risk and fraud in the financial system, he received from this investment the grand total of $5,000. He probably doesn't know much about the details of the Grand Casino that our financial system has become, but he knows enough to diagnose the problem: "They're all crooks." The rest of us are also figuring it out in growing numbers, and we are on our way. . . .

Joel Roache
Salisbury, MD 21801

Thank You for My Lessons

Anonymous

To: Jay Mandelbaum, JP Morgan Chase

Dear Jay,

I just wanted to thank you for giving me a mortgage I couldn't afford in 2006. I was naïve. I had never bought a house before; but luckily I had a mortgage broker who was making a large amount of money for securing a very high mortgage for me and my family. You see, we lived in Florida and in 2006, I was afraid if we didn't buy a home immediately, we would be locked out forever. Again, I was young and naïve and didn't understand what it would mean for the "bubble to burst."

My mortgage broker assured me that we had sufficient income to buy this house and the bank agreed. We were making about $50,000 annually as a married couple with one child. Our 1,200 square-foot, two-bedroom, two-bathroom house was $165,000. We thought the right thing to do would be to put our savings into the home and pay 20% down. So that's what we did. We also put $10,000 in upgrades and repairs so we could increase the equity in our home. After all, our home was the safest place to put it, right? It was all relative to the market and the market was doing fantastic. We could even make money off of our home someday. We weren't planning to do this, but what a great option to have. We escrowed our taxes and insurance and our payment was $900 month. A little steep for our modest income, but we were going to make it work no matter what. They also sold us a fifty-year mortgage to lower the payment. But it was a fixed rate and we were told this was what we wanted in order to have a predictable mortgage, so we felt comfortable. After all, we were going to live here forever or for a long time. And in ten or so years, we should have some decent equity in the home and might even be able to sell it.

But then our taxes went up and so did our insurance, and our payment went up to $1,700 month. It was also peculiar that only $15 per month of that amount was going to principal and the rest to interest. That's when I learned that we had a negative amortization loan. We would never really be able to outrun the interest because we would never pay enough on principal. We didn't have anything extra to send in with a $1,700 month payment. Talk about some serious stress at this point. *We'll just cut back*, we thought. We shut off our cable, got rid of our cell phones. Bought cheap food. But we couldn't make it happen.

Two years into the mortgage, and after our mortgage had been sold three times, we asked for a loan modification. We were told we weren't behind in payments, so we had to stop sending them. The representative said we should save those payments because we would use them for a new down payment when we were approved for the modification. So we did exactly as we were told. But, once we were assigned to a modification caseworker, we could never get her on the phone. Ever. It took six months for first contact. Then, we were served foreclosure papers. I begged and pleaded and frantically reminded the call center representatives every day that we had only done what we were told. I advised [them] we had saved all of the payments and had six months' worth of payments in the bank that I would hand over now. They said they could not accept payments on a property in foreclosure.

We hired an attorney and they eventually offered to modify the loan after a couple of years of fighting it, but we would also owe $8,000 in their attorney's fees. We were not willing to do this, since we had only done what they advised us to do. We realized later that we had a mortgage servicer, who was on your side, Mr. Bank Official, not ours. So, we were treated like criminals every time we talked to someone at the servicer. You were, after all, the servicer's client. I was not.

Our home has been worth $60,000 since 2008. We put down $30,000, completed $10,000 in upgrades in the first year and paid $40,000 in payments in the first two years before the modification mess occurred. Our total investment: $80,000. The house is worth $60,000 and we now owe more than we financed due to late fees, attorney's fees, and mortgage payments. We have been forced into bankruptcy because there is no other option at this point. Sure, one of the many servicers that have managed our loan has offered us a modification, but we would have to sign our rights to bankruptcy away, pay their attorney's fees, and accept many other conditions that our attorneys have advised us to not agree to.

We take responsibility for not educating ourselves more before we entered into the very serious contract of mortgaging a home. We wish the industry would have taken this contract much more seriously as well. If they had, they would have denied us the loan, knowing very well that we would not be able to sustain the payments long-term. I also wish there were requirements such as classes that better explain things like what a rise in escrow cost might mean for the bottom line of your mortgage payment. We must have asked twenty times at closing what our final payment would be and we were told over and over: $900. We were never told that our exemptions were different than those of the widow who sold us the home, so our escrow would increase for the negative amount as well as an additional collection to pad for the following year. But we should have researched more before entering into such a serious agreement.

Thank you again for ruining our financial life. We have gained much experience, and for that we are thankful. We know that owning an overpriced mortgage on a devalued home is not our American Dream. We know that we will never borrow money from anyone for anything ever again. We know that our possessions do not define us, but our ability to survive and learn and love does. We know that we are blessed to have jobs and families that love us. We know that we are so sorry you could not take our payments when you made a mistake because we wanted to honor our debts, even if it was a nightmare situation. Most of all, we know that we will be okay because our money and possessions do not define us, but our integrity and compassion do. We wish the same for you and your employees and hope you can someday learn the lessons we have.

How We're Doing Out Here

Anonymous

To: Susan S. Bies, Bank of America

Dear Ms. Bies:

I read that a lot of Wall Street executives do not understand why the Occupy Wall Street protesters are doing this. I thought it might help if you knew a little about life in a different part of America.

I live in a small town in Illinois. Years ago there was a manufacturing plant here and a thriving downtown business district. But the manufacturing work moved overseas, where I'm sure it could be done more cheaply, and the plant closed.

Over the years, we have lost most of the local businesses, including both of our grocery stores. In the last few months, the pharmacy and hardware store closed. Our newspaper had to lay off all but one part-time employee. Our school district is in desperate financial straits—they have cut spending so deeply that there is now only one English teacher for the entire high school. And still, the board just received a projection that it will run out of money to operate the schools within two years.

Almost 15% of us are out of work—and that doesn't include many of us who are employed at minimum wage ($8.75/hour) jobs like clerking at Walmart, which is an hour round-trip drive from here with gas at $3.40. More than half of the children at the school qualify for free or reduced lunches because their family incomes are so low. Our food pantry says it served over 10% of the families in our community in the last year. Imagine that you've worked hard all your life and now, with your children watching, you have to line up for a hand-out at the food pantry.

There are coffee cans on the counter of the convenience store for people with cancer or injured kids without medical insurance. You throw in your change and hope it will help somehow.

Our neighbors, with teenagers our children grew up with, are about to be evicted from their house. Their car was repossessed. Their father works in construction, and there hasn't been much of that going on since the real estate market crashed, which you may remember. Whose fault was that—his? He does any work he can get now, and so does his wife. They can't get enough to keep a roof over their heads.

People have nowhere to live, while houses stand empty. Teachers have been thrown out of work, while the school has no one to teach the kids. The road to the town north of us is closed indefinitely because the bridge is unsafe. We have people in town with the skills to fix it who need the work desperately, but there is no money to pay for it.

I have had the privilege of relatively high-paying work at times in my life, and I know that being comfortable or well-off can insulate a person from the reality that others are not. You're working hard, you feel you deserve to be well paid, and everyone else should just do the same. But that is an easy and false conclusion—most people do not have the opportunity you have been fortunate to receive.

I hope this picture of how some of the other 99% are doing sheds light on what Occupy Wall Street is all about. The enormous disparity of incomes in this country is unjust and growing. People in your world are doing great (from what we hear, "great" doesn't begin to describe it), while the rest of us are going down. It is a disaster and it cannot continue.

I Didn't Buy a House

Pamila Payne

I knew I couldn't afford a house, but I hoped that someday if I kept working hard, I'd be able to. Those zero-money-down, everybody-qualifies loan offers flooded my mailbox, but I didn't bite because I knew my income couldn't carry that much debt.

I've been a renter my whole life. Thanks to the actions of a greedy few, the economy has tanked and living the American Dream is farther out of reach for people like me than ever.

When people play by the rules but don't get rewards, and see others cheating and being rewarded despite the harm they cause, deep, seething anger is the result.

This social movement to hold financial institutions accountable for wrongdoing and to create a system of economic justice for all is just getting started.

We will create change because we're not just disaffected hippies. We're the disaffected middle class. And we're huge.

Like a large majority of the middle class, I don't have a ton of money in one of your banks, but I have a regular paycheck and savings that I cultivate consistently. Very soon, I'll be closing my accounts and moving to a credit union or a small community bank. I'll do everything I can, socially, politically, and economically, to help move the society I live in out of corporate domination and into a state of proper democracy where citizens can play by fair rules and reap earned rewards.

I'm willing to wait for my house. I'm willing to work for a better future not just for myself, but for future generations as well. There's a lot of people like me out there.

How many of you are there? What are you willing to work for?

Pamila Payne
Los Angeles, CA 90068

New York Times

The op-ed of the year, by a large margin, came from a formerly unknown South African equity-derivatives banker in London. In a self-serving but extremely powerful and resonant statement, he took on Goldman Sachs from the pages of the *New York Times* and won a book deal and a news cycle or three in the process. Greg Smith's criticisms weren't new, but this was the first time they'd come from inside rather than outside the company, giving them unprecedented and undeniable heft. For most of the rest of the year, Goldman found itself on the back foot, defending itself from the impression the op-ed created.

Greg Smith

22. Why I Am Leaving Goldman Sachs

Today is my last day at Goldman Sachs. After almost twelve years at the firm—first as a summer intern while at Stanford, then in New York for ten years, and now in London—I believe I have worked here long enough to understand the trajectory of its culture, its people, and its identity. And I can honestly say that the environment now is as toxic and destructive as I have ever seen it.

To put the problem in the simplest terms, the interests of the client continue to be sidelined in the way the firm operates and thinks about making money. Goldman Sachs is one of the world's largest and most important investment banks, and it is too integral to global finance to continue to act this way. The firm has veered so far from the place I joined right out of college that I can no longer in good conscience say that I identify with what it stands for.

It might sound surprising to a skeptical public, but culture was always a vital part of Goldman Sachs's success. It revolved around teamwork, integrity, a spirit of humility, and always doing right by our clients. The culture was the secret sauce that made this place great and allowed us to earn our clients' trust for 143 years. It wasn't just about making money; this alone will not sustain a firm for so long. It had something to do with pride and belief in the organization. I am sad to say that I look around today and see virtually no trace of the culture that made me love working for this firm for many years. I no longer have the pride, or the belief.

But this was not always the case. For more than a decade I recruited and mentored candidates through our grueling interview process. I was selected as one of ten people (out of a firm of more than 30,000) to appear on our recruiting video, which is played on every college campus we visit around the world. In 2006 I managed the summer intern program in sales and trading in New York for the eighty college students who made the cut, out of the thousands who applied.

I knew it was time to leave when I realized I could no longer look students in the eye and tell them what a great place this was to work.

When the history books are written about Goldman Sachs, they may reflect that the current chief executive officer, Lloyd C. Blankfein, and the president, Gary D. Cohn, lost hold of the firm's culture on their watch. I truly believe that this decline in the firm's moral fiber represents the single most serious threat to its long-run survival.

Over the course of my career I have had the privilege of advising two of the largest hedge funds on the planet, five of the largest asset managers in the United States, and three of the most prominent sovereign wealth funds in the Middle East and Asia. My clients have a total asset base of more than a trillion dollars. I have always taken a lot of pride in advising my clients to do what I believe is right for them, even if it means less money for the firm. This view is becoming increasingly unpopular at Goldman Sachs. Another sign that it was time to leave.

How did we get here? The firm changed the way it thought about leadership. Leadership used to be about ideas, setting an example and doing the right thing. Today, if you make enough money for the firm (and are not currently an ax murderer) you will be promoted into a position of influence.

What are three quick ways to become a leader? a) Execute on the firm's "axes," which is Goldman-speak for persuading your clients to invest in the stocks or other products that we are trying to get rid of because they are not seen as having a lot of potential profit. b) "Hunt Elephants." In English: get your clients—some of whom are sophisticated, and some of whom aren't—to trade whatever will bring the biggest profit to Goldman. Call me old-fashioned, but I don't like selling my clients a product that is wrong for them. c) Find yourself sitting in a seat where your job is to trade any illiquid, opaque product with a three-letter acronym.

Today, many of these leaders display a Goldman Sachs culture quotient of exactly zero percent. I attend derivatives sales meetings where not one single minute is spent asking questions about how we can help clients. It's purely about how we can make the most possible money off of them. If you were an alien from Mars and sat in on one of these meetings, you would believe that a client's success or progress was not part of the thought process at all.

It makes me ill how callously people talk about ripping their clients off. Over the last twelve months I have seen five different managing directors refer to their own clients as "muppets," sometimes over internal e-mail. Even after the SEC, Fabulous Fab, Abacus, God's work, Carl Levin, Vampire Squids? No humility? I mean, come on. Integrity? It is eroding. I don't know of any illegal behavior, but will people push the envelope and pitch lucrative and complicated products to clients even if they are not the simplest investments or the ones most directly aligned with the client's goals? Absolutely. Every day, in fact.

It astounds me how little senior management gets a basic truth: If clients don't trust you they will eventually stop doing business with you. It doesn't matter how smart you are.

These days, the most common question I get from junior analysts about derivatives is, "How much money did we make off the client?" It bothers me every time I hear it, because it is a clear reflection of what they are observing from their leaders about the way they should behave. Now project ten years into the future: You don't have to be a rocket scientist to figure out that the junior analyst sitting quietly in the corner of the room hearing about "muppets," "ripping eyeballs out," and "getting paid" doesn't exactly turn into a model citizen.

When I was a first-year analyst I didn't know where the bathroom was or how to tie my shoelaces. I was taught to be concerned with learning the ropes, finding out what a derivative was, understanding finance, getting to know our clients and what motivated them, learning how they defined success and what we could do to help them get there.

My proudest moments in life—getting a full scholarship to go from South Africa to Stanford University, being selected as a Rhodes Scholar national finalist, winning a bronze medal for table tennis at the Maccabiah Games in Israel, known as the Jewish Olympics—have all come through hard work, with no shortcuts. Goldman Sachs today has become too much about shortcuts and not enough about achievement. It just doesn't feel right to me anymore.

I hope this can be a wake-up call to the board of directors. Make the client the focal point of your business again. Without clients you will not make money. In fact, you will not exist. Weed out the morally bankrupt people, no matter how much money they make for the firm. And get the culture right again, so people want to work here for the right reasons. People who care only about making money will not sustain this firm—or the trust of its clients—for very much longer.

ProPublica

ProPublica's Jake Bernstein draws you right into the story of Joe Caramadre with a beautifully crafted description of a Rhode Island lawyer whose avidness for playing the angles may have taken him too far. Did Caramadre sharply exploit a legal loophole to extract a bonanza from an insurance product called a "variable annuity," or did he commit fraud at the expense of dying people and their families? According to Rhode Island law, Caramadre or one of his clients could buy an annuity on the life of someone who was not expected to live long and then pocket a profit when that person died. A little unsavory, perhaps, but was it also illegal? Insurance companies were losing on that claim in civil suits, but then came the criminal charges.

Jake Bernstein

23. Death Takes a Policy

How a Lawyer Exploited the Fine Print and Found Himself Facing Federal Charges

Joseph Caramadre has spent a lifetime scouring the fine print. He's hardwired to seek the angle, an overlooked clause in a contract that allows him to transform a company's carelessness into a personal windfall. He calls these insights his "creations," and he numbers them. There have been about nineteen in his lifetime, he says. For example, there was number four, which involved an office superstore coupon he parlayed into enough nearly free office furniture to fill a three-car garage. Number three consisted of a sure-fire but short-lived system for winning money at the local dog track. But the one that landed him on the evening news as a suspect in a criminal conspiracy was number 18, which promised investors a unique arrangement: You can keep your winnings and have someone else cover your losses.

Caramadre portrays himself as a modern-day Robin Hood. He's an Italian kid from Providence, R.I., who grew up modestly, became a certified public accountant, and then put himself through night school to get a law degree. He has given millions to charities and the Catholic Church. As he tells his life story, his native ability helps him outsmart a phalanx of high-priced lawyers, actuaries, and corporate suits. Number 18 came to fruition, he says, when a sizeable segment of the life-insurance industry ignored centuries of experience and common sense in a heated competition for market share.

Federal prosecutors in Rhode Island and insurance companies paint a very different picture of Caramadre: They say he's an unscrupulous con artist who engaged in identity theft, conspiracy, and two different kinds of fraud. Prosecutors contend he deceived the terminally ill to make millions for himself and his clients. For them, Caramadre's can't-miss investment strategy was an illusion in which he preyed on the sick and vulnerable.

ProPublica has taken a close look at the Caramadre case because it offers a window into a larger issue: The transformation of the life-insurance industry away from its traditional business of insuring lives to peddling complex financial products. This shift has not been a smooth one. Particularly during the lead up to the financial crisis, companies wrote billions worth of contracts that now imperil their financial health.

In a series of detailed interviews, Caramadre said the companies designed the rules; all he did was exploit them. Their hunger for profits in a period of dizzying growth and competition, he contends, left them vulnerable to someone with his unusual acumen. The companies have argued in court that Caramadre is a fraud artist who should return every last dime he made. In his rulings to date, the federal judge hearing the civil cases has agreed with Caramadre's contention that he was doing what the fine print allowed.

The secret to Caramadre's scheme can be glimpsed in a 2006 brochure for the ING GoldenSelect Variable Annuity. On the cover is a photo of a youthful older couple. The woman sits next to a computer, sporting a stylish haircut and wire-framed glasses. A man with graying hair and an open collared shirt, presumably her husband, is draped over her in a casual loving way. Images of happy vibrant seniors enjoying their golden years together—frolicking on the beach, laughing in chinos next to a gleaming classic car, enjoying the company of grandkids—populate the sales material for life insurance's hottest product—the variable annuity.

As outlined in the brochure and in countless others like it, the contracts worked this way: The smiling couple gives money to ING in return for the promise of future payments. The consumer chooses how the money is invested, usually in mutual-like funds that have stocks, bonds, or money-market instruments. This is the "variable" part of the equation.

There are two main benefits to this arrangement not found in the ordinary mutual funds sold by brokers and financial advisers. Taxes on variable annuities are deferred until the consumer takes out cash, which means it's possible to move your money among funds without paying taxes until the money is withdrawn. (An investor who cashes in shares of a mutual fund must pay taxes on any gains.)

Variable annuities also typically include a life-insurance component called a guaranteed death benefit. With this guarantee, if the market crashes—but you die before your investment recovers—your beneficiary still gets a lump sum equal to either the death benefit or the value of the investments in your account, whichever is greater.

The target audience for brochures like that of ING's are people nearing retirement with a nest egg to safeguard and perhaps grow a bit. It's a huge and growing market. In 2011, as the first wave of baby boomers began to retire, there were more than 40 million people age sixty-five or over. Between 2001 and 2010, life insurance companies sold about $1.4 trillion worth of variable annuities, according to LIMRA, an industry association.

Caramadre got the seeds of his idea in the mid-nineties when he attended an investment seminar for insurance agents. He quickly saw how variable annuities could be a hot product for insurance companies—particularly when they could charge hefty fees for attractive goodies like the guaranteed death benefit.

Caramadre decided that he wouldn't offer variable annuities to clients in the way the insurance companies envisioned. It was too expensive. "They are just whacking you for fees," he says.

What Caramadre wanted was a way to get his clients the benefits without their having to die.

• • •

Society has long frowned on certain behaviors. Taking out an insurance policy on a friend or neighbor and killing them? Not acceptable. Taking out a life insurance policy that gambles your neighbor will die soon, even without your help, also crosses the line. Today, it is well-established law that one must have what is called an "insurable interest" before purchasing an insurance policy on someone else's life. The person who benefits from the policy must be a relative or business associate who himself would face financial or familial loss from the death.

Insurable interest worked fine for 200 years or so until the life-insurance business itself changed. Despite its name, the industry doesn't sell as much "life insurance" anymore. Life companies now peddle financial services, particularly annuities. Variable annuities were developed in the 1950s, initially as a way to give teachers retirement options. Insurable interest was not an issue and could have been an impediment to widespread adoption of the product.

Caramadre did his research and concluded that Rhode Island law did not require that people buying variable annuities have an insurable interest.

As imagined by the insurance companies, variable annuities have two participants. There's the investor, the person who puts up the money. That person typically also serves as the annuitant, or the "measuring life." If that person dies, the death benefit is paid to the beneficiary, usually a spouse or child.

Caramadre realized it didn't have to be that way. There was no requirement that the investor and the annuitant be the same person. In fact, as he read the contracts, the annuitant didn't need to have a relationship with the investor at all. Caramadre or one of his clients could buy an annuity on the life of someone who was not expected to live long and then pocket any profit when that person died.

"All we need to do is replace the necessity of the investor having to die, with someone else, dying," says Caramadre.

If they chose well, the account went up and they reaped the benefits. If they chose poorly, the death benefit kicked in and they recouped their original investment.

"If you won, you keep the winnings. If you lose, they give you your money back," says Caramadre.

There is something morally unsettling about this. Put simply: Caramadre was setting himself and his clients up to profit from the demise of strangers. While the macabre aspect of his scheme offends many, it did not make Caramadre squeamish. He rationalized that a lot of people—funeral homes, hospitals, and cemeteries—make money from the dead and dying, why not him?

Caramadre's insight might have remained a curiosity were it not for something called "the arms race." As competition intensified in the mid-2000s, many life-insurance companies launched an unprecedented war for customers, offering benefits they now acknowledge were far, far too favorable.

The insurance companies' contracts provided little defense against Caramadre's approach. For policies under a million dollars, they didn't check the health status of people receiving variable annuities. Instead, they limited the ages of annuitants or the amount that could be invested. All that the companies required for persons to serve as a measuring life was their signature, birthdate, and Social Security number. Some didn't even require the signature.

There was usually only a single line that touched on insurable interest in the contract. Companies would ask if a relationship existed between the investor and the annuitant. Caramadre and the men with whom he worked would either leave the answer blank or type in "none." The companies, eager for business, took the policy anyway.

There have been at least eight lawsuits filed in Rhode Island's federal district court relating to Caramadre's scheme. Insurance companies Nationwide, Transamerica, and Western Reserve have all sued. The companies have not fared well in civil court. United States District Court Judge William Smith keeps knocking out claims. The companies then refile new ones. As of this writing, Western Reserve has filed five successive complaints against Caramadre in the same case. When he dismissed Nationwide's complaint, Judge Smith questioned whether the company ignored its own contracts. In the Western Reserve case, Judge Smith wrote, "It is a bit ironic for Plaintiffs [the insurance companies] to suggest that they did not know the true nature of contracts that they themselves drafted."

The lawyer who represents both Transamerica and Western Reserve declined to comment.

The more serious charges are the criminal ones. Caramadre usually paid dying people between $3,000 and $10,000 for agreeing to serve as annuitants. He characterizes the arrangement as a win-win for everybody but the insurance companies. Prosecutors charge that he instructed participants in the scheme to lie, to steal identity information, and to forge the signatures of annuitants in an effort to defraud insurance and bond companies.

The story as told by prosecutors goes like this: In an effort to get rich, Caramadre and his associates enticed the dying to give up their vital information by offering them $2,000 as a charitable donation. More than 150 people received the $2,000. Of those, at least 44 went on to play a role in number 18.

The government alleges that Caramadre directed his associates to lie to both the annuitants and the insurance companies. Sometimes, prosecutors assert, the dying people had no idea someone else stood to profit. In other instances, the indictment says, dying people were told that their signatures were just for the receipt of the charitable donation. A Caramadre employee allegedly told other family members they would be the beneficiaries. In five cases, the government says, signatures were forged.

Caramadre denies the accusations. He says that he instructed his employees to properly explain the program to the annuitants and that he would never permit forgeries.

Youthful looking with a round expressive face etched with deep lines across his brow, Caramadre appears more like an eager-to-please bulldog than a criminal mastermind. During the arms race, he says, companies did not complain when Caramadre paid their hefty fees and later filed claims seeking death benefits. Family members didn't object either. Everything changed in 2009 with the financial crisis. Companies started to feel the consequences of the arms race, the insurance companies sued, and the FBI began visiting relatives and surviving annuitants. Today, some of those family members are the strongest witnesses for the prosecution.

"I lose my mom, who is my best friend, my world, and in me, losing my mother forever at the age of sixty-four, you, in turn, profit and get X amount of dollars," says Stephanie Porter, whose mother received $2,000 from Caramadre before she died of cancer. "It's slimy what the man did."

• • •

Caramadre learned to hustle early. He graduated from the University of Rhode Island in three years with an accounting and finance degree, supporting himself through odd jobs that included running his church's weekly bingo game. After graduation, he took a job at a bank preparing documents for trusts. A friend convinced him that his fastest track to becoming a millionaire would be to sell life insurance, so he took a job as an agent with the Penn Mutual Life Insurance Company.

Caramadre had landed in an industry on the cusp of a historic transformation.

Life insurance used to be safe and profitable. Many insurance companies had begun in the 1800s as mutual-aid societies. They were ostensibly owned by their customers, who sometimes even received dividends. The idea behind the business was simple: Collect premiums from lots of people at a price high enough to account for mortality, which can be quite accurately predicted. The companies invested their pools of money. When they wandered into trouble, it almost always involved poor investment choices rather than unforeseen behavior by policyholders. By 1985, annual compensation for a top company CEO could be in the high six figures. While this was not a Wall Street salary, the business had the benefit of comfortably predictable profits.

Insurance agents worked for specific companies and offered products only from that firm. The agent was a man of the community, hawking a service that few young and healthy people want to contemplate. The old adage in life insurance is that "it's sold, not bought." Agents sold a relationship and a vision for the future, encouraging clients to protect their family from a tragic event and, possibly, give their heirs a leg up.

By the 1990s, the business was changing.

Under pressure from banks offering new retirement products, including annuities, insurance companies decided to shed the cost of keeping large numbers of agents on their payroll. Rather than train, staff, and equip insurance agents, the industry moved increasingly to a freelance model. "Independent" insurance agents paid for their own offices and expenses solely through commissions earned on the policies they sold. Insurance companies like Prudential, which once had as many as 18,000 agents, whittled their in-house force down to about 2,500.

The rise of independent agents was accompanied by the widespread transformation of mutual companies. Between 1985 and 2003, more than twenty mutual-life-insurance firms converted themselves into stock companies, most of which were traded on Wall Street. This process heightened the focus on quarterly earnings and eventually helped lead to an increase in executives' pay. Rising stock prices meant bigger bonuses.

The change in culture and incentives in the life-insurance business created the perfect conditions for the arms race. It also made the business a prime target for Caramadre.

It wasn't until the 1990s that the growth of variable annuities took off. Between 1990 and 1999, the amount of variable annuities individuals purchased in the United States leapt from $3.5 billion to nearly $63 billion in 1999, according to the American Council of Life Insurers.

For the companies, it was easier to sell a product customers could use while still alive. Unlike life insurance, annuities did not require an expensive health examination. Life insurance was based on premium payments that remained steady. But the yearly fees charged on annuities, which sometimes topped 4 percent of the value of the account, would rise in line with those values. More money under management meant more fees, which buoyed the companies' stock prices and their executives' compensation.

Annuities were not a terrible idea. They fit a growing gap in the nation's pension system. The defined benefit plan, a retirement approach where the employer guaranteed a pension based on salary and years of service, was disappearing. From 1980 through 2008, the proportion of private sector American workers covered by company pensions fell from 38 percent to 20 percent, according to the Bureau of Labor Statistics. Meanwhile, a demographic bubble of baby boomers needed other retirement options. Annuities seemed to be tailor-made.

At Penn Mutual, Caramadre broke sales records, becoming at age twenty-four one of the youngest Golden Eagles—a recognition the company bestowed on top sales performers. Caramadre left Penn Mutual two years before the company ended its captive-agent system. As an independent agent he could find better deals for his customers on the open market. He became a student of insurance products, deconstructing the product software provided by the companies, delving deep into the contracts. It became almost like scouting a ball player, he says.

• • •

Caramadre says annuities provided only about 5 percent of the profits he made from his business. He says he took out policies for himself, family members, and clients. When he offered his "creation" to investors, Caramadre would either share the commission on the policy with brokers who worked in his office or, in a few cases, he would take a percentage of the gain on the account, he says. He says his lawyers have advised him not to reveal how much he made but it was likely in the millions. Prosecutors allege that he and his accomplices fraudulently obtained $15 million from insurance companies.

Caramadre anticipated that eventually companies would close the loopholes and shut him down. But what began in 1995 with AIDS patients grew over time to an effort that advertised weekly in a Catholic newspaper aimed at hospice patients.

By 2006, Caramadre had several people combing through the fine print of variable annuity prospectuses. He claims they looked at 680 of them that year. Most he could eliminate quickly. The companies were too small or had sub-par ratings. If they lost millions, they might go out of business, which would be bad for both Caramadre and the company.

Caramadre found that the companies with the best benefits were the ones who were most eager to expand their market share. ING Group, for example, was a favorite selection. The Netherlands-based company went on an acquisition spree in the 1990s in an effort to become a dominant player in the U.S. annuities business. ING spent most of the arms race fighting to stay in the top ten life insurance companies in variable-annuity sales. In 2004, ING had new annual variable-annuity sales of $7.7 billion. Four years later, that number had increased to $12.3 billion, according to Morningstar.

"When a company is pushing hard to sell bells and whistles on a product—they are desperate to get money through the door—either because they are in an expansionary phase or they want more assets under management in order to sell themselves to a bigger company," Caramadre says.

ING offered a bevy of benefits. It started with a "bonus credit." This became common by late 2006. In the case of ING's Golden Select Premium Plus variable annuity, the company promised to add 5 percent of the value of the contract. If you deposited a million dollars, the insurance company would add $50,000 on top of it.

Why would ING give away free money?

It never expected to pay the majority of the benefits it offered.

The 5 percent was added to the death benefit, which was held in a separate account known as a shadow account. The insurance company only paid the shadow account if the policyholder died and the money—the million dollars—in the real account had shrunk to a lesser value.

The companies' models of customer behavior, which were based on data collected before the 2008 financial collapse, predicted that the death benefit would rarely be paid. Something would happen. Policy makers would take the money out for a big purchase, surrendering their account. If the policyholder annuitized—started taking a stream of monthly payments—the shadow account disappeared. In any event, the rising market made it likely that the account would outperform the promises.

But the models turned out to be the insurance-industry equivalent of the housing bubble. When the market crashed, consumers began acting differently than they had in the past.

Perhaps the gaudiest of the benefits the companies never expected to pay was known as the "rachet." The idea was perfect for a steadily rising market. Say you had $1 million in your account in 2007 and your investment did well, boosting the value to $1.2 million. That amount would be set on a given date as your death benefit which you would be paid *no matter what had happened to your investment.*

If stocks cratered, as they did in 2008, and your account fell to, say, $600,000? The insurance company would still owe you $1.2 million when you died.

ING offered a quarterly ratchet—it set every four months—and charged only about a quarter of a percent annual fee to customers who wanted it. Many companies, including Nationwide Life and Annuity Insurance Company and Transamerica Life Insurance Company, offered monthly ratchets.

To differentiate themselves, companies also sold exotic investment options into which the buyers of the annuity could invest their funds. ING featured funds managed by reputable companies like Pimco, Fidelity, and T. Rowe Price. Each fund carried a fee that ING split with the fund manager. While ING provided aggressive growth and real-estate funds, many annuity companies went beyond that to give consumers a choice of funds that used derivatives to bet for or against the market, sometimes with multipliers, so-called double betas. For example, if the stock market plunged, investors could double their money.

"Double betas were crazy funds," says Caramadre. "It hyperinflates the problem."

Caramadre's first step was to make sure his clients qualified for every incentive. If there was a monthly ratchet and bonus, he might invest the funds in a money market account until the ratchet set with the bonus.

It was as if Caramadre was playing with the house's money and going straight to the blackjack tables. With decent gains locked in, he would take flyers on the riskiest investments possible. Sometimes, he would invest his clients' money in two variable annuities, one that paid out if the market went up and the other if it declined. It didn't matter. When the annuitant died, Caramadre's client, at the very least, would get both principals back plus the gains from whichever fund paid out.

Caramadre kept increasing the number of annuitants and placing big bets.

"It was pretty fun being in the market without the risk," he says.

• • •

The fun ended in 2009 when the insurance companies began to investigate. In March, Nationwide formally complained to the Rhode Island insurance supervisor, who didn't take any action.

Nationwide had calculated the fees it charged and the guarantees it offered based on the assumption that the policyholder would keep the product for a certain period of time, it told Rhode Island officials. Caramadre's treatment of the annuity as a short-term investment caused "a negative economic impact on annuity issuers such as Nationwide," the company wrote in its complaint.

Nationwide's main allegation involved a lack of insurable interest, the relationship between the investor and the annuitant. "It is Nationwide's position that the insurable interest statute applies to annuity contracts," the company wrote.

Attorneys for the two insurance brokers who worked with Caramadre, Edward Hanrahan and Edward Maggiacomo Jr., filed detailed responses to the Nationwide complaint with the Rhode Island state insurance regulator.

The company, the attorneys argued, had "no one to blame but itself."

"Having attracted buyers, Nationwide now seeks to evade its payment obligations, which arise from the very documents that Nationwide itself drafted," Hanrahan's response read.

In 2009, Alaska and Nebraska were the only two states with insurable-interest statutes that encompassed annuities in all circumstances, according to Adler, Pollock & Sheehan, one of the law firms that prepared the response. It said Rhode Island has no such requirement.

Nationwide filed suit against one of Caramadre's investors in May of that year, a suit it would lose. Transamerica and Western Reserve would wait until November to file their suits.

In June, Caramadre got word that the FBI had contacted one of the hospice nurses who had referred annuitants to him.

His lawyer, Robert Flanders Jr., a former state Supreme Court justice, asked for a meeting with prosecutors. He hoped to persuade them that the matter was best left to the civil courts. According to Flanders, at the meeting prosecutors let him know they didn't like Caramadre's creation regardless of whether it was criminal or not. "Here was a guy who was just throwing a few shekels at some poor sick people at the end of their lives, and he was reaping the lion's share," says Flanders. "They didn't like what they considered the inequity of it."

Flanders says he took the prosecutors' remarks as a threat. "At one point, the lead attorney there said to me, 'You know all that money your client made from the insurance companies?' I said, 'Yeah, what about it?' 'All that is now going to go from him to you, because during the course of this investigation, this is going to be a thing where he is going to be drained of all the money he made.'"

Asked specifically about the meeting and this accusation, a Department of Justice spokesman declined to comment.

An FBI agent started conducting interviews with hospice workers, investors, and family members of annuitants.

Investigators learned that most of the contact with the dying participants had occurred with Raymour Radhakrishnan, an employee Caramadre hired in the summer of 2007. A graduate of Wheaton College in Boston, Radhakrishnan was only twenty-three-years old at the time. His job would be to interact with the annuitants: assess their health, explain the program, get their signatures, and dispense the cash. Mainly, he would oversee a growing corporate bond program (creation 19).

The bond program had similarities to the variable annuity scheme. Caramadre would buy certain corporate bonds on the secondary market. After the financial crisis, these bonds were selling at a steep discount. As a sweetener, the companies that originally sold the bonds had included survivorship rights for co-owners.

For example, if you owned the bonds with your wife and she died, you didn't have to wait decades to redeem them. The company would buy them back at full value. Caramadre would "co-own" the bonds with a terminally ill person. When that person died, he would redeem the bonds at face value, reaping the value of the discount.

Radhakrishnan is a codefendant along with Caramadre in what the government contends was a vast criminal conspiracy. Reached through his public defender, Radhakrishnan declined to comment. He has pleaded not guilty to the charges.

Radhakrishnan's conversations with the terminally ill are at the heart of the criminal case against both men. Caramadre seldom met with the annuitants directly, but prosecutors allege that he instructed Radhakrishnan to deceive the potential annuitants. FBI reports, depositions, and interviews suggest that Radhakrishnan told different stories to different potential annuitants. The most serious charges against the men involve allegations that they forged signatures.

One forgery count in the indictment involves Stephanie Porter's mother, Bertha Howard. In January 2008, Radhakrishnan met with Howard and Porter at Fatima Hospital where she was being treated for lung cancer that had spread to her brain and spine, according to Porter. Radhakrishnan gave her mother a check for $2,000 and explained how Howard might be able to get more if she signed more documents. The next meeting between Radhakrishnan and Howard occurred in a nursing home a few weeks later. Porter was also present. She says her mother, shaky and heavily medicated, struggled to sign some forms. There was no additional explanation from Radhakrishnan, according to Porter. A week later, Howard died. Shortly after that Radhakrishnan called Porter to tell her that the company would not accept the signatures so there would be no more money forthcoming. Porter said it didn't matter since her mother was dead.

But a bond account was opened under Howard's name nonetheless. On the account are signatures that Porter does not recognize as those of her mother. The indictment charges that they are forgeries. Caramadre says it was a mistake, and documents he provided to *ProPublica* show that no money was ever put into the account.

The prosecution persuaded a judge to allow it to take depositions of dying participants in the schemes even though no charges had been filed at the time. Over a few weeks in hospitals and private homes, with tubes in their noses and a variety of high-powered medications in their bloodstreams, the annuitants testified that they did not understand the arrangement they had entered into with Caramadre and Radhakrishnan. Some denied writing their signatures on forms submitted to insurance and bond companies.

Caramadre believes the depositions show that the FBI and prosecutors misled witnesses and thus tainted their testimony. An FBI spokesman said the agency does not comment on active cases.

The *Wall Street Journal* wrote two stories on Caramadre's cases, one in February 2010 on variable annuities and another a month later on the corporate-bond program.

Two months later, the National Association of Insurance Commissioners held a hearing on stranger-originated annuities. Thomas R. Sullivan, a former Hartford Insurance executive and the state regulator from ING's home state of Connecticut, chaired the meeting.

"This is about embarrassment," says Caramadre. "Nobody ever complained about what I did until the insurance companies and the FBI came knocking."

In November 2011, after almost two years of work, a Rhode Island grand jury issued a sixty-six-count indictment against Caramadre and Radhakrishnan.

Their criminal trial is scheduled to begin in November.

Today, several of the companies Caramadre targeted have stopped selling variable annuities. ING has been forced to get out of the business and write down billions in losses. Others have had to boost their reserves. Transamerica is trying to buy back some of the variable annuities it sold to policyholders. The French insurer Axa is offering its variable annuity holders money if they surrender their death benefit guarantees.

Part VIII

Brave New World

New York Times Magazine

Charles Duhigg knows all about how to create little bursts of neurological pleasure: he wrote a best-selling book about them, called *Habit*. This fantastic article is a boiled-down version of the book and hits all the sweet spots that newspaper-feature readers love: a bit of neuroscience here, a bit of weight-loss advice there, and a large chunk of genuinely fascinating new material about the shadowy ways that large corporations like Target can anticipate your future behavior and try to influence it. Any predictive-analytics team would have known that this article would be a huge hit, and, of course, it was, especially because of the bit about how Target knew about one girl's pregnancy before her father did.

Charles Duhigg

24. How Companies Learn Your Secrets

Andrew Pole had just started working as a statistician for Target in 2002 when two colleagues from the marketing department stopped by his desk to ask an odd question: "If we wanted to figure out if a customer is pregnant, even if she didn't want us to know, can you do that?"

Pole has a master's degree in statistics and another in economics and has been obsessed with the intersection of data and human behavior most of his life. His parents were teachers in North Dakota, and while other kids were going to 4-H, Pole was doing algebra and writing computer programs. "The stereotype of a math nerd is true," he told me when I spoke with him last year. "I kind of like going out and evangelizing analytics."

As the marketers explained to Pole—and as Pole later explained to me, back when we were still speaking and before Target told him to stop—new parents are a retailer's holy grail. Most shoppers don't buy everything they need at one store. Instead, they buy groceries at the grocery store and toys at the toy store, and they visit Target only when they need certain items they associate with Target—cleaning supplies, say, or new socks or a six-month supply of toilet paper. But Target sells everything from milk to stuffed animals to lawn furniture to electronics, so one of the company's primary goals is convincing customers that the only store they need is Target. But it's a tough message to get across, even with the most ingenious ad campaigns, because once consumers' shopping habits are ingrained, it's incredibly difficult to change them.

There are, however, some brief periods in a person's life when old routines fall apart and buying habits are suddenly in flux. One of those moments—*the* moment, really—is right around the birth of a child, when parents are exhausted and overwhelmed and their shopping patterns and brand loyalties are up for grabs. But as Target's marketers explained to Pole, timing is everything. Because birth records are usually public, the moment a couple have a new baby, they are almost instantaneously barraged with offers and incentives and advertisements from all sorts of companies. Which means that the key is to reach them earlier, before any other retailers know a baby is on the way. Specifically, the marketers said they wanted to send specially designed ads to women in their second trimester, which is when most expectant mothers begin buying all sorts of new things, like prenatal vitamins and maternity clothing. "Can you give us a list?" the marketers asked.

"We knew that if we could identify them in their second trimester, there's a good chance we could capture them for years," Pole told me. "As soon as we get them buying diapers from us, they're going to start buying everything else, too. If you're rushing through the store, looking for bottles, and you pass orange juice, you'll grab a carton. Oh, and there's that new DVD I want. Soon, you'll be buying cereal and paper towels from us and keep coming back."

The desire to collect information on customers is not new for Target or any other large retailer, of course. For decades, Target has collected vast amounts of data on every person who regularly walks into one of its stores. Whenever possible, Target assigns each shopper a unique code—known internally as the Guest ID number—that keeps tabs on everything they buy. "If you use a credit card or a coupon or fill out a survey or mail in a refund or call the customer help line or open an e-mail we've sent you or visit our website, we'll record it and link it to your Guest ID," Pole said. "We want to know everything we can."

Also linked to your Guest ID is demographic information like your age, whether you are married and have kids, which part of town you live in, how long it takes you to drive to the store, your estimated salary, whether you've moved recently, what credit cards you carry in your wallet, and what websites you visit. Target can buy data about your ethnicity, job history, the magazines you read, if you've ever declared bankruptcy or got divorced, the year you bought (or lost) your house, where you went to college, what kinds of topics you talk about online, whether you prefer certain brands of coffee, paper towels, cereal, or applesauce, your political leanings, reading habits, charitable giving, and the number of cars you own. (In a statement, Target declined to identify what demographic information it collects or purchases.) All that information is meaningless, however, without someone to analyze and make sense of it. That's where Andrew Pole and the dozens of other members of Target's Guest Marketing Analytics department come in.

Almost every major retailer, from grocery chains to investment banks to the U.S. Postal Service, has a "predictive analytics" department devoted to understanding not just consumers' shopping habits but also their personal habits so as to more efficiently market to them. "But Target has always been one of the smartest at this," says Eric Siegel, a consultant and the chairman of a conference called Predictive Analytics World. "We're living through a golden age of behavioral research. It's amazing how much we can figure out about how people think now."

The reason Target can snoop on our shopping habits is that, over the past two decades, the science of habit formation has become a major field of research in neurology and psychology departments at hundreds of major medical centers and universities, as well as inside extremely well financed corporate labs. "It's like an arms race to hire statisticians nowadays," said Andreas Weigend, the former chief scientist at Amazon.com. "Mathematicians are suddenly sexy." As the ability to analyze data has grown more and more fine-grained, the push to understand how daily habits influence our decisions has become one of the most exciting topics in clinical research, even though most of us are hardly aware those patterns exist. One study from Duke University estimated that habits, rather than conscious decision making, shape 45 percent of the choices we make every day, and recent discoveries have begun to change everything from the way we think about dieting to how doctors conceive treatments for anxiety, depression, and addictions.

This research is also transforming our understanding of how habits function across organizations and societies. A football coach named Tony Dungy propelled one of the worst teams in the NFL to the Super Bowl by focusing on how his players habitually reacted to on-field cues. Before he became treasury secretary, Paul O'Neill overhauled a stumbling conglomerate, Alcoa, and turned it into a top performer in the Dow Jones by relentlessly attacking one habit—a specific approach to worker safety—which in turn caused a companywide transformation. The Obama campaign has hired a habit specialist as its "chief scientist" to figure out how to trigger new voting patterns among different constituencies.

Researchers have figured out how to stop people from habitually overeating and biting their nails. They can explain why some of us automatically go for a jog every morning and are more productive at work, while others oversleep and procrastinate. There is a calculus, it turns out, for mastering our subconscious urges. For companies like Target, the exhaustive rendering of our conscious and unconscious patterns into data sets and algorithms has revolutionized what they know about us and, therefore, how precisely they can sell.

• • •

Inside the Brain and Cognitive Sciences Department of the Massachusetts Institute of Technology are what, to the casual observer, look like dollhouse versions of surgical theaters. There are rooms with tiny scalpels, small drills, and miniature saws. Even the operating tables are petite, as if prepared for seven-year-old surgeons. Inside those shrunken ORs, neurologists cut into the skulls of anesthetized rats, implanting tiny sensors that record the smallest changes in the activity of their brains.

An MIT neuroscientist named Ann Graybiel told me that she and her colleagues began exploring habits more than a decade ago by putting their wired rats into a T-shaped maze with chocolate at one end. The maze was structured so that each animal was positioned behind a barrier that opened after a loud click. The first time a rat was placed in the maze, it would usually wander slowly up and down the center aisle after the barrier slid away, sniffing in corners and scratching at walls. It appeared to smell the chocolate but couldn't figure out how to find it. There was no discernible pattern in the rat's meanderings and no indication it was working hard to find the treat.

The probes in the rats' heads, however, told a different story. While each animal wandered through the maze, its brain was working furiously. Every time a rat sniffed the air or scratched a wall, the neurosensors inside the animal's head exploded with activity. As the scientists repeated the experiment, again and again, the rats eventually stopped sniffing corners and making wrong turns and began to zip through the maze with more and more speed. And within their brains, something unexpected occurred: as each rat learned how to complete the maze more quickly, its mental activity *decreased.* As the path became more and more automatic—as it became a habit—the rats started thinking less and less.

This process, in which the brain converts a sequence of actions into an automatic routine, is called "chunking." There are dozens, if not hundreds, of behavioral chunks we rely on every day. Some are simple: you automatically put toothpaste on your toothbrush before sticking it in your mouth. Some, like making the kids' lunch, are a little more complex. Still others are so complicated that it's remarkable to realize that a habit could have emerged at all.

Take backing your car out of the driveway. When you first learned to drive, that act required a major dose of concentration, and for good reason: it involves peering into the rearview and side mirrors and checking for obstacles, putting your foot on the brake, moving the gearshift into reverse, removing your foot from the brake, estimating the distance between the garage and the street while keeping the wheels aligned, calculating how images in the mirrors translate into actual distances, all while applying differing amounts of pressure to the gas pedal and brake.

Now, you perform that series of actions every time you pull into the street without thinking very much. Your brain has chunked large parts of it. Left to its own devices, the brain will try to make almost any repeated behavior into a habit, because habits allow our minds to conserve effort. But conserving mental energy is tricky, because if our brains power down at the wrong moment, we might fail to notice something important, like a child riding her bike down the sidewalk or a speeding car coming down the street. So we've devised a clever system to determine when to let a habit take over. It's something that happens whenever a chunk of behavior starts or ends—and it helps to explain why habits are so difficult to change once they're formed, despite our best intentions.

To understand this a little more clearly, consider again the chocolate-seeking rats. What Graybiel and her colleagues found was that as the ability to navigate the maze became habitual, there were two spikes in the rats' brain activity—once at the beginning of the maze, when the rat heard the click right before the barrier slid away, and once at the end, when the rat found the chocolate. Those spikes show when the rats' brains were fully engaged, and the dip in neural activity between the spikes showed when the habit took over. From behind the partition, the rat wasn't sure what waited on the other side, until it heard the click, which it had come to associate with the maze. Once it heard that sound, it knew to use the "maze habit," and its brain activity decreased. Then at the end of the routine, when the reward appeared, the brain shook itself awake again, and the chocolate signaled to the rat that this particular habit was worth remembering, and the neurological pathway was carved that much deeper.

The process within our brains that creates habits is a three-step loop. First, there is a cue, a trigger that tells your brain to go into automatic mode and which habit to use. Then there is the routine, which can be physical or mental or emotional. Finally, there is a reward, which helps your brain figure out if this particular loop is worth remembering for the future. Over time, this loop—cue, routine, reward; cue, routine, reward—becomes more and more automatic. The cue and reward become neurologically intertwined until a sense of craving emerges. What's unique about cues and rewards, however, is how subtle they can be. Neurological studies like the ones in Graybiel's lab have revealed that some cues span just milliseconds. And rewards can range from the obvious (like the sugar rush that a morning doughnut habit provides) to the infinitesimal (like the barely noticeable—but measurable—sense of relief the brain experiences after successfully navigating the driveway). Most cues and rewards, in fact, happen so quickly and are so slight that we are hardly aware of them at all. But our neural systems notice and use them to build automatic behaviors.

Habits aren't destiny—they can be ignored, changed, or replaced. But it's also true that once the loop is established and a habit emerges, your brain stops fully participating in decision making. So unless you deliberately fight a habit—unless you find new cues and rewards—the old pattern will unfold automatically.

"We've done experiments where we trained rats to run down a maze until it was a habit, and then we extinguished the habit by changing the placement of the reward," Graybiel told me. "Then one day, we'll put the reward in the old place and put in the rat and, by golly, the old habit will re-emerge right away. Habits never really disappear."

• • •

Luckily, simply understanding how habits work makes them easier to control. Take, for instance, a series of studies conducted a few years ago at Columbia University and the University of Alberta. Researchers wanted to understand how exercise habits emerge. In one project, 256 members of a health-insurance plan were invited to classes stressing the importance of exercise. Half the participants received an extra lesson on the theories of habit formation (the structure of the habit loop) and were asked to identify cues and rewards that might help them develop exercise routines.

The results were dramatic. Over the next four months, those participants who deliberately identified cues and rewards spent twice as much time exercising as their peers. Other studies have yielded similar results. According to another recent paper, if you want to start running in the morning, it's essential that you choose a simple cue (like always putting on your sneakers before breakfast or leaving your running clothes next to your bed) and a clear reward (like a midday treat or even the sense of accomplishment that comes from ritually recording your miles in a log book). After a while, your brain will start anticipating that reward—craving the treat or the feeling of accomplishment—and there will be a measurable neurological impulse to lace up your jogging shoes each morning.

Our relationship to e-mail operates on the same principle. When a computer chimes or a smartphone vibrates with a new message, the brain starts anticipating the neurological "pleasure" (even if we don't recognize it as such) that clicking on the e-mail and reading it provides. That expectation, if unsatisfied, can build until you find yourself moved to distraction by the thought of an e-mail sitting there unread—even if you know, rationally, it's most likely not important. On the other hand, once you remove the cue by disabling the buzzing of your phone or the chiming of your computer, the craving is never triggered, and you'll find, over time, that you're able to work productively for long stretches without checking your in-box.

Some of the most ambitious habit experiments have been conducted by corporate America. To understand why executives are so entranced by this science, consider how one of the world's largest companies, Procter & Gamble, used habit insights to turn a failing product into one of its biggest sellers. P&G is the corporate behemoth behind a whole range of products, from Downy fabric softener to Bounty paper towels to Duracell batteries and dozens of other household brands. In the mid-1990s, P&G's executives began a secret project to create a new product that could eradicate bad smells. P&G spent millions developing a colorless, cheap-to-manufacture liquid that could be sprayed on a smoky blouse, stinky couch, old jacket, or stained car interior and make it odorless. In order to market the product—Febreze—the company formed a team that included a former Wall Street mathematician named Drake Stimson and habit specialists, whose job was to make sure the television commercials, which they tested in Phoenix, Salt Lake City, and Boise, Idaho, accentuated the product's cues and rewards just right.

The first ad showed a woman complaining about the smoking section of a restaurant. Whenever she eats there, she says, her jacket smells like smoke. A friend tells her that if she uses Febreze, it will eliminate the odor. The cue in the ad is clear: the harsh smell of cigarette smoke. The reward: odor eliminated from clothes. The second ad featured a woman worrying about her dog, Sophie, who always sits on the couch. "Sophie will always smell like Sophie," she says, but with Febreze, "now my furniture doesn't have to." The ads were put in heavy rotation. Then the marketers sat back, anticipating how they would spend their bonuses. A week passed. Then two. A month. Two months. Sales started small and got smaller. Febreze was a dud.

The panicked marketing team canvassed consumers and conducted in-depth interviews to figure out what was going wrong, Stimson recalled. Their first inkling came when they visited a woman's home outside Phoenix. The house was clean and organized. She was something of a neat freak, the woman explained. But when P&G's scientists walked into her living room, where her nine cats spent most of their time, the scent was so overpowering that one of them gagged.

According to Stimson, who led the Febreze team, a researcher asked the woman, "What do you do about the cat smell?"

"It's usually not a problem," she said.

"Do you smell it now?"

"No," she said. "Isn't it wonderful? They hardly smell at all!"

A similar scene played out in dozens of other smelly homes. The reason Febreze wasn't selling, the marketers realized, was that people couldn't detect most of the bad smells in their lives. If you live with nine cats, you become desensitized to their scents. If you smoke cigarettes, eventually you don't smell smoke anymore. Even the strongest odors fade with constant exposure. That's why Febreze was a failure. The product's cue—the bad smells that were supposed to trigger daily use—was hidden from the people who needed it the most. And Febreze's reward (an odorless home) was meaningless to someone who couldn't smell offensive scents in the first place.

P&G employed a Harvard Business School professor to analyze Febreze's ad campaigns. They collected hours of footage of people cleaning their homes and watched tape after tape, looking for clues that might help them connect Febreze to people's daily habits. When that didn't reveal anything, they went into the field and conducted more interviews. A breakthrough came when they visited a woman in a suburb near Scottsdale, Ariz., who was in her forties with four children. Her house was clean, though not compulsively tidy, and didn't appear to have any odor problems; there were no pets or smokers. To the surprise of everyone, she loved Febreze.

"I use it every day," she said.

"What smells are you trying to get rid of?" a researcher asked.

"I don't really use it for specific smells," the woman said. "I use it for normal cleaning—a couple of sprays when I'm done in a room."

The researchers followed her around as she tidied the house. In the bedroom, she made her bed, tightened the sheet's corners, then sprayed the comforter with Febreze. In the living room, she vacuumed, picked up the children's shoes, straightened the coffee table, then sprayed Febreze on the freshly cleaned carpet.

"It's nice, you know?" she said. "Spraying feels like a little minicelebration when I'm done with a room." At the rate she was going, the team estimated, she would empty a bottle of Febreze every two weeks.

When they got back to P&G's headquarters, the researchers watched their videotapes again. Now they knew what to look for and saw their mistake in scene after scene. Cleaning has its own habit loops that already exist. In one video, when a woman walked into a dirty room (cue), she started sweeping and picking up toys (routine), then she examined the room and smiled when she was done (reward). In another, a woman scowled at her unmade bed (cue), proceeded to straighten the blankets and comforter (routine), and then sighed as she ran her hands over the freshly plumped pillows (reward). P&G had been trying to create a whole new habit with Febreze, but what they really needed to do was piggyback on habit loops that were already in place. The marketers needed to position Febreze as something that came at the end of the cleaning ritual, the reward, rather than as a whole new cleaning routine.

The company printed new ads showing open windows and gusts of fresh air. More perfume was added to the Febreze formula, so that instead of merely neutralizing odors, the spray had its own distinct scent. Television commercials were filmed of women, having finished their cleaning routine, using Febreze to spritz freshly made beds and just-laundered clothing. Each ad was designed to appeal to the habit loop: when you see a freshly cleaned room (cue), pull out Febreze (routine), and enjoy a smell that says you've done a great job (reward). When you finish making a bed (cue), spritz Febreze (routine), and breathe a sweet, contented sigh (reward). Febreze, the ads implied, was a pleasant treat, not a reminder that your home stinks.

And so Febreze, a product originally conceived as a revolutionary way to destroy odors, became an air freshener used once things are already clean. The Febreze revamp occurred in the summer of 1998. Within two months, sales doubled. A year later, the product brought in $230 million. Since then Febreze has spawned dozens of spinoffs—air fresheners, candles, and laundry detergents—that now account for sales of more than $1 billion a year. Eventually, P&G began mentioning to customers that, in addition to smelling sweet, Febreze can actually kill bad odors. Today it's one of the top-selling products in the world.

• • •

Andrew Pole was hired by Target to use the same kinds of insights into consumers' habits to expand Target's sales. His assignment was to analyze all the cue-routine-reward loops among shoppers and help the company figure out how to exploit them. Much of his department's work was straightforward: find the customers who have children and send them catalogues that feature toys before Christmas. Look for shoppers who habitually purchase swimsuits in April and send them coupons for sunscreen in July and diet books in December. But Pole's most important assignment was to identify those unique moments in consumers' lives when their shopping habits become particularly flexible and the right advertisement or coupon would cause them to begin spending in new ways.

In the 1980s, a team of researchers led by a UCLA professor named Alan Andreasen undertook a study of peoples' most mundane purchases, like soap, toothpaste, trash bags, and toilet paper. They learned that most shoppers paid almost no attention to how they bought these products, that the purchases occurred habitually, without any complex decision making. Which meant it was hard for marketers, despite their displays and coupons and product promotions, to persuade shoppers to change.

But when some customers were going through a major life event, like graduating from college or getting a new job or moving to a new town, their shopping habits became flexible in ways that were both predictable and potential gold mines for retailers. The study found that when someone marries, he or she is more likely to start buying a new type of coffee. When a couple move into a new house, they're more apt to purchase a different kind of cereal. When they divorce, there's an increased chance they'll start buying different brands of beer.

Consumers going through major life events often don't notice, or care, that their shopping habits have shifted, but retailers notice, and they care quite a bit. At those unique moments, Andreasen wrote, customers are "vulnerable to intervention by marketers." In other words, a precisely timed advertisement, sent to a recent divorcee or new homebuyer, can change someone's shopping patterns for years.

And among life events, none are more important than the arrival of a baby. At that moment, new parents' habits are more flexible than at almost any other time in their adult lives. If companies can identify pregnant shoppers, they can earn millions.

The only problem is that identifying pregnant customers is harder than it sounds. Target has a baby-shower registry, and Pole started there, observing how shopping habits changed as a woman approached her due date, which women on the registry had willingly disclosed. He ran test after test, analyzing the data, and before long some useful patterns emerged. Lotions, for example. Lots of people buy lotion, but one of Pole's colleagues noticed that women on the baby registry were buying larger quantities of unscented lotion around the beginning of their second trimester. Another analyst noted that sometime in the first twenty weeks, pregnant women loaded up on supplements like calcium, magnesium, and zinc. Many shoppers purchase soap and cotton balls, but when someone suddenly starts buying lots of scent-free soap and extra-big bags of cotton balls, in addition to hand sanitizers and washcloths, it signals they could be getting close to their delivery date.

As Pole's computers crawled through the data, he was able to identify about twenty-five products that, when analyzed together, allowed him to assign each shopper a "pregnancy prediction" score. More important, he could also estimate her due date to within a small window, so Target could send coupons timed to very specific stages of her pregnancy.

One Target employee I spoke to provided a hypothetical example. Take a fictional Target shopper named Jenny Ward, who is twenty-three, lives in Atlanta, and in March bought cocoa-butter lotion, a purse large enough to double as a diaper bag, zinc and magnesium supplements, and a bright blue rug. There's, say, an 87 percent chance that she's pregnant and that her delivery date is sometime in late August. What's more, because of the data attached to her Guest ID number, Target knows how to trigger Jenny's habits. They know that if she receives a coupon via e-mail, it will most likely cue her to buy online. They know that if she receives an ad in the mail on Friday, she frequently uses it on a weekend trip to the store. And they know that if they reward her with a printed receipt that entitles her to a free cup of Starbucks coffee, she'll use it when she comes back again.

In the past, that knowledge had limited value. After all, Jenny purchased only cleaning supplies at Target, and there were only so many psychological buttons the company could push. But now that she is pregnant, everything is up for grabs. In addition to triggering Jenny's habits to buy more cleaning products, they can also start including offers for an array of products, some more obvious than others, that a woman at her stage of pregnancy might need.

Pole applied his program to every regular female shopper in Target's national database and soon had a list of tens of thousands of women who were most likely pregnant. If they could entice those women or their husbands to visit Target and buy baby-related products, the company's cue-routine-reward calculators could kick in and start pushing them to buy groceries, bathing suits, toys, and clothing, as well. When Pole shared his list with the marketers, he said, they were ecstatic. Soon, Pole was getting invited to meetings above his paygrade. Eventually his paygrade went up.

At which point someone asked an important question: How are women going to react when they figure out how much Target knows?

"If we send someone a catalogue and say, 'Congratulations on your first child!' and they've never told us they're pregnant, that's going to make some people uncomfortable," Pole told me. "We are very conservative about compliance with all privacy laws. But even if you're following the law, you can do things where people get queasy."

About a year after Pole created his pregnancy-prediction model, a man walked into a Target outside Minneapolis and demanded to see the manager. He was clutching coupons that had been sent to his daughter, and he was angry, according to an employee who participated in the conversation.

"My daughter got this in the mail!" he said. "She's still in high school, and you're sending her coupons for baby clothes and cribs? Are you trying to encourage her to get pregnant?"

The manager didn't have any idea what the man was talking about. He looked at the mailer. Sure enough, it was addressed to the man's daughter and contained advertisements for maternity clothing, nursery furniture, and pictures of smiling infants. The manager apologized and then called a few days later to apologize again.

On the phone, though, the father was somewhat abashed. "I had a talk with my daughter," he said. "It turns out there's been some activities in my house I haven't been completely aware of. She's due in August. I owe you an apology."

When I approached Target to discuss Pole's work, its representatives declined to speak with me. "Our mission is to make Target the preferred shopping destination for our guests by delivering outstanding value, continuous innovation and exceptional guest experience," the company wrote in a statement. "We've developed a number of research tools that allow us to gain insights into trends and preferences within different demographic segments of our guest population." When I sent Target a complete summary of my reporting, the reply was more terse: "Almost all of your statements contain inaccurate information and publishing them would be misleading to the public. We do not intend to address each statement point by point." The company declined to identify what was inaccurate. They did add, however, that Target "is in compliance with all federal and state laws, including those related to protected health information."

When I offered to fly to Target's headquarters to discuss its concerns, a spokeswoman e-mailed that no one would meet me. When I flew out anyway, I was told I was on a list of prohibited visitors. "I've been instructed not to give you access and to ask you to leave," said a very nice security guard named Alex.

Using data to predict a woman's pregnancy, Target realized soon after Pole perfected his model, could be a public-relations disaster. So the question became: how could they get their advertisements into expectant mothers' hands without making it appear they were spying on them? How do you take advantage of someone's habits without letting them know you're studying their lives?

• • •

Before I met Andrew Pole, before I even decided to write a book about the science of habit formation, I had another goal: I wanted to lose weight.

I had got into a bad habit of going to the cafeteria every afternoon and eating a chocolate-chip cookie, which contributed to my gaining a few pounds. Eight, to be precise. I put a Post-it note on my computer reading "NO MORE COOKIES." But every afternoon, I managed to ignore that note, wander to the cafeteria, buy a cookie, and eat it while chatting with colleagues. Tomorrow, I always promised myself, I'll muster the willpower to resist.

Tomorrow, I ate another cookie.

When I started interviewing experts in habit formation, I concluded each interview by asking what I should do. The first step, they said, was to figure out my habit loop. The routine was simple: every afternoon, I walked to the cafeteria, bought a cookie, and ate it while chatting with friends.

Next came some less obvious questions: What was the cue? Hunger? Boredom? Low blood sugar? And what was the reward?

The taste of the cookie itself? The temporary distraction from my work? The chance to socialize with colleagues?

Rewards are powerful because they satisfy cravings, but we're often not conscious of the urges driving our habits in the first place. So one day, when I felt a cookie impulse, I went outside and took a walk instead. The next day, I went to the cafeteria and bought a coffee. The next, I bought an apple and ate it while chatting with friends. You get the idea. I wanted to test different theories regarding what reward I was really craving. Was it hunger? (In which case the apple should have worked.) Was it the desire for a quick burst of energy? (If so, the coffee should suffice.) Or, as turned out to be the answer, was it that after several hours spent focused on work, I wanted to socialize, to make sure I was up to speed on office gossip, and the cookie was just a convenient excuse? When I walked to a colleague's desk and chatted for a few minutes, it turned out, my cookie urge was gone.

All that was left was identifying the cue.

Deciphering cues is hard, however. Our lives often contain too much information to figure out what is triggering a particular behavior. Do you eat breakfast at a certain time because you're hungry? Or because the morning news is on? Or because your kids have started eating? Experiments have shown that most cues fit into one of five categories: location, time, emotional state, other people, or the immediately preceding action. So to figure out the cue for my cookie habit, I wrote down five things the moment the urge hit:

Where are you? (Sitting at my desk.)

What time is it? (3:36 p.m.)

What's your emotional state? (Bored.)

Who else is around? (No one.)

What action preceded the urge? (Answered an e-mail.)

The next day I did the same thing. And the next. Pretty soon, the cue was clear: I always felt an urge to snack around three-thirty.

Once I figured out all the parts of the loop, it seemed fairly easy to change my habit. But the psychologists and neuroscientists warned me that, for my new behavior to stick, I needed to abide by the same principle that guided Procter & Gamble in selling Febreze: to shift the routine—to socialize, rather than eat a cookie—I needed to piggyback on an existing habit. So now, every day around three-thirty, I stand up, look around the newsroom for someone to talk to, spend ten minutes gossiping, then go back to my desk. The cue and reward have stayed the same. Only the routine has shifted. It doesn't feel like a decision, any more than the MIT rats made a decision to run through the maze. It's now a habit. I've lost twenty-one pounds since then (twelve of them from changing my cookie ritual).

• • •

After Andrew Pole built his pregnancy-prediction model, after he identified thousands of female shoppers who were most likely pregnant, after someone pointed out that some of those women might be a little upset if they received an advertisement making it obvious Target was studying their reproductive status, everyone decided to slow things down.

The marketing department conducted a few tests by choosing a small, random sample of women from Pole's list and mailing them combinations of advertisements to see how they reacted.

"We have the capacity to send every customer an ad booklet, specifically designed for them, that says, 'Here's everything you bought last week and a coupon for it,'" one Target executive told me. "We do that for grocery products all the time." But for pregnant women, Target's goal was selling them baby items they didn't even know they needed yet.

"With the pregnancy products, though, we learned that some women react badly," the executive said. "Then we started mixing in all these ads for things we knew pregnant women would never buy, so the baby ads looked random. We'd put an ad for a lawn mower next to diapers. We'd put a coupon for wineglasses next to infant clothes. That way, it looked like all the products were chosen by chance.

"And we found out that as long as a pregnant woman thinks she hasn't been spied on, she'll use the coupons. She just assumes that everyone else on her block got the same mailer for diapers and cribs. As long as we don't spook her, it works."

In other words, if Target piggybacked on existing habits—the same cues and rewards they already knew got customers to buy cleaning supplies or socks—then they could insert a new routine: buying baby products, as well. There's a cue ("Oh, a coupon for something I need!") a routine ("Buy! Buy! Buy!"), and a reward ("I can take that off my list"). And once the shopper is inside the store, Target will hit her with cues and rewards to entice her to purchase everything she normally buys somewhere else. As long as Target camouflaged how much it knew, as long as the habit felt familiar, the new behavior took hold.

Soon after the new ad campaign began, Target's Mom and Baby sales exploded. The company doesn't break out figures for specific divisions, but between 2002—when Pole was hired—and 2010, Target's revenues grew from $44 billion to $67 billion. In 2005, the company's president, Gregg Steinhafel, boasted to a room of investors about the company's "heightened focus on items and categories that appeal to specific guest segments such as mom and baby."

Pole was promoted. He has been invited to speak at conferences. "I never expected this would become such a big deal," he told me the last time we spoke.

• • •

A few weeks before this article went to press, I flew to Minneapolis to try and speak to Andrew Pole one last time. I hadn't talked to him in more than a year. Back when we were still friendly, I mentioned that my wife was seven months pregnant. We shop at Target, I told him, and had given the company our address so we could start receiving coupons in the mail. As my wife's pregnancy progressed, I noticed a subtle upswing in the number of advertisements for diapers and baby clothes arriving at our house.

Pole didn't answer my e-mails or phone calls when I visited Minneapolis. I drove to his large home in a nice suburb, but no one answered the door. On my way back to the hotel, I stopped at a Target to pick up some deodorant, then also bought some T-shirts and a fancy hair gel. On a whim, I threw in some pacifiers, to see how the computers would react. Besides, our baby is now nine months old. You can't have too many pacifiers.

When I paid, I didn't receive any sudden deals on diapers or formula, to my slight disappointment. It made sense, though: I was shopping in a city I never previously visited, at nine-forty-five p.m. on a weeknight, buying a random assortment of items. I was using a corporate credit card and, besides the pacifiers, hadn't purchased any of the things that a parent needs. It was clear to Target's computers that I was on a business trip. Pole's prediction calculator took one look at me, ran the numbers, and decided to bide its time. Back home, the offers would eventually come. As Pole told me the last time we spoke: "Just wait. We'll be sending you coupons for things you want before you even know you want them."

Wired

What could possibly be interesting about the glass in your smartphone? Much more than you would imagine. Bryan Gardiner tells the unexpectedly enthralling tale of the slab of glass our thumbs have come to know so well. Corning developed the forerunner of Gorilla Glass fifty years ago but shelved it shortly thereafter when demand failed to appear. It wasn't until 2007, after Steve Jobs came calling, that the company first mass-produced the glass, and it now sells $700 million of it a year. You can't sell stuff if you can't make it, a truism that's usually lost on a business press far more prone to focus on earnings reports than manufacturing processes. Gardiner navigates the intersection of science and business to show how basic research, patience, and institutional memory lead to a breakthrough product.

Bryan Gardiner

25. Glass Works: How Corning Created the Ultrathin, Ultrastrong Material of the Future

Don Stookey knew he had botched the experiment. One day in 1952, the Corning Glass Works chemist placed a sample of photosensitive glass inside a furnace and set the temperature to 600 degrees Celsius. At some point during the run, a faulty controller let the temperature climb to 900 degrees C. Expecting a melted blob of glass and a ruined furnace, Stookey opened the door to discover that, weirdly, his lithium silicate had transformed into a milky white plate. When he tried to remove it, the sample slipped from the tongs and crashed to the floor. Instead of shattering, it bounced.

The future National Inventors Hall of Fame inductee didn't know it, but he had just invented the first synthetic glass-ceramic, a material Corning would later dub Pyroceram. Lighter than aluminum, harder than high-carbon steel, and many times stronger than regular soda-lime glass, Pyroceram eventually found its way into everything from missile nose cones to chemistry labs. It could also be used in microwave ovens, and in 1959

Pyroceram debuted as a line of Space Age serving dishes: Corningware.

The material was a boon to Corning's fortunes, and soon the company launched Project Muscle, a massive R&D effort to explore other ways of strengthening glass. A breakthrough came when company scientists tweaked a recently developed method of reinforcing glass that involved dousing it in a bath of hot potassium salt. They discovered that adding aluminum oxide to a given glass composition before the dip would result in remarkable strength and durability. Scientists were soon hurling fortified tumblers off their nine-story facility and bombarding the glass, known internally as 0317, with frozen chickens. It could be bent and twisted to an extraordinary degree before fracturing, and it could withstand 100,000 pounds of pressure per square inch. (Normal glass can weather about 7,000.) In 1962 Corning began marketing the glass as Chemcor and thought it could work for products like phone booths, prison windows, and eyeglasses.

Yet while there was plenty of initial interest, sales were slow. Some companies did place small orders for products like safety eyeglasses. But these were recalled for fear of the potentially explosive way the glass could break. Chemcor seemed like it would make a good car windshield too, and while it did show up in a handful of Javelins, made by American Motors, most manufacturers weren't convinced that paying more for the new muscle glass was worth it—especially when the laminated stuff they'd been using since the thirties seemed to work fine.

Corning had invented an expensive upgrade nobody wanted. It didn't help that crash tests found that "head deceleration was significantly higher" on the windshields—the Chemcor might remain intact, but human skulls would not.

After pitches to Ford Motors and other automakers failed, Project Muscle was shut down and Chemcor was shelved in

1971. It was a solution that would have to wait for the right problem to arise.

• • •

From above, Corning's headquarters in upstate New York looks like a Space Invaders alien: Designed by architect Kevin Roche in the early nineties, the structure fans out in staggered blocks. From the ground, though, the tinted windows and extended eaves make the building look more like a glossy, futuristic Japanese palace.

The office of Wendell Weeks, Corning's CEO, is on the second floor, looking out onto the Chemung River. It was here that Steve Jobs gave the fifty-three-year-old Weeks a seemingly impossible task: Make millions of square feet of ultrathin, ultrastrong glass that didn't yet exist. Oh, and do it in six months. The story of their collaboration—including Jobs's attempt to lecture Weeks on the principles of glass and his insistence that such a feat could be accomplished—is well known. How Corning actually pulled it off is not.

Weeks joined Corning in 1983; before assuming the top post in 2005, he oversaw both the company's television and specialty-glass businesses. Talk to him about glass and he describes it as something exotic and beautiful—a material whose potential is just starting to be unlocked by scientists. He'll gush about its inherent touchability and authenticity, only to segue into a lecture about radio-frequency transparency. "There's a sort of fundamental truth in the design value of glass," Weeks says, holding up a clear pebble of the stuff. "It's like a found object; it's cool to the touch; it's smooth but has surface to it. What you'd really want is for this to come alive. That'd be a perfect product."

Weeks and Jobs shared an appreciation for design. Both men obsessed over details. And both gravitated toward big challenges and ideas. But while Jobs was dictatorial in his management style, Weeks (like many of his predecessors at Corning) tends to encourage a degree of insubordination. "The separation between myself and any of the bench scientists is nonexistent," he says. "We can work in these small teams in a very relaxed way that's still hyperintense."

Indeed, even though it's a big company—29,000 employees and revenue of $7.9 billion in 2011—Corning still thinks and acts like a small one, something made easier by its relatively remote location, an annual attrition rate that hovers around 1 percent, and a vast institutional memory. (Stookey, now ninety-seven, and other legends still roam the halls and labs of Sullivan Park, Corning's R&D facility.) "We're all lifers here," Weeks says, smiling. "We've known each other for a long time and succeeded and failed together a number of times."

One of the first conversations between Weeks and Jobs actually had nothing to do with glass. Corning scientists were toying around with microprojection technologies—specifically, better ways of using synthetic green lasers. The thought was that people wouldn't want to stare at tiny cell-phone screens to watch movies and TV shows, and projection seemed like a natural solution. But when Weeks spoke to Jobs about it, Apple's chief called the idea dumb. He did mention he was working on something better, though—a device whose entire surface was a display. It was called the iPhone.

Jobs may have dismissed green lasers, but they represented the kind of innovation for innovation's sake that defines Corning. So strong is this reverence for experimentation that the company regularly invests a healthy 10 percent of its revenue in R&D. And that's in good times *and* in bad. When the telecom bubble burst in 2000 and cratering fiber-optic prices sent Corning's stock from $100 to $1.50 per share by 2002, its CEO at the time reassured scientists that not only was Corning still about research but that R&D would be the path back to prosperity.

"They're one of the very few technology-based firms that have been able to reinvent themselves on a regular basis," says Rebecca Henderson, a professor at Harvard Business School who has studied Corning's history of innovation. "That's so easy to say, and it is so hard to do." Part of that success lies in the company's ability not only to develop new technologies but to figure out how to make them on a massive scale. Still, even when Corning succeeds at both, it can often take the manufacturer decades to find a suitable—and profitable enough—market for its innovations. As Henderson notes, innovation at Corning is largely about being willing and able to take failed ideas and apply them elsewhere.

The idea to dust off the Chemcor samples actually cropped up in 2005, before Apple had even entered the picture. Motorola had recently released the Razr V3, a flip phone that featured a glass screen in lieu of the typical high-impact plastic. Corning formed a small group to examine whether an 0317-like glass could be revived and applied to devices like cell phones and watches. The old Chemcor samples were as thick as 4 millimeters. But maybe they could be made thinner. After some market research, executives believed the company could even earn a little money off this specialty product. The project was codenamed Gorilla Glass.

By the time the call from Jobs came in February 2007, these initial forays hadn't gotten very far. Apple was suddenly demanding massive amounts of a 1.3-mm, chemically strengthened glass—something that had never been created, much less manufactured, before. Could Chemcor, which had never been mass-produced, be married to a process that would yield such scale? Could a glass tailored for applications like car windshields be made ultrathin and still retain its strength? Would the chemical strengthening process even work effectively on such a glass? No one knew. So Weeks did what any CEO with a penchant for risk-taking would do. He said yes.

• • •

For a material that's so familiar as to be practically invisible, modern industrial glass is formidably complex. Standard soda-lime glass works fine for bottles and lightbulbs but is terrible for other applications because it can shatter into sharp pieces. Borosilicate glass like Pyrex may be great at resisting thermal shock, but it takes a lot of energy to melt it. At the same time, there are really only two ways to produce flat glass on a large scale, something called fusion draw and the float-glass process, in which molten glass is poured onto a bed of molten tin. One challenge a glass company faces is matching a composition, with all its desired traits, to the manufacturing process. It's one thing to devise a formula. It's another to manufacture a product out of it.

Regardless of composition, the main ingredient in almost all glass is silicon dioxide (a.k.a. sand). Because it has such a high melting point (1,720 degrees C), other chemicals, like sodium oxide, are used to lower the melting temperature of the mixture, making it easier to work with and cheaper to produce. Many of these chemicals also happen to imbue glass with specific properties, such as resistance to X rays, tolerance for high temperatures, or the ability to refract light and disperse colors. Problems arise, though, when the composition is changed; the slightest tweak can result in a drastically different material. Throwing in a dense element like barium or lanthanum, for example, will decrease the melting temperature, but you risk not getting a homogeneous mixture. And maxing out the overall strength of a glass means you're also making that glass more likely to fracture violently when it *does* fail. Glass is a material ruled by trade-offs. This is why compositions, particularly those that are fine-tuned for a specific manufacturing process, are fiercely guarded secrets.

One of the pivotal steps in glassmaking is the cooling. In large-scale manufacturing of standard glass, it's essential for the material to cool gradually and uniformly in order to minimize the internal stresses that would otherwise make it easier to break. This is called annealing. The goal with tempered glass, however, is to *add* stress between the inner and outer layer of the material. This, paradoxically, can make the glass stronger: Heat a sheet of glass until it softens, then rapidly cool, or quench, its outer surfaces. This outside shell quickly contracts while the inside remains molten. As the center of the glass cools, it tries to contract, pulling on the outer shell. A zone of tension forms in the center, while the outer surfaces are even more tightly compressed. Tempered glass will eventually break if you chip through this toughened outer compressive layer into the zone of tension. But even thermal tempering has its limits. The amount of strengthening you can achieve is dependent on how much the glass contracts upon cooling, and most compositions will shrink only modestly.

The interplay between compression and tension is best demonstrated by something called a Prince Rupert's drop. Formed by dripping globs of molten glass into ice water, the quickly cooled and compressed heads of these tadpole-shaped droplets can withstand massive amounts of punishment, including repeated hammer blows. The thin glass at the end of the tail is more vulnerable, however, and if you break it the fracture will propagate through the drop at 2,000 miles per hour, releasing the inner tension. Violently. In some cases, a Prince Rupert's drop can explode with such force that it will actually emit a flash of light.

Chemical strengthening, the method of fortifying glass developed in the sixties, creates a compressive layer, too, through something called ion exchange. Aluminosilicate compositions like Gorilla Glass contain silicon dioxide, aluminum, magnesium, and sodium. When the glass is dipped in a hot bath of molten potassium salt, it heats up and expands. Both sodium and potassium are in the same column on the periodic table of elements, which means they behave similarly. The heat from the bath increases the migration of the sodium ions out of the glass, and the similar potassium ions easily float in and take their place. But because potassium ions are larger than sodium, they get packed into the space more tightly. (Imagine taking a garage full of Fiat 500s and replacing most of them with Chevy Suburbans.) As the glass cools, they get squeezed together in this now-cramped space, and a layer of compressive stress on the surface of the glass is formed. (Corning ensures an even ion exchange by regulating factors like heat and time.) Compared with thermally strengthened glass, the "stuffing" or "crowding" effect in chemically strengthened glass results in higher surface compression (making it up to four times as strong), and it can be done to glass of any thickness or shape.

• • •

By the end of March, Corning was closing in on its formula. But the company also needed to manufacture it. Inventing a new manufacturing process was out of the question, as that could take years. To meet Apple's deadline, two of Corning's compositional scientists, Adam Ellison and Matt Dejneka, were tasked with figuring out how to adapt and troubleshoot a process the company was already using. They needed something capable of spitting out massive quantities of thin, pristine glass in a matter of weeks.

There was really only one choice: fusion draw. In this technique, molten glass is poured from a tank into a trough called an isopipe. The glass overflows on each side, then the two streams rejoin under the isopipe. It's drawn down at a prescribed rate by rollers to form a continuous sheet. The faster it's drawn, the thinner the glass.

Corning's one fusion-capable factory in the United States is in Harrodsburg, Kentucky. In early 2007, that plant's seven fifteen-foot-tall tanks were going full blast, each churning out more than 1,000 pounds per hour of sold-out LCD glass for TV panels. One tank could meet Apple's initial request. But first the old Chemcor compositions had to be reformulated. The glass not only needed to be 1.3 mm now, it also had to have better visual characteristics than, say, a pane in a telephone booth. Ellison and his team had six weeks to nail it. To be compatible with the fusion process, the glass also needed to be extra stretchy, like chewing gum, at a fairly low temperature. The problem was, anything you do to increase a glass's gooeyness also tends to make it substantially more difficult to melt. By simultaneously altering seven individual parts of the composition—including changing the levels of several oxides and adding one new secret ingredient—the compositional scientists found they were able to ramp up the viscosity while also producing a finely tuned glass capable of higher compressive stress and faster ion exchange. The tank started in May 2007. By June, it had produced enough Gorilla Glass to cover seven football fields.

In just five years, Gorilla Glass has gone from a material to an aesthetic—a seamless partition that separates our physical selves from the digital incarnations we carry in our pockets. We touch the outer layer and our body closes the circuit between an electrode beneath the screen and its neighbor, transforming motion into data. It's now featured on more than 750 products and 33 brands worldwide, including notebooks, tablets, smartphones, and TVs. If you regularly touch, swipe, or caress a gadget, chances are you've interacted with Gorilla.

Corning's revenue from the glass has skyrocketed, from $20 million in 2007 to $700 million in 2011. And there are other uses beyond touch screens. At this year's London Design Festival, Eckersley O'Callaghan—the design firm responsible for some of Apple's most iconic stores—unveiled a serpentine-like glass sculpture made entirely from Gorilla Glass. It may even end up on windshields again: The company is in talks to install it in future sports car models.

Today, two yellow robotic arms grab five-foot-square panels of Gorilla Glass with special residue-limiting suction cups and place them in wooden crates. From Harrodsburg, these crates are trucked to Louisville and loaded on a westbound train. Once they hit the coast, the sheets get loaded onto freight ships for their eventual date at one of Corning's "finisher" facilities in China, where they get their molten potassium baths and are cut into touchable rectangles.

Of course, for all its magical properties, a quick scan of the Internet will reveal that Gorilla Glass does fail, sometimes spectacularly so. It breaks when phones are dropped, it spiders if they bend, it cracks when they're sat on. Gorilla Glass is, after all, glass. Which is why a small team at Corning spends a good portion of the day smashing the hell out of the stuff.

"We call this a Norwegian hammer," says Jaymin Amin, pulling a metal cylinder out of a wooden box. The tool is usually wielded by aircraft engineers to test the sturdiness of a plane's aluminum fuselage. But Amin, who oversees all new glass development in the Gorilla family, pulls back the spring-loaded impact hammer and releases 2 joules of impact energy onto a 1-mm-thick piece of glass, enough to put a big dent in a block of wood. Nothing happens.

The success of Gorilla Glass presents some unique challenges for Corning. This is the first time the company has faced the demands of such rapid iteration: Each time a new version of the glass is released, the way it performs in the field has to be monitored for reliability and robustness. To that end, Amin's team collects hundreds of shattered Gorilla Glass phones. "Almost all breakage, whether it's big or small, begins at one spot," says senior research scientist Kevin Reiman, pointing to a nearly invisible chip on an HTC Wildfire, one of a handful of crunched phones on the table in front of him. Once you actually locate that spot, you can start to measure the crack to get an idea of how the tension was applied to the glass; if you can reproduce a break, you can study how it propagated and attempt to prevent it, either compositionally or through chemical strengthening.

Armed with this information, the rest of the group jumps in to re-create that precise kind of failure over and over. They use lever presses; drop testers with granite, concrete, and asphalt surfaces; free-gravity ball drops; and various industrial-looking torture devices armed with an arsenal of diamond tips. There's even a high-speed camera capable of filming at 1 million frames per second to study flexure and flaw propagation.

All this destruction and controlled mayhem has paid off. Compared with the first version of the glass, Gorilla Glass 2 is 20 percent stronger (a third version is due out early next year). The Corning composition scientists have accomplished this by pushing the compressive stress to its limit—they were being conservative with the first version of Gorilla—while managing to avoid the explosive breakage that can come with that increase. Still, glass is a brittle material. And while brittle materials tend to be extremely strong under compression, they're also extremely weak under tension: If you bend them, they can break. The key to Gorilla Glass is that the compression layer keeps cracks from propagating through the material and catastrophically letting tension take over. Drop a phone once and the screen may not fracture, but you may cause enough damage (even a microscopic nick) to critically sap its subsequent strength. The next drop, even if it isn't as severe, may be fatal. It's one of the inevitable consequences of working with a material that is all about trade-offs, all about trying to create a perfectly imperceptible material.

• • •

Back at the Harrodsburg plant, a man wearing a black Gorilla Glass T-shirt is guiding a 100-micron-thick sheet of glass (about the thickness of aluminum foil) through a series of rollers. The machine looks like a printing press, and, appropriately, the glass that comes off it bends and flexes like a giant glimmering sheet of transparent paper. This remarkably thin, rollable material is called Willow. Unlike Gorilla Glass, which is meant to be used as armor, Willow is more like a raincoat. It's durable and light, and it has a lot of potential. Corning imagines it will facilitate flexible smartphone designs and *Über*-thin, roll-up OLED displays. An energy company could also use Willow for flexible solar cells. Corning even envisions e-books with glass pages.

Eventually, Willow will ship out on huge spools, like movie reels, each holding up to 500 feet of glass. That is, once someone places an order. For now, rolls of glass sit on the Harrodsburg factory floor, a solution waiting for the right problem to arise.

New York Times

The robots are coming for the last of the manufacturing jobs, as John Markoff writes in this fascinating look at the future of building things. This isn't science fiction or futurism. It's already happening, and it raises critical questions for society as a whole. At Tesla, the assembly-line workers have "a slightly menacing 'Terminator' quality" as the ten-foot-tall robots weld, rivet, and install parts. An electronic voice that Kroger workers call "The Brain" directs those humans on the warehouse floor who haven't already been replaced by the machines. And at Philips Electronics, robots "bend wires with millimetric accuracy, set toothpick-thin spindles in tiny holes, grab miniature plastic gears and set them in housings" to make electric razors. As these machines get ever cheaper and more powerful, the outlook for low- and medium-skilled blue-collar workers looks bleak.

John Markoff

26. Skilled Work, Without the Worker

Drachten, the Netherlands—At the Philips Electronics factory on the coast of China, hundreds of workers use their hands and specialized tools to assemble electric shavers. That is the old way.

At a sister factory here in the Dutch countryside, 128 robot arms do the same work with yoga-like flexibility. Video cameras guide them through feats well beyond the capability of the most dexterous human.

One robot arm endlessly forms three perfect bends in two connector wires and slips them into holes almost too small for the eye to see. The arms work so fast that they must be enclosed in glass cages to prevent the people supervising them from being injured. And they do it all without a coffee break—three shifts a day, 365 days a year.

All told, the factory here has several dozen workers per shift, about a tenth as many as the plant in the Chinese city of Zhuhai.

This is the future. A new wave of robots, far more adept than those now commonly used by automakers and other heavy manufacturers, are replacing workers around the world in both manufacturing and distribution. Factories like the one here in the Netherlands are a striking counterpoint to those used by Apple and other consumer electronics giants, which employ hundreds of thousands of low-skilled workers.

"With these machines, we can make any consumer device in the world," said Binne Visser, an electrical engineer who manages the Philips assembly line in Drachten.

Many industry executives and technology experts say Philips's approach is gaining ground on Apple's. Even as Foxconn, Apple's iPhone manufacturer, continues to build new plants and hire thousands of additional workers to make smartphones, it plans to install more than a million robots within a few years to supplement its work force in China.

Foxconn has not disclosed how many workers will be displaced or when. But its chairman, Terry Gou, has publicly endorsed a growing use of robots. Speaking of his more than one million employees worldwide, he said in January, according to the official Xinhua news agency: "As human beings are also animals, to manage one million animals gives me a headache."

The falling costs and growing sophistication of robots have touched off a renewed debate among economists and technologists over how quickly jobs will be lost. This year, Erik Brynjolfsson and Andrew McAfee, economists at the Massachusetts Institute of Technology, made the case for a rapid transformation. "The pace and scale of this encroachment into human skills is relatively recent and has profound economic implications," they wrote in their book, *Race Against the Machine*.

In their minds, the advent of low-cost automation foretells changes on the scale of the revolution in agricultural technology over the last century, when farming employment in the United States fell from 40 percent of the work force to about 2 percent today. The analogy is not only to the industrialization of agriculture but also to the electrification of manufacturing in the past century, Mr. McAfee argues.

"At what point does the chainsaw replace Paul Bunyan?" asked Mike Dennison, an executive at Flextronics, a manufacturer of consumer electronics products that is based in Silicon Valley and is increasingly automating assembly work. "There's always a price point, and we're very close to that point."

But Bran Ferren, a veteran roboticist and industrial product designer at Applied Minds in Glendale, Calif., argues that there are still steep obstacles that have made the dream of the universal assembly robot elusive. "I had an early naiveté about universal robots that could just do anything," he said. "You have to have people around anyway. And people are pretty good at figuring out, how do I wiggle the radiator in or slip the hose on? And these things are still hard for robots to do."

Beyond the technical challenges lies resistance from unionized workers and communities worried about jobs. The ascension of robots may mean fewer jobs are created in this country, even though rising labor and transportation costs in Asia and fears of intellectual property theft are now bringing some work back to the West.

Take the cavernous solar-panel factory run by Flextronics in Milpitas, south of San Francisco. A large banner proudly proclaims "Bringing Jobs & Manufacturing Back to California!" (Right now China makes a large share of the solar panels used in this country and is automating its own industry.)

Yet in the state-of-the-art plant, where the assembly line runs twenty-four hours a day, seven days a week, there are robots everywhere and few human workers. All of the heavy lifting and almost all of the precise work is done by robots that string together solar cells and seal them under glass. The human workers do things like trimming excess material, threading wires, and screwing a handful of fasteners into a simple frame for each panel.

Such advances in manufacturing are also beginning to transform other sectors that employ millions of workers around the world. One is distribution, where robots that zoom at the speed of the world's fastest sprinters can store, retrieve, and pack goods for shipment far more efficiently than people. Robots could soon replace workers at companies like C & S Wholesale Grocers, the nation's largest grocery distributor, which has already deployed robot technology.

Rapid improvement in vision and touch technologies is putting a wide array of manual jobs within the abilities of robots. For example, Boeing's wide-body commercial jets are now riveted automatically by giant machines that move rapidly and precisely over the skin of the planes. Even with these machines, the company said it struggles to find enough workers to make its new 787 aircraft. Rather, the machines offer significant increases in precision and are safer for workers.

And at Earthbound Farms in California, four newly installed robot arms with customized suction cups swiftly place clamshell containers of organic lettuce into shipping boxes. The robots move far faster than the people they replaced. Each robot replaces two to five workers at Earthbound, according to John Dulchinos, an engineer who is the chief executive at Adept Technology, a robot maker based in Pleasanton, Calif., that developed Earthbound's system.

Robot manufacturers in the United States say that in many applications, robots are already more cost-effective than humans.

At an automation trade show last year in Chicago, Ron Potter, the director of robotics technology at an Atlanta consulting firm called Factory Automation Systems, offered attendees a spreadsheet to calculate how quickly robots would pay for themselves.

In one example, a robotic manufacturing system initially cost $250,000 and replaced two machine operators, each earning $50,000 a year. Over the fifteen-year life of the system, the machines yielded $3.5 million in labor and productivity savings.

The Obama administration says this technological shift presents a historic opportunity for the nation to stay competitive. "The only way we are going to maintain manufacturing in the U.S. is if we have higher productivity," said Tom Kalil, deputy director of the White House Office of Science and Technology Policy.

Government officials and industry executives argue that even if factories are automated, they still are a valuable source of jobs. If the United States does not compete for advanced manufacturing in industries like consumer electronics, it could lose product engineering and design as well. Moreover, robotics executives argue that even though blue-collar jobs will be lost, more efficient manufacturing will create skilled jobs in designing, operating, and servicing the assembly lines, as well as significant numbers of other kinds of jobs in the communities where factories are.

And robot makers point out that their industry itself creates jobs. A report commissioned by the International Federation of Robotics last year found that 150,000 people are already employed by robotics manufacturers worldwide in engineering and assembly jobs.

But American and European dominance in the next generation of manufacturing is far from certain.

"What I see is that the Chinese are going to apply robots too," said Frans van Houten, Philips's chief executive. "The window of opportunity to bring manufacturing back is before that happens."

A Faster Assembly Line

Royal Philips Electronics began making the first electric shavers in 1939 and set up the factory here in Drachten in 1950. But Mr. Visser, the engineer who manages the assembly, takes pride in the sophistication of the latest shavers. They sell for as much as $350 and, he says, are more complex to make than smartphones.

The assembly line here is made up of dozens of glass cages housing robots made by Adept Technology that snake around the factory floor for more than one hundred yards. Video cameras atop the cages guide the robot arms almost unerringly to pick up the parts they assemble. The arms bend wires with millimetric accuracy, set toothpick-thin spindles in tiny holes, grab miniature plastic gears and set them in housings, and snap pieces of plastic into place.

The next generation of robots for manufacturing will be more flexible and easier to train.

Witness the factory of Tesla Motors, which recently began manufacturing the Tesla S, a luxury sedan, in Fremont, Calif., on the edge of Silicon Valley.

More than half of the building is shuttered, called "the dark side." It still houses a dingy, unused Toyota Corolla assembly line on which an army of workers once turned out half a million cars annually.

The Tesla assembly line is a stark contrast, brilliantly lighted. Its fast-moving robots, bright Tesla red, each has a single arm with multiple joints. Most of them are imposing, eight to ten feet tall, giving them a slightly menacing Terminator quality.

But the arms seem eerily human when they reach over to a stand and change their "hand" to perform a different task. While the many robots in auto factories typically perform only one function, in the new Tesla factory a robot might do up to four: welding, riveting, bonding, and installing a component.

As many as eight robots perform a ballet around each vehicle as it stops at each station along the line for just five minutes. Ultimately as many as eighty-three cars a day—roughly 20,000 are planned for the first year—will be produced at the factory. When the company adds a sport utility vehicle next year, it will be built on the same assembly line, once the robots are reprogrammed.

Tesla's factory is tiny but represents a significant bet on flexible robots, one that could be a model for the industry. And others are already thinking bigger.

Hyundai and Beijing Motors recently completed a mammoth factory outside Beijing that can produce a million vehicles a year using more robots and fewer people than the big factories of their competitors and with the same flexibility as Tesla's, said Paul Chau, an American venture capitalist at WI Harper who toured the plant in June.

The New Warehouse

Traditional and futuristic systems working side by side in a distribution center north of New York City show how robotics is transforming the way products are distributed, threatening jobs. From this warehouse in Newburgh, C & S, the nation's largest grocery wholesaler, supplies a major supermarket chain.

The old system sprawls across almost half a million square feet. The shelves are loaded and unloaded around the clock by hundreds of people driving pallet jacks and forklifts. At peak times in the evening, the warehouse is a cacophony of beeping and darting electric vehicles as workers with headsets are directed to cases of food by a computer that speaks to them in four languages.

The new system is much smaller, squeezed into only 30,000 square feet at the far end of the warehouse and controlled by just a handful of technicians. They watch over a four-story cage with different levels holding 168 "rover" robots the size of go-carts. Each can move at twenty-five miles an hour, nearly as fast as an Olympic sprinter.

Each rover is connected wirelessly to a central computer and on command will race along an aisle until it reaches its destination—a case of food to retrieve or the spot to drop one off for storage. The robot gathers a box by extending two-foot-long metal fingers from its side and sliding them underneath. It lifts the box and pulls it to its belly. Then it accelerates to the front of the steel cage, where it turns into a wide lane where it must contend with traffic—eight robots are active on each level of the structure, which is twenty aisles wide and twenty-one levels high.

From the aisle, the robots wait their turn to pull into a special open lane where they deposit each load into an elevator that sends a stream of food cases down to a conveyor belt that leads to a large robot arm.

About ten feet tall, the arm has the grace and dexterity of a skilled supermarket bagger, twisting and turning each case so the final stack forms an eight-foot cube. The software is sophisticated enough to determine which robot should pick up which case first, so when the order arrives at the supermarket, workers can take the cases out in the precise order in which they are to go on the shelves.

When the arm is finished, the cube of goods is conveyed to a machine that wraps it in clear plastic to hold it in place. Then a forklift operator summoned by the computer moves the cube to a truck for shipment.

Built by Symbotic, a start-up company based in the Boston area, this robotic warehouse is inspired by computer designers who created software algorithms to efficiently organize data to be stored on a computer's hard drive.

Jim Baum, Symbotic's chief executive, compares the new system to a huge parallel computer. The design is efficient because there is no single choke point; the cases of food moving through the robotic warehouse are like the digital bits being processed by the computer.

Humans' Changing Role

In the decade since he began working as a warehouseman in Tolleson, Ariz., a suburb of Phoenix, Josh Graves has seen how automation systems can make work easier but also create new stress and insecurity. The giant facility where he works distributes dry goods for Kroger supermarkets.

Mr. Graves, twenty-nine, went to work in the warehouse, where his father worked for three decades, right out of high school. The demanding job required lifting heavy boxes and the hours were long. "They would bring in fifteen guys, and only one would last," he said.

Today Mr. Graves drives a small forklift-like machine that stores and retrieves cases of all sizes. Because such workers are doing less physical labor, there are fewer injuries, said Rome Aloise, a Teamsters vice president in Northern California. Because a computer sets the pace, the stress is now more psychological.

Mr. Graves wears headsets and is instructed by a computerized voice on where to go in the warehouse to gather or store products. A centralized computer the workers call The Brain dictates their speed. Managers know exactly what the workers do, to the precise minute.

Several years ago, Mr. Graves's warehouse installed a German system that automatically stores and retrieves cases of food. That led to the elimination of 106 jobs, roughly 20 percent of the work force. The new system was initially maintained by union workers with high seniority. Then that job went to the German company, which hired nonunion workers.

Now Kroger plans to build a highly automated warehouse in Tolleson. Sixty union workers went before the City Council last year to oppose the plan, on which the city has not yet ruled.

"We don't have a problem with the machines coming," Mr. Graves told city officials. "But tell Kroger we don't want to lose these jobs in our city."

Some jobs are still beyond the reach of automation: construction jobs that require workers to move in unpredictable settings and perform different tasks that are not repetitive; assembly work that requires tactile feedback like placing fiberglass panels inside airplanes, boats, or cars; and assembly jobs where only a limited quantity of products are made or where there are many versions of each product, requiring expensive reprogramming of robots.

But that list is growing shorter.

Upgrading Distribution

Inside a spartan garage in an industrial neighborhood in Palo Alto, Calif., a robot armed with electronic "eyes" and a small scoop and suction cups repeatedly picks up boxes and drops them onto a conveyor belt.

It is doing what low-wage workers do every day around the world.

Older robots cannot do such work because computer vision systems were costly and limited to carefully controlled environments where the lighting was just right. But thanks to an inexpensive stereo camera and software that lets the system see shapes with the same ease as humans, this robot can quickly discern the irregular dimensions of randomly placed objects.

The robot uses a technology pioneered in Microsoft's Kinect motion sensing system for its Xbox video game system.

Such robots will put automation within range of companies like Federal Express and United Parcel Service that now employ tens of thousands of workers doing such tasks.

The start-up behind the robot, Industrial Perception Inc., is the first spinoff of Willow Garage, an ambitious robotics research firm based in Menlo Park, Calif. The first customer is likely to be a company that now employs thousands of workers to load and unload its trucks. The workers can move one box every six seconds on average. But each box can weigh more than 130 pounds, so the workers tire easily and sometimes hurt their backs.

Industrial Perception will win its contract if its machine can reliably move one box every four seconds. The engineers are confident that the robot will soon do much better than that, picking up and setting down one box per second.

"We're on the cusp of completely changing manufacturing and distribution," said Gary Bradski, a machine-vision scientist who is a founder of Industrial Perception. "I think it's not as singular an event, but it will ultimately have as big an impact as the Internet."

Mother Jones

When *Mother Jones*'s Mac McClelland took a temporary warehouse job, she ran into a woman, who offered advice: "You'll see people dropping all around you. But don't take it personally and break down or start crying when they yell at you." The warehouse, designed to get online purchases to customers as quickly as possible, is a worker's hell—made possible by people's desperation for jobs. Temporary workers face firing for infringements including even a moment's tardiness during the first week and are constantly pressured to work faster. "Pickers" in McClelland's warehouse speed-walk an average of twelve miles a day on cold concrete; their breaks are shortened by having to pass through metal detectors to make sure they aren't stealing; and McClelland and other workers quickly accumulate severe aches, pains, and shocks. McClelland doesn't name the Internet-based retail company to reinforce the notion that these conditions are not limited to one company or site but are endemic to the Web-based free-shipping economy.

Mac McClelland

27. I Was a Warehouse Wage Slave

"Don't take anything that happens to you there personally," the woman at the local chamber of commerce says when I tell her that tomorrow I start working at Amalgamated Product Giant Shipping Worldwide Inc. She winks at me. I stare at her for a second.

"*What?*" I ask. "Why, is somebody going to be mean to me or something?"

She smiles. "Oh, yeah." This town somewhere west of the Mississippi is not big; everyone knows someone or *is* someone who's worked for Amalgamated. "But look at it from their perspective. They need you to work as fast as possible to push out as much as they can as fast as they can. So they're gonna give you goals, and then you know what? If you make those goals, they're gonna increase the goals. But they'll be yelling at you all the time. It's like the military. They have to break you down so they can turn you into what they want you to be. So they're going to tell you, 'You're not good enough, you're not good enough, you're not good enough,' to make you work harder. Don't say, 'This is the best I can do.' Say, 'I'll try,' even if you know you can't do it. Because if you say, 'This is the best I can do,' they'll let you go. They hire and fire constantly, every day. You'll see people dropping all around you. But don't take it personally and break down or start crying when they yell at you."

Several months prior, I'd reported on an Ohio warehouse where workers shipped products for online retailers under conditions that were surprisingly demoralizing and dehumanizing, even to someone who's spent a lot of time working in warehouses, which I have. And then my editors sat me down. "We want you to go work for Amalgamated Product Giant Shipping Worldwide Inc.," they said. I'd have to give my real name and job history when I applied, and I couldn't lie if asked for any specifics. (I wasn't.) But I'd smudge identifying details of people and the company itself. Anyway, to do otherwise might give people the impression that these conditions apply only to one warehouse or one company. Which they don't.

So I fretted about whether I'd have to abort the application process, like if someone asked me why I wanted the job. But no one did. And though I was kind of excited to trot out my warehouse experience, mainly all I needed to get hired was to confirm twenty or thirty times that I had not been to prison.

The application process took place at a staffing office in a rundown city, the kind where there are boarded-up businesses and broken windows downtown and billboards advertising things like "Foreclosure Fridays!" at a local law firm. Six or seven other people apply for jobs along with me. We answer questions at computers grouped in several stations. Have I ever been to prison? the system asks. No? Well, but have I ever been to prison for assault? Burglary? A felony? A misdemeanor? Raping someone? Murdering anybody? Am I sure? There's no point in lying, the computer warns me, because criminal-background checks are run on employees. Additionally, I have to confirm at the next computer station that I can read, by taking a multiple-choice test in which I'm given pictures of several album covers, including Michael Jackson's *Thriller*, and asked what the name of the Michael Jackson album is. At yet another set of computers I'm asked about my work history and character. How do I feel about dangerous activities? Would I say I'm not really into them? Or *really* into them?

In the center of the room, a video plays loudly and continuously on a big screen. Even more than you are hurting the company, a voice-over intones as animated people do things like accidentally oversleep, you are hurting yourself when you are late because you will be penalized on a point system, and when you get too many points, you're fired—unless you're late at any point during your first week, in which case you are instantly fired. Also because when you're late or sick you miss the opportunity to maximize your overtime pay. And working more than eight hours is mandatory. Stretching is also mandatory, since you will either be standing still at a conveyor line for most of your minimum-ten-hour shift or walking on concrete or metal stairs. And be careful, because you could seriously hurt yourself. And watch out, because some of your coworkers will be the kind of monsters who will file false workers' comp claims. If you know of someone doing this and you tell on him and he gets convicted, you will be rewarded with $500.

The computers screening us for suitability to pack boxes or paste labels belong to a temporary-staffing agency. The stuff we order from big online retailers lives in large warehouses, owned and operated either by the retailers themselves or by third-party logistics contractors, a.k.a. 3PLs. These companies often fulfill orders for more than one retailer out of a single warehouse. America's largest 3PL, Exel, has 86 million square feet of warehouse in North America; it's a subsidiary of Deutsche Post DHL, which is cute because Deutsche Post is the German post office, which was privatized in the 1990s and bought DHL in 2002, becoming one of the world's biggest corporate employers. The $31 billion "value-added warehousing and distribution" sector of 3PLs is just a fraction of what large 3PLs' parent companies pull in. UPS's logistics division, for example, pulls in more than a half a billion, but it feeds billions of dollars of business to UPS Inc.

Anyhow, regardless of whether the retailer itself or a 3PL contractor houses and processes the stuff you buy, the actual stuff is often handled by people working for yet another company—a temporary-staffing agency. The agency to which I apply is hiring 4,000 drones for this single Amalgamated warehouse between October and December. Four thousand. Before leaving the staffing office, I'm one of them.

I'm assigned a schedule of Sunday through Thursday, seven a.m. to five-thirty p.m. When additional overtime is necessary, which it will be soon (Christmas!), I should expect to leave at seven or seven-thirty p.m. instead. Eight days after applying, i.e., after my drug test has cleared, I walk through a small, desolate town nearly an hour outside the city where I was hired. This is where the warehouse is, way out here, a long commute for many of my coworkers. I wander off the main road and into the chamber of commerce to kill some afternoon time—though not too much since my first day starts at five a.m.—but I end up getting useful job advice.

"Well, what if I do start crying?" I ask the woman who warns me to keep it together no matter how awfully I'm treated. "Are they really going to fire me for that?"

"Yes," she says. "There's sixteen other people who want your job. Why would they keep a person who gets emotional, especially in this economy?"

Still, she advises, regardless of how much they push me, don't work so hard that I injure myself. I'm young. I have a long life ahead of me. It's not worth it to do permanent physical damage, she says, which, considering that I got hired at eleven-something dollars an hour, is a bit of an understatement.

As the sun gets lower in the curt November sky, I thank the woman for her help. When I start toward the door, she repeats her "number-one rule of survival" one more time.

"Leave your pride and your personal life at the door." If there's any way I'm going to last, she says, tomorrow I have to start pretending like I don't have either.

• • •

Though it's inconvenient for most employees, the rural location of the Amalgamated Product Giant Shipping Worldwide Inc. warehouse isn't an accident. The town is bisected by a primary interstate, close to a busy airport, serviced by several major highways. There's a lot of rail out here. The town became a station stop on the way to more important places a hundred years ago, and it now feeds part of the massive transit networks used to get consumers anywhere goods from everywhere. Every now and then, a long line of railcars rolls past my hotel and gives my room a good shake. I don't ever get a good look at them because it's dark outside when I go to work and dark again when I get back.

Inside Amalgamated, an employee's first day is training day. Though we're not paid to be here until six, we have been informed that we need to arrive at five. If we don't show up in time to stand around while they sort out who we are and where they've put our ID badges, we could miss the beginning of training, which would mean termination. "I was up half the night because I was so afraid I was going to be late," a woman in her sixties tells me. I was, too. A minute's tardiness after the first week earns us 0.5 penalty points, an hour's tardiness is worth 1 point, and an absence 1.5; 6 is the number that equals "release." But during the first week even a minute's tardiness gets us fired. When we get lined up so we can be counted a third or fourth time, the woman conducting the roll call recognizes the last name of a young trainee. "Does your dad work here? Or uncle?" she asks. "Grandpa," he says, as another supervisor snaps at the same time, sounding not mean but very stressed out, "We gotta get goin' here."

The culture is intense, an Amalgamated higher-up acknowledges at the beginning of our training. He's speaking to us from a video, one of several videos—about company policies, sexual harassment, etc.—that we watch while we try to keep our eyes open. We don't *want* to be so intense, the higher-up says. But our customers demand it. We are surrounded by signs that state our productivity goals. Other signs proclaim that a good customer experience, to which our goal-meeting is essential, is the key to growth, and growth is the key to lower prices, which leads to a better customer experience. There is no room for inefficiencies. The gal conducting our training reminds us again that we cannot miss any days our first week. There are *NO* exceptions to this policy. She says to take Brian, for example, who's here with us in training today. Brian already went through this training, but then during his first week his lady had a baby, so he missed a day and he had to be fired. Having to start the application process over could cost a brand-new dad like Brian a couple of weeks' worth of work and pay. Okay? Everybody turn around and look at Brian. Welcome back, Brian. Don't end up like Brian.

Soon, we move on to practical training. Like all workplaces with automated and heavy machinery, this one contains plenty of ways to get hurt, and they are enumerated. There are transition points in the warehouse floor where the footing is uneven, and people trip and sprain ankles. Give forklifts that are raised up several stories to access products a wide berth: "If a pallet falls on you, you won't be working with us anymore." Watch your fingers around the conveyor belts that run waist-high throughout the entire facility. People lose fingers. Or parts of fingers. And about once a year, they tell us, someone in an Amalgamated warehouse gets caught by the hair, and when a conveyor belt catches you by the hair, it doesn't just take your hair with it. It rips out a piece of scalp as well.

If the primary message of one-half of our practical training is Be Careful, the takeaway of the other half is Move As Fast As

Humanly Possible. Or superhumanly possible. I have been hired as a picker, which means my job is to find, scan, place in a plastic tote, and send away via conveyor whatever item within the multiple stories of this several-hundred-thousand-square-foot warehouse my scanner tells me to. We are broken into groups and taught how to read the scanner to find the object among some practice shelves. Then we immediately move on to practicing doing it faster, racing each other to fill the orders our scanners dictate, then racing each other to put all the items back.

"Hurry up," a trainer encourages me when he sees me pulling ahead of the others, "and you can put the other items back!" I roll my eyes that my reward for doing a good job is that I get to do more work, but he's got my number: I am exactly the kind of freak this sort of motivation appeals to. I win, and set myself on my prize of the bonus errand.

That afternoon, we are turned loose in the warehouse, scanners in hand. And that's when I realize that for whatever relative youth and regular exercise and overachievement complexes I have brought to this job, I will never be able to keep up with the goals I've been given.

The place is immense. Cold, cavernous. Silent, despite thousands of people quietly doing their picking, or standing along the conveyors quietly packing or box-taping, nothing noisy but the occasional whir of a passing forklift. My scanner tells me in what exact section—there are nine merchandise sections, so sprawling that there's a map attached to my ID badge—of vast shelving systems the item I'm supposed to find resides. It also tells me how many seconds it thinks I should take to get there. Dallas sector, section yellow, row H34, bin 22, level D: wearable blanket. Battery-operated flour sifter. Twenty seconds. I count how many steps it takes me to speed-walk to my destination: twenty. At five-foot-nine, I've got a decently long stride, and I only cover the twenty steps *and* locate the exact shelving unit in the allotted time if I don't hesitate for one second or get lost or take a drink of water before heading in the right direction as fast as I can walk or even occasionally jog. Olive-oil mister. Male libido enhancement pills. Rifle strap. Who the fuck buys their paper towels off the internet? Fairy calendar. Neoprene lunch bag. Often as not, I miss my time target.

Plenty of things can hurt my goals. The programs for our scanners are designed with the assumption that we disposable employees don't know what we're doing. Find a Rob Zombie Voodoo Doll in the blue section of the Rockies sector in the third bin of the A-level in row Z42, my scanner tells me. But if I punch into my scanner that it's not there, I have to prove it by scanning every single other item in the bin, though I swear on my life there's no Rob Zombie Voodoo Doll in this pile of thirty individually wrapped and bar-coded batteries that take me quite a while to beep one by one. It could be five minutes before I can move on to, and make it to, and find, my next item. That lapse is supposed to be mere seconds.

This week, we newbies need to make 75 percent of our total picking-volume targets. If we don't, we get "counseled." If the people in here who've been around longer than a few weeks don't make their *100* percent, they get counseled. *Why* aren't you making your targets? the supervisors will ask. You *really* need to make your targets.

From the temp agency, Amalgamated has ordered the exact number of humans it should take to fill this week's orders if we work at top capacity. Lots of retailers use temporary help in peak season, and online ones are no exception. But lots of warehousing and distribution centers like this also use temps year-round. The Bureau of Labor Statistics found that more than 15 percent of pickers, packers, movers, and unloaders are temps. They make three dollars less an hour on average than permanent workers. And they can be "temporary" for years. There are so many temps in this warehouse that the staffing agency has its own office here.

Industry consultants describe the temp-staffing business as "very, very busy." "On fire." Maximizing profits means making sure no employee has a slow day, means having only as many employees as are necessary to get the job done, the number of which can be determined and ordered from a huge pool of on-demand labor literally by the day. Often, temp workers have to call in before shifts to see if they'll get work. Sometimes, they're paid piece rate, according to the number of units they fill or unload or move. Always, they can be let go in an instant and replaced just as quickly.

Everyone in here is hustling. At the announcement to take one of our two fifteen-minute breaks, we hustle even harder. We pickers close out the totes we're currently filling and send them away on the conveyor belt, then make our way as fast as we can with the rest of the masses across the long haul of concrete between wherever we are and the break room, but not before passing through metal detectors, for which there is a line—we're required to be screened on our way out, though not on our way in; apparently the concern is that we're sneaking Xbox 360s up under our shirts, not bringing in weapons. If we *don't* set off the metal detector and have to be taken aside and searched, we can run into the break room and try to find a seat among the rows and rows and long-ass rows of tables. We lose more time if we want to pee—and I do want to pee, and when amid the panic about the time constraints it occurs to me that I don't have my period I toss a fist victoriously into the air—between the actual peeing and the waiting in line to pee in the nearest one of the two bathrooms, which has eight stalls in the ladies' and I'm not sure how many in the men's and serves thousands of people a day. Once I pare this process down as much as possible, by stringing a necktie through my belt loops because I can't find a metal-less replacement for my belt at the local Walmart—and if my underwear or butt-crack slips out, I've been warned, I can get penalized—and by leaving my car keys in the break room after a manager helps me find an admittedly "still risky" hiding place for them because we have no lockers and "things get stolen out of here all the time," I get myself up to seven minutes' worth of break time to inhale as many high-fat and -protein snacks as I can. People who work at Amalgamated are always working this fast. Right now, because it's almost Black Friday, there are just more of us doing it.

Then as quickly as we've come, we all run back. At the end of the fifteen minutes, we're supposed to be back at whichever far-flung corner of the warehouse we came from, scanners in hand, working. We run to grab the wheeled carts we put the totes on. We run past each other and if we do say something, we say it as we keep moving. "How's the job market?" a supervisor says, laughing, as several of us newbies run by. "Just kidding!" Ha ha! "I know why you guys are here. That's why I'm here, too!" At another near collision between employees, one wants to know how complaining about not being able to get time off went and the other spits that he was told he was lucky to *have* a job. This is no way to have a conversation, but at least conversations are not forbidden, as they were in the Ohio warehouse I reported on—where I saw a guy get fired for talking, specifically for asking another employee, "Where are you from?" So I'm allowed the extravagance of smiling at a guy who is always so unhappy and saying, "How's it goin'?" And he can respond, "Terrible," as I'm running to the big industrial cage-lift that takes our carts up to the second or third floors, which involves walking under a big metal bar gating the front of it, and which I should really take my time around. Within the last month, three different people have needed stitches in the head after being clocked by these big metal bars, so it's dangerous. Especially the lift in the Dallas sector, whose bar has been installed wrong, so it is extra prone to falling, they tell us. Be careful. Seriously, though. We really need to meet our goals here.

Amalgamated has estimated that we pickers speed-walk an average of twelve miles a day on cold concrete, and the twinge in my legs blurs into the heavy soreness in my feet that complements the pinch in my hips when I crouch to the floor—the pickers' shelving runs from the floor to seven feet high or so—to retrieve an iPad protective case. iPad anti-glare protector. iPad one-hand grip-holder device. Thing that looks like a landline phone handset that plugs into your iPad so you can pretend that rather than talking via iPad you are talking on a phone. And dildos. Really, a staggering number of dildos. At breaks, some of my coworkers complain that they have to handle so many dildos. But it's one of the few joys of my day. I've started cringing every time my scanner shows a code that means the item I need to pick is on the ground, which, in the course of a 10.5-hour shift—much less the mandatory 12-hour shifts everyone is slated to start working next week—is literally hundreds of times a day. "How has OSHA signed off on this?" I've taken to muttering to myself. "*Has* OSHA signed off on this?" ("The thing about ergonomics," OSHA says when I call them later to ask, "is that OSHA doesn't have a standard. Best practices. But no laws.") So it's a welcome distraction, really, to imagine all these sex toys being taken out from under a tree and unwrapped. Merry Christmas. I got you this giant black cock you wanted.

At lunch, the most common question, aside from "Which offensive dick-shaped product did you handle the most of today?" is "Why are you here?" like in prison. A guy in his mid-twenties says he's from Chicago, came to this state for a full-time job in the city an hour away from here because "Chicago's going down." His other job doesn't pay especially well, so he's here—pulling 10.5-hour shifts and commuting two hours a day—anytime he's not there. One guy says he's a writer; he applies for grants in his time off from the warehouse. A middle-aged lady near me used to be a bookkeeper. She's a peak-season hire, worked here last year during Christmas, too. "What do you do the rest of the year?" I ask. "Collect unemployment!" she says, and laughs the sad laugh you laugh when you're saying something really unfunny. All around us in the break room, mothers frantically call home. "Hi, baby!" you can hear them say; coos to children echo around the walls the moment lunch begins. It's brave of these women to keep their phones in the break room, where theft is so high—they can't keep them in their cars if they want to use them during the day because we aren't supposed to leave the premises without permission, and they can't take them onto the warehouse floor because "nothing but the clothes on your backs" is allowed on the warehouse floor (*anything* on your person that Amalgamated sells can be confiscated—"And what does Amalgamated sell?" they asked us in training. "Everything!"). I suppose that if I were responsible for a child, I would have no choice but to risk leaving my phone in here, too. But the mothers make it quick. "How are you doing?" "Is everything okay?" "Did you eat something?" "I love you!" and then they're off the phone and eating as fast as the rest of us. Lunch is twenty-nine minutes and fifty-nine seconds—we've been reminded of this: "Lunch is *not* thirty minutes and one second"—that's a penalty-point-earning offense—and that includes the time to get through the metal detectors and use the disgustingly overcrowded bathroom—the suggestion board hosts several pleas that someone do something about that smell—and time to stand in line to clock out and back in. So we chew quickly, and are often still chewing as we run back to our stations.

The days blend into each other. But it's near the end of my third day that I get written up. I sent two of some product down the conveyor line when my scanner was only asking for one; the product was boxed in twos, so I should've opened the box and separated them, but I didn't notice because I was in a hurry. With an hour left in the day, I've already picked 800 items. Despite moving fast enough to get sloppy, my scanner tells me that means I'm fulfilling only 52 percent of my goal. A supervisor who is a genuinely nice person comes by with a clipboard listing my numbers. Like the rest of the supervisors, she tries to create a friendly work environment and doesn't want to enforce the policies that make this job so unpleasant. But her hands are tied. She needs this job, too, so she has no choice but to tell me something I have never been told in nineteen years of school or at any of some dozen workplaces. "You're doing really bad," she says.

I'll admit that I did start crying a little. Not at work, thankfully, since that's evidently frowned upon, but later, when I explained to someone over Skype that it hurts, oh, how my body hurts after failing to make my goals despite speed-walking or flat-out jogging and pausing every twenty or thirty seconds to reach on my tiptoes or bend or drop to the floor for 10.5 hours, and isn't it awful that they fired Brian because he had a baby, and, in fact, when I was hired I signed off on something acknowledging that anyone who leaves without at least a week's notice—whether because they're a journalist who will just walk off or because they miss a day for having a baby and are terminated—has their hours paid out not at their hired rate but at the legal minimum. Which in this state, like in lots of states, is about seven dollars an hour. Thank God that I (unlike Brian, probably) didn't need to pay for opting into Amalgamated's "limited" health insurance program. Because in my 10.5-hour day I'll make about sixty dollars after taxes.

"This is America?" my Skype pal asks, because often I'm abroad.

Indeed, and I'm working for a gigantic, immensely profitable company. Or for the staffing company that works for that company, anyway. Which is a nice arrangement, because temporary-staffing agencies keep the stink of unacceptable labor conditions off the companies whose names you know. When temps working at a Walmart warehouse sued for not getting paid for all their hours and for then getting sent home without pay for complaining, Walmart—not technically their employer—wasn't named as a defendant. (Though Amazon has been named in a similar suit.) Temporary staffers aren't legally entitled to decent health care because they are just short-term "contractors" no matter how long they keep the same job. They aren't entitled to raises, either, and they don't get vacation and they'd have a hell of a time unionizing and they don't have the privilege of knowing if they'll have work on a particular day or for how long they'll have a job. And that is how you slash prices and deliver products superfast and offer free shipping and still post profits in the millions or billions.

"This really doesn't have to be this awful," I shake my head over Skype. But it is. And this job is just about the only game in town, like it is in lots of towns, and eventually will be in more towns, with U.S. Internet retail sales projected to grow 10 percent every year to $279 billion in 2015 and with Amazon, the largest of the online retailers, seeing revenues rise 30 to 40 percent year after year and already having sixty-nine giant warehouses, seventeen of which came online in 2011 alone. So butch up, Sally.

• • •

"You look way too happy," an Amalgamated supervisor says to me. He has appeared next to me as I work, and in the silence of the vast warehouse, his presence catches me by surprise. His comment, even more so.

"Really?" I ask.

I don't really *feel* happy. By the fourth morning that I drag myself out of bed long before dawn, my self-pity has turned into actual concern. There's a screaming pain running across the back of my shoulders. "You need to take 800 milligrams of Advil a day," a woman in her late fifties or early sixties advised me when we all congregated in the break room before work. When I arrived, I stashed my lunch on a bottom ledge of the cheap metal shelving lining the break room walls, then hesitated before walking away. I cursed myself. I forgot something in the bag, but there was no way to get at it without crouching or bending over, and any extra times of doing that today were times I couldn't really afford. The unhappy-looking guy I always make a point of smiling at told me, as we were hustling to our stations, that this is actually the second time he's worked here: A few weeks back he missed some time for doctors' appointments when his arthritis flared up, and though he had notes for the absences, he was fired. He had to start the application process over again, which cost him an extra week and a half of work. "Zoom zoom! Pick it up! Pickers' pace, guys!" we were prodded this morning. Since we already felt like we were moving pretty fast, I'm quite dispirited, in fact.

"*Really?*" I ask.

"Well," the supervisor qualifies. "Just everybody else is usually really sad or mad by the time they've been working here this long."

It's my twenty-eighth hour as an employee.

I probably look happier than I should because I have the extreme luxury of not giving a shit about keeping this job. Nevertheless, I'm tearing around my assigned sector hard enough to keep myself consistently light-headed and a little out of breath. I'm working in books today. "Oh," I smiled to myself when I reached the paper-packed shelves. I love being around books.

Picking books for Amalgamated has a disadvantage over picking dildos or baby food or Barbies, however, in that the shelving numbers don't always line up. When my scanner tells me the book I need is on the lowest level in section 28 of a row, section 28 of the eye-level shelf of that row may or may not line up with section 28 of the lowest level. So when I spot eye-level section 28 and squat or kneel on the floor, the section 28 I'm looking for might be five feet to my right or left. Which means I have to stand up and crouch back down again to get there, greatly increasing the number of times I need to stand and crouch/kneel in a day. Or I can crawl. Usually, I crawl. A coworker is choosing the crouch/kneel option. "This gets so tiring after a while," he says when we pass each other. He's twenty. It's 9:07 a.m.

There are other disadvantages to working in books. In the summer, it's the heat. Lots of the volumes are stored on the second and third floors of this immense cement box; the job descriptions we had to sign off on acknowledged that temperatures can be as low as sixty and higher than ninety-five degrees, and higher floors tend to be hotter. "They had to get fans because in the summer people were dying in here," one of the supervisors tells us. The fans still blow now even though I'm wearing five shirts. "If you think it's cold in *here*," one of my coworkers told me when she saw me rubbing my arms for warmth one morning, "just hope we don't have a fire drill." They evacuated everyone for one recently, and lots of the fast-moving employees had stripped down to T-shirts. They stood outside, masses of them, shivering for an hour as snow fell on their bare arms.

In the books sector, in the cold, in the winter dryness, made worse by the fans and all the paper, I jet across the floor in my rubber-soled Adidas, pant legs whooshing against each other, thirty seconds according to my scanner to take thirty-five steps to get to the right section and row and bin and level and reach for *Diary of a Wimpy Kid* and "FUCK!" A hot spark shoots between my hand and the metal shelving. It's not the light static-electric prick I would terrorize my sister with when we got bored in carpeted department stores, but a solid shock, striking enough to make my body learn to fear it. I start inadvertently hesitating every time I approach my target. One of my coworkers races up to a shelving unit and leans in with the top of his body first; his head touches the metal, and the shock knocks him back. "Be careful of your head," he says to me. In the first two hours of my day, I pick 300 items. The majority of them zap me painfully.

"Please tell me you have suggestions for dealing with the static electricity," I say to a person in charge when the morning break comes. This conversation is going to cost me a couple of my precious few minutes to eat/drink/pee, but I've started to get paranoid that maybe it's not good for my body to exchange an electric charge with metal several hundred times in one day.

"Oh, are you workin' in books?"

"Yeah."

"No. Sorry." She means this. I feel bad for the supervisors who are trying their damnedest to help us succeed and not be miserable. "They've done everything they can"—"they" are not aware, it would appear, that antistatic coating and matting exist—"to ground things up there but there's nothing you can do."

I produce a deep frown. But even if she did have suggestions, I probably wouldn't have time to implement them. One suggestion for minimizing work-related pain and strain is to get a stepladder to retrieve any items on shelves above your head rather than getting up on your toes and overreaching. But grabbing one of the stepladders stashed few and far between among the rows of merchandise takes time. Another is to alternate the hand you use to hold and wield your cumbersome scanner. "You'll feel carpal tunnel start to set in," one of the supervisors told me, "so you'll want to change hands." But that, too, he admitted, costs time, since you have to hit the bar code at just the right angle for it to scan, and your dominant hand is way more likely to nail it the first time. Time is not a thing I have to spare. I'm still only at 57 percent of my goal. It's been ten years since I was a mover and packer for a moving company, and only slightly less since I worked ridiculously long hours as a waitress and housecleaner. My back and knees were younger then, but I'm only thirty-one and feel pretty confident that if I were doing those jobs again I'd still wake up with soreness like a person who'd worked out too much, not the soreness of a person whose body was staging a revolt. I can break into goal-meeting suicide pace for short bouts, sure, but I can't keep it up for 10.5 hours.

"Do not say that," one of the workampers tells me at break. Workampers are people who drive RVs around the country, from temporary job to temporary job, docking in trailer camps. "We're retired but we can't . . ." another explains to me about himself and his wife, shrugging, "*make* it. And there's no jobs, so we go where the jobs are."

Amalgamated advertises positions on websites workampers frequent. In this warehouse alone, there are hundreds of them.

"Never say that you can't do it," the first workamper emphasizes. "When they ask you why you aren't reaching your goals—"

"Say, 'It's because they're totally unreasonable'?" I suggest.

"Say you'll do better, even if you know you can't," she continues, ignoring me. "Say you'll try harder, even if the truth is that you're trying your absolute hardest right now, no matter how many times they tell you you're not doing good enough."

There *are* people who make the goals. One of the trainers does. She works here all year, not just during Christmas. "I hated picking for the first month," she told me sympathetically the other day. "Then you just get used to it." She's one of many hardcore workers here, a labor pool studded with dedicated and solid employees. One of the permanent employees has tried to encourage me by explaining that he *always* makes his goals, and sometimes makes 120 percent of them. When I ask him if that isn't totally exhausting, he says, "Oh yeah. You're gonna be crying for your mommy when today's over." When I ask him if there's any sort of incentive for his overperformance, if he's rewarded in any way, he says occasionally Amalgamated enters him in drawings for company gift cards. For fifteen or twenty dollars. He shrugs when he admits the size of the bonus. "These days you need it." Anyway, he says, he thinks it's important to have a good attitude and try to do a good job. Even some of the employees who are total failures are still trying really hard. "I heard you're doing good," one of the ladies in my training group says to me. Her eyebrows are heavy with stress. I am still hitting less than 60 percent of my target. Still, that's better than she's doing. "Congratulations," she says and smiles sadly.

We will be fired if we say we just can't or won't get better, the workamper tells me. But so long as I resign myself to hearing how inadequate I am on a regular basis, I can keep this job. "Do you think this job has to be this terrible?" I ask the workamper.

"Oh, no," she says, and makes a face at me like I've asked a stupid question, which I have. As if Amalgamated couldn't bear to lose a fraction of a percent of profits by employing a few more than the absolute minimum of bodies they have to, or by storing the merchandise at halfway ergonomic heights and angles. But that would cost space, and space costs money, and money is not a thing customers could possibly be expected to hand over for this service without huffily taking their business elsewhere. Charging for shipping does cause high abandonment rates of online orders, though it's not clear whether people wouldn't pay a few bucks for shipping, or a bit more for the products, if they were guaranteed that no low-income workers would be tortured or exploited in the handling of their purchases.

"The first step is awareness," an e-commerce specialist will tell me later. There have been trickles of information leaking out of the Internet Order Fulfillment Industrial Complex: an investigation by the Allentown, Pennsylvania, *Morning Call* in which Amazon workers complained of fainting in stifling heat, being disciplined for getting heat exhaustion, and otherwise being "treated like a piece of crap"; a workampers' blog picked up by *Gizmodo*; a *Huffington Post* exposé about the lasting physical damage and wild economic instability temporary warehouse staffers suffer. And workers have filed lawsuits against online retailers, their logistics companies, and their temp agencies over off-the-clock work and other compensation issues, as well as at least one that details working conditions that are all too similar. (That case has been dismissed but is on appeal.) Still, most people really don't know how most Internet goods get to them. The e-commerce specialist didn't even know, and she was in charge of choosing the 3PL for her midsize online-retail company. "These decisions are made at a business level and are based on cost," she says. "I never, ever thought about what they're like and how they treat people. Fulfillment centers want to keep clients blissfully ignorant of their conditions." If you called major clothing retailers, she ventured, and asked them "what it was like at the warehouse that ships their sweaters, no one at company headquarters would have any fucking clue."

Further, she said, now that I mentioned it, she has no idea how to go about getting any information on the conditions at the 3PL she herself hired. Nor how to find a responsible one. "A standard has to be created. Like fair trade or organic certification, where social good is built into the cost. There is a segment of the population"—like the consumers of her company's higher-end product, she felt—"that cares and will pay for it."

If they are aware how inhumane the reality is. But awareness has a long way to go, and logistics doesn't just mean online retail; food packagers and processors, medical suppliers, and factories use mega-3PLs as well. And a whole lot of other industries—hotels, call centers—take advantage of the price controls and plausible deniability that temporary staffing offers.

"Maybe awareness will lead to better working conditions," says Vinod Singhal, a professor of operations management at Georgia Tech. "But . . ." Given the state of the economy, he isn't optimistic.

This is the kind of resignation many of my coworkers have been forced to accept. At the end of break, the workamper and I are starting to fast-walk back to our stations. A guy who's been listening to our conversation butts in. "They can take you for everything you've got," he says. "They know it's your last resort."

At today's pickers' meeting, we are reminded that customers are waiting. We *cannot* move at a "comfortable pace," because if we are comfortable, we will never make our numbers, and customers are not willing to wait. And it's Christmastime. We got 2.7 million orders this week. People need—*need*—these items and they need them right now. So even if you've worked here long enough to be granted time off, you are not allowed to use it until the holidays are over. (And also forget about Election Day, which is today. "What if I want to vote?" I ask a supervisor. "I think you should!" he says. "But if I leave I'll get fired," I say. To which he makes a sad face before saying, "Yeah.") No time off includes those of you who are scheduled to work Thanksgiving. There are two Amalgamated-catered Thanksgiving dinners offered to employees next week, but you can only go to one of them. If you attend one, your employee badge will be branded with a nonremovable sticker so that you cannot also attempt to eat at the other. Anyway, good luck, everybody. Everybody back to work. Quickly!

Speed-walking back to the electro-trauma of the books sector, I wince when I unintentionally imagine the types of Christmas lore that will prevail around my future household. I feel genuinely sorry for any child I might have who ever asks me for anything for Christmas, only to be informed that every time a "Place Order" button rings, a poor person takes four Advil and gets told they suck at their job.

I suppose this is what they were talking about in the radio ad I heard on the way to work, the one that was paid for by a coalition of local businesses, gently begging citizens to buy from them instead of off the Internet and warning about the importance of supporting local shops. But if my coworker Brian wants to feed his new baby any of these twenty-four-packs of Plum

Organics Apple & Carrot baby food I've been picking, he should probably buy them from Amazon, where they cost only $31.16. In my locally owned grocery store, that's $47.76 worth of sustenance. Even if he finds the time to get in the car to go buy it at a brick-and-mortar Target, where it'd be less convenient but cost about the same as on Amazon, that'd be before sales tax, which physical stores, unlike Amazon, are legally required to charge to help pay for the roads on which Brian's truck and, more to the point, Amazon's trucks drive.

Back in books, I take a sharp shock to my right hand when I grab the book the scanner cramping my left hand demands me to and make some self-righteous promises to myself about continuing to buy food at my more-expensive grocery store because I can. Because I'm not actually a person who makes $7.25 an hour, not anymore, not one of the one in three Americans who is now poor or "near poor." For the moment, I'm just playing one.

"Lucky girl," I whisper to myself at the tail of a deep breath, as soon as fresh winter air hits my lungs. It's only lunchtime, but I've breached the warehouse doors without permission. I've picked 500 items this morning and don't want to get shocked anymore or hear from the guy with the clipboard what a total disappointment I am. "Lucky girl, lucky girl, lucky girl," I repeat on my way to my car. I told the lady from my training group who's so stressed about her poor performance to tell our supervisor not to look for me—and she grabbed my arm as I turned to leave, looking even more worried than usual, asking if I was sure I knew what I was doing. I don't want our supervisor to waste any time; he's got goals to make, too. He won't miss me, and nobody else will, either. The temp agency is certainly as full of applicants as it was when I went to ask for a job.

"Just look around in here if you wanna see how bad it is out there," one of the associates at the temp office said to me, unprompted, when I got hired. It's the first time anyone has ever tried to comfort me *because* I got a job, because he knew, and everyone in this industry that's growing wildfire fast knows, and accepts, that its model by design is mean. He offered me the same kind of solidarity the workers inside the warehouse try to provide each other at every break: *Why are you here? What happened that you have to let people treat you like this?* "We're all in the same boat," he said, after shaking my hand to welcome me aboard. "It's a *really* big boat."

New York Times

More than one hundred workers at an Apple supplier in China were injured when they were forced to use a poisonous chemical to clean iPhone screens. Meanwhile, two people were killed immediately, twelve died later, and others were injured in an explosion in the section of the same FoxConn factory in Chengdu. Charles Duhigg and David Barboza of the *New York Times* carefully document the troubling conditions endured by Chinese workers who produce Apple products amid "onerous work environments and serious—sometimes deadly—safety problems." Apple's own audits document the problems but don't necessarily fix them. Duhigg and Barboza report on the constant pressure Apple puts on vendors to keep prices low, allowing suppliers the narrowest of profits. "If you squeeze margins, you're forcing them to cut safety," a former Apple executive notes, while another observes that "right now, customers care more about a new iPhone than working conditions in China."

Charles Duhigg and
David Barboza

28. In China, Human Costs Are Built Into an iPad

The explosion ripped through Building A5 on a Friday evening last May, an eruption of fire and noise that twisted metal pipes as if they were discarded straws.

When workers in the cafeteria ran outside, they saw black smoke pouring from shattered windows. It came from the area where employees polished thousands of iPad cases a day.

Two people were killed immediately and over a dozen others hurt. As the injured were rushed into ambulances, one in particular stood out. His features had been smeared by the blast, scrubbed by heat and violence until a mat of red and black had replaced his mouth and nose.

"Are you Lai Xiaodong's father?" a caller asked when the phone rang at Mr. Lai's childhood home. Six months earlier, the twenty-two-year-old had moved to Chengdu, in southwest China, to become one of the millions of human cogs powering the largest, fastest, and most sophisticated manufacturing system on earth. That system has made it possible for Apple and hundreds of other companies to build devices almost as quickly as they can be dreamed up.

"He's in trouble," the caller told Mr. Lai's father. "Get to the hospital as soon as possible."

In the last decade, Apple has become one of the mightiest, richest, and most successful companies in the world, in part by mastering global manufacturing. Apple and its high-technology peers—as well as dozens of other American industries—have achieved a pace of innovation nearly unmatched in modern history.

However, the workers assembling iPhones, iPads, and other devices often labor in harsh conditions, according to employees inside those plants, worker advocates, and documents published by companies themselves. Problems are as varied as onerous work environments and serious—sometimes deadly—safety problems.

Employees work excessive overtime, in some cases seven days a week, and live in crowded dorms. Some say they stand so long that their legs swell until they can hardly walk. Underage workers have helped build Apple's products, and the company's suppliers have improperly disposed of hazardous waste and falsified records, according to company reports and advocacy groups that, within China, are often considered reliable, independent monitors.

More troubling, the groups say, is some suppliers' disregard for workers' health. Two years ago, 137 workers at an Apple supplier in eastern China were injured after they were ordered to use a poisonous chemical to clean iPhone screens. Within seven months last year, two explosions at iPad factories, including in Chengdu, killed four people and injured seventy-seven. Before those blasts, Apple had been alerted to hazardous conditions inside the Chengdu plant, according to a Chinese group that published that warning.

"If Apple was warned, and didn't act, that's reprehensible," said Nicholas Ashford, a former chairman of the National Advisory Committee on Occupational Safety and Health, a group that advises the United States Labor Department. "But what's morally repugnant in one country is accepted business practices in another, and companies take advantage of that."

Apple is not the only electronics company doing business within a troubling supply system. Bleak working conditions have been documented at factories manufacturing products for Dell, Hewlett-Packard, IBM, Lenovo, Motorola, Nokia, Sony, Toshiba, and others.

Current and former Apple executives, moreover, say the company has made significant strides in improving factories in recent years. Apple has a supplier code of conduct that details standards on labor issues, safety protections, and other topics. The company has mounted a vigorous auditing campaign, and when abuses are discovered, Apple says, corrections are demanded.

And Apple's annual supplier-responsibility reports, in many cases, are the first to report abuses. This month, for the first time, the company released a list identifying many of its suppliers.

But significant problems remain. More than half of the suppliers audited by Apple have violated at least one aspect of the code of conduct every year since 2007, according to Apple's reports, and in some instances have violated the law. While many violations involve working conditions rather than safety hazards, troubling patterns persist.

"Apple never cared about anything other than increasing product quality and decreasing production cost," said Li Mingqi, who until April worked in management at Foxconn Technology, one of Apple's most important manufacturing partners. Mr. Li, who is suing Foxconn over his dismissal, helped manage the Chengdu factory where the explosion occurred.

"Workers' welfare has nothing to do with their interests," he said.

Some former Apple executives say there is an unresolved tension within the company: executives want to improve conditions within factories, but that dedication falters when it conflicts with crucial supplier relationships or the fast delivery of new products. Tuesday, Apple reported one of the most lucrative quarters of any corporation in history, with $13.06 billion in profits on $46.3 billion in sales. Its sales would have been even higher, executives said, if overseas factories had been able to produce more.

Executives at other corporations report similar internal pressures. This system may not be pretty, they argue, but a radical overhaul would slow innovation. Customers want amazing new electronics delivered every year.

"We've known about labor abuses in some factories for four years, and they're still going on," said one former Apple executive who, like others, spoke on the condition of anonymity because of confidentiality agreements. "Why? Because the system works for us. Suppliers would change everything tomorrow if Apple told them they didn't have another choice."

"If half of iPhones were malfunctioning, do you think Apple would let it go on for four years?" the executive asked.

Apple, in its published reports, has said it requires every discovered labor violation to be remedied and suppliers that refuse are terminated. Privately, however, some former executives concede that finding new suppliers is time-consuming and costly. Foxconn is one of the few manufacturers in the world with the scale to build sufficient numbers of iPhones and iPads. So Apple is "not going to leave Foxconn and they're not going to leave China," said Heather White, a research fellow at Harvard and a former member of the Monitoring International Labor Standards committee at the National Academy of Sciences. "There's a lot of rationalization."

Apple was provided with extensive summaries of this article, but the company declined to comment. The reporting is based on interviews with more than three dozen current or former employees and contractors, including a half-dozen current or former executives with firsthand knowledge of Apple's supplier responsibility group, as well as others within the technology industry.

In 2010, Steven P. Jobs discussed the company's relationships with suppliers at an industry conference.

"I actually think Apple does one of the best jobs of any companies in our industry, and maybe in any industry, of understanding the working conditions in our supply chain," said Mr. Jobs, who was Apple's chief executive at the time and who died last October.

"I mean, you go to this place, and, it's a factory, but, my gosh, I mean, they've got restaurants and movie theaters and hospitals and swimming pools, and I mean, for a factory, it's a pretty nice factory."

Others, including workers inside such plants, acknowledge the cafeterias and medical facilities but insist conditions are punishing.

"We're trying really hard to make things better," said one former Apple executive. "But most people would still be really disturbed if they saw where their iPhone comes from."

The Road to Chengdu

In the fall of 2010, about six months before the explosion in the iPad factory, Lai Xiaodong carefully wrapped his clothes around his college diploma, so it wouldn't crease in his suitcase. He told friends he would no longer be around for their weekly poker games and said goodbye to his teachers. He was leaving for Chengdu, a city of 12 million that was rapidly becoming one of the world's most important manufacturing hubs.

Though painfully shy, Mr. Lai had surprised everyone by persuading a beautiful nursing student to become his girlfriend. She wanted to marry, she said, and so his goal was to earn enough money to buy an apartment.

Factories in Chengdu manufacture products for hundreds of companies. But Mr. Lai was focused on Foxconn Technology, China's largest exporter and one of the nation's biggest employers, with 1.2 million workers. The company has plants throughout China and assembles an estimated 40 percent of the world's consumer electronics, including for customers like Amazon, Dell, Hewlett-Packard, Nintendo, Nokia, and Samsung.

Foxconn's factory in Chengdu, Mr. Lai knew, was special. Inside, workers were building Apple's latest, potentially greatest product: the iPad.

When Mr. Lai finally landed a job repairing machines at the plant, one of the first things he noticed were the almost blinding lights. Shifts ran twenty-four hours a day, and the factory was always bright. At any moment, there were thousands of workers standing on assembly lines or sitting in backless chairs, crouching next to large machinery, or jogging between loading bays. Some workers' legs swelled so much they waddled. "It's hard to stand all day," said Zhao Sheng, a plant worker.

Banners on the walls warned the 120,000 employees: "Work hard on the job today or work hard to find a job tomorrow." Apple's supplier code of conduct dictates that, except in unusual circumstances, employees are not supposed to work more than sixty hours a week. But at Foxconn, some worked more, according to interviews, workers' pay stubs, and surveys by outside groups. Mr. Lai was soon spending twelve hours a day, six days a week inside the factory, according to his paychecks. Employees who arrived late were sometimes required to write confession letters and copy quotations. There were "continuous shifts," when workers were told to work two stretches in a row, according to interviews.

Mr. Lai's college degree enabled him to earn a salary of around twenty-two dollars a day, including overtime—more than many others. When his days ended, he would retreat to a small bedroom just big enough for a mattress, a wardrobe, and a desk where he obsessively played an online game called Fight the Landlord, said his girlfriend, Luo Xiaohong.

Those accommodations were better than many of the company's dorms, where 70,000 Foxconn workers lived, at times stuffed twenty people to a three-room apartment, employees said. Last year, a dispute over paychecks set off a riot in one of the dormitories, and workers started throwing bottles, trash cans, and flaming paper from their windows, according to witnesses. Two hundred police officers wrestled with workers, arresting eight. Afterward, trash cans were removed, and piles of rubbish—and rodents—became a problem. Mr. Lai felt lucky to have a place of his own.

Foxconn, in a statement, disputed workers' accounts of continuous shifts, extended overtime, crowded living accommodations, and the causes of the riot. The company said that its operations adhered to customers' codes of conduct, industry standards, and national laws. "Conditions at Foxconn are anything but harsh," the company wrote. Foxconn also said that it had never been cited by a customer or government for underage or overworked employees or toxic exposures.

"All assembly line employees are given regular breaks, including one-hour lunch breaks," the company wrote, and only 5 percent of assembly line workers are required to stand to carry out their tasks. Work stations have been designed to ergonomic standards, and employees have opportunities for job rotation and promotion, the statement said.

"Foxconn has a very good safety record," the company wrote. "Foxconn has come a long way in our efforts to lead our industry in China in areas such as workplace conditions and the care and treatment of our employees."

Apple's Code of Conduct

In 2005, some of Apple's top executives gathered inside their Cupertino, Calif., headquarters for a special meeting. Other companies had created codes of conduct to police their suppliers. It was time, Apple decided, to follow suit. The code Apple published that year demands "that working conditions in Apple's supply chain are safe, that workers are treated with respect and dignity, and that manufacturing processes are environmentally responsible."

But the next year, a British newspaper, *The Mail on Sunday*, secretly visited a Foxconn factory in Shenzhen, China, where iPods were manufactured and reported on workers' long hours, push-ups meted out as punishment, and crowded dorms. Executives in Cupertino were shocked. "Apple is filled with really good people who had no idea this was going on," a former employee said. "We wanted it changed, immediately."

Apple audited that factory, the company's first such inspection, and ordered improvements. Executives also undertook a series of initiatives that included an annual audit report, first published in 2007. By last year, Apple had inspected 396 facilities—including the company's direct suppliers, as well as many of those suppliers' suppliers—one of the largest such programs within the electronics industry.

Those audits have found consistent violations of Apple's code of conduct, according to summaries published by the company. In 2007, for instance, Apple conducted over three dozen audits, two-thirds of which indicated that employees regularly worked more than sixty hours a week. In addition, there were six "core violations," the most serious kind, including hiring fifteen-year-olds as well as falsifying records.

Over the next three years, Apple conducted 312 audits, and every year, about half or more showed evidence of large numbers of employees laboring more than six days a week as well as working extended overtime. Some workers received less than minimum wage or had pay withheld as punishment. Apple found seventy core violations over that period, including cases of involuntary labor, underage workers, record falsifications, improper disposal of hazardous waste, and more than a hundred workers injured by toxic chemical exposures.

Last year, the company conducted 229 audits. There were slight improvements in some categories, and the detected rate of core violations declined. However, within ninety-three facilities, at least half of workers exceeded the sixty-hours-a-week work limit. At a similar number, employees worked more than six days a week. There were incidents of discrimination, improper safety precautions, failure to pay required overtime rates, and other violations. That year, four employees were killed and seventy-seven injured in workplace explosions.

“If you see the same pattern of problems, year after year, that means the company’s ignoring the issue rather than solving it,” said one former Apple executive with firsthand knowledge of the supplier-responsibility group. “Noncompliance is tolerated, as long as the suppliers promise to try harder next time. If we meant business, core violations would disappear.”

Apple says that when an audit reveals a violation, the company requires suppliers to address the problem within ninety days and make changes to prevent a recurrence. “If a supplier is unwilling to change, we terminate our relationship,” the company says on its website.

The seriousness of that threat, however, is unclear. Apple has found violations in hundreds of audits, but fewer than fifteen suppliers have been terminated for transgressions since 2007, according to former Apple executives.

“Once the deal is set and Foxconn becomes an authorized Apple supplier, Apple will no longer give any attention to worker conditions or anything that is irrelevant to its products,” said Mr. Li, the former Foxconn manager. Mr. Li spent seven years with Foxconn in Shenzhen and Chengdu and was forced out in April after he objected to a relocation to Chengdu, he said. Foxconn disputed his comments and said, “both Foxconn and Apple take the welfare of our employees very seriously.”

Apple's efforts have spurred some changes. Facilities that were reaudited "showed continued performance improvements and better working conditions," the company wrote in its 2011 supplier-responsibility progress report. In addition, the number of audited facilities has grown every year, and some executives say those expanding efforts obscure year-to-year improvements.

Apple also has trained over a million workers about their rights and methods for injury and disease prevention. A few years ago, after auditors insisted on interviewing low-level factory employees, they discovered that some had been forced to pay onerous "recruitment fees"—which Apple classifies as involuntary labor. As of last year, the company had forced suppliers to reimburse more than $6.7 million in such charges.

"Apple is a leader in preventing underage labor," said Dionne Harrison of Impactt, a firm paid by Apple to help prevent and respond to child labor among its suppliers. "They're doing as much as they possibly can."

Other consultants disagree.

"We've spent years telling Apple there are serious problems and recommending changes," said a consultant at BSR—also known as Business for Social Responsibility—which has been twice retained by Apple to provide advice on labor issues. "They don't want to preempt problems, they just want to avoid embarrassments."

"We Could Have Saved Lives"

In 2006, BSR, along with a division of the World Bank and other groups, initiated a project to improve working conditions in factories building cell phones and other devices in China and elsewhere. The groups and companies pledged to test various ideas. Foxconn agreed to participate.

For four months, BSR and another group negotiated with Foxconn regarding a pilot program to create worker "hotlines" so that employees could report abusive conditions, seek mental counseling, and discuss workplace problems. Apple was not a participant in the project, but was briefed on it, according to the BSR consultant, who had detailed knowledge.

As negotiations proceeded, Foxconn's requirements for participation kept changing. First, Foxconn asked to shift from installing new hotlines to evaluating existing hotlines. Then Foxconn insisted that mental-health counseling be excluded. Foxconn asked participants to sign agreements saying they would not disclose what they observed and then rewrote those agreements multiple times. Finally, an agreement was struck, and the project was scheduled to begin in January 2008. A day before the start, Foxconn demanded more changes, until it was clear the project would not proceed, according to the consultant and a 2008 summary by BSR that did not name Foxconn.

The next year, a Foxconn employee fell or jumped from an apartment building after losing an iPhone prototype. Over the next two years, at least eighteen other Foxconn workers attempted suicide or fell from buildings in manners that suggested suicide attempts. In 2010, two years after the pilot program fell apart and after multiple suicide attempts, Foxconn created a dedicated mental-health hotline and began offering free psychological counseling.

"We could have saved lives, and we asked Apple to pressure Foxconn, but they wouldn't do it," said the BSR consultant, who asked not to be identified because of confidentiality agreements. "Companies like HP and Intel and Nike push their suppliers. But Apple wants to keep an arm's length, and Foxconn is their most important manufacturer, so they refuse to push."

BSR, in a written statement, said the views of that consultant were not those of the company.

"My BSR colleagues and I view Apple as a company that is making a highly serious effort to ensure that labor conditions in its supply chain meet the expectations of applicable laws, the company's standards and the expectations of consumers," wrote Aron Cramer, BSR's president. Mr. Cramer added that asking Apple to pressure Foxconn would have been inconsistent with the purpose of the pilot program, and there were multiple reasons the pilot program did not proceed.

Foxconn, in a statement, said it acted quickly and comprehensively to address suicides, and "the record has shown that those measures have been successful."

A Demanding Client

Every month, officials at companies from around the world trek to Cupertino or invite Apple executives to visit their foreign factories, all in pursuit of a goal: becoming a supplier.

When news arrives that Apple is interested in a particular product or service, small celebrations often erupt. Whiskey is drunk. Karaoke is sung.

Then, Apple's requests start.

Apple typically asks suppliers to specify how much every part costs, how many workers are needed, and the size of their salaries. Executives want to know every financial detail. Afterward, Apple calculates how much it will pay for a part. Most suppliers are allowed only the slimmest of profits.

So suppliers often try to cut corners, replace expensive chemicals with less costly alternatives, or push their employees to work faster and longer, according to people at those companies.

"The only way you make money working for Apple is figuring out how to do things more efficiently or cheaper," said an executive at one company that helped bring the iPad to market. "And then they'll come back the next year, and force a 10 percent price cut."

In January 2010, workers at a Chinese factory owned by Wintek, an Apple manufacturing partner, went on strike over a variety of issues, including widespread rumors that workers were being exposed to toxins. Investigations by news organizations revealed that over a hundred employees had been injured by n-hexane, a toxic chemical that can cause nerve damage and paralysis.

Employees said they had been ordered to use n-hexane to clean iPhone screens because it evaporated almost three times as fast as rubbing alcohol. Faster evaporation meant workers could clean more screens each minute.

Apple commented on the Wintek injuries a year later. In its supplier responsibility report, Apple said it had "required Wintek to stop using n-hexane" and that "Apple has verified that all affected workers have been treated successfully, and we continue to monitor their medical reports until full recuperation." Apple also said it required Wintek to fix the ventilation system.

That same month, a *New York Times* reporter interviewed a dozen injured Wintek workers who said they had never been contacted by Apple or its intermediaries and that Wintek had pressured them to resign and take cash settlements that would absolve the company of liability. After those interviews, Wintek pledged to provide more compensation to the injured workers and Apple sent a representative to speak with some of them.

Six months later, trade publications reported that Apple significantly cut prices paid to Wintek.

"You can set all the rules you want, but they're meaningless if you don't give suppliers enough profit to treat workers well," said one former Apple executive with firsthand knowledge of the supplier responsibility group. "If you squeeze margins, you're forcing them to cut safety."

Wintek is still one of Apple's most important suppliers. Wintek, in a statement, declined to comment except to say that after the episode, the company took "ample measures" to address the situation and "is committed to ensuring employee welfare and creating a safe and healthy work environment."

Many major technology companies have worked with factories where conditions are troubling. However, independent monitors and suppliers say some act differently. Executives at multiple suppliers, in interviews, said that Hewlett-Packard and others allowed them slightly more profits and other allowances if they were used to improve worker conditions.

"Our suppliers are very open with us," said Zoe McMahon, an executive in Hewlett-Packard's supply chain social and environmental responsibility program. "They let us know when they are struggling to meet our expectations, and that influences our decisions."

The Explosion

On the afternoon of the blast at the iPad plant, Lai Xiaodong telephoned his girlfriend, as he did every day. They had hoped to see each other that evening, but Mr. Lai's manager said he had to work overtime, he told her.

He had been promoted quickly at Foxconn, and after just a few months was in charge of a team that maintained the machines that polished iPad cases. The sanding area was loud and hazy with aluminum dust. Workers wore masks and earplugs, but no matter how many times they showered, they were recognizable by the slight aluminum sparkle in their hair and at the corners of their eyes.

Just two weeks before the explosion, an advocacy group in Hong Kong published a report warning of unsafe conditions at the Chengdu plant, including problems with aluminum dust. The group, Students and Scholars Against Corporate Misbehavior, or SACOM, had videotaped workers covered with tiny aluminum particles. "Occupational health and safety issues in Chengdu are alarming," the report read. "Workers also highlight the problem of poor ventilation and inadequate personal protective equipment."

A copy of that report was sent to Apple. "There was no response," said Debby Chan Sze Wan of the group. "A few months later I went to Cupertino, and went into the Apple lobby, but no one would meet with me. I've never heard from anyone from Apple at all."

The morning of the explosion, Mr. Lai rode his bicycle to work. The iPad had gone on sale just weeks earlier, and workers were told thousands of cases needed to be polished each day. The factory was frantic, employees said. Rows of machines buffed cases as masked employees pushed buttons. Large air ducts hovered over each station, but they could not keep up with the three lines of machines polishing nonstop. Aluminum dust was everywhere.

Dust is a known safety hazard. In 2003, an aluminum dust explosion in Indiana destroyed a wheel factory and killed a worker. In 2008, agricultural dust inside a sugar factory in Georgia caused an explosion that killed fourteen.

Two hours into Mr. Lai's second shift, the building started to shake, as if an earthquake was under way. There was a series of blasts, plant workers said.

Then the screams began.

When Mr. Lai's colleagues ran outside, dark smoke was mixing with a light rain, according to cell-phone videos. The toll would eventually count four dead, eighteen injured.

At the hospital, Mr. Lai's girlfriend saw that his skin was almost completely burned away. "I recognized him from his legs, otherwise I wouldn't know who that person was," she said.

Eventually, his family arrived. Over 90 percent of his body had been seared. "My mom ran away from the room at the first sight of him. I cried. Nobody could stand it," his brother said. When his mother eventually returned, she tried to avoid touching her son, for fear that it would cause pain.

"If I had known," she said, "I would have grabbed his arm, I would have touched him."

"He was very tough," she said. "He held on for two days."

After Mr. Lai died, Foxconn workers drove to Mr. Lai's hometown and delivered a box of ashes. The company later wired a check for about $150,000.

Foxconn, in a statement, said that at the time of the explosion the Chengdu plant was in compliance with all relevant laws and regulations, and "after ensuring that the families of the deceased employees were given the support they required, we ensured that all of the injured employees were given the highest quality medical care." After the explosion, the company added, Foxconn immediately halted work in all polishing workshops and later improved ventilation and dust disposal and adopted technologies to enhance worker safety.

In its most recent supplier-responsibility report, Apple wrote that after the explosion, the company contacted "the foremost experts in process safety" and assembled a team to investigate and make recommendations to prevent future accidents.

In December, however, seven months after the blast that killed Mr. Lai, another iPad factory exploded, this one in Shanghai. Once again, aluminum dust was the cause, according to interviews and Apple's most recent supplier-responsibility report. That blast injured fifty-nine workers, with twenty-three hospitalized.

"It is gross negligence, after an explosion occurs, not to realize that every factory should be inspected," said Nicholas Ashford, the occupational safety expert, who is now at the Massachusetts Institute of Technology. "If it were terribly difficult to deal with aluminum dust, I would understand. But do you know how easy dust is to control? It's called ventilation. We solved this problem over a century ago."

In its most recent supplier responsibility report, Apple wrote that while the explosions both involved combustible aluminum dust, the causes were different. The company declined, however, to provide details. The report added that Apple had now audited all suppliers polishing aluminum products and had put stronger precautions in place. All suppliers have initiated required countermeasures, except one, which remains shut down, the report said.

For Mr. Lai's family, questions remain. "We're really not sure why he died," said Mr. Lai's mother, standing beside a shrine she built near their home. "We don't understand what happened."

Hitting the Apple Lottery

Every year, as rumors about Apple's forthcoming products start to emerge, trade publications and websites begin speculating about which suppliers are likely to win the Apple lottery. Getting a contract from Apple can lift a company's value by millions because of the implied endorsement of manufacturing quality. But few companies openly brag about the work: Apple generally requires suppliers to sign contracts promising they will not divulge anything, including the partnership.

That lack of transparency gives Apple an edge at keeping its plans secret. But it also has been a barrier to improving working conditions, according to advocates and former Apple executives.

This month, after numerous requests by advocacy and news organizations, including the *New York Times*, Apple released the names of 156 of its suppliers. In the report accompanying that list, Apple said they "account for more than 97 percent of what we pay to suppliers to manufacture our products."

However, the company has not revealed the names of hundreds of other companies that do not directly contract with Apple but supply the suppliers. The company's supplier list does not disclose where factories are, and many are hard to find. And independent monitoring organizations say when they have tried to inspect Apple's suppliers, they have been barred from entry—on Apple's orders, they have been told.

"We've had this conversation hundreds of times," said a former executive in Apple's supplier-responsibility group. "There is a genuine, companywide commitment to the code of conduct. But taking it to the next level and creating real change conflicts with secrecy and business goals, and so there's only so far we can go." Former Apple employees say they were generally prohibited from engaging with most outside groups.

"There's a real culture of secrecy here that influences everything," the former executive said.

Some other technology companies operate differently.

"We talk to a lot of outsiders," said Gary Niekerk, director of corporate citizenship at Intel. "The world's complex, and unless we're dialoguing with outside groups, we miss a lot."

Given Apple's prominence and leadership in global manufacturing, if the company were to radically change its ways, it could overhaul how business is done. "Every company wants to be Apple," said Sasha Lezhnev at the Enough Project, a group focused on corporate accountability. "If they committed to building a conflict-free iPhone, it would transform technology."

But ultimately, say former Apple executives, there are few real outside pressures for change. Apple is one of the most admired brands. In a national survey conducted by the *New York Times* in November, 56 percent of respondents said they couldn't think of anything negative about Apple. Fourteen percent said the worst thing about the company was that its products were too expensive. Just 2 percent mentioned overseas labor practices.

People like Ms. White of Harvard say that until consumers demand better conditions in overseas factories—as they did for companies like Nike and Gap, which today have overhauled conditions among suppliers—or regulators act, there is little impetus for radical change. Some Apple insiders agree.

"You can either manufacture in comfortable, worker-friendly factories, or you can reinvent the product every year, and make it better and faster and cheaper, which requires factories that seem harsh by American standards," said a current Apple executive.

"And right now, customers care more about a new iPhone than working conditions in China."

Gu Huini contributed research.

Wired

People report on computer security flaws every day, and too often we ignore those stories. But you can't ignore Mat Honan's first-person story of how his life was upended by a blasé yet sociopathic hacker. The dreadful experience for Honan was something of a blessing for those of us who hadn't yet turned on dual-factor authentication in Gmail or remembered to back up our computers recently. It also persuaded Apple to fix a big hole in its security systems. This story, told with the immediacy of something that was very fresh in Honan's mind, is ultimately much more *real* than just about anything else written on this subject.

Mat Honan

29. How Apple and Amazon Security Flaws Led to My Epic Hacking

In the space of one hour, my entire digital life was destroyed. First my Google account was taken over then deleted. Next my Twitter account was compromised and used as a platform to broadcast racist and homophobic messages. And worst of all, my AppleID account was broken into, and my hackers used it to remotely erase all of the data on my iPhone, iPad, and MacBook.

In many ways, this was all my fault. My accounts were daisy-chained together. Getting into Amazon let my hackers get into my Apple ID account, which helped them get into Gmail, which gave them access to Twitter. Had I used two-factor authentication for my Google account, it's possible that none of this would have happened because their ultimate goal was always to take over my Twitter account and wreak havoc. Lulz.

Had I been regularly backing up the data on my MacBook, I wouldn't have had to worry about losing more than a year's worth of photos, covering the entire lifespan of my daughter, or documents and e-mails that I had stored in no other location.

Those security lapses are my fault, and I deeply, deeply regret them.

But what happened to me exposes vital security flaws in several customer service systems, most notably Apple's and Amazon's. Apple tech support gave the hackers access to my iCloud account. Amazon tech support gave them the ability to see a piece of information—a partial credit card number—that Apple used to release information. In short, the very four digits that Amazon considers unimportant enough to display in the clear on the web are precisely the same ones that Apple considers secure enough to perform identity verification. The disconnect exposes flaws in data-management policies endemic to the entire technology industry and points to a looming nightmare as we enter the era of cloud computing and connected devices.

This isn't just my problem. Since Friday, August 3, when hackers broke into my accounts, I've heard from other users who were compromised in the same way, at least one of whom was targeted by the same group.

Moreover, if your computers aren't already cloud-connected devices, they will be soon. Apple is working hard to get all of its customers to use iCloud. Google's entire operating system is cloud-based. And Windows 8, the most cloud-centric operating system yet, will hit desktops by the tens of millions in the coming year. My experience leads me to believe that cloud-based systems need fundamentally different security measures. Password-based security mechanisms—which can be cracked, reset, and socially engineered—no longer suffice in the era of cloud computing.

I realized something was wrong at about five p.m. on Friday. I was playing with my daughter when my iPhone suddenly powered down. I was expecting a call, so I went to plug it back in.

It then rebooted to the setup screen. This was irritating, but I wasn't concerned. I assumed it was a software glitch. And my phone automatically backs up every night. I just assumed it would be a pain in the ass, and nothing more. I entered my iCloud login to restore, and it wasn't accepted. Again, I was irritated but not alarmed.

I went to connect the iPhone to my computer and restore from that backup—which I had just happened to do the other day. When I opened my laptop, an iCal message popped up telling me that my Gmail account information was wrong. Then the screen went gray and asked for a four-digit PIN.

I didn't have a four-digit PIN.

By now, I knew something was very, very wrong. For the first time it occurred to me that I was being hacked. Unsure of exactly what was happening, I unplugged my router and cable modem, turned off the Mac Mini we use as an entertainment center, grabbed my wife's phone, and called AppleCare, the company's tech support service, and spoke with a rep for the next hour and a half.

It wasn't the first call they had had that day about my account. In fact, I later found out that a call had been placed just a little more than a half an hour before my own. But the Apple rep didn't bother to tell me about the first call concerning my account, despite the ninety minutes I spent on the phone with tech support. Nor would Apple tech support ever tell me about the first call voluntarily—it only shared this information after I asked about it. And I only knew about the first call because a hacker told me he had made the call himself.

At 4:33 p.m., according to Apple's tech support records, someone called AppleCare claiming to be me. Apple says the caller reported that he couldn't get into his Me.com e-mail—which, of course was my Me.com e-mail.

In response, Apple issued a temporary password. It did this despite the caller's inability to answer security questions I had set up. And it did this after the hacker supplied only two pieces of information that anyone with an Internet connection and a phone can discover.

At 4:50 p.m., a password-reset confirmation arrived in my inbox. I don't really use my me.com e-mail and rarely check it. But even if I did, I might not have noticed the message because the hackers immediately sent it to the trash. They then were able to follow the link in that e-mail to permanently reset my AppleID password.

At 4:52 p.m., a Gmail password-recovery e-mail arrived in my me.com mailbox. Two minutes later, another e-mail arrived notifying me that my Google account password had changed.

At 5:02 p.m., they reset my Twitter password. At 5:00 they used iCloud's "Find My" tool to remotely wipe my iPhone. At 5:01 they remotely wiped my iPad. At 5:05 they remotely wiped my MacBook. Around this same time, they deleted my Google account. At 5:10, I placed the call to AppleCare. At 5:12 the attackers posted a message to my account on Twitter taking credit for the hack.

By wiping my MacBook and deleting my Google account, they now not only had the ability to control my account but were able to prevent me from regaining access. And crazily, in ways that I don't and never will understand, those deletions were just collateral damage. My MacBook data—including those irreplaceable pictures of my family, of my child's first year and relatives who have now passed from this life—weren't the target. Nor were the eight years of messages in my Gmail account. The target was always Twitter. My MacBook data was torched simply to prevent me from getting back in.

Lulz.

I spent an hour and a half talking to AppleCare. One of the reasons it took me so long to get anything resolved with Apple during my initial phone call was because I couldn't answer the security questions it had on file for me. It turned out there's a good reason for that. Perhaps an hour or so into the call, the Apple representative on the line said "Mr. Herman, I . . ."

"Wait. What did you call me?"

"Mr. Herman?"

"My name is Honan."

Apple had been looking at the wrong account all along. Because of that, I couldn't answer my security questions. And because of that, it asked me an alternate set of questions that it said would let tech support let me into my me.com account: a billing address and the last four digits of my credit card. (Of course, when I gave them those, it was no use, because tech support had misheard my last name.)

It turns out, a billing address and the last four digits of a credit card number are the only two pieces of information anyone needs to get into your iCloud account. Once supplied, Apple will issue a temporary password, and that password grants access to iCloud.

Apple tech support confirmed to me twice over the weekend that all you need to access someone's AppleID is the associated e-mail address, a credit card number, the billing address, and the last four digits of a credit card on file. I was very clear about this. During my second tech support call to AppleCare, the representative confirmed this to me. "That's really all you have to have to verify something with us," he said.

We talked to Apple directly about its security policy, and company spokesperson Natalie Kerris told *Wired*, "Apple takes customer privacy seriously and requires multiple forms of verification before resetting an Apple ID password. In this particular case, the customer's data was compromised by a person who had acquired personal information about the customer. In addition, we found that our own internal policies were not followed completely. We are reviewing all of our processes for resetting account passwords to ensure our customers' data is protected."

On Monday, *Wired* tried to verify the hackers' access technique by performing it on a different account. We were successful. This means, ultimately, all you need in addition to someone's e-mail address are those two easily acquired pieces of information: a billing address and the last four digits of a credit card on file. Here's the story of how the hackers got them.

On the night of the hack, I tried to make sense of the ruin that was my digital life. My Google account was nuked, my Twitter account was suspended, my phone was in a useless state of restore, and (for obvious reasons) I was highly paranoid about using my Apple e-mail account for communication.

I decided to set up a new Twitter account until my old one could be restored, just to let people know what was happening. I logged into Tumblr and posted an account of how I thought the takedown occurred. At this point, I was assuming that my seven-digit alphanumeric AppleID password had been hacked by brute force. In the comments (and, oh, the comments) others guessed that hackers had used some sort of keystroke logger. At the end of the post, I linked to my new Twitter account.

And then, one of my hackers @ messaged me. He would later identify himself as Phobia. I followed him. He followed me back.

We started a dialogue via Twitter direct messaging that later continued via e-mail and AIM. Phobia was able to reveal enough detail about the hack and my compromised accounts that it became clear he was, at the very least, a party to how it went down. I agreed not to press charges, and in return he laid out exactly how the hack worked. But first, he wanted to clear something up:

"didnt guess ur password or use bruteforce. i have my own guide on how to secure emails."

I asked him why. Was I targeted specifically? Was this just to get to Gizmodo's Twitter account? No, Phobia said they hadn't even been aware that my account was linked to Gizmodo's, that the Gizmodo linkage was just gravy. He said the hack was simply a grab for my three-character Twitter handle. That's all they wanted. They just wanted to take it, and fuck shit up, and watch it burn. It wasn't personal.

"I honestly didn't have any heat towards you before this. i just liked your username like I said before" he told me via Twitter Direct Message.

After coming across my account, the hackers did some background research. My Twitter account linked to my personal website, where they found my Gmail address. Guessing that this was also the e-mail address I used for Twitter, Phobia went to Google's account recovery page. He didn't even have to actually attempt a recovery. This was just a recon mission.

Because I didn't have Google's two-factor authentication turned on, when Phobia entered my Gmail address, he could view the alternate e-mail I had set up for account recovery. Google partially obscures that information, starring out many characters, but there were enough characters available, m••••n@me.com. Jackpot.

This was how the hack progressed. If I had some other account aside from an Apple e-mail address or had used two-factor authentication for Gmail, everything would have stopped here. But using that Apple-run me.com e-mail account as a backup meant told the hacker I had an AppleID account, which meant I was vulnerable to being hacked.

"You honestly can get into any email associated with apple," Phobia claimed in an e-mail. And while it's work, that seems to be largely true.

Since he already had the e-mail, all he needed was my billing address and the last four digits of my credit card number to have Apple's tech support issue him the keys to my account.

So how did he get this vital information? He began with the easy one. He got the billing address by doing a whois search on my personal web domain. If someone doesn't have a domain, you can also look up his or her information on Spokeo, WhitePages, and PeopleSmart.

Getting a credit card number is trickier, but it also relies on taking advantage of a company's back-end systems. Phobia says that a partner performed this part of the hack but described the technique to us, which we were able to verify via our own tech-support phone calls. It's remarkably easy—so easy that *Wired* was able to duplicate the exploit twice in minutes.

First you call Amazon and tell them you are the account holder, and want to add a credit card number to the account. All you need is the name on the account, an associated e-mail address, and the billing address. Amazon then allows you to input a new credit card. (*Wired* used a bogus credit card number from a website that generates fake card numbers that conform with the industry's published self-check algorithm.) Then you hang up.

Next you call back, and tell Amazon that you've lost access to your account. Upon providing a name, billing address, and the new credit card number you gave the company on the prior call, Amazon will allow you to add a new e-mail address to the account. From here, you go to the Amazon website and send a password reset to the new e-mail account. This allows you to see all the credit cards on file for the account—not the complete numbers, just the last four digits. But, as we know, Apple only needs those last four digits. We asked Amazon to comment on its security policy but didn't have anything to share by press time.

And it's also worth noting that one wouldn't have to call Amazon to pull this off. Your pizza guy could do the same thing, for example. If you have an AppleID, every time you call Pizza Hut, you've giving the sixteen-year-old on the other end of the line all he needs to take over your entire digital life.

And so, with my name, address, and the last four digits of my credit card number in hand, Phobia called AppleCare, and my digital life was laid waste. Yet still I was actually quite fortunate.

They could have used my e-mail accounts to gain access to my online banking or financial services. They could have used them to contact other people and socially engineer them as well. As Ed Bott pointed out on TWiT.tv, my years as a technology journalist have put some very influential people in my address book. They could have been victimized too.

Instead, the hackers just wanted to embarrass me, have some fun at my expense, and enrage my followers on Twitter by trolling.

I had done some pretty stupid things. Things you shouldn't do.

I should have been regularly backing up my MacBook. Because I wasn't doing that, if all the photos from the first year and a half of my daughter's life are ultimately lost, I will have only myself to blame. I shouldn't have daisy-chained two such vital accounts—my Google and my iCloud account—together. I shouldn't have used the same e-mail prefix across multiple accounts—mhonan@gmail.com, mhonan@me.com, and mhonan@wired.com. And I should have had a recovery address that's only used for recovery without being tied to core services.

But, mostly, I shouldn't have used Find My Mac. Find My iPhone has been a brilliant Apple service. If you lose your iPhone, or have it stolen, the service lets you see where it is on a map. The *New York Times*'s David Pogue recovered his lost iPhone just last week thanks to the service. And so, when Apple introduced Find My Mac in the update to its Lion operating system last year, I added that to my iCloud options too.

After all, as a reporter, often on the go, my laptop is my most important tool.

But as a friend pointed out to me, while that service makes sense for phones (which are quite likely to be lost) it makes less sense for computers. You are almost certainly more likely to have your computer accessed remotely than physically. And even worse is the way Find My Mac is implemented.

When you perform a remote hard-drive wipe on Find my Mac, the system asks you to create a four-digit PIN so that the process can be reversed. But here's the thing: If someone else performs that wipe—someone who gained access to your iCloud account through malicious means—there's no way for you to enter that PIN.

A better way to have this set up would be to require a second method of authentication when Find My Mac is initially set up. If this were the case, someone who was able to get into an iCloud account wouldn't be able to remotely wipe devices with malicious intent. It would also mean that you could potentially have a way to stop a remote wipe in progress.

But that's not how it works. And Apple would not comment as to whether stronger authentification is being considered.

As of Monday, both of these exploits used by the hackers were still functioning. *Wired* was able to duplicate them. Apple says its internal tech-support processes weren't followed, and this is how my account was compromised. However, this contradicts what AppleCare told me twice that weekend. If that is, in fact, the case—that I was the victim of Apple not following its own internal processes—then the problem is widespread.

I asked Phobia why he did this to me. His answer wasn't satisfying. He says he likes to publicize security exploits so companies will fix them. He says it's the same reason he told me how it was done. He claims his partner in the attack was the person who wiped my MacBook. Phobia expressed remorse for this, and says he would have stopped it had he known.

"yea i really am a nice guy idk why i do some of the things i do," he told me via AIM. "idk my goal is to get it out there to other people so eventually every1 can over come hackers"

I asked specifically about the photos of my little girl, which are, to me, the greatest tragedy in all this. Unless I can recover those photos via data-recovery services, they are gone forever. On AIM, I asked him if he was sorry for doing that. Phobia replied, "even though i wasnt the one that did it i feel sorry about that. Thats alot of memories im only 19 but if my parents lost and the footage of me and pics i would be beyond sad and im sure they would be too."

But let's say he did know and failed to stop it. Hell, for the sake of argument, let's say he *did* it. Let's say he pulled the trigger. The weird thing is, I'm not even especially angry at Phobia or his partner in the attack. I'm mostly mad at myself. I'm mad as hell for not backing up my data. I'm sad, and shocked, and feel that I am ultimately to blame for that loss.

But I'm also upset that this ecosystem that I've placed so much of my trust in has let me down so thoroughly. I'm angry that Amazon makes it so remarkably easy to allow someone into your account, which has obvious financial consequences. And then there's Apple. I bought into the Apple account system originally to buy songs at ninety-nine cents a pop, and over the years that same ID has evolved into a single point of entry that controls my phones, tablets, computers, and data-driven life. With this AppleID, someone can make thousands of dollars of purchases in an instant or do damage at a cost that you can't put a price on.

Additional reporting by Roberto Baldwin and Christina Bonnington. Portions of this story originally appeared on Mat Honan's Tumblr.

Permissions

"The Fallen: The Sharp, Sudden Decline of America's Middle Class," by Jeff Tietz, *Rolling Stone*, July 5, 2012. Copyright © 2012 Rolling Stone LLC. All Rights Reserved. Reprinted by permission.

"The Great American Foreclosure Story," by Paul Kiel. Published by *ProPublica*, April 10, 2012. © ProPublica. Reprinted by permission. www.propublica.org

"Bad to the Bone: A Medical Horror Story," by Mina Kimes, from *Fortune* magazine, September 18, 2012. © 2012 Time Inc. Used under license. *Fortune* and Time Inc. are not affiliated with and do not endorse products or services of Licensee.

"Prescription for Addiction," by Thomas Catan, Devlin Barrett, and Timothy W. Martin. Reprinted with permission of *The Wall Street Journal*. © 2012 Dow Jones & Company. All rights reserved.

"Anemia Drugs Made Billions, but at What Cost?" by Peter Whoriskey, from the *Washington Post*, July 19, 2012. © 2012 The Washington Post. All rights reserved. Used by permission and protected by the Copyright Laws of the United States. The printing, copying, redistribution, or retransmission of the Material without express written permission is prohibited. www.washingtonpost.com.

"Making the World's Largest Airline Fly," by Drake Bennett. Originally published by *BusinessWeek*, February 2, 2012. Used with permission from Bloomberg Businessweek Copyright © 2012. All rights reserved.

"Gusher—*The New Yorker*, April 9, 2012," from *Private Empire: ExxonMobil and American Power*, by Steve Coll, copyright © 2012 by Steve Coll. Used by permission of The Penguin Press, a division of Penguin Group (USA) Inc.

"Vast Mexico Bribery Case Hushed Up by Wal-Mart After Top-Level Struggle," by David Barstow, from the *New York Times*,

April 22, 2012. © 2012 The New York Times. All rights reserved. Used by permission and protected by the Copyright Laws of the United States. The printing, copying, redistribution, or retransmission of this Content without express written permission is prohibited. www.nytimes.com.

"Chesapeake and Rival Plotted to Suppress Land Prices," by Brian Grow, Joshua Shneyer, and Janet Roberts. © Thomson Reuters 2012. All rights reserved. Republication or redistribution of Thomson Reuters content, including by framing or similar means, is expressly prohibited without the prior written consent of Thomson Reuters. Thomson Reuters and its logo are registered trademarks or trademarks of the Thomson Reuters group of companies around the world. Thomson Reuters journalists are subject to an Editorial Handbook, which requires fair presentation and disclosure of relevant interests. www.reuters.com.

"Fear Fans Flames for Chemical Makers," by Patricia Callahan and Sam Roe. From the *Chicago Tribune*, May 6, 2012, © 2012 Chicago Tribune. All rights reserved. Used by permission and protected by the Copyright Laws of the United States. The printing, copying, redistribution, or retransmission of the Material without express written permission is prohibited.

"His. Hers," by Jessica Pressler. Published in *New York*, February 20, 2012. © 2012 New York Media. Reprinted by permission of New York Media.

"Top Five Ways *Bleacher Report* Rules the World!" by Joe Eskenazi. First published in *San Francisco Weekly*, October 3, 2012. © by SF Weekly, L.P. Reprinted by permission of Village Voice Media Holding LLC.

"Citizens Jain: Why India's Newspaper Industry Is Thriving," by Ken Auletta. First published in *The New Yorker*, October 8, 2012. © Ken Auletta. Reprinted by permission of the author.

"The Frequent Fliers Who Flew Too Much," by Ken Bensinger, published May 5, 2012. Copyright © 2012 Los Angeles Times. Reprinted with permission.

"Trade-offs Between Inequality, Productivity, and Employment," by Steve Randy Waldman. First published by *Interfluidity*, July 31, 2012. © 2012 by Steve Randy Waldman. Reprinted by permission of the author.

"The Naked and the TED," by Evgeny Morozov. First published in *The New Republic*, August 2, 2012. © 2012 by Evgeny Morozov. Reprinted by permission of the author.

"Wall Street Bonus Withdrawal Means Trading Aspen for Coupons" by Max Abelson, from *Bloomberg News*, February 29, 2012. © Bloomberg News. Reprinted by permission.

"The Tale of a Whale of a Fail" by Matt Levine, published by *Dealbreaker.com* on May 11, 2012. © 2012 Breaking Media, Inc. Reprinted by permission of Breaking Media, Inc.

"Case Against Bear and JPMorgan Provides Little Cheer," by Bethany McClean. © Thomson Reuters 2012. All rights reserved. Republication or redistribution of Thomson Reuters content, including by framing or similar means, is expressly prohibited without the prior written consent of Thomson Reuters. Thomson Reuters and its logo are registered trademarks or trademarks of the Thomson Reuters group of companies around the world. Thomson Reuters journalists are subject to an Editorial Handbook, which requires fair presentation and disclosure of relevant interests. www.reuters.com.

"How ECB Chief Outflanked German Foe in Fight for Euro," by Brian Blackstone and Marcus Walker. Reprinted with permission of the *Wall Street Journal*. © 2012 Dow Jones & Company. All rights reserved.

"Please Don't Harass My Father Any Further," by Deena DeNaro; "My Furnace Guy," by Joel Roache; "Thank You for My Lessons," by anon.; "How We're Doing Out Here," by anon.; and

"I Didn't Buy a House," by Pamila Payne. Reprinted from *The Trouble Is the Banks*, edited by Mark Greif, Dayna Tortorici, Kathleen French, Emma Janaskie, and Nick Werle. Published in 2012 by n+1 Foundation. © n+1 Foundation. Reprinted by permission of the publisher.

"Why I Am Leaving Goldman Sachs," by Greg Smith, from the *New York Times*, March 14, 2012. © 2012 The New York Times. All rights reserved. Used by permission and protected by the Copyright Laws of the United States. The printing, copying, redistribution, or retransmission of this Content without express written permission is prohibited. www.nytimes.com.

"Death Takes a Policy," by Jake Bernstein. Published by ProPublica, August 24, 2012 © ProPublica. Reprinted by permission. www.propublica.org.

"Psst, You in Aisle 5" ("How Companies Learn Your Secrets"), by Charles Duhigg, from the *New York Times Magazine*, February 19, 2012. © 2012 The New York Times. All rights reserved. Used by permission and protected by the Copyright Laws of the United States. The printing, copying, redistribution, or retransmission of this Content without express written permission is prohibited. www.nytimes.com.

"Glass Works: How Corning Created the Ultrathin, Ultrastrong Material of the Future." Copyright © 2012 Condé Nast. All Rights Reserved. Article by Bryan Gardiner originally published in *Wired*. Reprinted by permission

"Skilled Work, Without the Worker," by John Markoff, from the *New York Times*, August 19, 2012. © 2012 The New York Times. All rights reserved. Used by permission and protected by the Copyright Laws of the United States. The printing, copying, redistribution, or retransmission of this Content without express written permission is prohibited. www.nytimes.com.

"I Was a Warehouse Wage Slave," by Mac McClelland. First published in *Mother Jones* March/April 2012. © 2012 by Foundation for National Progress. Reprinted by permission of Foundation for National Progress.

"In China, Human Costs Are Built Into an iPad," by Charles Duhigg and David Barboza, from the *New York Times*, January 26, 2012. © 2012 The New York Times. All rights reserved. Used by permission and protected by the Copyright Laws of the United States. The printing, copying, redistribution, or retransmission of this Content without express written permission is prohibited. www.nytimes.com.

"How Apple and Amazon Security Flaws Led to My Epic Hacking." Copyright © 2012 Condé Nast. All Rights Reserved. Article by Mat Honan originally published in *Wired*. Reprinted by permission.

Contributors

Max Abelson is a reporter at Bloomberg News and was previously a staff writer at the *New York Observer.* He is a graduate of Yale University

Ken Auletta has written for *The New Yorker* since 1992. He is the author of eight books, including *Three Blind Mice: How the TV Networks Lost Their Way*; *Greed and Glory on Wall Street: The Fall of The House of Lehman*; and, most recently, *Googled: The End of the World as We Know It.*

David Barboza is a correspondent for the *New York Times* based in Shanghai, China. He writes primarily for the Business section. He was part of a team that was named a finalist for a Pulitzer Prize in 2002. In 2005, he was one of five *Times* reporters awarded the Gerald Loeb Award.

Devlin Barrett is a *Wall Street Journal* reporter covering security and law enforcement.

David Barstow joined the *New York Times* in 1999. His reporting on workplace safety in America won the Pulitzer Prize for public service in 2004, and in 2009 he won the Pulitzer for articles that exposed a covert Pentagon campaign to use retired military officers, working as analysts for television and radio networks, to reiterate administration "talking points" about the war on terror.

Drake Bennett is a staff writer with *Bloomberg BusinessWeek*, where he covers the economy, politics, and the people that drive both. He was a previously a reporter for the *Boston Globe.*

Ken Bensinger, a two-time Loeb award winner, is an enterprise reporter at the *Los Angeles Times* after arriving as a business reporter in 2007. He started his career at the *Wall Street Journal*, worked as a freelancer in Mexico City, and was a staff writer at *SmartMoney* magazine.

Jake Bernstein is a Pulitzer Prize–winning business reporter for ProPublica. Before joining ProPublica, Bernstein served as the executive editor of the investigative biweekly *The Texas Observer*.

Brian Blackstone joined Dow Jones in 1997. He has covered the Federal Reserve, fixed-income markets, telecommunications, and antitrust and currently reports on European monetary and economic policy.

Patricia Callahan is an investigative reporter on the *Chicago Tribune*'s Watchdog Team and was part of a team that won the 2008 Pulitzer Prize for Investigative Reporting. Before joining the *Tribune* in 2006, she was a beat reporter at the *Wall Street Journal* in Chicago. She shared a Pulitzer Prize for Breaking News Reporting for coverage of the Columbine High School shootings. She graduated from Northwestern University's Medill School of Journalism.

Thomas Catan is a staff reporter in the Washington bureau of the *Wall Street Journal* covering the Justice Department and legal affairs. He joined the paper in October 2008 as the correspondent in Madrid. Mr. Catan had previously reported for the *Times* of London and was energy correspondent and an investigative reporter for the *Financial Times*. He holds a bachelor's degree from the London School of Economics.

Steve Coll is a writer for *The New Yorker* and author of the Pulitzer Prize–winning book *Ghost Wars: The Secret History of the CIA, Afghanistan, and Bin Laden, from the Soviet Invasion to September 10, 2001*. He is president of the New America Foundation, a public-policy institute in Washington, D.C. Previously he served, for more than twenty years, as a reporter, foreign correspondent, and, ultimately, managing editor of the *Washington Post*.

Charles Duhigg is a staff writer for the *New York Times* where he writes for the business section and has contributed to series that received the George Polk, Loeb, and other awards. He is also author of *The Power of Habit: Why We Do What We Do in Life and Business*.

Joe Eskenazi is a staff writer at *San Francisco Weekly*. He was born in San Francisco, raised in the Bay Area, and educated at U.C. Berkeley. He never left. While primarily a government and politics reporter at *SF Weekly*, during his tenure there Eskenazi has sweated through a Bikram yoga session with a world-champion boxer, spent fifty-plus hours in a piano bar, conducted jailhouse interviews with a mentally retarded man who stole more than $200,000 worth of art, and traveled from San Francisco to Los Angeles solely via public transportation. He lives with his wife in the Lower Haight, 1.9 miles from his birthplace and 5,474 from hers.

Bryan Gardiner is an Oakland-based freelance journalist. His writing has appeared in *Wired*, *Popular Science*, *Gizmodo*, and other publications.

Mark Greif is a cofounder and coeditor of *n+1*, a magazine of literature, culture, and politics, where **Dayna Tortorici** is an associate editor. With **KATHLEEN FRENCH**, **EMMA JANASKIE**, and **NICK WERLE**, they are the editors of the volume *The Trouble Is the Banks: Letters to Wall Street.* The letters by Deena DaNaro, Joel Roche, Pamila Payne, and other anonymous authors first appeared on the Occupy the Boardroom website created by volunteers from community and labor organizations as well as the Occupy movement to allow everyday Americans to send personal e-mails to the nation's top bank and corporate executives.

BRIAN GROW is a special enterprise correspondent for Reuters based in Atlanta. He joined Thomson Reuters in 2010 as a senior staff writer covering legal affairs. Previously, he was a project director at the Center for Public Integrity in Washington and reported for *BusinessWeek*. He has won eighteen awards for his work. He graduated from the University of Notre Dame and the Johns Hopkins School of Advanced International Studies.

MAT HONAN is a senior writer at *Wired* and was a former senior writer for *Gizmodo*.

PAUL KIEL is a reporter at ProPublica, where his foreclosure coverage won a 2011 Scripps Howard Award for business and economics reporting. Before ProPublica, Paul wrote for TPMmuckraker, a unit of *Talking Points Memo. TPM*'s coverage of the firings of U.S. attorneys and politicization of the Department of Justice won a George Polk Award for legal reporting.

MINA KIMES is a writer for *Fortune*. She received the Nellie Bly Cub Reporter award from the New York Press Club in 2009. Before joining Fortune, Kimes was a reporter at *Fortune Small Business*. She graduated summa cum laude from Yale University.

MATT LEVINE is at Breaking Media after a stint at Goldman Sachs. Before Goldman, Matt was a lawyer at Wachtell Lipton. Before that he graduated from Yale Law School. Before law school, Matt graduated from Harvard College.

John Markoff is a senior writer at the *New York Times* for the paper's science section.

Timothy W. Martin is an Atlanta-based reporter for the *Wall Street Journal*, covering the U.S. prescription-drug supply chain and public health. Martin is a 2006 graduate of Eastern Illinois University, where he studied journalism. Before joining the *Wall Street Journal*, Martin taught English and studied Korean in South Korea, where he was born.

Mac McClelland is a reporter at *Mother Jones*, where she writes "The Rights Stuff." Her work has also appeared in *The Nation, GQ South Africa, Orion*, and *Hustler*, among other publications, and she is the author of *For Us Surrender Is Out of the Question: A Story From Burma's Never-Ending War.*

Bethany McLean is a contributing editor at *Vanity Fair* and co-author, with Joe Nocera, of *All the Devils Are Here: The Hidden History of the Financial Crisis*. Her first book, *The Smartest Guys in the Room*, about the fall of Enron, cowritten with Peter Elkind, became an Academy Award–nominated documentary.

Evgeny Morozov is a writer and researcher who studies the political and social implications of technology. A visiting scholar at Stanford University, he is the author of *The Net Delusion: The Dark Side of Internet Freedom* and a contributing editor of and blogger for *Foreign Policy* magazine.

Jessica Pressler is a senior contributing editor and columnist at *New York* magazine. Her work has appeared in *GQ*, *Elle*, and other publications. She graduated magna cum laude from Temple University.

Janet Roberts is a reporter and editor on the data team at Thomson Reuters and a former projects editor with the *New York Times* and database editor at the *Saint Paul Pioneer Press.* She graduated from the University of North Carolina at Chapel Hill.

Sam Roe reports on topics, including public health, product safety, corporate wrongdoing, and criminal justice for the *Chicago Tribune.* Roe was part of the reporting team that won the 2008 Pulitzer Prize for Investigative Reporting, and he was a Pulitzer finalist in 2000 and in 2011. He teaches investigative reporting at Columbia College Chicago

Joshua Schneyer is U.S. oil correspondent at Thomson Reuters and a former reporter at Bloomberg News. He studied at the London School of Economics and Political Science, the University of London, and McGill University.

Greg Smith resigned in the spring of 2012 as the head of Goldman Sachs's U.S. equity derivatives business in Europe, the Middle East, and Africa. Born in South Africa, Smith graduated from Stanford.

Jeff Tietz holds an MFA in literary nonfiction from Columbia University. His work has appeared in many publications and has been nominated for the National Magazine Award, the Pushcart Prize, and a Livingstone Journalism Award. His work has also appeared in the anthologies *Best American Magazine Writing* and *Best American Crime Writing.*

Steve Randy Waldman writes the *Interfluidity* blog, which provides commentary on macroeconomic developments, hedge funds, and financial markets.

Marcus Walker is the European economics correspondent for the *Wall Street Journal* covering politics, economics, and general news in Germany and the euro zone. Before joining the *Journal* in 2000, Walker worked as a staff reporter for *Euromoney Magazine* and as a research analyst for Royal United Services Institute for Defense and Security Studies. He has bachelor's and master's degrees from Oxford.

Peter Whoriskey is a staff writer for the *Washington Post* covering unemployment issues, manufacturing, and the auto industry. He began covering national business news, and the recession, after covering Hurricane Katrina as the *Post*'s Southern bureau chief.